Irit Amit Cohen • Ruth Kark

Yehoshua
HANKIN
Two Loves

Israel Academic Press

Yehoshua Hankin • *Two Loves*
by Irit Amit Cohen and Ruth Kark

Published by ISRAEL ACADEMIC PRESS, New York

(A subsidiary of MultiEducator, Inc.)

553 North Avenue • New Rochelle, NY 10801

Email: info@Israelacademicpress.com

ISBN # 978-1-885881-69-4

© 2022 Israel Academic Press

Acknowledgement

The authors thank all those who assisted in the preparation of the manuscript for publication. Special thanks to the late Yosef Alkoni and Milo Publishing House who published this book in Hebrew in 1996. We thank Fern Seckbach the translator of the book, who took care to translate every word and maintain the style of the Hebrew writing spirit. Thanks are due to Solly (Shlomo) Avi-No'am, a decendent of the Hankin and Tzukerman families, whose contribution enabled the translation of the book into English. We also thank Roni Lee Gilad for helping to create the land purchase maps in which Yehoshua Hankin was involved. We also thank the historical archives in Rishon Lezion, Gedera, Hadera, and the Central Zionist Archive in Jerusalem.

The roots of the creation of a nation—are in the earth.
Even the piece of sky that will be told "you are mine,"
is actually being directed
to none other than the plot of land in one's possession.

— H. N. Bialik

Contents

List of Photographic Images

List of Maps

Land purchases by Yehoshua Hankin in Eretz Israel in the years 1890–1942

Summer, 1943

They had made the hole in the fourth-floor tile in the fifth row and marked its location with a star. The cleaning ladies already knew that it should be left open and not covered with the rug, and the rug had to be as far away as possible so the wheelchair, always set at the same distance from the star, would not come into contact with it, making him lose his balance. The hooligans attending him knew to place the chair at a precise distance of ten tiles from the hole. They did not have to count them since the drag marks left by the chair were deeply etched into the mosaic of small stones that made up the tiles. The cleaning ladies, no matter how hard they tried to scrub and polish, could not obliterate those signs—they attested to "his desire" to lug the chair, to get close to the hole, and to hear voices rising from it, or to hurl the chair away so he could stretch out on the floor and press his eye to the hole to catch a glimpse of parts of arms and legs or facial features, and with the help of the voices identify their owners.

Today, too, the hooligans had appeared unannounced. They noisily opened the front door and asked if he had forgotten to take his cane and the quilt that Sarah had made from the strands of lambs' wool she had collected one by one from the Arab women and then spun—she did not buy ready-made. Sarah had given him the blanket on the day he married Olga, but Olga was no longer with us; she had only left him a blanket to warm his legs. And the rascals, after casting curious looks at what had gone on in his bed and glancing to see what was new on his table, placed him in the chair and wheeled him down the steps toward the waiting car. These two did not give a thought to the stillness of the house nor his pains, and they did not take the time to see if the checkered blanket wrapped his legs well, even though he had warned them time and again that the chill first hurt his legs and then spread to other parts of his body, and he had not forgotten to stress that his own doctor had warned him to stay away from the cold and to protect his weak lungs.

The trip lasted just a few minutes. As usual, he sat in the back while they perched in the front, forgetting all about him as they discussed the wiles of women. Also, as usual, the car stopped in front of the entrance to the tall building, and as had happened in the past few months, no one waited, even today, for his arrival. Of course, he had gotten used to this, but he was still not ready to forget other days on which they had opened his car door and greeted him warmly and brought him up the steps, two marching in front and two in back. He sighed, happy that they did not see him in his weakness.

The gateman opened the car door, first for the driver, then for the hooligan sitting next to him, finally remembering him as well. The hooligans and the gateman kept on nattering, artlessly lifting him and treating him as always, a routine act. Then, they placed him in the wheelchair again and pushed him, one hooligan on either side. If he hadn't reminded them about the blanket and the cane, they would have left them on the back seat, rendering him without support, to suffer from the cold that had been seizing him of late with no means to ward it off. The driver went and fetched the blanket and put it over his knees; the fellow's dissatisfaction showed in the twitch of his face along with the feeling of annoyance he roused in him. The two did not say a word—not out of respect for him, he knew, but owing to their mockery of his caring for the little things— and they hurried to lug the chair and carry him up the stairs to the second story, to the room with the hole in the floor.

With a push of a shoulder, they opened the door and then vied between themselves to see if they could manage to put the chair down at precisely a distance of 10 tiles from the hole without looking at the floor. The chair was shoved, rolling from hooligan to hooligan, neither of them being bothered by the sounds of the groans and belabored breathing coming from it. Finally, when they realized they could not set it precisely on the right spot without looking, they pulled the handles, made sure the chair was stable, positioned him wherever he was, and left him alone.

Now he sat, and the very sitting bothered him; he was sorry they had rushed to go out. He did not know how many hours he would sit while waiting for the vote to be taken in the large hall below.

Shadows engulfed the room. For some reason, the voting was delayed, and he wanted to know the time, but he did not like to wear ticking watches that showed the hour and minute, reminding one of the obligations not fulfilled on time. He preferred a different rhythm of life, bound by laws he determined;

he loved to feel the passing time that changed with the colors of the day and the seasons. But precisely today, times had confused him, and by the light coming in from outside, he could not guess the hour.

A mixture of voices rose from the hole, accompanied by the slamming of the doors by those coming in and going out. He was fed up with sitting there and wanted to see the faces of those present in the hall, to hear their orderly voices putting together words and sentences. So, he decided to drag the chair and himself and come close to the hole. He put the cane in front of him, lifted his body, put his weight on the cane, and pulled the chair; and again, he put the cane forward, dragged the chair, and paused, with both hands leaning on the backrest and the cane at his side. He debated with himself whether to sit again. He knew himself and his weaknesses full well: if he sat, he would not manage to lift his body again, but if he continued to stand, his feet would fall asleep and tremble, and sweat would engulf him. He decided to wait a bit, for only one more lunge, and he would be at the hole.

As he stood hunched over, he surveyed the walls. He already knew them well, every crack, every hair left by the brush when the walls had been whitewashed. And then, as always happened, his hands began to shake and not obey him, and he could not control their trembling. He had to hold on to something steady to tame the tremors and turned himself toward the seat while conjuring up its markings and each lump in the weaving. The minutes seemed like an eternity until his hand took hold of the backrest and allowed his body to relax and tumble into the chair.

Now he sat down, not really sitting, but taking a weak pose, and he figured out how to straighten up without moving the chair or rocking it. Oh so very slowly, he moved himself, for fear he would go beyond the edge of the seat, and thought about what would happen if he fell from it. Somehow, he managed to position himself steadily. Yet, he was surprised at how he was able to sit on the whole seat.

Sweat flowed all along his spine and pinned his shirt to his body, setting him aquiver, but slowly his breathing settled down and took on a constant, uniform rhythm until finally, he heard the people below filling the room, and he calmed down.
The wind breezed in through the open windows, dried his perspiration, and cooled his body. He slowly relaxed and expanded his lungs as his glances scanned the room's corners, revealing the signs of mold beneath the window and the overlooked cobwebs.

He loved open windows. They gave him a good reason for covering up with the patchwork quilt and feeling its woolliness through his clothes, and it was all the same to him, be it an autumn day or sweltering summer. The cleaning women knew about this love of his and always left the windows open. They thought he preferred open windows for reasons of health and considered this an oddity of the elderly who follow every bit of advice they receive from eccentrics. But they did not know that the family doctor had forbidden him to expose his body to the wind.

The same way he loved the woolliness of the blanket, he also enjoyed street noises: the sounds of rushing, honking cars; the shouts from the English-speaking soldiers who needed rides, and the calls from the Arab drivers arguing among themselves and raising their voices: who will be the first to take the initiative and drive the beret wearers, with neither rider nor driver understanding each other. But he smiles since he understands each word of their language.

Once he felt his strength coming back, he inhaled deeply and pulled his body above the seat, lifted the cane, and set it in front of him. Then he stood up and, while leaning on the backrest, pushed the wheelchair with his body. The outline of the star marked on the floor began to waver before his eyes, but he knew that the blurring came from his nearsightedness, and the hole was nearby, very close. He tensed his muscles and gave a final push—and the chair stood precisely over the hole. Now, he only had to stabilize the chair and himself. He grabbed the backrest and let the cane fall. He slowly sat down and adjusted his body to the depression in the seat, rubbing vertebra by vertebra against the backrest and expanding his lungs in preparation for prolonged sitting.

The noises from outside declined. Each driver received his daily livelihood and the soldiers scattered. It was now afternoon when it was customary to take afternoon tea. He smiled to himself for knowing each one's way of life, down to the minutest details. Then he leaned his body over until his face was near the hole.

New voices rose from below. He did not trust his hearing and wanted to see facial features. Perhaps he could identify those sitting in the hall? He bent his torso, and his eye spied a brimmed hat and a coat sleeve, discerning movement, and motion. He understood people had taken their places and were now waiting for their turn to speak. "Nu, in any event, they've started the meeting," he thought. He straightened out, sat erect in his chair, and smiled into his beard.

He does not need to listen, for he knows what they will talk about. Following his long-standing custom, he had thoroughly read the pages that had been sent to him in advance. He had perused them all, not skipping even one letter, lest his hearing fail him and he would not catch an important note or nuance.

"This time, I really didn't have to read," he thought to himself aloud. Yet, he had gone over the material, since he did not trust those people; for many months now, they had been dealing with his land and were incapable of reaching a decision. He had pressed and protested, and they remained complaisant. They did not feel the land was slipping through their fingers while they went on discussing a comma here, a comma there, and places of honor where the name of each bureaucrat would be signed. Finally, they decided on a date for voting, to decide whether to divide the land or leave it as one bloc. He, of course, had already given his opinion, and they only had to give their approval. He knew each of them—even the "new ones," who hadn't yet been involved in even one purchase. All of them loved to argue and voice an opinion, and the newcomers, if they didn't argue, who would get to know them? How would their placement on the name roster be determined? He decided to wait patiently since, in just a bit, they would strike the gavel and vote on the proposal.

Everything always takes place in a set order: First, everyone directs their glance toward the ceiling, and then they bend an ear to listen to the pounding of the cane. One strike means agreement with the proposal raised in the discussion; two strikes indicate disapproval. Then, after his decision is clear to them, the people crowd around the table and vote, and the majority opinion does not differ from his … The gavel has not yet struck. Why are they dillydallying, he thinks to himself.

The shadows in the room stretched even longer. Outside, streetlamps were lit, and their glow was swallowed in the twilight. He felt it had been quite a while since he had moved the chair and looked through the hole. He decided to try to bend over again and, with great effort, arched his back. Unfortunately, the light in the hall blinded him, and he had to close his eyes, and when he opened them, he saw the visage of Squareface, who was standing at the head of the table, directly under the hole.

He was taken aback. The unrest and anxiety gnawed at him from sitting so long only heightened his fears. He did not understand what the brimmed-hat wearer was doing in the position of the chairman. Why had they invited him to the vote?

Everyone knew how much he hated him and about the great dispute. Perhaps something else had been put on the agenda and displaced the issue of his land? For sure, they did not want to bother him, and they did not hurry to report to him since they knew it was a minor matter. When they finished with this other issue, the turn of his land would come. He lifted his eyes away from the hole, dried them, and looked through the opening—he was not satisfied with the conclusion he had drawn. His heart pounded desperately, and his fear intensified: Why specifically Squareface? And if they had invited him to the meeting, they should have included this in the pages, since he was an influential director, almost as important as he. It must have been a mistake, he decided. Yes, merely a mistake.

He listened closely and paid attention to every word. The words coming up through the hole were clear and sharp. No, there was no mistake here—they were dealing with his land. There was no striking of the gavel, and they were raising nothing for discussion, and their eyes did not look up to catch the stamping of his cane. They were not interested in his pounding. His opinion didn't count. He couldn't believe this. They had to hear, to listen for the cane. That was what they had agreed upon; that's how it always was …

He recoiled and abandoned the hole. The view became blurry, so he rubbed his eyes and looked again and saw the brimmed hat wearer getting out of his seat and waving his arms, and he heard whispered murmurings passing through the assembly like waves and unclear words swallowed up in one another. Maybe they will take a stance in any event? Perhaps their sanity will return? He will get the cane ready and pound twice. He will stamp it with all his might, and they will all know that he is against any division of the land. He won't let them damage the land, chopping it into tiny pieces. More than once, they had countered his opinion and afterward admitted he had been right. But some of them were not among his admirers since they had been captivated by Squareface's hatred, but he forgave them. As time passed, they acknowledged their mutual love, theirs and his—love for the land—and like him, they understood the value of one solid unit and the drawbacks of piecemeal. He had trained many disciples who would follow in his wake, and he heard them quoting — land is acquired as an entity, maintained as an entity, and the more it is divided, the more quarrels will result.

His hand hurt and holding onto the cane was difficult for him. He sharpened his gaze and saw that Squareface was still speaking. His eyes sought the gavel, but the table was empty. Again, his eyes were teary, and his vision blurred; he had to unbend and sit erect in his chair. He paused for a minute, straightened his back, and then bent over again. He only saw dark; in the hall, the lights grew dim, and he had difficulty identifying whose hat it was and to whom the arm belonged. Rage began to well in him, and he could feel his patience giving out and his loss of self-control. Once more, he did not think. He threw the cane aside, putting his hands in front of him for support, and let his body fall and roll on the floor. With the impact of the fall, the wheelchair turned over and moved a few tiles away from the hole. He didn't pay attention to that and did not let his gaze venture from the thin strip of light breaking through from below. Instead, he pulled his body until his eye was right above the hole. Despite the dimness, by dint of effort, he managed to discern the members of the Limited Actions Committee gathered around Squareface and raising their hands to vote, the secretary counted their fingers, one by one. He tallied them quickly, standing firm, and when he finished, he wrote a note and passed it to Squareface. The latter looked it over, lifted his head, and raised his eyes to the hole in the ceiling, with a smirk on his face.

They had decided.

They did not wait for the pounding of the cane, and they did not hear whether he agreed or not; he knew full well that their decision was entirely different than his. He couldn't hear them talking, but he saw the look of victory on Squareface's face and his confident hand movement.

No one wanted to hear his opinion. No one cared for his cane, the one they had given him as a present at the jubilee celebrations. His stampings had turned into annoyances for them, and it was like he didn't exist — in fact, he didn't exist.

He would still show them. He would not give up, not yet. He put his mouth over the hole and whispered into it, "My pounding, you did not hear my pounding," but no one turned his head toward the murmuring.

He raised his voice, "Looters! Warmongers! Land is good only when it is sold as a whole and settled in its entirety and not when it is parceled into small lots. And what do you want? To see it snatched away, cut into pieces shifting from hand to hand to whoever pays more? And not one of the many interested buyers will intend to work them and settle them. They are all speculators. It is not settlement they wish to promote but rather to make themselves wealthier and walk about town with full pockets."

No one heard his cries, and everyone continued to speak all at once, their voices stronger than his. He beat his fists on the floor; his hands hurt, but he couldn't help himself.

In the hall below, chairs were moved; they were getting ready to leave. He yelled out again, and his voice was strong, his words aimed at Squareface: "Mountain man, you grabbed importance, you loved authority, a great deal of land as much as could be taken, you destroyed the Fund, and your eyes are blind, me you sent to the devil, you aim to acquire land, but the land does not obey you …" He is hoarse. The street sounds of late evening have come in through the windows and swallowed his cries. Honking cut through the air; girls mumbled something in garbled English and were answered with giggles. He was silent; what's the use?

❧

After a while, he wanted to get up, but there was nothing to hold on to. The wheelchair had been tossed a short distance from him, while the cane was lying near him though he had no strength to lift it, so he just continued to lay there with his eye pasted to the hole. To himself, he said he would have to wait until someone in the room below would remember him and send the hooligans to take him. And they, as usual, would play dumb about the late evening hour and about the light they had forgotten to turn on, and once again, they would put him in the wheelchair and roll him down the stairs. At the entrance, he would meet a few of the new ones who were taking their time so they could mingle with the senior members. Some of the latter who wanted to take in any tidbit of news, and both groups would look at him and his chair and nod their heads in pity and then, not to his face, whisper, "crazy," "old nut," and if they knew his name, they would add, "Crazy Yehoshua."

Spring, 1915

The train took the curves awkwardly, rising above the hilly region, whistling, screeching, and shattering the silence. Slowing before each turn, it gathered its power, sped up again, and climbed, leaving behind a plume of rising smoke between the hills, the only evidence of its journey. The snow was soft. The railroad ties and green blotches poked out from it, but it was still enough to make the rocky, hilly surface slippery. The engine blasted its horn and passed by a wooden house plastered to the mountainside; its plumes mixed with the structure's chimney smoke. No one could be seen. Only a herd of black goats that skipped on the path–no-path stopped alongside the track; the goats huddled next to each other, hiding their heads in each other's wool. Once the train had passed, they scattered, and now were no more than dispersed black patches moving into the distance in the gleaming snow.

The train whistled and entered the plains of the Anatolian Plateau, drawing distant from the peaks of the mountains of Armenia, looking like a crown seen from afar. During its run, it crossed river channels etched very deeply into the stony ground, tossing up lumps of mud, and the crescendos from the flowing river waters competed with the clacking of the train wheels.

Morning rose.

The train's curtains were down, trying to fend off the light seeking to burst in through the windows, drawing away yesterday's night like a blanket over one's head. Whoever was teased by the morning light tried to banish it and go back to sleep, to gain a bit more respite from the rattling of the wheels, the desolation of the plateau, the smell of perspiration mingled with those of clotted blood, garlic, and onions.

The train was packed more tightly than ever. Soldiers occupied the central cars. Some of them were wounded—the first to return home, dreaming in their heart of hearts of returning home to the glory of victors at the gates to their cities— while others, healthy, were on their way to Adana from where they would be sent to the battlefields, not knowing their precise destinations. The hale sat next to the ill and crowded the wagons, with the journey being longer and more exhausting than the war. They hunched over in wrinkled dress uniforms, their copper buttons unpolished. Stubble covered their cheeks. And crumbs clung to the ends of their mustaches. There was no one before whom they had to rise or stand erect or create straight lines shoulder to shoulder. They needed the blast of a whistle to return them to military dignity, but the whistle was nestled in the pocket of one of the officers, who had dozed off in the sleeping car near the end of the train, among the other vehicles reserved for diplomats.

Unlike in the other cars, the diplomats hurried to awaken. They devoted a long time to bathing themselves, and they liked to precede the rural people and the soldiers and stand first in line for the washing facilities. The gentlemen opened doors and peeked into the corridors, closed the beds, turning them into benches; a medley of languages flooded the passageways. Women called the "boy" and grumbled that he had not hurried to come, and forgetting they were unkempt, they left the cabins and raised their voices. Men asked the "boy" to bring hot water and shaving foam, and they jostled each other to see who would get served first. The "boy" scurried between the engine and the wagons, between men and women, lugging a bowl of steaming water up and back, with the water splashing on the splay-footed rubes sitting in the corridors, nothing interfering with their placidness. These yokels sat leaning on their bundles, looking with eyes half-open/half-closed at the morning tumult waging around them and stretched out their hands to feel their bundles and straighten them out beneath their heads, and with a wave of a hand dispelled the noise and went back to drowsing knowing Constantinople was still far ahead.

❧

At the entrance to the last car sat a napping gendarme, whose inhaling and exhaling shook his mustache. Above his stretched-out legs mounded his belly and on it was a rifle, which swayed from side to side and was pushed and sliding at a steady rate. He leaned his head on the door of the car as it jumped and moved up and down in time with the shaking of the train. No lock was on the door, so a rope had been tied to the handle and the other end to the gendarme's hand. Because of the shifting, the door alternately closed and opened, and the gendarme's head would slide, and his hand reach out; he would open his eyes, scratch behind his ear with his free hand, change position, and go on dozing. Whenever the train made a sharp turn, increasing its curvature, the crack between the lintel and door would widen, and it was possible to see the passengers in the last car.

There were four of them. They had gotten on in Damascus, accompanied by a Turkish policeman, and when the policeman showed his authorization and their arrest document, the training officer was frightened and pushed them into the last car. He then wrote with chalk on the wooden beams "Convicted" and warned the gendarme not to let them wander between the vehicles. By the time they reached Aleppo, all the riders on the train knew about the passengers in the last wagon—and whispered among themselves "traitors," "dangerous," "have to stay away from them," "being taken to exile in Turkey, to Sivas." One of the passengers laughed out loud, then whispered, "They all die in Sivas. A swift hanging in the plazas of Aleppo and Damascus are better than the sufferings of famine and plagues." A few of the riders chimed in, repeating "Sivas" "Sivas," spitting along with their murmuring and the clack of the masbaha beads. Despite the overcrowding of the train cars, the floor near the last carriage stayed clear, and the gendarme could spread his legs and stretch out without worrying about visits from officers higher in rank than he.

After Alexandretta, the chalk marking above the door of the last car was erased. The cramping became more severe, and the bare floor drew soldiers and peasants to it. They no longer spoke about the "convicted," and the gendarme sometimes had to bend his legs. With a thunderous voice, the man succeeded in clearing space for himself from time to time, to straighten out his legs, give himself a shake, without forgetting to curse those sitting in the last carriage as well as the villagers who were not paying him enough respect. Only "the boy" who ran between the cars and brought water to the doorway of the last one, continued to splash a few drops on the door and to spit three times against the evil influence of its inhabitants, whispering, "May Allah have mercy, may Allah have mercy, in Sivas they no longer bury the dead"; he would then set down the bowl of water and flee, short of breath and trembling. The peasants nodded their heads after him and shot looks at the wagon door, peeking through the crack, but they asked no questions. The journey continued. Other peasants replaced the villagers, and more soldiers got on, and no further glances were aimed at the last car. And only "the boy" continued to sprinkle water on the door.

❧

Sitting next to the door was Yehoshua. His hair was long, longer than ever, shoved behind his ears, and his eyebrows were distinctly prominent, separating a high, etched forehead from deeply set eyes. A tangled beard covered his cheeks and stroked his chin—for many a day it had not been cared for. His shoulders sloped and pulled his body downward, so he sat hunched over, leaning on large hands, too large. He was wearing a gray, faded student's coat, with a closed row of buttons, two of which were new, while the others' shininess had dulled. The coat clung to his body, the frame of a young fellow, and emphasized his thinness. But he was no youth. He stared at the woman sitting next to him, with her head on his shoulder, who had pushed in beside him and taken up the entire seat.

He smiled into his beard when he looked at her, and with his grinning, the lines etched in his forehead deepened, and his eyes sunk further: she had gone with him. She had preferred a trial in Damascus and exile in Sivas over the ill patients and the women suffering their labor pains in Palestine. She wanted to take care of him since she considered him a child who needed tending. He caressed her head, put back a hair that had fallen out of place, and then mussed others. He stretched out a finger and drew it along the lines of her broad, slightly square face and patted her matted eyebrows, shadowing huge eyes. He knew their color, their size. They were black and deep. His fingers fluttered over her thin lips, almost always clenched, those of someone who knows what she wants and does not utter a superfluous word. Now, her lips were parted, and she breathed lightly, giving a little shake, entirely relaxed.

So heavy, so wide. He loved her in her sleep. She was sixty-three, and he was thirteen years younger. But next to her, he was ever so much older. His finger continued to caress her and count her wrinkles, and then stopped above the cleft that divided her chin into two. Olga felt his touch and changed position; her serenity vanished, and she snuggled against him. Her head sought the dip in his shoulder. Her body was stretched out, so her hands sought a grip, but finally, she interlaced her fingers and hid them in the folds of her blouse. She stopped moving and again breathed lightly. He looked at the pleats of her blouse, at the curly ruffles on the edges of its lapels. They were already two weeks on the way. She—her blouse was ironed, but he—his coat was filthy, with unraveled threads next to the pockets and holes in the sleeves. He was embarrassed by his coat and tried to fold up the sleeves, but the shirtsleeves underneath it were no better. The meagerness of his clothing and their tears made him blush. He was ashamed for her to see him like that. He was always embarrassed when she saw him that way and tried to hide the clumps of earth stuck to his clothes and the gaping soles of his boots. He was afraid of her look, of her silence, and knew deep down that she did not want to hurt him. They did not talk very much with each other, since they did not need many words, but sometimes he was saddened by their lengthy silence.

Who knows? If they spoke, perhaps their suffering would be minimized, and their pain diminished and understood and divided between them, not be taken in and turned into a heavy lump blocking off their innermost feelings. He looked at her again and at her calm, and he took hold of the bun of hair rolled on her neck and relaxed in his seat. He did not want to disturb her peace. But, as usual, he did not make her party to his fear. His legs had fallen asleep, and he did not want to stretch them out lest he wake her again. He straightened his toes out one by one, and he felt little tingles spreading from the soles to the ankle and climbing up to the thigh. For a moment, he tried to forget his almost numb legs and focused his thoughts on the train's destinations and the people sitting with them in the carriage. He looked at a man and woman huddled together. A moment of peace was visited upon them, he thought, the war has done them good.

⸙

Mania was no longer a young woman, but her hair was like a high school student's—smooth and short, surrounding a sharp-featured face, falling on prominent cheek bones and refusing to be held with a single hair clip. Freckles were rife beneath her eyes but were swallowed up in the shadows cast by her long eyelashes, which neither Israel nor Hassan Bey could withstand.

In comparison to Mania, Israel was diminutive. Yehoshua was pedantic about calling him Israel Shochat to keep him separate from his two brothers-in-law: the Israel of Fanny, Olga's sister, and Israel Belkind, Olga's brother. But for whatever reason, he could not attach the name Shochat to Mania. For him, she was always simply Mania, and he felt ever so much closer to her. He never managed to penetrate the depths of Israel's soul though he did pity him. And the more profound the crises between Israel and Mania became, and the more the rumors about his infidelity grew, the more Yehoshua's sympathy for Israel grew but not for Mania. She was strong, while he was left with his weakness.

The war subdued Israel while it toughened Mania. His hair was shot with gray, and more wrinkles appeared on his face, and Yehoshua did not know if he could endure a long exile. He looked at Mania again and felt bad that she was being sent into it. When he had met her, she had been a young lass, and he considered her his daughter, the one he and Olga had never had. In time, he learned that Mania needed neither a father's nor a mother's love but only required friends, equal to her and larger-than-life like she was. He settled his glance on Israel and wondered if he would ever understand that Mania needed no one and that whoever became too attached to her would end up hurt. Yehoshua's thoughts kept wandering until the tingling in his feet stopped, and he could relax his muscles and lean backward.

⚐

When she was put on the train, Mania could not stand on her own two feet and could barely bend her knees to sit. Her flogged feet were swollen, a doughy mass of wounds and contusions. Israel bandaged them with torn strips of clothing soaked in plant extractions he had discovered on his travels and kept in his pockets wherever he went. Now they were used for Mania, and he patted her wounds with his soft touch and tears in his eyes. They covered her puffy feet with an Arab dress made of fringed strips, and no one could see she was barefoot, since no shoe large enough for her to wear had been found as she went into exile. Yehoshua was not used to seeing her in a dress because she always wore pants, and with her short hair, people thought she was a young man and not a woman, which is how she wanted it. In jail, they had taken Mania's clothes, burned them, and given her a dress of one of the Arab women. They also took her boots and only gave them back after nail by nail had been removed from the soles so they could check that no notes were hidden in them. Now, the boots were tied to one of the bundles, and the dress they had given her in the jail was still draped on her, many sizes too large for her.

They had arrested Mania at the end of the summer, a few days after the war broke out. Hassan Bey himself came to Sejera to seize her; he showed her the arrest order and called her "traitor" and "danger to the kingdom." When she laughed at him, he could not stand her ridiculing him and asked one of his soldiers to tie her hands. The story of her bravery spread from place to place throughout the country. It was also told that Hassan Bey put Mania in a closed, sealed, mule-driven carriage and brought her in the middle of the night from the mountain to the valley, with him riding beside her, with his stuffed ears so as not to hear her fearless, mocking cackles.

That very night the Turkish officer brought her to the detention center in Haifa, where he harassed her, trying to find out about "the members" and about "Hashomer." Right in front of her, he waved the loaded bandolier that he usually wore around his chest and pulled out bullet after bullet, threatening to torture her with the same number of torments as the bullets. Mania derided his threats, so he bound her hands to the seat of the chair and hit her legs, but she just laughed. When they put her legs in a brace and turned her topsy-turvy, so her head sank, she laughed. And when they touched her body with a glowing piece of coal, she turned her head aside; and when they then poured water over her, she smiled again, since she could no longer laugh.

When Mania was placed under arrest, Israel was not there. At that time, they were following separate paths: Mania stayed at Sejera, and among her other activities, she also reared their two children, while Israel roamed in Galilee and collected idlers and reckless fellows to turn them into soldiers. He trained them in how to hide, attack, and fight. He taught them the pathways through Galilee, as well. He educated them in the science of medicinal plants and the secrets of the waterholes among the rocks. When he found out that Mania had been arrested, he suddenly remembered his love for her and left his "soldiers"; he rushed to Haifa and looked for her, going from one detention center to another. But for Israel, that was not enough—he became an Ottoman national and paid the tax for becoming an Ottoman so people could not say that they were not citizens of the Ottoman Empire. But whoever knew Israel was aware of how much he hated the Ottomans and how much he despised and mocked anyone carrying in his pocket the red scrap of paper to prove Ottoman citizenship.

His searching did not last long, since two days after his arrival in Haifa, he was arrested and sent to solitary confinement facing the ocean. The man with the unkempt hair hoped that the coins sewn into the linings of his sleeves would be enough to bribe the guard and to find out from him what had happened to Mania. But unfortunately, it took one day, and many coins to unfetter the guard's tongue and learn that Mania had been transferred to the women's prison in Jerusalem, accused of treason, and sentenced to death.

For five months, Israel did not see Mania. He was shackled in his cell, and the guard would give him snippets of news, information in exchange for a coin. That was how he learned that implementation of her verdict had been postponed, and she had been put in the same cell with women accused of theft, prostitution, and insanity. Among them was a thief who was famous in all of Jerusalem. A large, gangly woman who had a hand in everything. She took Mania under her wing and treated her wounds. Woe to anyone who dared to come to Mania to take care of her or say something to her. Mania herself was afraid of this thief and waited for the moment when they would bring a new woman to the cell, and she would no longer be favored. But it was Mania she clung to, and Mania, who feared for her outcome, curled up on the mat in her corner and tried to leave space between her and the mat on which the woman laid down.

The crazy woman held with them in the cell had many visitors: mad people, male and female beggars who pawed through garbage cans, market thieves, beggars who were missing arms, and people missing a leg whose artificial limb was tied to them artfully and who had learned to get around better on one leg than people who walked on two. They would stand behind the cell window that faced the alley, pass food remnants through the window's bars, and relate the news to the mad inmate, who would then tell it to the other prisoners. From those visitors, Mania learned that Israel had been arrested, as had Yehoshua with a charge of sedition as well as the pretext that they knew too much, so they were dangerous to the government. Hankin's arrest surprised her, since he was known for his closeness with the Turkish officers and rulers; he negotiated with them over land matters and had visited the Turkish capital, but the war had turned everything upside down, and friends had become enemies. Israel and Yehoshua were placed in jail in the al-Adas quarter of Jerusalem for those condemned to death.

⌖

Yehoshua's comfortable sitting pose lasted a short time as his internal disquiet returned and overwhelmed him. The serenity of the three others suddenly angered him, and he envied them their amnesia at a time when he was once again flooded with the memories that weighed him down. Added to these remembrances was the fear of an unclear future. The prisoners had sat for five months waiting for the imposition of their verdict. Five months they had looked, each in his own cell, at the sun rising at daybreak and setting in the evening, and they were sure it was their last day on earth. The authorities had rushed them from trial to trial and repeated the same accusation, "belonging to the Hashomer movement and therefore responsible for the weakness of the Turkish army." Now, they were sitting near each other, with Olga at his side, and they had no inkling what tomorrow would bring. Four going into exile, who knows for how long?

Yehoshua remembered the letter he had sent to the American ambassador in Constantinople through the boy who had brought his bowl of food to his cell. After the boy took the bundle of money that contained the letter, Yehoshua never saw him again.

He tried to shake off these thoughts, but they were relentless. How could the letter help? And why should the ambassador try to help him? He wanted to believe that the diplomat would exchange exile in horrible Sivas for exile in Bursa. Everyone was talking about the terrible plague in Sivas, rumormongering not only in the train wagons but also in Damascus and Palestine. They already feared to mention the city's name and only said "there" or "in that place." Soldiers were afraid to approach the fences and threw food sacks over them; exiles would wallow in the filth, looking for peels. Yehoshua shuddered and, with a sharp movement, placed his hand on the sleeping Olga's hair and snuggled her head to his shoulder, for he wanted to feel the warmth of her body as close as possible. Afterward, he gently lifted her head and, with his free hand, pulled one of their bundles toward them, put it beneath him, and raised her feet, laughing out loud at the sight of the bench that was too narrow to hold her. Hearing his own guffaws, he put his hand over his mouth in embarrassment. He did love her with all her girth, with her silence; he relished seeing her movements and the way she managed no matter where and how everyone listened to her.

At the Afula train station, Olga had joined the three accused who were going to Damascus for trial. She took the guilt upon herself, even though she had never hurt anyone nor broken the law. She said to the gendarme that he had to arrest her and seat her in the last wagon together with the other dangerous characters, because, like them, she was a traitor and a danger to the Empire, and only by mistake had they forgotten to arrest her. The gendarme thought she was "crazy" and refused to let her enter the carriage, but she would not relent and gave him one of those smiles she kept in reserve for times of distress, and into his hand, she thrust a little sack of money and a bag of lentils. These enticed the guard, and since he saw no one was watching him, he pushed her into the car, insisting, "If your esteemed self wants to go into exile, so be it, but you must heed my instructions, first—sew on a button for me; second, sing me one of those songs the Russians sing; third—prepare me lentil pottage." Olga was happy to be in Yehoshua's company, and she had no qualms about complying with the gendarme's quirks. Thinking about this incident made Yehoshua laugh, and he forgot the others were sleeping: "The policeman was looking at you." Olga moved in discomfort but was not awakened, and he regained his composure and stopped laughing.

Yehoshua rose from the bench, stretched his limbs, and sensed his bones one by one. After that, he approached the door and peeked into the swaying corridor through the slit. Then he returned to the center of the wagon where everyone was still sleeping and turned to look through the heavily barred window, smiling at seeing the grating. In Damascus, the window had been latticed at the train engineer's request after his verdicts were read to him. To where would they escape, to the Syrian deserts? To the wilderness of Anatolia? To the mountains of Armenia? The other three did not like the bars, and Olga would say that they also penned within them the expanses of the hilly regions — when they would look out to the mountains and hills, the shadows cast by the bars would cut them into long strips. Yehoshua didn't care; he was very familiar with the look of the highlands, every hillock, every curve that could be seen. He had ridden the same train to Damascus, to Adana, and to Constantinople so many times. But, of course, he had never sat in the last wagon, as he now did, but in the diplomats' carriage, for he was a notable person, *hawaja*, and rated his own jug of steaming coffee and bowl of hot water. And when he clapped his hands, "the boy" had hastened to come to shave him and to pat his face with a moist towel. But now, they had placed him in the last wagon and used a rope to tie the door handle to the hand of the rotund Turkish guard and installed bars on the windows. They no longer addressed him as *hawaja* but whispered: traitor and dangerous. Yet, all his treachery was linked to the land he loved.

This was the second time he had been sent into exile. He snickered inwardly—and for the same accusation, land dealer, incorrigible speculator, great expert, knows everything that is forbidden to know, provocateur, works by himself, and has no competitors. But, though the charges were the same, the exiles had changed as had the deporters; the first exile had been foisted upon him by Jews, but this, the second one—by Turks. The first he had experienced by himself, he had fallen and wallowed in a dunghill, not believing he would be able to extricate himself from it—but he had endured and continued to acquire land and even attained great stature. Now he was en route to a second exile and did not know if it would end.

Yehoshua sat and looked out through the barred window. The train dashed through the hills of the plateau, and the more it turned west, the more the flocks increased, impeding the journey. Now, the sun was high in the sky, and Yehoshua felt its heat. He sat again at Olga's feet, stretching out his hand and crushing the material of her dress. He knew that people were laughing at him behind his back and sniping at him, "She's older than you and will also grow old before you, and you will remain alone, left only with memories."

1A. Rishon LeZion first years (1890s-1900) Source: Rishon LeZion Archive.

1B. Rishon LeZion first years (1890s-1900) Source: Rishon LeZion Archive.

1C. Rishon LeZion first years (1890s-1900) Source: Rishon LeZion Archive.

1D.   Rishon LeZion first years (1890s-1900) Source: Rishon LeZion Archive.

2. Members of the Feinberg and Belkind families, 1913.
Seated, from left to right: Olga Hankin, Mania, Eliezer, and Shifra Belkind.
Source: Tanhum Hankin Family Private Archive

ᘓᕈ

He was 19 the first time he met her in Rishon Lezion, and when he came to his father to tell him of his love, he was told, "Youthful nonsense. Wait, there will be others." But when Yehoshua was not convinced, his father went on, "She's intelligent and educated. She dresses like the city women of Petersburg and has many suitors. Why get involved?" Thirty years had passed, and there were no others. There was only her, and he loved to bury his head in her chest and to dwarf himself next to her and to be only "Jashiya," without the other honorifics that had increased in time the more respected he became. He never had enough of hearing her whisper, "You are mine, the second Jashiya, the second Joshua." And when she would go on to say, "The first conquered the land with his legs, taking it by force. The second took it with love," he would answer, "Not second, for you—first." Now she was accompanying him and was willing to share a second exile with him.

Rishon Lezion, February 1885

Night. The street of the moshava had emptied. At night the houses seemed whiter, calmer. On the boulevard, the trees had already grown taller. At first, they had planted palm trees with the hope that they would grow tall like the Egyptian palms with straight trunks and a thin crown of leaves; then they had listened to the advice of the gardener Digour and replaced them with cypress trees, since he was a great expert on them and wanted to make the moshava's street like the Paris boulevards where the trees on both sides were pruned into triangular, square, or arched gate shapes. The farmers did not prune them; the gardener was replaced; a new administrator came who occupied himself with other minor issues; the trees grew tall, and the bougainvillea that had been planted alongside them, to serve as a fence, climbed on them, with their purple blossoms striking the eye.

Along the side of the paved street, Yehoshua walked carefully, so as to not step in the dirt—maybe at least one time he would not get his boots dusty. The street's silence stressed his loneliness. The oil lamp was burning in the home of Fanny and Israel Feinberg. Yehoshua tapped lightly on the door and, not waiting for a reply, went in.

Israel was reading the newspaper *Ha-Melitz*. He certainly heard Yehoshua's steps and recognized the slapping of his soles, but he did not lift his head. Few in the small moshava walked about late at night and visited each other. On many an occasion, Yehoshua had turned to their house just at a time when the moshava residents were huddled in for the night. Since he was like one of the family, they thought he needed no attention. Now, Yehoshua approached the big stove and poured tea for himself from the brass samovar atop of it. Among the cups on the shelf, he saw a saucer with jam and took it down. He brought it near his nose and sniffed the aroma of sugared grapes. Then he moved toward Israel with the cup and jam saucer in hand and stood in front of him; he sipped tea and gave voice to his pleasure—and Israel just went on pretending as if he hadn't heard him and hid behind his newspaper so hid face could not be seen at all and stretched his legs in front of him. Yehoshua put the cup on the floor and dragged a stool near Israel. He settled on it and lifted the saucer with the jam, bringing it right in front of Israel. Facing the oil lamp, flames flickered in the glass cup and took on the color of the jam.

"Grapes!? Grapes in our places?" he cried out. "How can that be? Let the accused proceed to the witness chair and testify whether these are Rishon Lezion grapes or grapes from Jaffa. For jam made of Rishon Lezion grapes is forbidden to use and forbidden to be seen, while Jaffa jam is certainly allowed."

From behind *Ha-Melitz* came a restrained snort, but Yehoshua continued his declaration, "May the accused read to me the rules of Rishon Lezion: grape harvest—forbidden; winemaking—forbidden; eating grapes—forbidden. Gleanings of grapes may be left in the vineyard—as food for wild birds."

Now, Israel was rocking in his chair, the paper resting on his stomach, and mighty peals of laughter were making his body shake. From one outburst of laughter to the next, he, too, added to the clamor and called out, "The Alsatian is coming! The Alsatian is coming!" Then he got up and approached Yehoshua's stool and grabbed its legs while Yehoshua bent down and took hold of Israel's shoulders. They stood that way and made their declaration until the stool toppled over and the friendly duo rolled on the floor laughing uncontrollably. "Lolik," Yehoshua huffed, "where is the jam from?"

No one in the moshava called Israel Feinberg by his given name but only with the nickname "Lolik." Since he was the youngest in his family, they had shortened his name and called him "Lulo." His brothers did not stop there but lengthened the nickname and dubbed him — "Lolik." Were it not for his figure, and everyone would have thought they were talking about a spineless wimp. But Israel was tall and ungainly, with a booming voice, and all the Arabs in the surroundings shuddered when they saw him and called out as he passed by, "The giant is coming, *hawaja* Lulu!"

Yehoshua rose first from the floor, straightened his coat, and put a handout for Israel. Like Fanny, he knew well his good-heartedness and his gentleness. Lolik pulled him after him toward the window facing the street, moved the curtain aside, and opened the shutter, so the dark night engulfed them. The two looked toward the edge of the moshava and saw the Administration Center bathed in light.

"The Alsatian is celebrating," said Lolik. "He's sitting there with the clerk Ossowetzky, and the secretary Benshimol and the three of them are busy with writing new regulations. They don't have time to wonder about the plate of jam sitting on my shelf."

"He'll still think about it, have no doubt," Yehoshua said to him. "His eyes and hands are in everything, and the more the Baron threatens to cut off his support for the farmers, the heavier the hand of the Alsatian. Wusses all of them, cowards."

Wanting to calm him down, Lolik closed the window and adjusted the curtain until the lights from the Administration Center were no longer visible. Then he sat Yehoshua down on the Damask sofa that seated two, knowing how much Yehoshua loved to find serenity on their sofa. Lolik loved to talk; Yehoshua loved to hold his peace. Lolik was aware of all the news in the moshava. From Fanny and her friends and from his brother Yosef and from the Arabs who worked in the fields, he would hear the news and be sure to tell it to others. The moshava, even though it was small, had lots of news: who had joined the moshava, who had left, who was employing the new workers, and what had been written on the post in the courtyard of the administrator Ossowetzky's house. That way, Israel was the first in the moshava to spread the news that Hirsch, the Baron's director, who lived in Mikveh Israel and mediated between the Baron and the settlers, had been at one time an officer in the Russian army and fought in Alsace and been awarded many medals. For that, they called him "the Alsatian." Lolik also knew to tell that when the Baron had asked him to go to Palestine to manage his colonies, and that after he had accepted, he showed up one day in the Jaffa port with a single suitcase in hand stuffed with medals. From then on, the man used to command his clerks as if they were junior officers and the farmers—simple soldiers who obeyed their orders.

Lolik and Yehoshua sat and slowly slipped cups of tea in silence. Yehoshua's eyes were closed, and his head rested on his friend's shoulder. But Lolik did not keep still for long, and when he spoke again, his words angered Yehoshua. Lolik rose from the sofa, saying, "All summer, Ossowetzky did nothing for the moshava. He did not buy plows, and he did not seal the granaries, and the wheat rotted in the fields. On Sukkot two years ago, he ordered to plant grapes, so the farmers went to the field and plowed and turned over the clods of earth and planted grapes—and now he has forbidden to pick them. There is no reaping and no grape harvest. There is financial support; every month, the farmers stand at the entrance to the Administration Center to get payment from the masters and to wait disheartened for the Alsatian's arrival. And the man comes into the gates of the Administration Center in a Jaffa carriage, and from the height of his seat tosses bundles of money, calling out, 'Take, eat money! From the bundles, salvation will sprout for you and not from the fields.' The farmers hear and bow their heads, and from month to month, they grow shorter. But they continue to take the bundles, taking them and keeping quiet, and when they pass the post, they look to see if a new decree has been levied against them. How long with they keep still? How long will they let themselves be trampled?

A week ago, they put up a notice: "The proletariat has no place in the Baron's colonies." My brother Yosef went to get permission to bring workers, especially for the grape harvest. The administrator told him a new decree had been imposed—it is forbidden to harvest grapes until they get authorization from the Baron's advisers. And the advisers are sitting in the capitals of France and Morocco and want to learn from there about the fields of Rishon Lezion and its vineyards. How can that be? Last week they forbade the pharmacist from selling quinine to 'radicals.' Yesterday ...

Yehoshua blocked his ears—he, too, belonged to the "radicals," he and all the Hankin family, the Feinberg family, and the Belkind family, and they were joined by the seasonal workers. The Alsatian and Ossowetzky did not like them; they were afraid of them, since the "radicals" refused to obey and follow the new regulations. Since he had listened to Lolik's speech, Yehoshua was sure that the Feinberg family had decided to harvest the grapes, in spite of the clerks' opposition and without the help of the laborers but by themselves, and they had even made grape jam.

A smile spread on his face erasing the signs of anger, and Yehoshua brought his hand to the jam saucer, dipped a finger in it, and licked it. He found the jam's flavor very delicious. Israel saw that Yehoshua no longer covered his ears, so he went on from where he had stopped, "Yesterday, the town crier went through the moshava and announced that from today all the farmers of Rishon Lezion have been declared day laborers and the administration has the right to fire them at any time and to evict them from the land and do whatever it wants with it. By payment of bundles of money, they took the lands." Israel paused here and scrutinized Yehoshua to see if he had managed again to make him angry.

Yehoshua could not stand what Lolik was saying. He knew him and his prattling well, but this time he had gone too far — informing him of so many bad things all at once as if he had slung rocks at him, and he had no way to defend himself. He got up from the couch and felt his hand trembling, fearing the jam saucer would slip through his fingers. "Why should he touch the lands? They do not belong to the Baron. The farmers bought them with a great deal of money," he blurted out.

"Fool," Lolik nodded his head:

You have a short memory. Two years have gone by since my brother Yosef went to the Baron and asked for his help in drilling a well for the moshava. He groveled and pleaded, and what did the Baron answer him? He would consider his request. And now he has thought and dug the well and given the farmers an allotment, and in exchange for that and in exchange for the water, he took the lands. Not only that—he limited his generosity only to whoever would accept his decrees. The others—they were forbidden from using the water. As he sees it, let them die of thirst, unless they change their minds and come to him and hand over their land. He would hold the land as custody, he promised, until all of them would be 'real farmers.' And what are real farmers? Those who obey him and answer 'Amen.' For a long while now, Yosef has stopped walking about the moshava in public since he is embarrassed to raise his head and look straight at the farmers.

Now, the sweetness of the jam choked Yehoshua's throat. Lolik's bitterness took hold of him, and he felt the rage making his skin tingle, so he dug his nails into his palms to hold himself back from exploding. Lolik was right. The administrators were running Rishon Lezion under the guise of advisers: a French gardener, a French agronomist, a French wine expert. And he tried to ignore what was going on in Rishon Lezion, to rise early each morning before the other farmers and to go down to the vineyard to trim the dry branches and in the evening after them to water the almond seedlings and not see those standing in line in the administration courtyard.

"What will be with the grapes?" he muttered. "They are bursting with sweetness, and the birds are pecking them. By the end of the month, they will be rotten."

Upon noticing Yehoshua's fit of temper, Lolik became frightened, especially since he was not used to seeing him like this. He took him by the shoulders and forcibly sat him down, and put the cup of tea in his hand, seeking a way to draw his attention and put a smile on his face. Since he was a born storyteller, he began to relate the tale of the saucer with the jam and was soon able to distract Yehoshua.

ᏋᏜ

In the early morning, Fanny went to Yosef's vineyard. Yosef, having already been burned, had stopped taking care of his vineyard and had begun to deal with milch cows, spending his days milking and making cheese. He had, of course, looked for Jewish workers to whom he could turn over the work of tending the vineyard, but since the administrators did not approve employment of Jewish laborers in the moshava, claiming they were too expensive and would cause riots, he had asked Fanny to take care of the grapes in the meantime. All winter, Fanny took care of the vineyard: she had straightened the branches and prepared the irrigation channels; the vines had begun to produce fruit, and now the time had come to harvest them. Fanny knew of the prohibition but laughed at it, since she had an excuse—it was her brother-in-law's vineyard, so she was not harvesting her own grapes. In the early hours, she woke Israel and told him where she was headed; when he tried to dissuade her and enumerated all the dangers, she laughed and said, "They wouldn't dare strike a woman," and she left.

On her way, she called Rivka Yavetz, her neighbor, to go with her. Since the Yavetz family was not considered "radical," so to avoid frightening Rivka, Fanny did not tell her where they were headed. "Let's go out to the fields," she said to her, "to see the early birds hopping about and collecting seeds on these lovely summer days."

And Rivka, who loved Fanny's quirks, agreed to go with her, but when she saw Fanny leading her to the vineyard and then harvesting grapes and filling her basket, she yelled, "Taboo, taboo, the regulations don't allow it," and fled from there as fast as she could run. Later, in the moshava, they said that Rivka had run, with her hair flying, as if possessed by demons, and looked for men who would go and take Fanny away from among the grapevines. But at that hour of the morning, she only saw toddlers in the yards.

Fanny calmly finished harvesting, filling two bushels, and returned to the moshava. Although she knew that Rivka was hiding from her, she stopped by the Javetz family on her way home and left a basket overflowing with bunches of grapes in front of the old woman who sat in the doorway; she told her they were good for wine, and if not for wine, then for jam. The elderly woman, who was deaf and was not aware of the regulations, took one grape, scrutinized it as if it were a marvelous wonder, put it in her mouth, and set the basket on her knees, like a child holding a toy and not willing to let it go.

Fanny hurried home and made jam from the clusters in her bushel, enjoying the fragrances coming from the pot and filling the house and the street.

When Lolik finished telling Fanny's story, he was elated, and mischievousness danced in his eyes. Just then, Yehoshua remembered he had not asked about Fanny since he was so used to finding her always with Israel.

"Where's Fanny," he wondered.

"She went to her brother's," laughed Lolik. "To the home of Shimshon Belkind. All the family is gathering there. Didn't you hear? Fanny's parents and her sister Olga have come to the moshava. They came in the Jaffa coach together with the architect Baruch Papiermeister. You must remember him. He was the first to buy additional land in Ayun Kara and joined Rishon Lezion, but the last to settle on them. Finally, the architect, expert in life in the world at large and for whom the matters of the moshava are too petty, has kindly agreed to visit his holdings, and he has brought guests with him. You should only have seen how the moshava girls stared at him and at the young woman who sat next to him. As if they had never seen such a handsome Odessa or Petersburg couple. And that woman had had the nerve to turn her head and refuse the architect when he put out his hand to help her alight from the carriage. If she had only known how many girls were ready to change places with her and take his outstretched hand. But she—she didn't even look at him, descended, and trod on the carriage lane as if she had known the moshava and its paths forever."

"She was wearing a black skirt, and the girls said it was made of pure silk, and a white shirt closed with silver buttons and a wide sash belt emphasizing her waist. Her arms were covered with puff sleeves with a decorated ribbon at their ends. Fanny said this is the latest fashion in Europe." Israel specified the details, and when he spoke, a tone of admiration crept in.

Yehoshua wanted to hear more, since something in Lolik's description differed from the tall tales he usually told. His friend noticed this yearning and went on,

"She brought boxes of books with her. In all of Rishon Lezion, I have never seen so many books. She asked the carriage driver to ride after her and to unload the books at her brother Shimshon's house, and when he said that he first had to off-load the architect's belonging, she went and told Mr. Papiermeister without hesitation, 'Excuse me, sir, would you be so good as to take your items with you so the driver can take my books?' The entire street looked at her and admired her language and her nerve. Before, she had refused to take his hand, but now she was asking him to give in to her, and while doing so, she already knew he would agree. The architect didn't give a peep, took his suitcase, and toddled down the dusty path.

"Fanny also related that her sister Olga had been a telegrapher in the Mogilev train station. Not only that she was a midwife, and women came to her house in Petersburg to give birth in secret. She even raised an infant after the daughter of a marquis had given birth to an illegitimate child. And now someone such as this has come to Rishon Lezion, educated, intelligent, sharp-tongued. Everyone will flock to her, and she will look down at them contemptuously with her knowledge. Just like that architect who remained a man of the big world, she won't last in the small moshava," Lolik concluded. His tone had changed. He was no longer admiring and telling wondrous things but only complaining about Fanny.

"Since the afternoon, she had been visiting her family. She only popped back here in the evening and handed me the saucer with the jam, with no greeting or asking how I'm doing, and back to her family. She has forgotten she is a married woman ..."

The last part Yehoshua did not hear, since he had fallen asleep, with Lolik sitting next to him on the Damask sofa and holding his tongue.

Since there was no one listening to whom he could pour out his soul, he thought about Fanny. He envisioned her as the first time he saw her, so blond with two large eyes, wide open with a kind of wonder mixed with naiveté, and they were drinking in everything her new surroundings offered. Lolik could not resist Fanny's gaze; he, too, was drawn into her eyes in captivation, and again he did not manage to free himself of it, nor did he want to.

Three years earlier, ten families had come to the lands of Rishon Lezion, among them the Hankin family, the Feinberg family, and Shimshon Belkind.

A few months later, Shimshon was joined by a brother and sister, Israel and Fanny. The two had arrived with a group of Bilu [Beit Ya'akov Lechu Venelcha] members to help the moshava's farmers and intended to continue on to Gedera. But Israel Belkind became enchanted by the charms of the moshava, and Fanny with the charm of Israel Feinberg. Fanny assisted the moshava's doctor and even received a salary from the administration, but a year after he arrived, Israel Belkind, her brother, was no longer under the spell of the moshava, so he moved away and left his plot to his brother so that he would work it for him— other places and people attracted him with their enticements.

The young, delicate Fanny did not join her younger brother and stayed in the moshava in the home of Shimshon Belkind. Some predicted that by the end of the year, she would break down since she would not be able to face the hardships of the place, but the vilifiers were proven wrong. The first time she called Israel Feinberg "Lolik," and they saw how he melted when she called him, they no longer spoke about her or shook their heads. They knew she would stay. At the first moshava party, right after they had finished building the Administration Center and hoped for salvation for the moshava, Fanny and Lolik announced their engagement, and at Passover time, they were married.

Both Hirsch and Ossowetzky came to the wedding. They brought 12 glass goblets—a present from the administration—as well as a glass cabinet covered by a delicate iron mesh, lest the glass should break, and the shards shatter the goblets. Now the cabinet stood proudly next to the stove, and only rarely did they take the goblets out of it, for there was no reason to celebrate.

Lolik touched Yehoshua's arm lightly and roused him, asking if he would like to stay overnight in their home. Yehoshua politely refused and got up from the soft sofa swaying and then set off into the night with the dampness and coolness waking him fully, and he felt as if he had just awoken from a deep sleep.

He thought this time of the night, when the moshava was asleep and closed-up in its houses, was beautiful. Drops of dew sparkled on the bougainvillea leaves, and Yehoshua was no longer worried about his boots becoming covered with the dust of the path. It was the new Russian woman he thought about and wondered whether she was similar to Fanny.

3. Olga Hankin 26 years old • 4. Yehoshua Hankin 22 years old.
Source: Rishon Lezion Archive.

Vue de la Rue „Rothschild" à „Richon-le-Zion" près Jaffa. Palestine.

5. Rishon LeZion Colony in Late 19th Century.
Source: Rishon Lezion Archive.

RISCHON LE ZION : DIE HAUPTSTRASSE.

6. Postcard of Rishon LeZion Colony, 1912 • Source: Rishon Lezion Archive.

September, 1885

At the end of September, Yehuda Leib Hankin decided to carry out the harvest. No one else was party to this decision, but his entire family said "Amen" to it.

At an early morning hour, the caravan was ready to set out. At its head stood the sole wagon owned by the family, and it was full of baskets and bushels. Tanhum, the youngest son, was standing on the wagon, declaring with a triumphant shout through a homemade megaphone of rolled newspaper, "Rise, O sleeping ones, the harvest time has come."

Sitting on the edges of the wagon were Israel and Yosef Feinberg, garden shears in hand, and blessing each other, "May you do likewise." Mendel and Ya'akov, Yehuda Leib's two oldest sons, were holding impatient mules that were spewing froth and stamping their legs, trying to gallop off.

Behind the Hankin, family cart stood that of Shimshon Belkind. Though not meant for heavy loads, it could carry the young daughters of the Hankin family—Haya, Rosa, and Rivka. The two toddler girls, ages three and two, were being kept at home. Now, both of them stood at the entrance to the yard and were engulfed in the apron of A-lya, the Arab woman who had lived with the family since the Russians had come to the lands of Ayun Kara, namely, Rishon Lezion. One of the girls cried because she wanted to join the others; her sister clung to her and copied her, wailing without understanding anything.

Yehoshua was the last to wake up, when all the tumult was almost over. Just this morning, it was hard for him to rise. He wanted to ignore the daylight and go on sleeping for some reason, but the little girls' unceasing wails disturbed him, and he finally got up. He remembered his father's plans and felt bad that he was delaying them all. He washed his face in ice-cold water that flowed from a wooden bowl and drained into the yard. On his way, he lifted his two sobbing sisters, one under each arm, and jiggled them until they calmed down. He gave them back to A-lya and joined Fanny and Sarah, his mother. His mother stood on her tiptoes, and her son bent his head toward her until she could tousle his hair. She was surprised by his tardiness and hoped to get an explanation from him. But Yehoshua only smiled at her and cast down his eyes, while taking from her hands two large jars dripping cold water and loading them on the wagon. Now, the caravan was set to go.

Curious people crowded the entrances to the yards; children surrounded the wagons, the Yavetz family opened their door, faces peeked out from a narrow slit, and immediately closed the door again.

Yehuda Leib sat on the platform at his wagon's front, lifted his long whip, and yelled out, "Let's go!"

And his cry merged with the snap of the leather strand slicing the air. Mendel and Yaakov let go of the reins, and the mules began to gallop, someone calling after them, "Come back, give it up!" But they did not pay attention to that shout, and clouds of dust-covered those staying behind, while the wagons disappeared as the road rose. Finally, at the end of the moshava, three more people joined them: David Zeiberg and Ostashinsky, two of the farmers belonging to the radicals, and the laborer who worked for them, Michael Halperin. The first two jumped on the cart as it was moving, with only Michael running after it, sticking his embroidered shirt into his pants and closing a button, his beard flying and his eyes shining. Then, filled with joy and dancing about, he shouted, "Amen, Amen, may it be Thy will."

When the caravan passed the Administration Center, its members increased the noise level. Fanny stood on the basket-loaded wagon, waved her apron, and was about to start dancing. Michael Halperin reached out his hand toward her and skipped alongside the cart and flapped the handkerchief he held, and Tanhum hummed through the paper megaphone; the Feinberg brothers put their fingers in their mouths and whistled. The Administration Center remained sealed as if emptied of its inhabitants, and only Sarah noticed a raised shutter and piercing eyes looking at them; she pulled at Yehoshua's shirt to show him, but he refused to look, putting his hand on her shoulder, and pointing toward the girls searching among the baskets. Sarah shrugged and averted her eyes, "Well, they're always hungry."

The procession descended the hill and crossed over Levontin's land that stretched along the settlement's edges and passed by the new lands of Ayun Kara, and soon, once again, there was no sign at all of the moshava's homes. The carts hobbled on a narrow, dusty path of dry, lumpy clods that snaked their way to the vineyards. Unkempt, untended vines drifted onto the path, and the weight of the clusters pulled them down. The wagons continued to roll between the vines and finally halted next to a sign with eroded letters, "Hankin Vineyard."

Yehuda Leib jumped down first. He rolled one of the bushels off the wagon and beckoned to the riders to hurry up and follow him. Then he entered the row of grapes and was swallowed up among them, only his silvery hair poking out from among the green leaves. At the end of the row, he paused and waited for the others who were slowly gathering around him. Once he had several witnesses, he harvested the first cluster and recited the *Shehecheyanu* prayer heard on special occasions, plucked a grape, and put it in his mouth. The smacking of his lips made the others drool. Yehuda Leib finished chewing and swallowed the grape. He was followed by the young Tanhum and then the rest. The cluster shifted from hand to hand, like a cup of kiddush wine on Sabbath eve. The sounds of enjoyment reverberated, and each, in turn, recited the blessing. In the end, only the pips remained from the first cluster, and they mingled among the clods of earth and were no longer visible.

The people scattered among the rows with great joy and laughter and began harvesting clusters of grapes and tossing them into the bushels, and slowly they filled to overflowing. Time passed quickly, a hot mountain wind replaced the morning breeze, and instead of rushed activity and joyous sounds came to the fatigue of the toilers. When high noon came, the sweaty harvesters took a break and left the orderly rows to sit in the shade of the wagon and eat their lunch.

While everyone was resting, a new group came and joined the grape gathers: women taking time off from their tasks, children who had escaped from the Talmud Torah, and farmers who had mustered courage despite the order from the Alsatian and found encouragement from seeing that the Administration Center stayed closed, and neither Ossowetzky nor Hirsch were walking about in the moshava. Among those who came was Olga. She was elegantly dressed, as if she were about to go to a dance, and the harvesters just gaped at her. Haya and Rosa took hold of a pleat of her dress, felt its silk, and reached out to touch her wide-brimmed hat, bedecked with ribbons. Olga was embarrassed by never having been at a harvest; Fanny, seeing her confusion, went to her and tied her own apron around her sister's waist. For a moment, Olga blushed and then tied the ends of the apron together, making a basket out of them and joined Fanny, and the two dived back into the rows of grapes as full of joy as two young girls.

As evening approached, the wagon was full of bushels, and whatever could not fit was put in Belkind's small cart as well. The first to tire was Yehuda Leib. He put down his pruning shears, sat on the edge of the wagon, and closed his eyes, with his lips murmuring a silent prayer. Then, Tanhum and the girls crowded next to him like a band of chicks and fell asleep on his chest, tired from the day's hustle-bustle. Then the others began to leave the vineyard one by one, each immersed in his thoughts and his fatigue. Some sat on the carts, while others sat on the parched clods, all of them drinking from the water jars and waiting for the wagons to move. Fanny sat next to Lolik with her head resting on his broad shoulder; Yosef slouched on a rock with his hat over his eyes. All of them were there—except for Yehoshua, the last one in the vineyard, looking for any remaining clusters hiding among the leaves.

Yehoshua was glad to be the last since he found the quiet among the clusters pleasant, and he wished to engulf himself in it for a few moments more. However, sweat blurred his vision and his mouth tasted liked dust. When he reached the end of the row, he wanted to go back—then he heard a voice above him, "Thou shalt not wholly reap the corner of thy field ... And thou shalt not glean thy vineyard." Upon listening to this, he straightened up, wiped the dampness from his eyes, and saw Fanny's sister, Olga Belkind. Yehoshua was embarrassed by his soiled, splattered clothes and his dusty face, with rills on it made by his sweating, and he did not understand what she was doing in his father's vineyard.

"Miss Belkind?!" He tried hard to hide his astonishment.

She stood there in front of him, wearing a graceful dress covered by a spotless apron; she was simply inconceivable. Everyone talked about her from the day she arrived in the moshava accompanied by her parents and that architect. She was invited to almost every event and was the object of conversation among the young people in the moshava. And he, even though she was on his mind, had never found the nerve to overcome his shyness, which was stronger than his will. But now she was standing opposite him, so close, and he could not find the words to start speaking with her. He wanted to throw the grape cluster in his hand at her purely white apron to stain it purple and red, break down the distance and bring her close to him. But he was embarrassed even thinking this.

He tried to hide his confusion and blurted out without knowing what he was saying, "Did you come now at noon with the other women and toddlers?" And when she nodded her head, he hurriedly went on and added, "I heard the children's quarrels and the cries of the mothers, but I preferred the sweetness of the grapes and the murmuring of the leaves over gossipy lunch."

"You run away from them, while I love their joy and the noise of the children and the infants' cries," she laughed. Yehoshua looked at her again; she was tall and different from the other young women in the moshava. She still seemed snobbish to him, but her laughter had softened her features. He liked her square chin, with the cleft in the middle, her broad cheekbones, and her slightly almond-shaped eyes with her thick brows that almost touched overshadowing them, and he did not know what else to say, so he was quiet.

Finally, Olga proffered her hand to him, and he stuck his out, not for her to take but to show her just how scratched and sticky his hand was and not fit even for becoming acquainted. But Olga did not withdraw her hand and only stretched out her arm to take hold of his. Yehoshua was startled and pulled his arm toward his chest clumsily. Olga chuckled and put her hand back in the folds of her apron, while Yehoshua already felt sorry for maybe not having behaved properly and missing a chance to get to know her.

She had only wanted to take something out of her apron that was serving as a container, a cluster of exquisite grapes. She lifted it up and picked a handful of its fruit. Then she neared Yehoshua with a smile flickering in her eyes and tried to shove the grapes into his mouth. Yehoshua turned his face away from her and refused to put even one more grape in it; he stepped back and stumbled into the vines. The peals of laughter that reverberated among the bushes overcame his embarrassment and the unease he felt. Now, when she put out her hand, he saw fit to take hold of it and no longer refused. Olga looked at him with mischief in her eyes and let her hand rest in his for a moment and then again took it away and put it in the folds of her apron.

The two of them straightened up. They shook off the remnants of leaves and dry branches and walked together. She was in front and he behind her, his eyes watching her every move, each pleat of her dress, and he wondered why she had gone to look for him among the grapevines. He preferred not to ask and not to be too surprised about it. He was afraid, but he could not take his eyes off her silhouette.

An afternoon breeze dried Yehoshua's sweat; insects scurried between the clods of earth, and Yehoshua took care not to step on them or to turn the clumps over and expose their beds to the burning sun. Olga marched confidently, paying no heed to the spiny branches striking her or to the hum of bees flying around the juice of the grapes, and, opening a gap, she went ahead of Yehoshua. She never once turned to look back since she knew he was trailing after her.

When Olga appeared from between the vines, everybody was sitting down, worn out and waiting for the sign from Yehuda Leib to move out, so no one lifted their eyes up to wonder about her tardiness. But when Yehoshua came out of the vineyard, they all began to look from her to him, and smiles spread on their faces. Fanny winked at Yehoshua, went to Olga, and elbowed her in the ribs. Yehuda Leib's call, "On the road, to the moshava," put an end to the growing merriment and saved the two from questions and curious glances, and everyone rushed to climb on the wagon or to walk alongside it.

On the way back to the settlement, people were quiet, barely talking.

Only Yehuda Leib sat restlessly. The closer they came to the moshava, the straighter he sat up, to the point that he finally rose and stood on the wagon, holding the whip, and the last rays of sun of the month of Elul toyed with his hair and turned the white stands to golden threads.

Strong sunlight shined into everyone's eyes and lent a golden glow to the roofs of the first houses espied by those coming from the hilltop. Yehuda Leib recalled that this was just the way he had stood and seen the houses in his mind's eye when he approached the lands of Ayun Kara three years ago. It was summertime then, too, the beginning of August.

Then, nine young fellows had sat in the wagon, with all their money in their pockets. In Jaffa, they had bought the wagon and two mules; they loaded it with boards and mats, coal, and flour and vegetables. The family was put up at Hatzkel's small hotel, and the young men told the others they would be away for only a week, and then they would come to take them. Since they did not know where the Ayun Kara lands were, they hired, for a few pennies, a young man, a camel driver going from Jaffa to Gaza and from Gaza to Egypt, who was familiar with the pathways of the Land of Israel and who agreed to lead them. At the same time, he rode his camel, and they followed in their wagon. At the last minute, some of them backed down and asked to stay in Jaffa, claiming they wanted to consult their families and listen to advice from an expert on agriculture and the conditions in the land. Yehuda Leib laughed at their doubts, "If we don't leave now, we will be late, and the landowners will look for other buyers." But his comrades were not convinced. So he rummaged through his pockets and took out nine rubles and gave one ruble to each member of the group, declaring that in exchange for ten rubles, he had bought the right to sit at the front of the wagon, along with the right to decide where it would head and where it would stop. Those who had trouble making up their mind took the ruble from him and climbed onto the wagon with the mules walking behind the camel.

Now, he was standing on the same wagon, with the same mules pulling it, but not all the ten riders were now with him. Some of them became enemies and split into camps: the camp of the "Baron's Guard" and the camp of the "Radicals." Some of them were lackeys dependent on Ossowetzky, while others had forgotten their promise to establish a moshava and be proud farmers who knew how to till the soil and earn from it their daily bread. All their pride had vanished as if it never existed, and their daring was replaced by fear: they were afraid of Hirsch, afraid of Ossowetzky, afraid to be farmers.

What had happened to all of them? He was angry. Why had they signed a lien and sold their land and their soul for bundles of cash tossed them every month? When they heard that he, Yehuda Leib, had refused to sign, they joined Ossowetzky's choir and bellowed to him, "Russian revolutionary" and "Radical."

Thoughts were running through his mind, and the reins went limp, and since he was deep in his musings, he had not paid attention to the mules who were slackening their pace. For sure, he would show everyone how to stomp on grapes and make wine. He would teach them that the taste of his wine was as good as French wine and prove to all the farmers and administrators that the land purchased at such great sacrifice would not be put on the market again.

While Yehuda Leib was still pondering, he straightened his back, pulled the harness, cracked the whip, and set the mules to galloping: He would still show them, show them, show...

The mules pulled the wagon uphill, and their noses quivered at the smell of fresh hay awaiting them in the stable. Once they entered the moshava, they slowed their blistering speed until they halted at the entrance to the yard of their driver. Night had fallen, and everyone stepped off the wagon and gathered in the yard next to the barn.

Yehuda Leib's house was the first in the moshava to be completed. Immediately afterward, the barn had been erected. At first, it was a community barn for all farmers in the settlement, but at the end of the first year, the communality had been dissolved, and wheat was no longer planted in the fields. So, the barn turned into a cowshed. They bought cows and milked them, but there was no one to sell them to. Then they became enslaved to the Baron, so they sold the cows, and the cowshed was turned into a winery. They dug a channel, poured concrete over it, and lined a cistern with stones. Then they connected the winery to the pit. They continued to call the winery "the granary" even though that had not been even one grain of wheat there for a long time. The winery's floor was dry and clean, since they had never crushed grapes on it. As in the morning, now too, the yard was filled with the bustling and movement of the curious, the children, and farmers who had dared to come under cover of darkness.

Yehuda Leib continued to sit high up on the wagon and waited until the yard was crammed full. As soon as it seemed to him that the entire moshava had gathered, and there were many witnesses to his actions, he alighted, chose an empty barrel, and rolled it to the barn. Then he went to the cart, took a bushel of grapes, carried it over, and emptied it into the barrel. Those standing near him rushed and took bushels as well and crammed as much as they could into the barrel. Once it was full, Yehuda Leib lifted his hand, and silence filled the yard. A few still held clusters, while others pulled back, and only the children came close to the barrel with bated breath.

Yehuda Leib grabbed his son Tanhum, set him in the barrel, and, for the second time that day, recited *Shehecheyanu*. Next, he patted the boy's bare feet and told him, "Stomp!"

Tanhum hesitated, frightened by everyone's stares, but his father's gaze encouraged him. He began to crush the grapes slowly; he would lift a foot and slip among the grapes, raise himself up, jump a bit, and then rise even higher and feel the cold of the night. Then he'd jump again and feel himself getting stronger as his leaps grew more powerful. Now, he was no longer thinking or seeing the people crowding around the barrel, and it seemed he was under a frenzied spell, up and down, up and down, and with his jumps, the murmurings grew bolder, reaching a mighty crescendo, "Stomp, Tanhum, stomp!" Suddenly a stream of first juice spurted out and spilled from the barrel into the concrete channel; eyes followed it passionately, and trembling fingers dipped in the juice.

With all the hoopla, no one paid any attention to the two approaching the yard with shirts buttoned to the neck and wearing ties, ironed pants, and striped jackets. These were Ossowetzky and the new administrator, a lackey who followed him everywhere—Benshimol. It was Benshimol's vigilance that had led them to Hankin's house. In the morning, from the window of the Administration Center, he had seen the wagons leaving the gate of the moshava. He waited for them all day, curious to know what they would bring with them, and when he saw bushels of grapes, he ran to Ossowetzky to prove his loyalty.

Now, the two were hiding among the cypresses, afraid to enter the yard. Israel Feinberg was the first to notice them, and he went to tell Yehuda Leib. The farmer did not glance their way but called to Yehoshua and whispered something while the others continued to fill the barrels and stomp on the grapes without being aware of anything else. Excitement and fervor had overwhelmed the grape crushers who had not stopped licking their fingers and gulping full cups of reddish juice nor singing and dancing.

Chief among the revelers was Michael Halperin. He grabbed the hands of those in the courtyard and pulled after him a procession of merrymakers reveling like himself. Yehoshua came to him and separated him from the line of dancers; the man wasn't feeling a thing and just continued to dance and prance, facing the juice flowing in the channel, until he stumbled upon a stone, and his long body wallowed in the dust. Yehoshua shook him, and when Michael stood up, he saw the two stodgy administrators, the bearded one and the one with fiery eyes, standing near the cypresses. Michael pulled himself away from Yehoshua's hold and went back to the juice makers, took a cup, and filled it with juice. Then he lifted it and, while dancing, approached the two; the fresh liquid spilled on his shirt, staining it.

First, Michael offered the cup to Ossowetzky. The administrator blushed, and the gold chain hanging over his suit jacket swayed with his breathing; he stepped back in fear of Halperin and perhaps—of juice stains. Benshimol stretched out his hand to take the cup, but the Ossowetzky grabbed his lapel and dragged him back. The two retreated, with Michael trodding after them, circling them, blocking their way. Somebody in the crowd noticed what Halperin was doing and came to watch the unfolding scene. Then, more and more people drew close. One small boy began to clap, and the adults joined in to provide the rhythm for Halperin's dance; with his steps growing wider and his hands waving, the juice spilled on his clothes. The Baron's two representatives were trapped between the gate and Michael, and the circle of people around them grew tighter.

Yehoshua felt that things had gone too far and the time had come to stop Halperin, so he called to his older brother Mendel and to Lolik, and together, the three marched into the wild crowd, with Lolik clearing the way. He went up to Halperin, lifted him like a baby, and took him out of the circle. Now, the people scattered, and the two administrators stood alone near the gate. For a moment, they froze in place and then hurried to disappear down the moshava's boulevard; they scurried along, casting occasional glances behind them to see if they were being chased. Only after they went quite a distance did Yehoshua return to the yard and join those stomping the grapes, but the flow rate of the juice became slower and slower.

In the wee hours of the night, people scattered, and only family remained to cork the barrels and roll them to the cellar beneath the barn. Olga, too, stayed to help Sarah Hankin seal the barrels and write down their measurements and capacity. Yehoshua approached them, looked at them, and scrutinized the differences between them: one had a narrow face and a kerchief on her head from which brown hair sprinkled with gray peeped out. The other had a square, flushed face, and her thick, black hair was combed into a bun—not even one curl peeked out. Yehoshua touched Olga's shoulder and said, "The kerosene in the lamp is almost finished, and it'll soon be morning. Come, I'll walk you to the Belkind home."

Olga took off the apron and handed it to Sarah, and for the second time that day, Yehoshua paid attention to her narrow waist and her silk dress that flapped with her every step.

They plodded slowly from sheer fatigue and made no effort to go any faster. A new day began to stir, and in the Yavetz house, people began to hitch the mules, and when they saw the two of them, they turned their backs on them. In the Zeiberg yard, Ostashinsky was milking the cows; and someone crossed the boulevard going early to say his morning prayers. Yehoshua offered a hand to Olga to make it easier for her to walk, and he noticed she was taller than he, while Olga, who read his mind, stood even straighter—but took his hand. He smiled at her and to himself and continued to march along that way until they neared the home of Shimshon Belkind. He was sorry the moshava was so small, and they had nowhere else to go. They stopped next to the stone gate, and Olga took her leave from him with a "Good morning" and rushed to go inside.

As he walked back to the Hankin house, Yehoshua strode quickly in the middle of the moshava's boulevard, picked a few of the bougainvillea flowers, and began tearing off their petals and tossing them along the way. The Hankin family yard was empty, with only A-lya, the Arab woman, who had not taken part in the excitement at night or the day before, walking about the yard feeding the chickens. He nodded to her and then dipped his face in cold water from the cistern and went to bed. Sleep did not come swiftly. The morning light crept in through the curtains, and strange, odd figures danced before his eyes. One of them alternately came and went—the figure of Ossowetzky with his red face and bulging eyes—and then that one was replaced with Olga's broad, ruddy face with her shining eyes. Again, the figure changed, and he had a hard time identifying it—a mouth, a woman's mouth; but the eyes, a man's eyes—and finally, he fell asleep.

7. Avshalom Feinberg 1907 • Source: Rishon LeZion Archive.

8. Belkind Family 1886 in Rishon LeZion • Source: Rishon LeZion Archive.

The Shot

Yehoshua went to the Belkind home to ask for Olga's hand a week before Hanukkah. That was a week of unceasing rain, and the path was full of puddles that had turned into open pits after the wagon wheels had left their mark on them. The Hankin family house was not far from that of the Belkind family, but since he had to skip over the puddles and go around the pits and since he wanted to keep his boots clean, Yehoshua's walk took longer. He did not know whether it was good to be late or if it would be better to hurry and be early, to be able to put an end to his fears.

How should he begin? He took counsel with himself. In what way could he impress Meir and Shifra, Olga's parents? From the day they had come to the moshava, they had been secluded in Shimshon's house, and except for events in the synagogue, he had not seen them, so he did not know them. Before he had gone out, Sarah dressed him in a summer suit jacket belonging to Yehuda Leib—she had made it clear to him he must not leave in his stained, worn-out student jacket. And Yehoshua had not argued. He did not have the strength to bicker with her, especially since he had not received his father's wholehearted agreement.

Yehuda Leib did not believe in marriage to an "intelligent, urbane woman, and even more so, one thirteen years older than Yehoshua." But as he walked, he felt the cold wind penetrating through the thick material of the coat and pricking his body and thought he should have, in any event, stuck to his guns and not agreed to wear summer clothing during a downpour. The issue of clothing so occupied him that he did not even realize he had already reached his destination.

The entrance to the Belkind family home was aglow with bright, shining light. Shimshon had brought the lamp with him from Russia, a memento from other houses and distant days. Still, since they had a hard time in Eretz Israel finding so many candles to light every night, they replaced the candle holders with small kerosene lamps. The lamp cast its radiant halo on the entrance hall, and whoever came in was seen by those sitting inside, but the entrant could not see them. Yehoshua did not like this entry to the house, and, on a regular day, he would go in through the kitchen door and announce his arrival from there. However, this time, he felt coming in through the back door did not suit his attire or the event.

Yehoshua knocked on the door, and from the low silhouette of the person who opened the door. He assumed it was Fanny standing before him. If Fanny was here, then so was Israel, he said to himself. It was only the laughter of these two that was missing. So it was that immediately upon entering he heard Fanny's teasing voice, "Look, just look! Like a groom in front of his *chuppah*." And Israel chiming in after her, "Where's the jacket from? For years I haven't seen you in a tailored coat. You look like a clerk. Did you find a job with the Baron?"

Fanny approached him and circled around him seven times, and on each turn, she straightened a fold, pulled down the edges, and cleaned off a crumb stuck on the jacket. Yehoshua's head was swimming because of the encircling, and his eyes sought Olga, since he missed having her in the room. And hadn't they agreed on his coming, and hadn't she promised him she would be waiting in the entry hall? Perhaps she was embarrassed? No, Olga wasn't afraid of anyone and did whatever her heart desired. Lolik nudged him and sat him next to him on the sofa, and the people sitting in the room went back to usual and again spoke about administrators and decrees.

Yehoshua did not hear what they were saying. He was still organizing his words in his mind and did not know how to begin. What should he say to them? That he loves Olga? Should he speak Yiddish? Perhaps Russian? Either way, they'll laugh at him. Then, finally, Olga came in. Yehoshua was sure that more than an hour had passed since Lolik had sat him down on the sofa. She came right from the kitchen, with floury hands, wearing regular clothes and the scent of honey engulfing her. Together with her mother, Shifra, she had been busy baking sweet rolls dipped in honey. When she saw Yehoshua, she grinned and rolled up her apron so it should not dirty anyone in the room and shoved it under her belt. Then she pushed Israel and Yehoshua until they made room for her, and she sat between them.

Olga knew Yehoshua well and understood just how hard it was for him to sit in the company of her parents when she was not present. However, she smiled to herself, seeing his discomfort, and relaxed. After all, wasn't she sitting in her home and aware of what she wanted; she had already known it since the grape harvest.

When the others saw how she was sitting next to Yehoshua comfortably and waiting, they stopped talking. Olga looked at those present one by one and turned her gaze to Yehoshua and whispered to him, "Now it's time." When Olga addressed Yehoshua, her voice became tender and whispery and aimed only at him. Yehoshua took heart and rose, standing for a minute and wiping his hands on the sides of his pants; then, he sat down again and looked down.

Olga put her head close to his, and her urgent murmuring tickled his ear lobe. Yehoshua took heart, held her hand, peeled the dough off her fingernails, and without looking up, said to them all, "I want her, want her to be my wife." He waited for their mockery, since he was sure that his request was a surprise to them and they would refuse him, arguing he was a mere lad who hadn't yet turned twenty. But they said nothing. For a moment, all was quiet, and then they were all chattering again. He had told them nothing new; they already knew what he wanted long before he was aware of it himself.

Indeed, the entire moshava knew. There was no one in the small settlement who had not noticed his caressing glances at Olga and his repeated attempts to get close to her. Of course, they had all been exchanging looks and whispering behind his back that he was blind and could not see what was taking place and that this was love based on a lad's admiration for the grown-ups, but Yehoshua did not hear and did not see their glances. He was steeped in love, so the family was not excited by his actions. If they had only known how many sleepless nights there had been until he had mustered the courage to ask for Olga's hand, he thought, and felt sick at heart. He had not noticed their murmurings the same way he now did not understand their silence. Olga understood his disappointment. She rose and approached her father and stood facing him until he had to pay attention to her and get up and hug her, and immediately go to Yehoshua and press his hand. Shifra saw what her husband had done and also got up. She took out small glasses from the cupboard, poured wine into them, and went back to check her baking sweet rolls. Only after everyone had seen the wine did they stir and begin to deal with the reason Yehoshua had come. They then set the wedding for a few days after Sukkot, after everyone would be finished harvest of the crops and picking fruit, as well as the wine grape harvest, and preparing for long winter days. They chose the time but did not know that a rebellion would break out before the wedding and interfere with the moshava's way of life.

☙

Things had not settled down in the moshava since the grape harvest in Yehuda Leib's vineyard. Every week new regulations were added, and they divided the farmers. At first, the moshava had a single association called "Rodef Shalom" [Pursuer of Peace], and everyone belonged to it: farmers, laborers, Maskilim [the Enlightened], and ordinary people—even the administrators were part of it. Every Sabbath, they would gather to discuss Talmudic issues and sing songs. They'd chatter about innovations in the Hebrew language published in Ben-Yehuda's paper, *HaZvi*, share information about what was being done in the field, like how to guard against the worm chewing the fruit and the mole that was nibbling at the roots.

The first to leave the association were the laborers, headed by Michael Halperin. They established their own society after the high and mighty Ossowetzky refused to sit at the same table with them. A few farmers joined the hired workers, while some stayed in the first society. Ossowetzky's wrath was ignited by those who left, and he began to split the farmers, promising a different payment to those who went along with him. When he learned that the breakaway farmers would not change their minds, he formed a third society that admitted only those closest to him—its name was "Agudat Re'ut" [Friendship Society]. Whoever feared for his own welfare, as well as for the support money, made every effort possible to join Ossowetzky's inner circle. And if not accepted into the inner circle, he'd mocked its members out of envy for them. However, if accepted, he'd scorn the farmers and hire workers who belonged to the first and second societies.

The entire moshava was fractured between the different societies and those willing to recite the new regulations orally and obey each order, inform on the identity of those refusing to do so, and those who refused to heed the administrator's voice. Very quickly, Ossowetzky realized the power he held through the regulations, which allowed him to force acceptance of his whims and to deter the farmers from opposing him, and he produced as many as he could. Daily, his workers hung a fresh page of restrictions on the pillar standing in the administration yard.

That was not enough for him. He also sent the town crier to announce that people should gather in the yard to hear the new restrictions read. When he felt all of that was insufficient to force his leadership on them, he would send a special messenger from house to house and make sure to have the residents sign that they had indeed heard the announcement. Then, in the evening, everyone would gather in the courtyard, and Ossowetzky would look them over and read the regulations to them out loud and then leave the people to hold discussions. At the same time, he went up to the veranda and observed the crowd from on high, enjoying power and eminence.

The courtyard thus became the center of life in the moshava, and Ossowetzky's actions pleased him no end. When the days began to get longer, the clerk Benshimol ordered an awning be built over the pillar. The kibitzers of the moshava joked that after the awning would come the walls, and the pillar with its regulations would be the support beam for a new community center and perhaps even for a theater.

A few days before Rosh Hashanah, a new decree was pinned to the pillar. This time Ossowetzky himself hung it, and not being satisfied with a single location, he went from one cypress tree to the next, and on each trunk, he tacked a copy of this announcement: "The Administration has the right to invalidate farming to anyone who is not loyal to the Baron and his emissaries."

Two days before Yom Kippur, he repeated this act. Alongside the older regulation, he hung a new one: "The farmers and hired workers must come to the Administration Building and sign a declaration of loyalty. Whoever does not sign will be called for disciplinary action by Samuel Hirsch, the supervising representative of the Baron's colonies."

Since the farmers were afraid of losing support money, they hurried to stand in line that very day in the administration yard to sign the declaration. Ossowetzky sat on the veranda and shook hands with each signer and showered him with compliments, and when no one was looking, he would wink to Benshimol and whisper the count to him, "Thirteen, fourteen, they all will come ..."

Among those refusing to sign were the Feinberg, Belkind, Eisenband, and Hankin families, and they were joined by the plot-less hired workers who belong to Michael Halperin's society.

The morning after the signing day, the announcements disappeared from the cypress trunks. Someone said he had seen Michael Halperin go by in the night and remove them. That very evening, the administration yard was abuzz with farmers and hired workers, both signees and those refusing to sign. All were shouting simultaneously and breaking into each other's words. Since it was impossible to hear, they raised their voices, and the clamor grew. Amid all the noise and tumult, suddenly Michael Halperin appeared. First, he stood on the side and listened; then, he rolled a rock over to the pillar and stood on it. Now all could see him elevated above them, and they quieted down.

Michael began speaking in a sing-song tone, drawing the crowd to listen to him and not miss a word. He was like a prophet; his eyes were shining, his thick beard was wild, his ritual fringes and shirttails were flapping about his trouser belt.

"We will organize into one society. He called to them, we will be the 'majority' and not the 'minority,'" we will be the 'majority.' "Unity will increase our strength. Unity of opinion and unity of deed will free us from the yoke of bureaucracy. Where is your pride? Where is the farmer who eats his bread by the sweat of his brow?"

"Talk! All talk!" shouted someone for the edges of the crowd. "We rebelled once, and we failed. We tried to plant wheat and live like the Arab *fellah*. The *fellah* was successful, his seeds germinated, and his crops' grains were full, and we, our grains were dried out and our sacks empty. And the Baron came to our aid and dug a well and extended credit and taught us how to plant, and you and your like come and kick and spit in the well, the money for whose digging came from the Baron. Who are you? An uppity hired worker, a delusional prophet ..."

Michael lifted his hand in dismissal of the farmer's statements. "Come, approach the light, you who quote Ossowetzky's word," he called to him. "Listen to other tones, to the sounds of the pickaxe and the hoe in the heavy earth, to the rustling of the seed sprouting and the stalk growing." As he spoke, his voice rose and spread wave after wave, and they no longer argued with him nor interrupted him.

Just then, the main door of the Administration Center opened, and Ossowetzky came close and stood at the edge of the circle of people. The stocky man was sure they would clear a path for him, for was he not the director of the moshava. But no one paid attention to him. So Ossowetzky pushed some of them and entered into the crowd, but still, no one even looked at him.

Finally, the administrator responsible for the moshava became angry and, while still inching forward, began calling out to the speaker standing on the stone, "Revolutionary! Radical!" And the closer he came, the more Halperin's face was harder to see since the crowd closed in and hid him from Ossowetzky's view. Yet, Ossowetzky still heard his quiet, rhythmic voice, "Unite. Say 'No'! No to the bundles of money."

For a moment, Ossowetzky was quiet as he continued clearing a path for himself through the crowd. As he approached, he repeated his words and even yelled in his direction, but Michael continued to speak to the open air and ignored the shouts aimed at him. The two were like a chorus of the deaf, with neither hearing the screams of the other nor his voice, but the crowd heard and looked on, enjoying the performance.

Ossowetzky moved near the pillar and stood next to the stone; he lifted his eyes toward Halperin, whom he realized was much higher up, and he panicked. Suddenly he felt like a midget about to be trampled.

"Go," he whispered to him, "Go." But Halperin continued to speak, pretending he did not hear him. "Go," screeched Ossowetzky, "this is the home of the administrator, and you are a hired worker, a revolutionary. Go quietly." Halperin cupped a hand to an ear, bent down toward the administrator, and said, "I heard a buzzing close to my ear; there are bees in the yard. Be careful. They sting."

Ossowetzky could no longer contain himself given the humiliating smiles on the faces of those standing around him, so he barked, "Get away from my house, get out of the moshava, an abomination, a curse on you and the society. Until you came to Rishon Lezion, no one dared to raise his voice against me. I was a director, the emissary of Hirsch and the Baron himself, and what are you? A laborer, a maniac. Leave and take all your helpers with you, and the moshava will settle down."

In the meantime, people gathered around and closed the circle around the two and waited for a battle since they knew how much Ossowetzky hated Michael Halperin. He had threatened to expel him from the settlement more than once, and he had sent letters to the farmers David Zeiberg and Ostashinsky telling them not to rent him a room. Since Halperin had become the leader of the workers' society, Ossowetzky considered him a competitor who was inciting all the hired workers against him. As for the farmers, most of them did not like Ossowetzky and were afraid of him. Now that administrator seemed to them like an insect pleading for his life from a giant, and this giant was none other than a simple laborer who was not scared and dared to open his mouth, to mock and ridicule him. And if a hired hand was allowed to do so, so were they. Halperin's confidence was contagious, and they began to move, whisper, and provoke each other.

Ossowetzky felt their hatred burning behind his back and tried to say something, but his voice was swallowed up, and no one heard him. He began to sweat and tremble and retreated slowly in fear and terror. Those standing near him saw his agitation and the drops of sweat gathering on his forehead, and they heard his heavy breathing; they were frightened by their own harshness, never having expected that they would go so far. He tried to step back, and when they opened a path for him, he saw the faces staring at him on both sides of the human walls, and he wished to etch them in his memory, but his vision was blurry, and he registered only a mob of eyes pitying him and scorning him.

Finally, he left the circle of the crowd. But no sooner had he exited, the walls closed, and the faces were turned from him to the man towering above them, impassioning them with his voice. Ossowetzky hurried to go up the steps to the veranda of the Administration Center, opened the door, went inside, and closed the shutters, trying to block out the voices from the yard, but in vain. Halperin's voice seeped through the walls and chased him even in his home. Then, deep within himself, the director of the settlement took a solemn decision. He had to eject Halperin from here, to send him as far away from him as possible.

᳐

The holiday season passed; the wedding of Yehoshua and Olga was postponed. They were waiting for calmer days when everyone would be ready for happy times. In the meantime, Olga joined Halperin's circle and often went to his room in the house of Zeiberg and Ostashinsky to listen, along with the other hired workers and farmers who joined his melodious voice. The meetings in Halperin's room went on into the deep of the cold nights. It reminded her of the times in Petersburg, the happy student days, when she went with Fanny and her brother Israel to hear the cry of "Let us go up [to the Land of Israel]," and become impassioned by the slogans and swear to live a simple life toward attaining the goal—to be free Jews in a new country. Yehoshua did not go with her; he helped Yaakov and Mendel in the barn and drained the water in the fields so they should not sweep away the soil and expose the roots of the young seedlings. The more Olga went to Halperin's room, the more often Yehoshua went down to the fields and immersed his hands in the mud to feel its warmth between his fingers.

It was then that Yehoshua discovered the land and learned to love it and to prefer it to the company of people. He found the serenity and quiet that he lacked. Its smell intoxicated him, and its colors dazzled his eyes. He became familiar with each hummock and each rock; he caressed them and felt them with his hands. Sometimes, it seemed to him that the land was competing with his love for Olga, returning his love without pressure; it was unchanging and ready to embrace all of him and drown him within it.

In those days, after he finished the work in the vineyard and the barn, he would take the mare and ride to the rained-moistened meadows and fields, to be among the green barley sprouts and the wild herbs and thorn bushes, with the aromas of the grasses engulfing and titillating his nostrils. That was how he became familiar with the Bedouin encampments, the sabra fences, and the clay houses in Naana and Azur villages. He memorized the language of the *fellahin* and learned their every movement and custom. And when the days grew shorter, he even stayed overnight in their tents and clay huts, distancing himself all the more from the moshava and its nonsense.

Two days before Hanukkah in 1885, an announcement was placed on the administration's pillar. Unlike the previous announcements, this was small and unobtrusive. Zeiberg was the first to read it when he was on his way to the field. He read and imagined his eyes were fooling him. When he reread it, his body shook, "*As of today, it is forbidden for any farmer or hired hand living permanently in the moshava to house in his home an outsider for more than 24 hours. The definition of an outsider is anyone who has no possessions and does not have permanent housing in the moshava and anyone who did not sign the loyalty letter.*"

Zeiberg returned and told Ostashinksy, who had been taking his time feeding his chickens, about the decree. The farmer was not astounded, and after he washed his hands using the barrel containing rainwater, he took out an envelope from his jacket pocket and put it in his friend's hand. "Just now it came. A few minutes after you left, Benshimol brought it."

Though the letter was short, many signatures were appended to it: the signatures of Ossowetzky, Samuel Hirsch the Alsatian, Benshimol, the banker Herzenstein who took care to send the money once a month from Jaffa to Rishon Lezion, and the top of page displayed the name of Baron Rothschild. The signatures blinded his eyes, and for a moment, Zeiberg could not go on reading the text. He again looked at Ostashinksy and then wiped his eyes, but letters began jumping again, "Michael Halperin is unwanted in the moshava. He arrived as an outside laborer and did not receive permission to stay in Rishon Lezion. According to the new regulations, he must leave the moshava within 24 hours. If he does not go, the right to farming will be taken away from Misters Zeiberg and Ostashinsky."

Zeiberg sat down, wringing his hands, and looked at his friend to give him advice.

"Ossowetzky cannot best Halperin," the farmer tried to calm his friend. "These two are like two rooted mountains that cannot be moved. Of course, they will grapple, but in the end, they will make up, and quiet will be restored," he said, but he didn't even believe himself.

On the first night of Hanukkah, the moshava was in a whirlwind. Pouring rain came down and caused people to scurry to their homes. Farmers and hired workers gathered in the house of Zeiberg and Ostashinsky. Everyone was waiting for the administrator to come and bring the order with him. They lit candles on time and put the menorah on the windowsill; now, they sat to wait in silence. In the meantime, more and more moshava residents flowed into the house, and the overcrowding became even worse.

A long time after the candles in the menorah had burned out, Ossowetzky came, accompanied by Hirsch and Benshimol. From outside, it looked to them as if the structure was about to explode, and they were uncertain whether they should all go in or just send in Ossowetzky by himself. The administrator did not want to exhibit the fears roiling his innards and decided to prove to his colleagues that he was still in control. So, he instructed Hirsch and Benshimol to wait for him outside in the lean-to protecting the work tools. What could happen anyway? Didn't all of them need him and the support money?!

Buoyed by the decision, the man inflated his chest and strode toward the house. The door was open, and there was no reason to ring the bell or to wait until they would come to call him. Ossowetzky wiped the soles of his boots on the boot scraper, straightened the gold chain peeping out of his pockets, and brushed his fingers over his hair, which was damp from raindrops, and went in, looking for the owner and the room renter—Halperin. The owner he saw leaning against the windowsill in the corner of the room, and he found Halperin by the noise coming from the center of the room. As usual, the hired worker stood surrounded by people, and his voice carried through the room, so everyone had to hear what he was saying. Many people were standing between Ossowetzky and Halperin and the homeowner blocking the way.

For a minute, the bureaucrat, the director of the moshava, hesitated. Then he removed an envelope from his pocket, straightened its edges, and handed it to the person closest to him. "Give this envelope to Mr. Ostashinsky. The noise and the overcrowding are barring me from approaching him," he said in a gentlemanly fashion, ensuring his voice should not tremble.

But the man just smiled at him, his legs apart and his hands in his pockets, and he was making no effort to take them out. Ossowetzky tried someone else, but that fellow pretended he did not hear. The administrator did not give up and waved the envelope over the heads of those present to draw Ostashinsky's attention. But Ostashinsky turned to face the people in the room, his glance passing over Ossowetzky as if he were air. Ossowetzky regretted he had come alone, and all his confidence drained away. Still holding the envelope, he debated with himself what to do and finally tore it open and unfolded the letter; he yelled, "Ostashinsky, I have a letter for you in my hand, a letter sent from the Baron." No one in the room paid any attention to him.

The chief administrator waited no longer and began reading the order loudly to overcome the noise. His screeching was unclear, so the people quieted down to try to hear him. From the garbled sentences and screaming, they understood that Ossowetzky had come to evacuate Halperin's room by order, to lock it, and forbid Ostashinsky and Zeiberg from renting it to anyone else. The clearer the words of Ossowetzky became, the more panicked eyes turned from Ostashinsky to Halperin and from Halperin to Ossowetzky; everyone waited for a signal to break the silence.

The quiet that dominated the room encouraged Ossowetzky, and his voice grew more assertive. "Where is Halperin's room," he thundered, and when there was no reply, he added, "Hirsch is waiting outside and has an eviction notice signed by the Baron."

People had not yet begun to talk, but the absolute silence began to shatter. Ostashinsky took his elbow off the windowsill and moved toward the administrator. His path was cleared until he stood face to face opposite him and said mildly, "Get out. No one asked you to come. I don't want you in my house."

Ossowetzky laughed mockingly. "Wanted? Since when does a director ask a subordinate if he is wanted?"

"Get out!" Ostashinsky raised his voice at him, "Get out! And if not, I won't be able to stop myself from hitting you. I won't be blamed; you will. You will be accused of trespassing."

Giggles were heard from the crowd. Someone went up to Ossowetzky and nudged him. Another pulled his jacket.

"Go, Go, Go." People began crowding him and shoving him. Ossowetzky moved back, and then someone opened the door, and the wind blew in, carrying cold raindrops. Ossowetzky kept on retreating from the men swarming him until he reached the entrance; then, he went out, and the door closed after him.

He found Hirsch and Benshimol waiting for him under the lean-to, wrapped in their coats and trembling from the cold and wet. Ossowetzky showed them the torn envelope and the crumpled stationery, and then he tossed them away without saying a word; they fell into the mud, became waterlogged, and were washed by the stream into the channel. The three hurried to leave the yard, to flee the raindrops and the eyes following them from the window of the house.

Inside the house, someone began to hum, "For the miracles and for the wonders," and swiftly, the buzzing turned into singing. Feet were lifted, hands clasped, shoulder put to shoulder, and all began dancing around Halperin, Zeiberg, and Ostashinsky, shoving aside the night and the rain and the fears for what tomorrow would bring.

In the morning, the rainstorm moved away, erasing all the troubles of the previous night. The men went out to work in the fields and orchard, shore up branches devastated by the storm, fill in the holes that opened in the soil, and straighten stakes supporting a leaning fence. Quiet reigned over the moshava.

Around ten o'clock, a group of lads saw Ossowetzky and Samuel Hirsch marching in the direction of Zev Yavetz's house. Working Yavetz's fields were two families of hired hands who lived in the farmyard, and that way, he could allow himself to stay at home and study a page of Talmud. To be sure, he was a strong, husky man like Lolik, and like him, he had come with the first settlers to Rishon Lezion, but unlike him, he walked bent over, spoke in a whisper, and kept his distance from the "radical" group of farmers. Yavetz was Ossowetzky's crony, and the latter had appointed him to represent the farmers in his contacts with them. The farmers, however, ignored this appointment and instead chose Levontin, who was the eldest among the farmers of Rishon Lezion and the first to buy a plot in Ayun Kara, for which they all respected him. When they had to send a message or an announcement, they went to Levontin, and he would give it to Yavetz, and Yavetz would take it to Ossowetzky. The result was that more than once, a decree or announcement reached Ossowetzky garbled, as did messages from him to the farmers. Yavetz understood the situation and did not fight for his appointment; he did everything he could not make the farmers nor the administrator angry at him.

The young fellows followed "the lordships" up to Yavetz's house and stood behind the door to hear the discussion. They heard the three arguing among themselves; the director tried to convince Yavetz to come with them "for the purpose of the signing," but Yavetz refused, despite threats by Hirsch to take away his farming rights and to besmirch his name. Afterward, the young men related that they had heard yelling and curses and finally silence. Next, the door of Yavetz's house opened, and they saw him going out with a Talmud volume in his hand, and Hirsch and Ossowetzky trailing behind him. Yavetz's elderly mother also came out, stopped at the threshold, and called the administrators rude names, her hoarse voice echoing all down the road, "What do you want from my son? Can't you make do with the hired workers? You also enjoy hurting the farmers?"

The rain had started to fall, and the three walked faster—with the young fellows behind them trying not to draw attention to themselves.

At the gate to Ostashinsky's yard, the Baron's emissaries halted. Then crossed the entry, one after the other, and walked around the house, pushing Yavetz in front of them. Finally, they stood by the low window of Halperin's room, which faced the yard, and its shutters were open, letting in the wind. A sycamore tree with spreading limbs cast a shadow on the window and shed its fruit all around it. Yavetz flinched and tried to get away from the other two, but Ossowetzky dragged him by his coat lapels and ordered him to take off his glasses. When he tried to disobey, Hirsch took the deed of trust out of his pocket, showed him the signature, and threatened to rip it up. Yavetz bent over and unenthusiastically crept to the window and removed the shutters, then he took the awl from Hirsch's outstretched hand and detached the window frame until the place where the window had been a large hole.

"Thus shall be done to the rebels," chuckled Ossowetzky; he dragged a crate lying in the yard and put it next to the wall. First, the two administrators climbed up and entered the house, while Yavetz stayed outside getting wet in the rain; his back stooped even more, and with a volume of Talmud in his hand, he mumbled a prayer. A moment later, Ossowetzky stuck his head outside of the opening in the wall and called him to join them, "The rebels in Rishon Lezion have to know that their brethren are shunning them and condemning their actions—and not only the Baron and his emissaries." Yavetz climbed on the crate and disappeared into the room.

A short time passed, and the young men heard sounds of explosion and breakage, and they saw objects being thrown out of the window: a chair and table legs, books, and a pile of clothing. None of those in the house paid any attention to the rain, and the yard filled with pages and furniture fragments that soon became waterlogged and sank into the mud.

When the three went away, the young fellows came closer and peeked through the gaping rectangle that was once a window: utensils tossed away, a smashed mirror, an upside-down water bowl whose contents were dripping on the clay floor. They wanted to riffle through it all to discover usable finds— weren't all the thrown away items now up for grabs—but fearing what this would look like, they finally stampeded out of the yard.

In the evening, people hurried to return from the fields to their homes, each steeped in his own thoughts and not talking with his comrades. Zeiberg, Ostashinsky's partner, was the first to reach home, and he immediately felt the wind blowing through the ravaged window opening, and he saw the items lying on the floor and peeking out from the mud in the yard. He cried out and ran to the boulevard and began calling, "Ostashinsky, Ostashinsky!" Some of the farmers saw him and tried to find out what had happened, but Zeiberg didn't answer and continued to run toward the outer edge of the moshava.

The distraught farmer met Ostashinsky plodding along, leading his mule uphill by the halter. Zeiberg did not stop running and almost crashed into his friend. Fortunately, Ostashinsky managed to turn aside, and Zeiberg flew past him. But unfortunately, he was so panicked that only after a few steps did he realize he had passed his partner and turned back. Breathing heavily and panting from the running, he slowed down and began walking alongside the mule owner, spewing out garbled half-sentences. Ostashinsky pulled the reins and stopped the mule; he grabbed Zeiberg by the shoulders and tried to calm him down. But the farmer, having found the person he sought, broke down; tears welled in his eyes, and his speech became even more unfathomable.

From the choppy phrases, Ostashinsky finally understood what had happened in his house, and he felt furious anger invading every cell in his body, threatening to explode uncontrollably.

The two neared the houses rising atop the hill, and people began to gather around them. Soon a large group was walking in the middle of the moshava's boulevard. Someone ran to the vineyard to call Halperin but did not find him. As usual, he was not in a hurry and was late to return. He was probably dawdling on the paths, looking at the migrating birds passing through the country's skies on their way south or picking a bunch of rose flax flowers and wondering about the split petals of the hollyhocks standing tall among the rocks.

When everyone reached the center of the settlement, the rumor was rampant. The young fellows who had followed Ossowetzky, Hirsch, and Yavetz were now heroes, and everyone asked them to repeat the morning scene. So, they repeated their version over and over, each time adding details and improving it until it was like a horror story.

In the meantime, Ostashinsky had arrived home. He entered it, went quickly through the rooms, glanced about, and saw the furniture fragments tossed in the yard and, without a peep, turned around and set out for Yavetz's house. Zeiberg, who had not gone into the house, hurried to follow him, and behind the two, the entire crowd surged. To Ostashinsky's surprise, Yavetz was waiting for them with his coat on, sitting on his chair at the entrance to his house, a volume of Talmud on his knees and his legs bent as if he intended to get up and go, waiting only for the call to move. When he saw them nearing him, he rose and stepped toward them, and without asking questions, marched with them and concealed his book under his long coat.

The procession shifted to the direction of the Administration Center. Next to the gate, they met Israel and Yosef Feinberg, as well as Shimshon, Yaakov, and Yehoshua Hankin. Fanny and Olga also came with them, and while they were still crowding around to enter the gate, they saw Halperin from afar, walking after a group of young children. The little ones slipped into their house, and the eccentric fellow with the thick, wild beard ran down the street, but when he saw the mob near the gate, he ceased running and joined it without knowing for what or for why.

The incensed crowd stopped, and the guard came out of the hut near the gate and sought to stop them, but someone pushed him, and he hurried to get away from there, since he was sure the stream of people would overwhelm the hut and trample the little structure with him inside it. Marchers amassed next to the steps to the veranda and began shouting, "Ossowetzky, come out! Ossowetzky, come out!"

The curtain was flicked aside, and the administrator's face became visible; all the while, the crowd kept calling. Finally, the man came out, with a hat in one hand and something hidden in the other. A few people noticed that he quickly hid it in his pocket. Then, he approached the staircase, standing above the people and sensing his weakness.

Michael Halperin emerged from the crowd, and drawing closer, stood on the bottom step, with his long shadow falling on the stairs. Yavetz was pushed after him, and Ostashinsky held on to his shirt. Behind their backs stood the farmers and the laborers, next to each other, and in the dark, they all blended.

Halperin stretched his foot out, intending to go up, and Ossowetzky was terrified, cold sweat washing over his body. He wanted to yell to him, "Stop!" but the cry stuck in his throat, and his eyes flicked left and right, seeking help. But he could not see the guard, Benshimol, or any familiar face in the sea of heads. He put his hand in his pocket and felt the cold, calming metal, and without overthinking, he hurried to draw out the pistol and started shooting in the air.

Echoes of the shot were heard within the closed courtyard and rang in the ears of those standing there. Shocked and disbelieving what they had heard, they did not move nor let out a peep. The first to leave were the people at the edges of the throng. On their tiptoes, they crept out, and then the others slowly dispersed. The yard emptied out, Halperin's shadow disappeared, Ostashinsky released Yavetz from his hold, and the last to leave the place were Yosef and Israel Feinberg. Ossowetzky remained by himself on the veranda, frightened by the sudden quiet and his isolation. He stepped back while facing the yard, the hand behind his back burned from contact with the gun, and he closed the door to the Administration Center.

Yosef and Israel went to Shimshon Belkind's house; Israel went to fetch Fanny and Yosef—because he did not want to be left by himself. The large lamp was burning in the entrance, and Yehoshua and Olga were already seated on straw stools, Halperin, Zeiberg, and Ostashinsky trying to decide what to do. All of them were convinced Ossowetzky would send someone to call the soldiers and accuse the moshava farmers of rebellion—and the first to be blamed would be those who had refused to sign.

Who wasn't familiar with the behavior of the administrator and his habit of blaming others but never himself? And who would dare to complain to the higher management and reveal that Ossowetzky had shot into the air? No one. Their word was worth nothing against his. Instead, he would accuse the farmers and provide a list of grievances against them: the grape harvest in Yehuda Leib's vineyard, the committee led by Michael Halperin, and the refusal of the "revolutionaries" to sign. He would find a common thread, one that would link the three families and make them out to be a group of rebels inciting all the farmers.

They sat in quiet, and finally, Yosef Feinberg broke the silence in an attempt to analyze things as they were and to organize them according to his logic: "Soldiers will come," he declared. "Because of that, we will turn to Yehuda Leib and ask him to present our issue—for the Turkish soldiers show great respect for anyone with gray hair and who also has a small potbelly." Hesitatingly, those sitting with him agreed, since they had no idea how to behave with Turkish soldiers. But on the other hand, Yehuda Leib knew soldiers, though not Turkish but Russian, and because of that, they hoped he would find a common language.

For a short while afterward, they continued to sit next to each other, deeply fearing what would emerge in the morning. The first to get up to go was Yehoshua, whom they had tasked with convincing his father and preparing him for the future; next, Olga rose to take leave from him. She offered her hand to him, and the heat of her hand in his made him forget a bit of the events of the night. He asked her to go outside with him and to accompany him on his way. She nodded yes and went to her room to take a scarf. Together, the two left the house and walked quite a distance, taking the morning air into their lungs, and whispering between themselves. They did not speak about their wedding, nor about Ossowetzky or Halperin. Rather, he told her about the beauty of the fields in the month of Kislev and the black color of the moist earth, the black goats climbing on the rocky hills, and the expanses that a human eye had never seen. Olga smiled at him and stayed quiet. Because she did not respond, he turned his head toward her and saw the smile at the corners of her mouth.

They halted next to a Washingtonia palm that had grown tall. Yehoshua stretched out a finger and patted the mouth of the woman next to him and the dimple in her chin. And when he wanted to express his love for her, she put her hand on his mouth and nodded as if hinting, "No need, I know." He kissed the fingers of her hand, and she laughed at him in her soft voice and held out her other hand.

A short time after Olga said goodbye to Yehoshua, soldiers came to the moshava. They were Turkish soldiers riding groomed horses adorned with strands of camel wool in red and blue. They wore pressed uniforms closed with copper buttons; on their feet were highly polished boots that reached to their knees. The entire caravan halted at the edge of the settlement, and only the commander left the group and galloped to the boulevard. The horse plodded in the mud and stopped at the first house; the officer dismounted and knocked on the door. Old Kanter came out to meet him, while stuffing his shirt into his trousers and combing his mustache to shake out the breakfast crumbs; the Turk addressed him in Turkish. At first, Kanter tried to understand him and even replied in Russian, sprinkled with the few Arabic words he knew. Still, when he realized it was useless to try to understand each other, he motioned to the Turk to follow him and plodded toward the house of Fanny and Lolik. Looking out the window, Lolik noticed Kanter and went out to greet him while holding a cup of coffee. When he saw the officer, he muttered angrily through pursed lips, "Ossowetzky did not wait for morning, under cover of darkness he raced and called the soldiers," and walked toward the Turk, calling him to join him in a friendly, welcoming tone.

After being impressed by Lolik's size, the man took a whistle out of his pocket and blew it to summon his soldiers. A few minutes later, the soldiers stood in a long row next to their commander and waited for orders.

Lolik waited no longer. He marched with head held high, and behind him, the officer's horse walked with a mincing gait, not deviating either right or left. Behind them was a crowded caravan of mounted soldiers. The children came out of the entrances of the houses to watch the impressive scene, and a few of them joined the riders and walked alongside the horses, trying to touch the fringes of the blankets descending from the animals' backs. Worried about their children, the mothers also joined the parade, and even they were amazed by the sheen of the bridles; early rising hired hands came as did farmers who had not yet gone out to the fields.

Lolik stopped next to Yehuda Leib's house, and behind him, the whole procession halted, too. Then, in his loud voice, the tall farmer called for Yehuda Leib to come out, and when Yehuda appeared, with his hat on his head, Lolik pointed to the Turk and went on, "The issue is in your hands—to expel or to bless." He stood at the threshold like a guard ready to spring to defense if only asked to do so.

Yehuda Leib dipped his head in greeting and invited the officer to drink his morning coffee with him. The gendarme entered the house, while the soldiers stayed in the yard and grinned at the group of children growing larger every minute. Since their commander was not present, discipline relaxed, and the riders dismounted to stretch their legs. The horses scattered in the yard looking for hay and grass, and the children came to pet them. The soldiers approached Lolik and repeatedly tapped his shoulders, and one could see that his very dimensions had enormously impressed them.

Inside sat Yehuda Leib and the officer pleasurably sipping their coffee; crowding around them were the older Hankin sons and young Tanhum, who could not stop staring at the officer's ranks and badges. The two finished drinking and smacked their lips; they spoke indirectly about Jaffa and its new houses, the steep rents, and the Jewish immigrants filling the streets. They spoke of Petach Tikva and the "Yarkonim" settlers, who were trying with all their might to hang on to the land, despite the malaria that was felling them. About the Germans living in the German "Colonies" in the cities, they built houses, dug cellars, and formed wagon caravans traveling between Jaffa and Jerusalem, while fighting among themselves and splitting up and founding agricultural settlements. They told each other different stories, while never touching upon the revolt.

Sarah offered refreshments. The Turk tasted different kinds of sweets dipped in sugar, and then yawned and made himself comfortable in his chair. He loosened the belt buckle holding up his pants, opened the uppermost button of his coat, and closed his eyes.

Time passed. Mendel left them, and Yosef took his place. He held on for only a few minutes and then went out to the yard, with Tanhum following him. Yosef stayed at Lolik's while Tanhum joined the children chasing the horses and congregating next to the soldiers. The only ones remaining in the house were Yehuda Leib, the officer, and the Hankin son, Yehoshua. Finally, when they all felt that the policeman's visit was only a courtesy call and the entire affair was basically an accident, the officer put his hand in his pocket and took out a silver tube, from which he pulled out a rolled-up paper and handed it to Yehoshua. Then, he touched his mustache, twisting the whiskers around his finger and pulling the mustache until it was as straight as an arrow stretched out under his nose.

Yehoshua read the letter and translated it out loud for his father. Then he took out a leather pouch and poured a pile of coins onto the table. The Turk took a handful of them, as was expected, to play with them, and unintentionally, as it were, rolled them up and dropped them into the silver tube he held.

Yehuda Leib smiled at the Turk and blurted out as if incidentally, "A colony of Jews in Rishon Lezion. The Jewish administrator, the men, a few with Russian citizenship and others with German, so what do Turkish soldiers have to do with the wars of the Jews?"

The officer nodded his head, "They sent someone to call me. They said there were riots in Rishon Lezion, shooting at Mr. Ossowetzky. Perhaps they only heard what they wanted to, and it is a matter of a lad who was shooting at pigeons or a wild boar. All's quiet with the Jews is what I'll report to my superior officer—a false alarm." The man laughed, moved his chair, and rose, and when he stood up, the coins in his pouch clinked.

He bid farewell to the people sitting there and went out to his soldiers, and when they saw him exiting the house, they hurried and mounted their horses. So, they thundered off on their way this time, and only the children ran after them. When they disappeared down the hillside of the moshava, Yosef called to Israel, his brother, and to Yehoshua and said to them, "It's time to go to the Administration Center."

The three of them put on their hats, slicked their hands down the fronts of their coats to brush off crumbs and straw stalks, and without saying a word, marched as a row across the entire width of the boulevard.

At the gate, the guard barred their entry and asked them to wait until he would inform Ossowetzky of their arrival. Yosef stopped him as he turned to go, showing him his hands, and saying, "They are empty, and we have good intentions." Then, he opened his coat, turned out his pockets, and undid his sleeves, and the guard relented and let them pass.

Someone had taken care to clean the yard and the steps, so no hint of the night's events remained. The callers knocked lightly on the door. Through slits in the curtains, Ossowetzky saw them, opened the door himself, and invited them in. He sat them down on the soft sofas and poured them vin clair. They all sipped the wine and kept their peace. The silence weighed heavily on them, and no one knew how to break it or who would be the first to speak. The guests were no longer the heroes they had been in the yard. At the time, the inflamed crowd had stood behind them. Ossowetzky—even he sat hesitantly on his easy chair since things had not happened the way he had expected, for the Turks had not led Halperin with his hands bound and tied to the mule as he had thought would be his lot and that of all the rebel leaders. Now they were sitting in front of him, and only Halperin was missing.

Ossowetzky cleared his throat and stutteringly asked about the damages from the most recent storm and about Yehuda Leib's daughters. When he received no reply, he sat silently. Then, finally, Yosef opened up and muttered, "We came to ask you to leave the moshava. Rishon Lezion can manage itself by itself. It does not need administrators and directors."

Ossowetzky played with his watch chain, moved in his chair, got up, walked about the room, and bitterly said, "You are rebels. All of you are upstarts. It is the Baron who appointed me administrator, and he will be the one to take the appointment from me." For a minute, he halted the flow of words, but then his voice became more robust, and the longer he talked, the more irritating his voice, "I'm not afraid of you nor from 'the bearded one' who calls himself the leader of the workers. You are radicals, refusing to sign. It is not the cowardly farmers who need monthly bundles who have sent you; that I know for sure. You have come only in your own name, a minority in Rishon Lezion."

Yosef's face turned red, and he lifted his hands to block his ears, so as not to hear this message. Then, a moment later, he got up and trod toward the administrator, reaching for his shoulder in an attempt to stop him and make the administrator turn to face him.

The administrator was alarmed and stepped back from him, but after he had recovered a bit, he burst out, "You intend to hit me? Many witnesses are around you, so you better be careful."

Yosef was enraged and moved away toward the door; the others also got out of their seats. "We are not radicals, not revolutionaries, and also not a minority," Lolik spoke in place of his brother. "In Rishon Lezion, the farmers want to work and not be involved in quarrels and break-ins to other people's houses. We don't need orders and decrees for that nor any threats from pistols. Go, go to Mikveh Israel, where they are used to receiving orders from directors."

Ossowetzky blushed and, with trembling voice, declared, "They rebelled against me. You saw it yourselves; they threatened me."

"You shot," called out Yosef disparagingly. "You couldn't control yourself. The farmers don't want you. Go." Now, Yosef also relented and approached his brothers, and Ossowetzky was frightened and hurriedly opened the door to call the guard.

"They're threatening me! They want to kill me!" His voice rang in the empty yard. The people sitting in the room did not wait for the guard but went out to the veranda and hurried out the gate without glancing back. Outside, the three separated: Yosef and Israel turned to go together, while Yehoshua headed to cross the boulevard.

He did not go to his room but circled his father's yard. He entered his room from behind, through a break in the raspberry bushes that climbed toward the barn and hastened to grow and cover the myrtle seedlings that Yehuda Leib planted on the day of the housewarming party in the hope that they would grow tall and provide a border between the front of the house and the street. Yehoshua stopped and leaned on one of the barn walls and visually measured the area that Yehuda Leib had allotted to him for building a house for himself and Olga. At that moment, he wanted to devote his energy to one project only: to drive four stakes into the dense soil, to stretch a rope around them to indicate the location of the walls, to set the first beam, and with all that to see to it that his wedding time would come sooner.

That very evening, Ossowetzky left the moshava. No one accompanied him, not even members of his society. The farmers came out of their houses as soon as the carriage was no longer visible and assembled on the boulevard, a group here, a group there, and the young men and hired hands and women and infants, gloom showing on every face. They knew for sure that Ossowetzky would return — and not alone. He would bring soldiers with him and a phalanx of clerks. When would they come? No one knew.

Over the next few hours, joining those gathered from among the residents of Rishon Lezion were also farmers from Gedera and Ekron. They had heard the rumor about the serious dispute and then had hurried to hitch the mules to a cart and come. Seemingly, they had come to calm things down and become partners in the developing crisis that would descend on the small moshava. Still, even more than they wanted to soothe the atmosphere, they were drawn by curiosity—to be part of what was about to happen in the tiny settlement.

The Tempest

On Saturday night after prayers, one of the farmers gave out the information that Ossowetzky intended to return to the colony on Sunday. "That's what I heard, and that's the word in all the moshavot of Judea, and only in Rishon Lezion do we refuse to hear this," he screamed.

Immediately after exchanging wishes for a "good week," those gathered were joined by guests from the moshavot near Rishon Lezion, and the boulevard was abuzz with curiosity seekers. Everyone was waiting to see what tomorrow would bring. At night, they continued to argue in the houses, and on Sunday morning, no one went out to work in the fields; the settlement wore a festive air. Pleasant coolness brought the people out to the boulevard; children played among the cypress trees, and women leisurely strolled to the top of the hill, casting brief glances at the road, and bending an ear to be the first to hear the wagon's bells.

Around ten o'clock, they heard the neighing of the horses, and the Jaffa carriage arrived, and to everyone's surprise, it was accompanied by neither policemen nor soldiers. Only three people occupied it: Samuel Hirsch, the general manager who lived permanently in Mikveh Israel; Sigmund Simmel, an associate of the Baron known for his loquaciousness; and Ossowetzky himself. Unfortunately, the road was blocked next to Yosef Feinberg's house, and the carriage could not continue on its way. Laborers from Halperin's society stood like a wall and informed the carriage driver that the wagon could enter the colony without Ossowetzky. Hirsch ordered the driver to ignore the hired hands' demand, but Lolik, who stood behind him, stopped him, saying, "Ossowetzky will not enter Rishon Lezion, even if he musters his superiors, it won't help him."

The wagoner pulled on the reins, and Hirsch descended from the carriage. In the meantime, the other farmers had come near, and Hirsch turned to them and promised a hefty reward to anyone who would come out to help in clearing away the obstructors—but no one moved. He tried again politely, attempting to make threats, but all held firm to their opinion. The sun began to turn west at the edges of the sky, and the crowd still congregated around the wagon to which Hirsch had returned, just as in the morning. The horses began moving restlessly, but nothing happened. The whole time, Ossowetzky was hiding in the back seat. He sat bent over with his face directed to the carriage floor, and he did not dare to raise his head. Finally, when it began to get dark, Hirsch understood nothing would shake the farmers from their stance, and he had to give in. He again got down from the wagon and promised that the carriage, with Ossowetzky in it, would move about one kilometer away, and only he and Simmel would enter the settlement.

And that's what happened. Hirsch and Simmel turned to go to the Administration Center, followed by the band of laborers, the farmers, and the merely curious, and no one turned his head to see if Ossowetzky stayed in the carriage, since they were sure he would do so.

Near the gate, Hirsch stopped and counted those entering the yard, and Simmel, who knew all of them—farmers of Rishon Lezion and hired workers of Ekron and plain riffraff—scrutinized the faces and wrote notes for himself. Then, he stood up straight, and since he knew everyone expected to hear a message from the Baron, began to praise him and enumerate his achievements in the colony near Rishon Lezion, Ekron. He spoke about "improvements" in the colonies under the aegis of the benefactor: about the well and the seed storage shed in Petach Tikva, about the cypress-lined thoroughfare in Rosh Pina, and someone in the audience called out, "Long live the Baron," while the rest chanted after him, "Long live, long live, long live."

Once the administrator understood he had captivated them, he took out the order and began reading it pleasantly, as if it was good news he was giving, "Michael Halperin will leave Rishon Lezion according to the order issued. The families of the farmers who refused to sign will now sign and declare their loyalty, and newly hired hands who come to work in the farmyards will need special approval in order to reside and work in the moshava. Once these conditions are met, Rishon Lezion, too, will enter a period of flourishing and receive aid."

When he finished reading, he bobbed his head in appreciation of their attention and wanted to leave. Still, Lolik blocked his way and turned to the crowd with a booming, confident voice and sparks of fury in his eyes, "The administrator is trying to sway your hearts. Don't believe him; don't be misled." Then he turned to face the Baron's emissaries and went on speaking, without a change in his tone, "Neither Hirsch nor Ossowetzky will lead Rishon Lezion. Whoever did not sign, will not sign; and whoever did sign, will rip up his signature." When he finished, he moved next to Simmel and showed him the way out with his hand. But the man was rooted to the ground, his eyes moving from Hirsch, who stood next to the gate, to the farmers and back again, and he did not know what to do. Lolik smiled at him, bowed toward him, and began to shift in the direction of the exit. And the community, as one, began to follow after Lolik and went out to the boulevard and dispersed.

Simmel and Hirsch, who remained alone in the yard, now realized that Rishon Lezion had declared a rebellion against the Baron's administration. So, silently, they stole back to the carriage waiting for them at the edge of the colony, climbed into it, and vanished as soon as they could.

Only two days after the administrators' visit, the town crier, who went from house to house, declared that the Baron had ceased support for Rishon Lezion. Each family closed itself in their only little world—going out in the morning to the fields, then returning at sunset and closing the shutters. The boulevard itself was forlorn; no one was there except the children, who kept running about among the cypresses, enjoying the empty road so they could play freely with their rag ball.

Purim passed. Even the children stopped dashing about the boulevard, and as soon as school finished for the day, they hurried to their homes. Outside the small settlement, inklings of spring were noticeable. Still, no one in it paid attention to the green barley stalks or the yellow splotches of chrysanthemums and the red poppies—everyone sat at home, dealing with the rebellion. In the meantime, Michael Halperin had left the settlement, and no one remembered that the revolt had begun because of Ossowetzky's hatred for him. The workers' society had fallen apart, and Ostashinsky and Zeiberg had not fixed the window in their house and were not looking for a hired hand to rent the room.

Since Ostashinsky's house no longer served as the meeting place for the young people in the moshava, Fanny and Lolik welcomed them, and their home turned into the center of debates and discussions. In that period, Olga spent a lot of time with them, and since she knew how to read and write Hebrew, she would sometimes read newspaper articles dealing with Rishon Lezion aloud to those gathered and write rebuttals to Yechiel Michal Pines, a Jewish community worker and activist in the settlements who often praised the Baron's projects and scorned the revolutionaries' acts in Rishon Lezion.

In the newspapers, Pines urged all the leaders of the Zionist associations and their center in Jaffa to not respond to requests for help from the farmers in the rebellious colony. Olga answered him in her pointed language, "Your actions are not out of Love for Zion, but out of love for yourself; what you want is to increase your favor in the eyes of the Baron."

In those days, Yehoshua followed his own ways and did not join Olga but stayed apart from her by going to the fields. His face became tanned, and his beard grew wildly, and only rarely did he calm down and take time to lay stone on stone in Yehuda Leib's yard and increase the height of the walls of the house he had promised to Olga. When he would go stealthily into Yehuda Leib's yard, Olga, too, would get out of her gatherings at the Feinberg home, attending to her task of reading the newspapers and preparing responses to Pines. Then, she'd sit herself down at the edges of the yard and lean her back against the trunk of the thick cypress that grew in the soil mixed with sand, while looking at her fingers. And when Yehoshua would finish laying a row of stones, she would come close and sit next to him, staying quiet, with only her fingers speaking, caressing his sunken eyes and his lips cracked from the sun, combing his dense beard. For a few minutes, they would forget the distance between them and the matter of the revolution, and his fingers would play with hers and roll through her hair and pet her neck and wish to go further, until she whispered to him, "The house will be finished, and we will be married; spring is coming."

Spring was well on its way, and with it came difficult times for the settlement. In a few homes, the granaries emptied, and some already said there wouldn't be credit to buy seeds for planting the fields at the end of the summer. Fear drew the people out of the houses, and outside new voices were heard insisting on going to apologize to the Baron. Replacing calls for rebellion and economic independence were accusatory looks, and their number increased daily, aimed at families that refused to sign. The more the granary floors could be seen, and with no new sacks available to cover them, the more insistent the voices grew against the Feinberg, Hankin, and Belkind families. On Passover, the farmers gathered in the home of the old man Cantor. They chose Baruch Papiermeister, the qualified architect who had arrived in the colony together with Olga, and Israel Nimtsovich, a chemist, and a doctor, who had often spoken with the farmers about modern industrial installations in the small colony, to travel to Paris and represent them. Both were wealthy and did not need support money, so the farmers felt they were most suitable for this mission.

The rebelling families were not party to the decision to send the two to plead for the moshava.

While the two emissaries were still sailing toward Paris, the Baron and his wife entered the gates of Jaffa. The Baron had not told anyone of his intention to visit Eretz Israel. After he learned of the revolt in Rishon Lezion from the newspapers, he took his wife to travel to Turkey by train. In Istanbul, he boarded a ship to Alexandria and from there to Jaffa.

A week after Passover, an announcement was sent from Mikveh Israel to Cantor that the Baron was coming soon to Rishon Lezion. This information spread in the settlement like a bolt out of the blue, and in a frenzy, the elderly farmer proceeded from house to house, asking the farmers, the school teachers, and the nursery school teachers to make sure to hang flags and dress festively to welcome the Baron. He did not go to the families who had refused to sign. Yehuda Leib learned of the announcement from his youngest son, Tanhum, and the Belkind family heard about it from their son Israel, who was staying in Jaffa having joined the committee of the Hovevei Zion functionaries and was on his way to visit his family in Rishon Lezion.

So it was that in May 1887, the Baron came to Rishon Lezion. He arrived in the evening, riding in a Jaffa carriage accompanied by a small donkey caravan and with mules carrying his and his wife's belongings. Besides Sigmund Simmel, none of the administrators living in Jaffa or Mikveh Israel came along with them. The carriage parked in the Administration yard, and the baggage was arranged in the Administration Center. Since Ossowetzky had left, nobody had opened the building, and only the gate guard had walked around it occasionally to check that everything was well. The farmers seldom visited the yard, the wooden pillar on which announcements were hung stood forlorn, and again there was no "news" in the settlement.

To be sure, Cantor took care to prepare the flags in advance. Still, neither he nor the others had thought that the Baron would arrive in the late evening hours, "since it does not befit barons to come like thieves in the night, but rather they should come in the light of day and in public view," complained Cantor when he found out about the arrival of the guests.

That evening the rumor spread from one to the other, and the farmers went out of their houses and crowded together next to the gate, asking the guard to let them in and peep, if not to see the Baron and his wife at least to look at the Jaffa carriage and the donkey caravan. The guard swelled with pride, and now, after several days when he had done nothing but check the fence surrounding the house, a task had been found for him—he asked for the names of those entering the yard—and he repeatedly told the gathering, "The Baron *himself* is staying in the house."

The evening of the Baron's arrival in Rishon Lezion, Yehoshua paid a visit to the home of Fanny and Lolik, intending to meet Israel Belkind. He was aware that the brother would be there and hoped Olga would also come and save him the need to go to Shimshon's house to find her. Not only were Israel and Olga present, but the entire family, Shifra and Meir, too, as well as Yosef Feinberg, all crowding together next to the window facing the boulevard and looking at the lights being turned on in the Administration Center, one after the other.

"What's going on?" wondered Yehoshua, and he stood close to Olga, hugging her to him.

She gently removed his hand, afraid of looks from the others in the room. However, Yehoshua did not give in and whispered in her ear, "You're mine."

"Not yet," She replied to him. "Look at the lights," she added, trying to make him forget his intentions.

Yehoshua looked out and saw the silhouettes scurrying in the Administration Center and the carriage and donkey caravan. His face grew grave, and he took his arm off Olga's shoulders and moved away from her; he went to sit next to Lolik and sink deep into the Damascus sofa.

"The Baron is in the colony," Lolik explained to him morosely. "He came this evening, and no one was waiting for him on the boulevard. Not even one flag was waved in his honor," he mocked. "He did not come to forgive us. Instead, he came to accuse, and we'll be the first to hear his allegations."

Yehoshua withdrew into himself, shrugged his shoulders, and closed his eyes. He saw the fields and open spaces in his mind's eye, the sabra bushes and the tents pitched on the crumbling earth. He knew his days in Rishon Lezion were numbered. But where would they go? And hadn't he promised to finish building the house for Olga in the spring. Suddenly he wanted to flee from the house, and his eyes pleaded with Olga that she should come with him and go out to breathe the night air. But she averted her eyes and continued to talk with Israel, her brother. He was jealous of him for a second, when he saw Olga's warm looks at him, and their heads bent together, practically touching. Then, finally, he bowed his head and saw the wrinkles in his pants and the mud stuck to the soles of his shoes and just sank deeper into the couch.

The farmers went out of their houses in the early morning, and the Jaffa carriage was still parked in the Administration Center's yard. They walked past the gate and did not stop, urging the children not to linger there and headed, as usual, to plow the fields but not knowing whether they would be able to plant, prune, or harvest the fruit.

In the later morning, the center's yard stirred with life, and the Baron and Baroness entered the carriage and set off toward the fields. From field to field, from orchard to orchard, the carriage rolled on, with the Baron stopping and alighting to talk with the farmer—for whom it was easy to pour out his heart to his listener when the two were truly alone.

Around noon, the carriage returned to the moshava, and this time children dressed in their holiday finery stood on both sides of the road, with colorful flags in hand, calling out, "Welcome to the benefactor, welcome."

The Baroness removed her hat, stood near the carriage seat, and waved her hand. The Baron stayed seated and did not wave, his face aimed toward the road.

In the afternoon, the farmers were called to the Administration yard. They all came—men, women, children, and hired workers—and they crowded near the balcony, waiting to see what would happen. The Baron and Baroness sat on the shaded balcony, and Cantor and Ze'ev Yavetz offered them bread and salt, along with a bowl of water. The Baron broke the bread and dripped a few drops of water onto the balcony tiles, his eyes wandering above the heads of the people packed in the yard.

The Baron spoke slowly. He told them of his great bitterness and reminded them of the years of near starvation, illness, and humiliation before the administrators had come to manage the settlement. The listeners, embarrassed, turned their faces toward the ground, remembering their shame and weakness. When he finished enumerating all of his good deeds, he scanned their faces and, continuing in the same tone, informed them that Ossowetzky would return to the moshava, and they would have to pledge in writing to obey all of his requests.

Total silence engulfed the yard. No one stirred; then, they turned pleading eyes to Yosef Feinberg, the spokesman for the rebels. Yosef cast his eyes down, trying to avoid the looks shooting towards his back and face, and finally, he took a step and came out of the crowd. He neared the balcony, holding a piece of paper containing signatures. While he went up the steps, he occasionally looked backward, as if looking for encouragement. When he did not find any in the eyes of the crowd in the yard, he moved more briskly and neared the Baron, his eyes not held high and not looking at the distinguished seated couple seated. He handed the sheet to the Baron, moved a bit away, and stood near the railing with his back to the gathering below.

The Baron rose and hastened to read the page; his face turned red. His hands grasping the railing trembled, and his voice screamed out, "Ingrates. You have chosen the counsel of Hushai for yourselves. Independence you want. Take a whole handful. But I will not change my mind; Rishon Lezion will no longer be one of my colonies." He scanned the heads, and his voice strengthened; his tone was harsh. "Go eat the husks in the fields and the blighted almonds and the wizened grapes, and may it be a delicacy for you." As soon as he finished his statement, he turned backward and slammed the door behind him, being swallowed up by the house.

The Baroness took off her hat, crushed the edges with her hands, put it on again, and hurried into the house, following her husband.

The shock passed after a short silence, and the yard began bubbling and surging. People elbowed each other and raised their voices in a fury at Yosef. "In whose name did you come?" "Who sent you?" "Why do we have to listen to the opinion of the radicals?" "Ossowetzky was right. The families that refused to sign must leave Rishon Lezion." "Once they go, we'll receive support again, and with it, calm will be restored." "Bring Yosef," they cried again and again. The children, too, were chanting without understanding a thing, "Yosef! Yosef!" But Yosef was no longer in the yard. As soon as the Baron turned his face away, Yosef left, quickly going as far as he could, hastening his steps, and in the end, running and disappearing on the rise of the boulevard.

When Olga heard the hubbub and realized the furor of the farmers, she looked around, seeking Yehoshua, and saw him standing next to the gate far away from the people crowding the yard, and she went to him.

She looked at his eyes and realized they were sunken. At that moment, it seemed to her that she had not looked into his eyes for several days nor smoothed the ends of his beard that had grown longer. She put out her hand and pulled him away from there. The two walked down the boulevard and turned to the dirt path leading to the vineyard. On the grapevines were the tender branches of early spring, and the soil had begun to dry out, the earth crumbling from the touch of their shoes. The wind played with the material of Olga's dress, lifting the hem that brushed Yehoshua's feet. Yehoshua tightened his hold on her hand, feeling her smooth skin contrasting with the roughness of his. They stopped when they came to the simple booth Tanhum had built for guarding the grapes during the summer against the Bedouins who raided the vineyards. They were alone; Olga blushed and was happy with the hut's drabness.

Olga sat on one of the rolled-up mats, and Yehoshua placed himself next to her, and that's how the two of them sat quietly, squeezing next to each other and listening to their breathing and feeling their body heat escaping through their clothes. Olga stretched her hand to Yehoshua's shock of hair, put her fingers into it, and combed and caressed it lightly. Then, she undid her hair and tried to arrange it again behind her earlobes. The aroma of the earth that clung to him suffused her, and his warmth surrounded her. She wanted him; all winter, she had wanted him, but she had waited for the spring, and then their wedding date had been pushed off, and Yehoshua had become distant from her and preferred his horse and the wide-open spaces. A tremor passed through her body, and Yehoshua did not know if it came from her desire or from the cold that had invaded the hut.

He swept his hand over her starched shirt, toyed with the round, fabric-covered buttons held by woven loops, and patted them; he caressed her body. She felt her skin tingling at his touch. She opened a button and drew his hand into the area around her neck, petting her while moving down, but she did not stop him now. Then he buried his head in her body, breathing in her fragrances and drawing her heat into his body. Olga responded to his caresses and held him fast, every movement of hers matching his.

Day turned into night, and a light breeze made its way in through the hut's gaping opening. The two trembled, and Yehoshua covered her with his body. Olga kissed his nose and the corners of his mouth, and then whispered in his ear,

"Let's go," and pushed him off her and straightened her dress and again pushed back hair that had broken loose from her bun on her neck; she asked for his help in fastening the large number of cloth buttons.

When they left the vineyard, Olga told Yehoshua, "I'll call Fanny and Rivka Yavetz and go the Baroness. Women understand each other." However, she made no mention of their house or their wedding.

Olga was right. Women do really understand each other.

After dinner, Rivka Yavetz and Fanny came to the Belkind family home and picked through the box of clothes standing in Olga's room, searching for scarves and sashes to adorn their clothes. They were sure the European fashion had changed, but they wanted to show Adelheid, the Baron's wife, that even in the moshavot of Eretz Israel, they know how to dress. They laughed and made merry like young girls when they tottered in sharp-pointed shoes and when they breathed heavily wearing a tight sash and almost forgot why they had decided to dress up. In the end, they were ready and went out into the night on their way to the illuminated house at the end of the boulevard, with their high heels leaving marks in the dry dust.

The Baroness received them happily, and when she told them the Baron had gone to Ekron, they were relieved. They made themselves comfortable in the Administration Center's easy chairs, sipped steaming tea, and nibbled at butter cookies while holding the thin handle of china cups, drinking without making sounds, and eating without leaving crumbs around their mouths. First, they spoke of women's matters—about fashion in the great cities of Europe and kinds of curative lotions—and then they moved on to tell about Ossowetzky. First, with a light touch, they giggled about his appearance and his clothing. Then they became serious and began to tell the story of Halperin, who had returned to Russia in the meantime and remarked on the regulations and tribulations of Rishon Lezion. But when they spoke, things didn't sound so threatening. Time flew by, and a plate of fruit replaced the plate of cookies, and at the end of their discussion, the Baroness promised them to help.

A day passed, and the Baron returned from his visit to Ekron, planning to pack his belongings and load them onto the donkeys' backs. This time, the children also waited for him with torches and flags in hand. At three, they had been placed on both sides of the boulevard, thoroughly uncomfortable in their festive clothing, and told to stand quietly until they heard the neighing of the horses. The wind blew out the torches, and the orderly row broke down whenever people tried to relight them. So, when the Baron finally arrived, the lines were not straight, the children's hair was uncombed, and the Baron himself looked tired.

The carriage stopped at the edge of the boulevard, and the somewhat round-shouldered man descended and walked between the two rows of children, immersed in his passing thoughts. One child approached him and gave him a flower; the Baron bent down and patted the boy's hair, almost inadvertently. He took his hand away and stopped, not knowing whether they were waiting for him to say something. He was hard put to forgive. But the large, innocent eyes of the child standing in front of him melted his heart, and he turned to the waiting crowd. Then, he began, in a trembling voice, "I have changed my mind. Ossowetzky will not be coming back to manage Rishon Lezion. Until another administrator is found, Samuel Hirsch will come to take his place. Tomorrow the farmers will present themselves and declare their loyalty." He was quiet for a moment, and then immediately went on, saying his final words quickly, "The families that caused the rebellion won't need to make a declaration. They will leave the colony, and their land will be sold to others …."

Not all of them heard the Baron's final words, for they were swept away with joy and the ringing roar, "Long live our benefactor! long live our redeemer!"

Circles of dancers formed and surrounded the Baron, accompanying him to the gate of the Administration Center yard. Only a few refused to take the outstretched hands and scurried quickly to their homes. Olga walked for some way next to Lolik until he parted from her to go to his house. She was left alone, wandering and puzzling where Yosef was and where Israel and her brother Shimshon had disappeared. She tried to locate Yehoshua and could not find him in Yehuda Leib's house nor in the yard. She went to Ostashinsky's house. She knocked on Lolik and Fanny's home door, but didn't find him there either. Knowing his habits, she feared that he might have taken his horse and escaped for fear of the decree. She went back to her brother's house, closed herself in her room, and waited; she finally fell asleep fully dressed in her clothes.

Late at night, Yehoshua returned. Olga's fears had been realized; he wanted to go far away from the settlement and not return to it and forget the rebellion, decree, and administrators. However, next to the tents of Duran (lands south of Rishon Lezion), he remembered his love, her hair in a bun, and the warmth of her body. So, he rode back slowly and let the mare lead him to Rishon Lezion.

After Yehoshua had returned the horse to the stable, given it water and some dry hay, he washed his face with cistern water and went to Shimshon Belkind's home. The entrance light had been extinguished long before, and no voices were heard from behind the door. For a moment, he thought about going around and knocking on the window of the room Olga lived in, but Olga shared it with her sister Sonia, and he did not want to wake her. So he left the yard and returned to his father's house. First, he went to the barn and examined the rows of bricks lying one atop the other. Then, he went inside, sat down in one of the corners, pulled up his knees, and fell asleep. Olga found him early in the morning, tucked into his coat and his hair dotted with dewdrops. She hurried to sit beside him and shook off the stalks of green grass stuck to his clothes. She sensed that the time would come when he would draw away from her and who knew if he would return.

The Baron and Baroness left, and life in the colony returned to routine, as if everyone had awakened after a long winter's hibernation. Again, the farmers stood beside the pole in the administration yard, read regulations, and shared the settlement news. At the entrances to the houses stood wagons full of sacks of seeds ready for planting at the end of the summer, and in the Administration Center, light shone every evening, and the farmers were frequented it.

As the Baron had promised, the Alsatian was not sent to manage the colony. Instead came a Moroccan-born functionary and teacher in Mikveh Israel named David Haim, and everyone called him, "soft-hearted and easy to get along with." Few noticed Yosef Feinberg leaving the moshava, and whoever asked received an evasive answer from Fanny and Lolik: He went to set up an olive press in Lydda, or perhaps he went to the desert to live as a recluse in the caves near Jericho. Lolik took care of the calves Yosef had left him, and Fanny learned how to make cheeses and distributed them in the settlement.

They no longer spoke openly about the conditions imposed on the families who refused to meet them, and they hoped the evil decree would be lifted. In the Belkind home, they even set a new date for the wedding of Olga and Yehoshua—

three days after Hoshana Rabba, so as to not mingle the festivities of Simchat Torah with the joy of the couple.

ᴄᴔ

At the end of Av, other winds began blowing in the colony. The Baron did not forget the conditions he had set, as they had all hoped. On the pole in the administration courtyard, new regulations were posted, and older ones were noted as well: forming associations was prohibited, hiring workers without the approval of the managerial administrator of the settlement was forbidden, and the farmers were ordered to sign on every decree.

One morning, the emissary came to Yehuda Leib's house and, without saying a thing, handed over a sealed letter and left. Yehuda Leib was afraid to open the envelope and waited until evening, when he would give it to Sarah to read in a minute of peace and quiet. Yet, in the evening, Sarah was busy cooking, so he had no choice but to gird his loins and open the letter. He hurriedly scanned it, taking in each word: The Baron was willing to forgive if the rebellious families would turn to him and sign, in the presence of witnesses, that from now on, they would be loyal to the administration's orders.

Yehuda Leib read it and laughed bitterly. Sarah came from the kitchen when she heard the cynical guffaw; she saw the letter, and her face fell.

That very evening the entire moshava learned about the letters. Not only Yehuda Leib refused to sign, so did Shimshon Belkind as well Yizhak Eisenband and Lolik—the only member of the Feinberg family still there. No one in the settlement accepted the refusal of the families. The farmers feared the implementation of the Baron's threats. They recalled memories of the empty granaries and the cows dying of starvation. Hence, their reaction was swift: the families refusing to sign were ostracized, and in the moshava, they stopped greeting them or asking their advice. Also, the hired hands who used to gather in Lolik's home stopped coming. The settlement's hostility toward them lay heavily on the families, and they found no common language even among themselves. Lolik and Fanny told Olga of their intention to move to Gedera and join the Bilu students from Kharkov.

"Our brother Israel lives there and also has a plot, so he will be able to help," said Fanny. But Olga shook her head. Like her younger sister, she was well aware of how hard life was for Israel Belkind, how many reservations he had, and how he wasn't able to find himself a permanent place.

Yehuda Leib became stooped; his hair turned gray, and he needed to walk with a cane. And Yehoshua and Olga did not talk about a date for their wedding.

The first evening of the month of Elul, after the New Moon prayers, the manager of the colony came to the Yehuda Leib's home. He did not make do with a messenger but came in person to try to persuade him with gentle speech. But Yehuda Leib refused to listen and turned away from him, so he went to Sarah and spoke with the boys and showed them the letter he had brought with him, "There's a suit against you, and the Baron won't give in. A company of soldiers will come to carry out the order, and what will you do? Will you rebel? Will you send soldiers? Give up, sign, and be like all the other farmers."

David Haim's approach aroused the anger of the older brothers, Yaakov and Mendel, and it was enough to look at their faces to see the administrator was not welcome.

The man rose, put the orders on the table, and directed his statement to Yehuda Leib, whose back faced him. Then, in a soft voice trying to convince him, "You'll take the one for you and the other two orders you will hand over to the other two families who like you are refusing to sign. Read it at your leisure and think again," he said, knowing that his words were falling on deaf ears.

The administrator, who was known in the colony for his ability to persuade people and create compromises between foes, had missed his chance. The families refusing to sign had made a firm decision to leave Rishon Lezion.

Later that night, Yehoshua delivered the orders to the other families. But first, he went to Shimshon Belkind's house, since he wanted to see Olga and find some consolation. He entered without knocking and was met by sounds of the piano flowing from the parlor. Olga sat and played a light air, the kind she had learned as a child, and with which he was not familiar. He stood at the entrance to the room. He did not announce his arrival and did not let out a peep, but looked at her fingers running over the keys; long, unadorned fingers he had promised would wear a ring after Simchat Torah.

Olga finished playing the piano, turned around in her seat, and saw him standing there with the letters in his hands. She rose, took the envelopes, opened the one intended for the Belkind family, and read the letter without asking anything. When she had finished, she wrapped a scarf around her shoulders and called to him; together, they walked to the home of Yizhak Eisenband and from there to Fanny and Lolik's house. They found them sitting, hugging each other, on the Damascus sofa, and showed them the order. Lolik shrunk into a corner of the sofa and folded his legs under him, making himself as small as possible and murmuring to himself and the others, "We are Russian citizens. Turkish soldiers will not come to arrest me, and a Turkish judge will not try me. I am eligible for defense by the Russian consul."

Fanny tried to quiet him down, but he went on and muttered, "If they don't want me in the Jewish colonies, I will go back to being a Russian, and accept the verdict of a Russian judge."

Olga listened to him, and he seemed to make sense. Perhaps, Lolik was right, and they had to choose their own emissary to go speak with the Russian consul in Jaffa. She shared this idea with Yehoshua, who knew this was nothing but an illusion, but he could not withstand her pleading eyes and nodded his head, his heart full of pity.

The following morning Meir and Shimshon Belkind rode to Jaffa to speak with the Russian consul. After the consul promised them to bring the issue before the court he was in charge of, the two went to the home of the Jewish functionaries in Jaffa to meet with them to convince them of their justness. First, they looked for the heads of the Jaffa committee of Hovevei Zion, but they had gone to Paris. Hearing this left a bitter taste in their mouths, since they knew well that if committee representatives had been sent to Paris, it would only be for meeting with the Baron, and that was bad news. Then, after some hesitation, they went to meet Yehoshua Barzilai, a member of the Hovevei Zion movement, who had immigrated to Israel in 1881 and whom they had known in Petersburg. Maybe some consolation would come from him. But he too was not in — just then, he had stayed in Egypt for his business. So, the father and son returned to the colony with no news other than the Russian consul's promise.

Olga met them when they entered the moshava, but they did not respond to her flood of questions and only shrugged their shoulders. The light in her eyes dimmed, and she no longer sought to change the evil decree. From that moment on, she stayed away from the parlor in her parents' home and from the house of Lolik and Fanny and immersed herself in her books, hiding herself in her room, waiting for the minute they would leave the settlement and go very far distant from it.

Rosh Hashanah passed, and Yom Kippur was approaching, and soon it would be a whole year since the revolt had broken out. Those who were early to rise to say *selichot* felt the coolness of the fall. The flowers of the b*ougainvillea* bushes that climbed on every post and tree fell, and the cypress tops were exposed; people took out scarves to wear. The gates to the yards of the holdouts against signing were kept locked to avoid the neighbors' prattling but the voices leaked through the fences.

The issue of those refusing to sign was the center of a great debate between two courts: a French court and a Russian court. The newspapers, the colony farmers, hired workers who had recently come, and municipal functionaries—everyone argued about those expelled. Again, no names were mentioned, and they forgot only a few families were involved. They dealt with important matters and asked themselves whether a certificate of citizenship and receiving citizenship were stronger than a letter of ownership over the land; was the power of a consul greater than that of a Turkish judge, and in general, what was the status of the Jews in Eretz Israel—foreign citizens? Turkish citizens? Or both?

Yehoshua refused to be cooped up in the Yehuda Leib's yard and rode long distances instead, and when he returned, he would prepare the fields for sowing, trim the grapevines, and clean the cisterns to ready them to receive rainwater. In addition, he continued building the house intended for him and Olga in the evenings. The backbreaking work stole his time and energy, but turned his mind away from the debates raging in the settlement.

In the Hankin house, as well as the Belkind house, people were looking for something to do, so they turned their attention to the wedding of Olga and Yehoshua. Olga immersed herself in sewing her wedding dress from lace remnants intended for a curtain. Sarah and Shifra competed over who was a bigger expert at baking and cooking. Sonia and other young Belkind girls ran around and got in the way—and the chief conductor of all the work was Fanny, whose joy was shared by all. Yehuda Leib frequently went to the synagogue to sit next to Meir Belkind and ignore the whispering behind his back. The two found a common language—they did not speak about the rebellion, nor the slanderous articles about them. Instead, they reminisced about the times of their long-ago weddings, and they relished their memories.

Two days before the Yom Kippur fast, the crier went through the colony and called for people to gather in the Administration Center yard shortly before sunset. The farmers hastened to return from the fields, to get washed, and pray. Even before tasting their evening meal, they hurried to the yard, which quickly filled up with people pushed near the pole and tried to guess what was so urgent. While people were still whispering, Samuel Hirsch, the Baron's emissary for settlement issues in Palestine, appeared and sat next to David Haim. Since the attempt to return Ossowetzky to the colony, the Alsatian administrator had not been seen there, but no everyone was surprised by his arrival. They were even more astonished when he got up to speak, and David Haim remained seated.

Hirsch moved to the railing, and without waiting for quiet, he unfolded a long roll of paper and waved it in front of the crowd, walking from one end of the balcony to the other to show everyone standing in the yard the written text.

Then, he read the following out loud in a booming voice, "Hirsch, don't be a devil. Hirsch, stop interfering in the matters of Rishon Lezion. Hirsch, pick yourself up and go and cancel the pending trial against the three farmers." He read it over and over again, as if wanting to etch the words on the hearts of those present.

"Devil? I'm Satan?" he raged. "And you, what are you? Revolutionaries, lovers of rebellions. Who took part in writing this letter?" he screamed. "Let him rise and confess, and if he does not confess, the whole moshava will be punished."

The crowd was silent. They did not know about the letter, and beyond this, none of those collected in the yard believed Yehuda Leib or anyone from the Belkind family had anything to do with its writing. They were torn between their faith in the farmers everyone called "revolutionaries" and their own fears. Those standing near the gate tried to make use of the opportunity to sneak out and escape the riot about to break out, but the Alsatian's voice stopped them, "Stay where you are. No one will leave the yard."

The old Cantor stepped out of the mob, and even though he was not used to speaking, he began for fear of Hirsch's fury and the unrest breaking out among the crowd. "The families of Rishon Lezion did not write the letter," he whispered. Then, raising his voice, he went on, "Go look among people of Gedera who support Mohilinsky. Who in the settlements is not familiar with the flightiness of the man, his desire to stir up controversy? He'll do anything to blacken the name of the Rishon Lezion farmers in the Baron's opinion. Go and check this out," he repeated and said emphatically, "Inquire among the Gedera farmers and watch your tongue. Don't accuse the innocent."

Hirsch bent over the railing and looked into the elderly man's eyes, as if wanting to determine if he was speaking the truth. Then he straightened up, and the anger that had been building in him for several days refused to dissolve. "All of you are a flock of revolutionaries," he cried. "It's the same to me whether the farmers of Rishon Lezion wrote this slanderous letter or those of Gedera. You're all the same to me—all of you are looking for a fight."

For a moment, he was quiet, while checking the impression his words had made on the crowds. Then, when he saw the dismay spread over their faces, he added, "You don't want me to make such parallels? Please, let the farmers who refuse to sign, in order to prove their innocence. Let them come and sign the loyalty document to the Baron and his administrators. And if they do not sign, they will be given a span of 48 hours to pack their belongings and leave the colony."

Hirsch finished speaking, with a trembling voice, red face, and neck veins still swollen. He rolled up the letter of denunciation, handed it to David Chaim, went into the house, and never looked back to see the impression his words had made. It was not necessary to see. It was enough to hear: the yard was seething, and everyone interrupted the other fellows' words. The name of Mohilinsky and that of Israel Feinberg were mentioned, "and perhaps this is the fault of Israel Belkind," yelled someone in the crowd. "They already wrote about him in one of the newspapers that he wants to inherit David Haim's place, and his sister Olga is helping him with that." They were all looking for someone to blame and upon whom to discharge their frustration.

David Haim continued to sit on the balcony, torn between Hirsch and the farmers and knowing full well that the farmers of Rishon Lezion were not to blame. Finally, one of the young people in the crowd waved a stick and urged the masses to join with him in punishing the guilty. Cantor stretched out his hand to grab the raised stick and tried to stop the crowd wild in anger, but the young men shoved him and pushed him aside.

"You want to catch the guilty, but you don't know whom to blame," Cantor continued to scream at them, but his broken voice was swallowed in the noise and cries. The group thirsting for a fight was urged on and marched toward the gate.

When the riot broke out, Yehoshua was not in the settlement. As usual, he was immersed in working in the fields and the vineyard, fleeing from himself and from the wedding preparations. When he returned to his father's house in the evening, no one was there, so he went to the barn intending to lay another row of bricks for his new house. The quiet in the yard surprised him since, generally, in those days, he would hear the bustling of wedding preparations. He went into the house again and flitted among the rooms; he entered the kitchen and saw on the table the bowl of flour, the raisin mixture, the sugar, and Sarah's abandoned apron. Now he was frightened and went out to the boulevard to look for all of them. He saw the Administration Center bathed in light from afar and people being pushed out through the gate and filling the street.

Something had happened! Yehoshua began to run, bumping into people without saying sorry. Olga, he must find Olga. But, since he could not identify her in the crowd, he went back and ran to Shimshon Belkind's house. At the entrance burned the Petersburg oil lamp; Yehoshua waited a bit until his breathing settled down, and he wondered why they had decided just today to light it, after they had refused to do so for several days. Then, finally, he entered the large room in the center of the house. Everyone was there: Yehuda Leib sat hunched over on a chair near the door, Sarah sat on a stool near him as if in mourning, her scarf undone. Yaakov and Mendel stood quietly in the company of Shimshon, staring at Yehoshua, who had just come in. Lolik and Fanny squeezed into one chair, holding on to each other. Only the young girls of Sarah and Shifra were happy with the chance to be together, and their laughter could be heard from the room that recently had been a sewing workshop. The little ones wrapped themselves in cloth remnants, covered their hair and faces with a veil, peeked through the parlor entry, and waited to hear the adult's reactions. But they were steeped in other matters and did not pay attention to the girls, so they continued to misbehave, and there was no one to reprimand them.

Yehoshua looked for Olga, and Fanny, seeing his eyes sweeping from corner to corner, pointed to the yard. He went there and found her leaning on the back doorway, with wisps of hair peeking out from beneath her kerchief and wearing a wrinkled apron. She was rummaging in the dry soil with the end of her shoe, and her lips were pursed to keep from crying. When she saw Yehoshua, she moved away from the wall, ran, and clung to him, breaking into tears that ran down her face. The two sat on the earth, hugging each other, and between outbursts of weeping, Yehoshua understood that the decree had been levied on them. He sat with her for a few moments; then, he got up and ran outside the yard, his eyes registering neither the people crowding the boulevard nor the lights flooding the administrator's house. He entered his father's yard with a kick to the gate and stopped next to the barn near the half-built house. He sat on a pile of burnt bricks, wanting to cry and make the walls tremble. Then, he grabbed a piece of gravel and threw it at the wall, wanting to see it break. But the pebble was small and rolled back down to the base of the wall, and he felt his weakness and uselessness.

❧

The next day was Yom Kippur. The men came in early from the fields to prepare for the fast. Yehuda Leib had already begun the fast in the morning. He sat on the ground in the yard, near the cistern, and prayed for forgiveness and advice—where should they go.

Olga had decided to spend the fast day in the Hankin family home. This was the first time since Yehoshua had asked for her hand that she had dared come to spend the night in their house. They gave her a bed in the room of Haya and Rivka, and both of them opened and closed the bag she had brought with her and examined its contents; they were thrilled to share their room with the woman so many years older than they.

The day was hot, one of those sharav heatwave days that come at the end of the summer, harassing the Yom Kippur fasters.

The heatwave continued the next day. People closed themselves in in the synagogue, and even the children, who usually ran about in the streets showing their tongues to each other to prove they were really fasting, while surreptitiously picking wood sorrels and sucking their stems, sat in the synagogue next to their parents, trying to follow the place in the prayer and the words to the singing by the Cantor. Even when the shofar was blown announcing the end of the fast, they did not tarry there as they had done in previous years, to show they were not gluttonous, but instead hurried home to eat their fill and return as fast as possible to routine life. The 48 hours were coming to an end.

On the night Yom Kippur ended, Olga dozed on the sofa and waited for Yehoshua. But by the time he arrived, she had fallen asleep and was breathing heavily. When Yehoshua lifted her head, sat himself down, and placed it on his knees, Olga had snuggled up near him and refused to wake up.

"It's almost morning," he whispered to her.

"Is the house finished?" she asked.

He laughed, "It's like a *sukkah*. We'll take it apart, carry it along, and erect it somewhere else."

Now she was awake and sat up. "Where?" she wondered.

Yehoshua caressed her face and her eyes, which were finding it hard to stay open. "In Gedera," he told her, running right on, giving her no chance to interrupt. "I'll go in advance to the small colony and prepare the ground, and maybe I'll manage to build a house. And when everything is ready, you'll come, and so will the others."

While Yehoshua was still speaking, Yehuda Leib entered the room and heard what his son was saying. Upon hearing them, he perked up and said, "We will go far away. There's a great deal of land in Eretz Yisrael. We'll find land, buy a plot, and even build a new house." He wanted to take a step and sit next to Olga, but suddenly he collapsed, and his cane fell noisily onto the floor. He was tired and weak from the long fast—and it seemed as if he had become old before his time. Yehoshua sat him in the easy chair, and he was sorry to see Yehuda Leib in his weakened state.

Gedera, 1887/1888

The day after Yom Kippur, the moshava calmed down. Everyone waited impatiently for the departure of the families who refused to sign. After several days, when no one came to visit or inquire how they were doing, people now came like pilgrims to ask if they needed help. Yehuda Leib kept the door closed, and Olga opened it to take out household goods and quilts for sale. In Jaffa, Yehoshua Barzilai continued to intercede on their behalf. Four days after the fast, he came to Rishon Lezion with a sealed envelope in hand: they were given an extension to find buyers for their farms and time to pack their belongings.

Since Barzilai belonged to neither the Baron's associates nor to the farmers' group and served as the secretary of Hovevei Zion in Jaffa, he was the one appointed to mediate between the farmers and the administrators, who were deciding the moshava's fate. To be sure, he was not familiar with the families who refused to sign, but one member of the Belkind family he knew quite well—Olga.

Yehoshua Barzilai remembered the young lady from the days of Petersburg, the times of parties and debates, the times of drawing rooms whose floors shined and whose chandeliers hung down from the ceiling, with their light reflected in the glittering tiles. When he heard that she was engaged to one of the farmers' sons, he could not believe it. He felt she belonged to the big city and not to a life of soil tillers in a small moshava. It was difficult for him to imagine her walking on the village paths, taking care not to soil her shoes in the mud, or going down to the almond orchard, squinting her eyes under the blazing sun. Finally, his curiosity got the better of him, and he asked to see if she had changed or, perhaps, was still that same girl who had always been surrounded by men, her dance card full. As a result, he decided to go to Rishon Lezion to actually see for himself rather than send a messenger to carry the envelope.

By the time Barzilai came to the moshava, Yehoshua was already no longer there. Two days earlier, he had left with his brothers Mendel and Yaakov. The three had packed a few belongings, put them on the wagon that had brought Yehuda Leib to Rishon Lezion, and set out after sunset; they left like thieves so as not to face the looks of the curious and not to hear their question—Where to?

Sarah came to see them off and took leave of them, knowing deep inside that they would not see each other for a long time. When Yehoshua tried to cheer her up and promised to prepare a land parcel for them wherever they settled anew, she hushed him and asked him not to be rash in making plans.

"Perhaps your father will agree to go to Jaffa," she said, noting that she preferred a town over a moshava with two houses, since she just didn't have the strength to work a new piece of land, and the girls and Tanhum needed her and a better life. In Jaffa, they knew Elazar Rokach, who supported the rebels of Rishon Lezion, and they could live with him for a few days hoping to find work. Should they not find employment in other people's businesses, she went on, Rokach would give them a loan, and Yehuda Leib would be able to rent a store and sell items the women of Jaffa needed. And if that did not go well, he could be a land agent for building houses. Sarah had heard that many Jews were coming to Jaffa, looking for land and a place to live, and the Arabs were sucking their money away from them like leeches and renting them a room at the price of a palace and a tiny space at the cost of a luxurious room. She had found out that acting as an agent was a good business and did not require riding a horse, slogging through mud, depending on rain coming on time, or fearing the coming of locusts with the desert winds.

Yehoshua hugged her and pressed her to him, telling her, "You will yet be a lady. Better days will come, and you will wear elegant dresses. You will sit in your doorway, polish silver spoons, and the wives of the rich men will come sit with you over steaming cups of coffee and lick their fingers when they eat your sesame-topped bagels and ask for the recipe, and you will wink your eye as if guarding a secret …"

Sarah laughed when she heard this—for a long while, Yehoshua had not seen her laugh like this—and promised to take care of Olga and to send her with a proper dowry. Then she hugged Mendel and Yaakov and turned away from them so they shouldn't see the tears pooling in the corners of her eyes, and the wagon creaked off into the dark.

In the stillness of the night, Yehoshua remembered the reaction of Fanny and Lolik. Behaving like children, they refused to speak and refused to act. When Yehoshua came to their home and told them he was moving to Gedera, Lolik told him he preferred to join Yosef in Lydda, but as the time approached for the departure of three of Yehuda Leib's sons, he changed his mind and asked to come with them. Nonetheless, Fanny stopped him from joining them and from talking about a plot of land in Gedera.

"None of the Kharkov people, the Bilu pioneers, stayed in Gedera. They scattered everywhere. The only ones to remain became stubborn farmers who aged before their time, and now, they are desperate for support—if not from the Baron, they'll take that of Hovevei Zion. Maybe we'll go to Jerusalem," she told Yehoshua, watching him to see the effect of her words, as if she awaited his approval. "We'll join a group of stonemasons and builders," she explained. "The kind that live from hand to mouth and for whom worries about tomorrow are far from their minds."

Fanny no longer wanted land that tied her down nor the company of traitorous farmers, and like his mother Sarah, she wanted a new, quieter life. "We'll leave Rishon Lezion and go far away and not be connected to anyone," she whispered to Yehoshua. "To be only for ourselves."

Later on, when the two came anyway to say goodbye to Yehoshua, Fanny put a letter to Sverdlov, a resident of Gedera, into his hand and explained, "Perhaps he'll remember the days of our youth." And when Lolik looked at her in astonishment, she quickly added, "Once we were young and looked for adventures and new beginnings. We called ourselves 'Biluim,' as you know, and we aimed to change the ways of the world...." She lowered her voice as if speaking to herself. Then, she took heart and went on with a smile on her lips," Sverdlov loved me, and because of that acquaintanceship, he'll take care of you, and who knows, maybe we, too, will need his help."

"What happened? Did you change your mind?" Lolik asked in amazement, and one could see in his eyes his latest attempts to convince her to go to Gedera and join Yehoshua. The separation from these three sons of Yehuda Leib Hankin was hard on him.

But Fanny shook her head strongly, "No, not now. Maybe in time, Yehoshua's success in Gedera will bring us to him; perhaps I'll have a child and need a crib and a permanent home. Look, my brother Yisrael also lives in Gedera. So, two families will settle there and take root, and there'll be place for a third one." She concluded with a shaky voice and lowered her eyes.

Yehoshua took the letter, stroked her hair to comfort her, and did not know what to say. Suddenly, Fanny looked old to him, a woman whose vivacity and joy of youth had vaporized completely. As the wagon moved away from the moshava, he kept seeing the image of the cupboard, goblets, the Damask sofa, and his two dear friends sitting on it tightly next to each other and giggling.

Mendel and Yaakov drowsed in the back, and Yehoshua felt the cold along with strong longings for Olga. He yearned for her, wanted to share the seat with her, and to feel her pressing against him. But Olga had stayed in Rishon Lezion to help with selling the plots. He had promised to marry her right after Simchat Tora and had not kept his word. He didn't even have a ring to give her. How long would she wait? These thoughts frightened him, and he returned to looking at his surroundings, his eyes penetrating through the mantle of darkness, trying to identify where they were.

The wagon entered the area of Bani Khirbat Duran. Yehoshua needed no memorable landmarks. He knew each pit and each stone; since it was to these fields and spaces that he would flee to escape the upheavals in the colony. He sat up straight and pulled on the harness for a moment, but when he saw that the horse knew the way well and did not require the whip or his calling, he sank back into his thoughts. The darkness and the silence of the night helped him clarify his thinking. Olga thought he used to run away to the fields because of her, since she was not sure of his love, and perhaps he had changed his mind? Maybe he was frightened by the bonds of marriage? And he had never spoken openly with her and never explained his reservations to her. He had not admitted that his other love was drawing him close with powerful ties, even to himself. He wrestled with his senses and tried to repress them. But when thoughts of regret would overpower him, and Olga's image would not leave him alone, he would engulf her in the scents of his other love and continue to flee, and in time he would return, with his silence strangling him.

"Strange how moments of solitude permit time for thinking and implant a feeling of confidence," he mused. After he had driven the wagon quite a long way and realized he was very far from an inhabited place, he called out into the night, "Land," and was not embarrassed to give voice to his other love. At that moment, memories of Rishon Lezion were shoved to the fringes, and only Land was with him, accompanying him, attracting him to her. He saw it as resembling a woman: surprising, coming closer, treacherous—as broad as Olga and as serene as she. Yehoshua laughed to himself and knew he would never be able to prefer one over the other; they were similar, and he loved both.

The cart continued to roll along the path that crossed unplowed land and on both sides of it stood fences of sabras made darker in the night and infinite plains, a bit of which had been planted with olives and most of which were thistles and thorns giving off the day's heat that had collected in them. From a distance, dogs' barking was heard, and the smell of dung campfires told Yehoshua that they were nearing the tents of Khirbat Duran. But, since he had no wish to meet early rising *fellahin* and the looks that would be sent his way and to his wagon, he left the pathway, going into rocky land, intending to bypass the tents. He walked alongside the wagon and let the horse go slowly, since he was in no hurry and wanted to reach Gedera after sunrise.

With the first rays of the sun, the cart returned to the path, leaving behind it the land of Duran. They approached the Arab village of Qatara, situated at the foot of the hill, on which the moshava of Gedera was built. The Arab village lands bordered those of the settlement. To reach the lane climbing toward the Jewish houses, one had to go through the village, whose inhabitants did not like the residents of Gedera nor their guests.

In the early morning hours, between the wooden huts and the clay houses, scurried women with runny-nosed children clinging to their dresses. One tot waved in greeting and jumped into their path, calling, "Al-Yahud!" but his mother pulled him toward her and tried to hide him between the folds of her dress. Yehoshua halted the wagon, smiled at the child, and looked into his pockets, maybe he would find something to give him, and he found a few nails of the kind he hammered into the wall of the house being built in Rishon Lezion. Since he didn't need them, he bent down and put them in the tot's hand, waved to him, and pulled on the reins.

The landscape quickly changed. The sun rose higher, and the rickety houses were replaced by fields of lupine and low-growing barley that had invaded the new olive and almond orchards that separated the Arab village from the young moshava. When he compared the meager field to the young orchard planted in orderly rows, Yehoshua understood the *fellahin's* hatred of the Russian farmers. This was not the first occasion on which he had crossed the fields of Qatara and the Gedera orchards. He had come with the farmers of Rishon Lezion several times to help put up a shelter for the horses in the settlement, or to lend a hand in digging cisterns. The Arab crowd would gather with axes and picks in hand and stand around the Gedera people, laughing at their attempts to dig in the rock and poke a spike into the hard soil. Laughing was not enough for some of them, and they would start disturbances. The farmers would dig, and the Arabs would fill in the holes; these would build, and those would destroy; and in the end, the Gedera men would light torches and repel the Arab villagers with shouts. The discord was so severe that the Qatara Arabs fenced off the village's well and would not allow the Jews of Gedera to draw water from it. But the Gedera people did not panic; they deepened the cisterns and collected water in catchments and containers, and sought donations from the wealthy so they could dig a well for themselves.

Yehoshua flicked the whip lightly over the horse's back and urged it to climb the mountain. The galloping of the horses awakened Mendel, and Yaakov—who slept alongside his brother, cuddling in his warmth—also woke up. They both wrapped themselves in their coats. They crowded onto the seat with Yehoshua, casting sleepy glances toward the hill rising above the Arab village, and took notice of the elongated cabin rising above the horizon, breaking the skyline.

Gedera was scarcely a settlement: on a barren hill stood one long, wooden house to which were attached stable and shaggy tents; while at a distance stood low huts, half of them of clay, half of interwoven branches, all of which seemed out of place and ready to fly from the hill in any substantial wind.

The horse plodded on the narrow, unpaved path climbing to this "settlement not settlement," easily seen as having been traveled by a few wagons. And Mendel and Yaakov went back to dozing sitting up, and, from time to time, Mendel would open an eye and ask, "Are we there yet?" and then his head would droop down again on Yehoshua's shoulder.

The wagon trundled into an olive grove, all of whose plantings were tiny seedlings, a few of which pushed through the soil and a few of which were bent and dried out, with only a smattering managing to stand upright. Yehoshua took care not to trample the remaining seedlings and neared the house built of long wooden beams with spaces between them that let the wind in from one direction and out the other unimpeded.

Yehoshua pulled up on the harness, jumped down from the wagon, stretched his back, gave himself a good shake, and knocked on the door. It was still early morning, and he did not know the colony's routine: whether people got up early or late, whether everyone went out to the fields, or the women stayed behind. The door was opened by an old, wrinkled, Russian-speaking woman who reminded Yehoshua of the tenants living on his father's estate before he had left for Palestine and of its workers, on whom the hand of time had left its mark on their faces and hands. In response to her guest's inquiries, the woman told him that anyone who knew how to hoe and clear stones rose early and set out for the field. "All of them are trying to reach there before the searing winds that erode the hill in the afternoon and toss anything they encounter on their way, "she complained, whining grudgingly against the wagon and the uninvited guests.

Now, Mendel and Yaakov got out of the wagon and listened to the conversation. When the old woman saw that the two of them were still brushing sleepy seeds from their eyes, she grumbled even more. Only after she scanned the cart and the bundles on it well did she offer to let them enter the house, where she would pour them a cup of tea from the samovar, and the three accepted her invitation.

Mendel and Yaakov hurried to go in, while Yehoshua stood a bit at the threshold. He looked around, and his eyes took in the few words scratched above the lintel: "The Pines Home." He hesitated for a moment as he remembered full well the slanderous letters and Olga's responses in the newspaper. "Pines' hand has a long reach," he mused. Then he sighed, banished this notion from his mind, pushed the door, and went in.

A long moment went by until Yehoshua adjusted to the room's dimness. His eyes searched for the samovar. He could not believe it when he saw it, shiningly clean in the poor, empty room, like the hill they had just climbed: rough clay floor tiles, mattresses piled on a raised wooden base that served as a wide bed, tins and frying pans hanging from a copper tray dangling from the ceiling. But, to his surprise, the hag had not lied to them. In the meager room, a samovar stood on a clay oven under which the coals glowed. That instrument in the sparsely furnished room was like a rogue plant, and the copper it was made of cast a sparkle all around. The three thanked the woman, and while she was pouring their tea and taking warm bread out of the *tabun* oven, they unloaded their belongings from the wagon and put them in one of the corners in the house. When they finished arranging their bundles, they sat on the mat near the stove.

The three sipped the tea and tasted the bread, with a hush settling over them— and Yehoshua understood they were far from Rishon Lezion. When they finished drinking, the old woman hinted to them to follow her into the yard, where she pointed a veiny finger to the far field, and said to Yehoshua, "Zuckerman's." When Mendel asked about Sverdlov, the crone lifted her shoulders, pursed her lips, and again assertively pointed out Zuckerman's field. Then, she turned her back on them and entered the cabin, slamming the door after her.

The brothers hesitated and stood still for a moment, but finally, Yehoshua walked away from the cabin, not in the direction she had shown them but toward the barren slope.

"Zuckerman can wait," determined Yehoshua, and the brothers did not oppose him; they walked after him, bringing the wagon with them. "The sooner we mark out a plot for ourselves, the easier it will be for the Gedera farmers to decide not to toss us out. Then they won't claim we are outsiders, and they won't cry, 'Rebels, rebels,' and perhaps they will even see fit to accept us into their group."

According to the signs given by Israel Belkind, Yehoshua found the plot that belonged to Israel. He chose an area at the plot's edge that had been straightened, an area in which the rocks outnumbered the available land. They put stones under the wagon wheels, released the mare, and bent over toward the soil without saying anything. Then, after checking its quality, they began to work: one began marking, by dragging his heels, a large square encompassing what could be taken in at a glance, while the other two removed stones and piled them one atop the other outside the perimeter of the plot. By noon, a fence consisting of two rows of stones was standing. By the time the sun had begun to glide toward the edge of the sky, and a hot wind had started to blow, tumbling weeds and dust, the brothers were joined by Shlomo Chazanov, his wife, Binyamin Fox, and Zuckerman, and towards sundown, Sverdlov came as well.

They had come owing to their acquaintance with Fanny and Israel Belkind, since they remembered them from the time when *Bilu* was established. However, the arrival of the Hankin brothers did not elate them. Besides nodding and setting a pitcher of water on the stone fence and motioning toward it for the brothers to come to drink and slake their thirst, they did nothing but stand at the edges of the plot, making no connection with those clearing stones. Only one did not hide her dissatisfaction, Chazanov's wife. She approached the three and spoke out—at first mumbling into her dress, and then she raised her head so they should hear her speaking. "Not everyone is happy that you've come," she said. "Many are afraid. They say Yehoshua Barzilai sent you to Gedera without consulting Hovevei Zion in Odessa and without checking if Hovevei Zion there is willing to support new families. People will still come from the main office in Jaffa and say the support has to be divided among all the families, new and old alike, and they will refuse to add to the budget and won't give even one measly coin or any cows or sacks of seeds. So how will Gedera hang on with three new families—especially ones inciting trouble?"

Speaking emboldened her, and she arched her back a bit to the rear, stuck out her chest, put her hands on her hips, and cast a glance at the workers in the field. Since they were all quiet and did not interfere, she took this as agreement and made her voice more strident, "Barzilai treats the money as his own. However, it was not meant for his pocket, but to support the toiling farmers. Yet he, instead of expelling the radicals of Rishon Lezion, reinforces them. All this because he was interested in one of the Belkind girls. In Jaffa, people say that even in Petersburg, he wooed her. And he did not know she had gone on *Aliyah* to Palestine, and when he found out, he lost his head."

Yehoshua heard these words and glared at the woman. Her last statements frightened him, since Olga had never told him anything about a connection between her and Barzilai and did not share with him previous experiences belonging to Petersburg. But after a short time, he just lowered his eyes and continued working, trying not to think about that.

Mendel, in contrast, did not give in. He straightened up and approached the woman to silence her, but Zuckerman stopped him, "Let it go," he said. "She's a bitter woman. She's had difficulties all her life." Mendel listened to him and left her alone. In the meantime, all of them had returned to their dealings, while the woman continued to blather, and the stone fence kept growing higher.

When the dark settled in, everyone returned to the cabin. The three brothers were allotted a corner, though not on the wooden platform, and a mat was stretched out for them. From among those who had not come to visit them in the field, some people came near to greet them and ask about the rebellion and the families that remained in Rishon Lezion. Others ignored them, and the three heard them whispering, and the words "support" and "radicals" were voiced repeatedly on purpose out loud.

Yehoshua did not forget to hand Fanny's letter to Sverdlov, but when he tried to read the man's expression, he failed. The man took the letter and quickly left the house, moving into the darkness. In the late hours, the brothers withdrew from the group gathering in the long cabin and lay down in their corner, covering themselves with their coats, and fell into dreamless sleep. Rishon Lezion was already far away.

Five days after the Hankin brothers' arrival, the Belkind family came to Gedera and joined the tract of the son and brother, Israel. Since Israel was spending time in Jaffa and making an effort to become associated with its functionaries, an empty house and a parcel to work were found for his parents and brother. About a week later, Fanny and Lolik came, too, and located themselves near Yehoshua's mat and then erected a tent, placing it close to one of the cabin walls. Three more families were added to Gedera, and with them, three land parcels.

2 HÉDÉRA - Orphelins juifs des pogroms ukrainiens au travail

9. Hedera 1892 • Source: Hedera Archive.

10. Rehovot 1899 • Source: Irit Amit Cohen Private Archive.

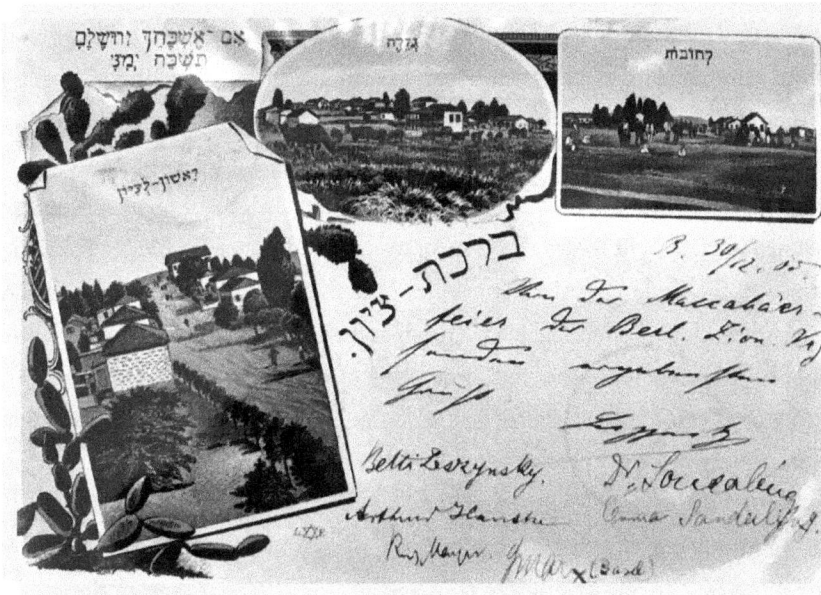

11. Postcard from Palestine • Source: Irit Amit Cohen Private Archive.

Olga was the first to adjust to Gedera. She hid her Rishon Lezion clothing in the big straw chest she had brought with her from Petersburg and arranged for farmers' clothes from Chanazov's wife and, in exchange, gave her wide material to make a bedspread. Then, she asked people to teach her how to plant and joined the families that embedded young twigs in the rocky soil; she competed with Yehoshua over whose hands were veinier and who would wash the mud off first. Yehoshua did not share her enthusiasm, for he did not like Gedera—not its houses nor its people. He, of course, tried hard not to show his attitude to the place, but his sour face, his tightly pressed lips, and his silence in the company of the farmers revealed his thoughts. He did not ask about Yehoshua Barzilai and did not want to know new details about him. Fortunately for him, the man's name only came up rarely, since everyone considered him a Jaffa hack, and in Gedera, people did not speak a lot about such people. Only when they praised the support reaching the colony on time at the beginning of every month did they also mention Barzilai's name. Since Yehoshua liked neither the talkers nor the topic, he turned a deaf ear to them.

Israel Belkind's plot and the one worked by the Hankin brothers were on Judith Mountain. The Gedera settlers had earmarked the mountain for planting a vineyard. Since the families had come from Rishon Lezion, they were familiar with vineyard tasks, so they were the first to plant grapevines there.

Olga loved the plot allotted to them—the lands sloped downward on the incline facing toward the Arab village of Qatara, and they were hidden from the houses of the Gedera farmers. Every now and then, when she tired of planting twigs or preparing supports for them, or removing stones from the land, she would sit on the stones that had been piled on the edges of the plot and look below at the homes and the people walking about. Between the houses, the women, bearing pottery jugs on their heads, filed along after the goats, swaying as they walked carefully, so as not to lose a drop of water. With the hand not holding onto the jug, they shooed away flies that swooped on the children's secretions. She barely saw village men and wondered about that. In the cabin, the farmers talked about the Arab villagers at length and their attempts to harass the Gedera residents. Yet, from the hillside, the Arab village looked as if it were immersed in bottomless quiet, and Olga loved this view; she did not even make Yehoshua part of it. It belonged only to her.

The small settlement was teeming with life. On Hanukkah, they celebrated three weddings—the wedding of Segalovitz, Leibowitz, and Binyamin Fox—while a date for the wedding of Olga and Yehoshua had not yet been set. In the meantime, they began building new cabins that were supported by the big cabin. Yehoshua dubbed them warts attached to a clump growing on the mountain, and he did not want to be part of them. When Olga's father Meir hinted to Yehoshua that the time had come to build his own house, he would shrug his shoulders and step away; he would go to his mat or out to the plot. And Olga did not speak of it or ask when. Instead, she remained in her parents' home, helped in the vineyard and orchard, and divided her time between the Hankin plot and the Belkind allotment, since the property of the new families grew, and they received additional land and planted olive trees on it.

⌖

The days passed quickly. The rains came, and the soil could not take in all the water; the overflow pooled and created puddles and chiseled rows in the land. On one of the winter days, Mendel wanted to go to Qatara to bring goat dung for fertilizing his orchards. He had learned that this was the proper season for fertilizing from reading books. In addition, Mendel had learned to distinguish between different types of manure and soil compositions, becoming a serious expert in new plantings. He asked Yehoshua to join him, mainly because he understood the language of the *fellahin,* and Mendel had a hard time understanding their tongue and carrying on a conversation with them. Olga, who had been listening to them talking, told Yehoshua that she wanted to ride with him to the village. Since the cart could not carry the three of them, Mendel gave up his seat and went to check the tender seedlings, while Yehoshua and Olga went by themselves.

For Olga, this was the first venture outside the colony since she had come to it, and inwardly she thanked Mendel, who had not argued nor demanded to go to the village himself. She sat impatiently on the wooden seat, her eyes wide open, and she wanted to share her experiences with Yehoshua. But Yehoshua was engaged in his attempts not to drive in the channels of mud lest the wheels sink in, and there would be no others to help release them. Olga laughed at his worries and told him she would be happy to finally be alone with him on the wagon. Yehoshua pretended not to hear and refused to react to her hints. Olga suffered her disappointment silently, and the wagon rolled along slowly down the slope of the hill until the beauty of the scenery displaced her distress. When they finally reached the bottom, Olga was taken aback by the village's appearance. It seemed so different to her from her usual view watching it from the heights of Judith Mountain— mounds of mud and tumbledown huts were immersed in ugly puddles that stood between wood clippings and floating tins.

Children in raggedy clothes jumped between the rickety huts and built bridges for themselves out of the tins and mud. When the little tykes saw the wagon enter the village, they halted their games and looked at it until it stopped next to one of the houses.

Yehoshua descended from the wagon and was swallowed up in fences of dry palm branches behind one house. Olga waited for a short time, but since Yehoshua did not come back, she alighted from the wagon and approached the house entrance to see what was going on inside. A group of women and children gathered around her; the giggling women pressed toward her and clandestinely felt her clothes. She liked their touch and was sorry she had worn simple farmer woman clothes and not something from the stored clothing in the wooden chest. She took the kerchief off her head and spread it out before them. Two women took hold of the scarf, one at each end, and examined its fringes and played with it: they put it on each other's shoulders, took it off and covered their veiled faces with it, and again hid it behind their back, and once more waved it in front of the other women. In the meantime, one of the women removed the cloth covering the entrance to the low house and hinted to Olga to enter.

She went in, followed by the other women, and it seemed to her she had been tossed into darkness. Slowly, her eyes adjusted to the dimness, and she managed to discern shadows and shapes around her. The woman sat her down on a pillow covered with scratchy wool material and walked around her and stood very close to her, and watched each movement she made. Olga laughed to them, and they laughed with her—since they had no other common language.

Suddenly, Olga heard an irritating, annoying cough, accompanied by stifled, strangled cries of pain, and then, once again, quiet reigned in the room. She rose from the pillow and mimed an expression of astonishment to the women. One of the women pointed to a corner of the room, while all the others acted as if they did not see her startled motion. When Olga wanted to go to that corner, they held her back, so she tried to gently push them away with a smile on her face; they distorted their faces and blocked her way. She sat down on the pillow again, realizing the cough was none of her business, but when she heard it break out another time, she could not contain her curiosity and stood on her tiptoes, looking over the women's shoulders.

On a pile of rugs, she saw a pregnant woman, bent over her stomach and gritting her teeth in pain, with every cough making her body tremble.

"There will soon be a birth," Olga knew. She did not wait for the women's permission and forcibly carved herself a path between them and approached the woman. The women, who had not expected such a reaction, stayed motionless, only their eyes following the stranger, darting here and there for fear they would miss any movement or slight action of hers. Olga bent down over the woman ready to give birth and felt a tingling spreading to the tips of her fingers and excitement washing over her.

Olga had not been practicing midwifery for three years now. She had not wiped a mother's sweaty face during the delivery nor whispered calming words to her. She had not held the screaming baby or presented a newborn to the mother who was still breathing heavily. Suddenly she wanted to be a midwife, to feel heartbeats and the baby's softness once again, to detach the umbilical cord, and to hear the first cry—nothing would stop her.

Olga bent her knees and sat near the woman, placing her hand on the heaving stomach. The women still had not moved. Olga forgot all about them and looked at the young woman, trying to peer deep into her black eyes. The frightened girl was confused by the touch of the woman leaning over her, and once more doubled over as pain tore through her.

Olga got up and rolled up a carpet that had been placed in a corner of the room and put it under the girl's body. Then, she pulled the young woman's legs until she was lying down. She needed water. Where could she take it from? She turned to the women standing a bit away, and with her hands, showed them what she needed, but they did not understand. She stood, straightened up, and looked about the room; when she espied a pottery jug, she went to it, took it, and presented it to one of the girls who had shortly before been playing with her scarf, which was still rolled on her arm covered by a black sleeve.

The young woman untied the scarf and tossed it on the floor at Olga's feet; she refused to take the jug and ran out of the tent. Olga did not know what to do and went back to the woman in labor, sat down next to her, trying to calm her and think of a way to solve the water problem. Someone tapped her on the shoulder, and when she turned her head, she saw an old woman bent over her. The woman said something to her in Arabic, but Olga didn't understand. The woman repeated her statement, speaking quickly in an angry tone; Olga, however, still didn't know what she meant. Finally, the old lady turned to face the other women and said something in a commanding manner. The women came near and stood between Olga and the rolled rug; they shoved the strange women to make her move away.

Olga tried to refuse; she pleaded with her eyes and tried to explain to them that she was indeed an expert, an experienced midwife, but there was no reaction in their eyes. Finally, she tried to get away and go back to the woman about to give birth, but the women were quicker than she and slowly, gently pushed her out until she burst out into the light of day.

The young woman who had been playing with the scarf and had thrown it on the floor, went after her and offered it to her. Olga grabbed the colorful kerchief from her outstretched hand and angrily moved away from the women crowding around the tent opening. She felt the looks aimed at her back and heard their silence, ruing her anger. Olga changed her mind and slowed her pace. Then, she turned around and walked toward them. She held the scarf out to them and left them alone. Once she was a bit away from then, she began running between the houses to look for the cart and for Yehoshua.

She found him loading manure onto the wagon. He was already tired, and his movements were labored. She stopped running; while panting. She tried to tell him what had happened, but her tears were choking her. Yehoshua saw she was terribly upset, so he stuck his pitchfork in the pile and took her arm, pulled her toward him, and gave her a hug. Olga yelled into his ear, "We will get married, we will get married and build a house. Not next spring but now."

Yehoshua sought to calm her, smoothed her wild hair, and answered, "After the summer, when the sesame will sprout in the fields."

She heard and nodded her head, but in her heart, she did not find his answer sufficient. So she turned her face away from him, wiped off her tears, climbed up to the wagon, and waited.

Yehoshua worked quickly and sent an occasional glance toward the cart, halting the motion of the pitchfork, and he saw her sitting on the wooden seat with a stormy face. He was angry at his weakness—after the summer, he had told her, and summer was still far off. At that moment she looked wilted, distant from him, and withdrawn deeply into herself.

Finally, the loading of the manure was finished, and Yehoshua climbed onto the wagon and hit the horse to urge him to leave the village. As they passed the listing house, they heard a baby's cry in it and saw a few young women standing near the doorway; one of them had wrapped her shoulders in Olga's kerchief.

The girl lifted her hand and waved shyly to Olga, but Olga did not react and only leaned toward Yehoshua and yelled to him, "Faster, faster!"

Yehoshua looked at Olga, looked at the girl, heard the cry, and was again saddened by his awkwardness and by his not knowing how to show the woman sitting next to him how worried he was. Suddenly, he wanted to halt the wagon and shout in the direction of the Arab women and tell them how much he loved that woman, but the cry was stuck in his throat, and Olga went on sitting silently and staring.

The summer ended, the holidays passed, and in Gedera, people no longer sufficed with wooden or clay houses close to the main cabin but erected individual houses on the shoulder of the hill. The first to build them were the

Zuckerman and Shimshon Belkind families, and they had the house warmings on Hanukah. Next, Binyamin Fox began constructing his house. Lolik and Fanny joined Shimshon's house, and Shifra and Meir's joy knew no end. Meir felt like a lord among his people, surrounded by sons and all of them holding steadfast to Gedera. He dreamt it would not be long before Yehoshua would also come and build a home for himself and bring Olga to it. After them, Israel would also settle and stop his wanderings between Jaffa and Jerusalem, between Jaffa and Gedera.

That summer, the older people hinted unceasingly to Yehoshua that he should set a date for his wedding. Olga, unlike her parents, did not annoy Yehoshua nor push him, but her pallor and silence grew until he could no longer see her pain. One evening, after Shifra and the younger girls had cleared the table, Yehoshua went to Olga and whispered, "On the twenty-second of Adar, we will be married after all the hoopla of Purim—between the end of winter and the start of spring." Olga did not reply, but her holding his hand attested to her excitement. Sonia, Olga's younger sister, took a piece of wood and a coal ember from the oven. She wrote the date in large, crooked letters and then asked Lolik to hang the piece above Yehoshua's bed, so he should see what was written every night when he went to sleep and every morning when he got up.

And Yehoshua began again building a house a year and a half after he had started to construct one next to the barn in the farmyard of Yehuda Leib's family. But unlike Zuckerman and Shimshon Belkind, he did not build a stone house but a wooden one. When he was asked the reason for the cabin, he said he had to finish building it by Purim, because if not, Sonia would hang him on the nail instead of the wooden piece now dangling there. But deep within, he knew they would not stay in Gedera for long.

⚜

On Purim, Sarah and Yehuda Leib came to Gedera along with Tanhum and the five girls seated in a wagon loaded with items and food from Jaffa. All of them had grown, and it was already difficult to identify them. Rivka had become a young lady with her braids wound around her head, above her ears, quiet and looking for corners to be by herself. Rosa was taller, and Tanhum was like a rooster who had just discovered his masculinity. He ambled from group to group of adults, sought to offer his knowledge and know-how on everything, and refrained from sitting with his little sisters. In the mornings, he often went with Mendel to help him in the orchard, and in the evenings, he joined the night owls sitting next to the fireplace, trading the news of Palestine among themselves. Stories of Jaffa filled Shimshon Belkind's house and, from it, made their way to other houses in the small colony spread out on the hill.

In those nighttime hours, some were envious of Yehuda Leib and Sarah and of glimpses of the big world, while Yehuda Leib envied the farmers and the smell of the earth and the grasses turning green on the slopes of the hills. This was a good kind of jealousy—each one exalted the deeds of the other, to the point that they competed over whose praise was greater.

For two weeks, they were occupied with cooking. The aromas intermingled, and it was difficult to distinguish between the smell of garlic and the scent of honey. The women learned from each other—they cooked and prepared dishes of Minsk alongside Odessa recipes, delicacies of Jaffa, as well as goodies from Gedera, everyone tasting from the others' pots, and the pile of baskets with the cookies and sweets and dry pulses grew higher.

Olga joined the women's tastings, the enthusiasm of the wedding preparations, and the sewing of the dresses. From her straw box, she took out the lace material she had begun to sew during the revolt and embroidered and pleated, hurrying to finish it so they should not use her sewing of the dress as an excuse to delay the wedding. Despite the hubbub, the excitement, and the joy, deep inside her, she did not believe the wedding ceremony would take place, so she tried to minimize her expectations and extinguish her delusions. Sometimes, she would stand in a corner of the house, hear the tumult all around, smell the abundance of aromas, and wonder who was all this for. She had waited so many days for Yehoshua, wanting a corner the two of them would call their own, and a piece of land and a deed of ownership with Yehoshua's signature in its margins, without any partners, to the point that she did not really believe that the wedding date had been set and marriage to her beloved was approaching.

Those days after Purim were days of joy in Gedera, not only because of the preparations for the wedding of Yehoshua and Olga. Yehiel Michel Pines had returned to live in Gedera. He entered the first cabin that displayed his name. He announced he did not intend to live in Jaffa anymore, nor talk about the matters regarding Gedera with the Hovevei Zion representatives who resided there. Still, he'd now let his message be heard from his hut in the colony.

The rebels of Rishon Lezion were not happy to welcome him. They had not forgotten his anger at them. They also claimed that with his appearance in Gedera and his declarations, he was similar to Ossowetzky. Like Ossowetzky, he was full of fancy speech and sought to unite the farmers around him so that they would accept his decisions unanimously. "And the worst thing of all," yelled Lolik, "he sees nothing wrong with the support allotments."

Of course, Pines remembered to differentiate between the bureaucracies and noted that the support by Hovevei Zion was not like that of Baron Rothschild and that the farmers could manage their affairs by themselves, but in the same breath, he knew to also add, "All the farmers lack training, so they are like fatherless children who need a leader to guide them and prepare them for the life of a tiller of the soil in Palestine." Naturally, the Rishon Lezion rebels did not like what he said, and Fanny mocked him, calling Pines "a trickster" and "a juggler." When he came to the home of Shimshon Belkind to announce that further building permits had been received as well as authorization to build a wall to separate them from the lands of Qatara, she laughed in his face and said bitterly, "The Arabs of Qatara will knock down the wall's stones with one pick-axe and the promises will fly in the wind."

The veteran Gedera farmers were angry at the reaction of the "people from Rishon" to Pines's arrival, and had it not been for the joy of the wedding mixed with the happiness at Pines's arrival, a huge quarrel would have developed. However, in the small colony, rumors and happy events continued to spread alongside each other. Sverdlov said that the Baron's anger at those who had revolted against him in Rishon Lezion, now living in Gedera, had abated. If so, he would provide money for digging a new well in the settlement and a loan for the farmers to expand the vineyard and the orchard. Israel Belkind brought news from Jaffa that the Baron did not intend to send clerks to Gedera, but he would send advisers, and Yehoshua Hankin promised to finish building his house by the time of the wedding.

In the Belkind family's home, the joy of the preparations continued and pulled in whoever was nearby. Yehoshua no longer escaped the noise but was part of it and repeatedly told himself that this was all in his honor. As had been customary at the time in Rishon Lezion, now, too, he sat until late in Olga's family's house, and the aroma of the rolls dipped in honey-filled it to the point that he could not taste them again. Fanny's laugh would travel through the house and draw in Lolik, and Lolik would get up and take hold of her and dance her round and round, and the dance would intoxicate Yehoshua, and he would join in, pulling Olga after him. Feet were stomping, and songs were ringing, and all of Gedera was happy and making merry.

Crowding increased in Shimshon Belkind's home as the wedding day approached. More guests came, more comforters were brought in, the *tabun* in the yard never stopped smoking, and the singing of the baking and cooking women became more forceful. The sunny days increased, the hill was covered with a mantle of green dotted with spots of groundsel and star hawkbit, and the scents of blossoming accompanied the people coming to the colony to take part in its joyous occasion. Yehoshua hurried to finish building his cabin, since abundant help was available—whoever was tired of sleeping all day or doing tastings the whole day through or spending hours prattling went to join the builders. And Yehuda Leib, who already needed a cane, was suddenly able to do without it. So he showed everyone the new expertise he had acquired from the Rokach family—planing of logs into boards, and he even asked those around him to go back to calling him "Diadka."

"The air of the hill makes my body younger and my spirit joyous," he explained to the astonished. "From the time of my youth, I was dubbed 'Diadka the mischievous,' let them go on calling me that on the day of the wedding of Yehoshua and his sweetheart."

Yehuda Leib had no competitors in the tiny colony, and very quickly, he became the center of attention in it. The builders crowded around him, examined his method for soaking the beams in water to make them flexible and smooth. They applauded his dexterity, and they, too, tried to do as he did. But while their hands stung with blisters, Yehuda Leib's stayed as unmarked as a baby's. In the meantime, the walls of the cabin grew higher, a window had already opened in them, and the roof beams were set in place.

The day after he finished building his home, Yehoshua Hankin took Olga Belkind for his wife. Yehiel Michel Pines came to marry them, and no one reminded him about his writings nor about Olga's responses in the *Hamelitz* newspapers. Even Fanny did not protest. And amid the clinking of the wine cups and the bubbling of the wine poured into them, Pines announced that the well would be dug after the Sabbath, as Baron Rothschild had promised. The joyousness grew, and joining the benches for the invited guests were people unrelated to the family of the groom or the bride who had come to Gedera only because of their exhilaration over the well.

When the blessings were finished, the parade of festive foods began. All the children came to help and carried trays laden with wondrous specialties. The tables were groaning, but the great abundance was quickly reduced to naught. So, the children came bearing overflowing bowls again, and the delightful aromas rising from them drew the celebrants to the tables. Once they finished tasting it all, the time came for circles of dancing. They arranged themselves in chains of dancers and wound round the tables, taking with them every crumb they had not wanted to leave in a dish. The dancers formed a moving snake of women and one of the men, who all drew closer around the bride and groom, then opened up again and wove between the tables.

Olga danced with gusto at the heart of the circle, tapping her feet and holding the lace woven around her with one hand and waving her scarf with the other, while winking enticingly to Yehoshua. Yehoshua responded with small steps, coming close and drawing back, offering her a handkerchief, and all his shyness melted away, surrounded by a cloud of aromas and singing and dancing.

In the wee hours of the morning, everything stopped. Those who remained moved the wooden benches and piled the pots, pans, and dishes to be washed later, and yawning, went into the house to spread out quilts for sleeping in the few nighttime hours left.

Yehoshua helped Olga clear the leftovers, but Shifra shooed them away, and she giggled at their embarrassment. Then, finally, they went out and turned toward their house.

The house stood off to itself, far from the stone and clay houses lined up in a single row on the shoulder of the hill, and it was still entirely exposed, with the lines of its silhouette prominent in the early glow of the morning. When they reached the cabin's doorway, Yehoshua bent down to pick up Olga in his arms to carry her over the threshold. But she slipped away from him. "You're adopting customs of the non-Jews," she chuckled. "Besides, I'm heavy and bigger than you."

Yehoshua pulled her to his body and bent over toward her earlobe and, kissing it, said, "Big, but mine. And the bigger you are, the more for me to hold onto."

Olga blushed, and Yehoshua noticed the redness spreading on her cheeks; he pushed the door with his elbow and pulled her after him, with his hand holding fast to hers. The room was spare and filled with the smell of new wood and the as yet not dry clay floor. Both stood on the threshold, breathing the scents in deeply, and looked at the bunch of wildflowers interlaced in a tin on the windowsill. Yehoshua turned his glance and looked at Olga; he saw her eyes shining and knew that she had cleaned and decorated the room in honor of both of them.

Then she pulled him after her, showed him every nook and cranny in the room, and told how she had come into the cabin the previous evening, after the builders had finished their job and gone back to their homes. She had cleaned the floor and the walls from the remnants of the cutting and planing until no sawdust remained in the cabin, and it was possible to walk about the room barefoot. When she had finished the cleaning, she went to pick chrysanthemums that grew on the side of the hill. She went as far as the edges of the lands of Qatara to gather stems of green barley that had just now ripened. After that, she returned to the cabin, interspersed the chrysanthemums among the barley stems, and joined them into one attractive bunch. In the wooden box, she had found rolls of material and sewn them together piece by piece until she had created a colorful bedspread. With a golden thread, she had embroidered the first two initials of their names in the left-hand corner of the counterpane and spread it over the bed. The letters twinkled now and winked to both of them. Yehoshua again drew her to his side, close to his body, but she had not yet finished showing him all of the room's new features. She pointed out the curtain she had sewn and hung in a corner of the room to hide the tools for working in the field. Next, she presented the wooden box standing in the middle of the room that served as a table and cabinet. She finally finished and could make out a smile nestling in the corners of Yehoshua's mouth. For a moment, she was silent and then responded to his hold and clung to him and whispered to him, "You are mine."

"And you are mine," he answered, "Olga Hankin." Even if the name sounded strange to him, he liked it better than Olga Belkind.

Unwillingly, Yehoshua pulled away from his wife and turned to the door to lock it. In the meantime, Olga had undone the tie that held back the curtain and spread out its folds in an attempt to prevent the sunlight from flooding the room. "If I could, I would close myself up with my man for quite a while and not let anything interrupt our life," she mused, "not the land luring him to her with magic strands and not the bitterness constantly knocking on the door." But Olga knew that it was only for a short time that they had lent Yehoshua to her, and then she would have to get used to sharing him with the expanses, with the happenings in the small settlement, and the awful things in Palestine.

She sat on the bed and waited for her spouse. He took off his boots slowly and placed them neatly in the corner bound by a curtain, then he walked barefoot and sat down next to her, feeling the bed sink. He wondered about that for a bit, since he had reinforced the boards, and then he smiled to himself. He had strengthened the boards according to his size, for he was not yet used to thinking for two. Yehoshua looked closely at the woman sitting comfortably, and she gave him her hand, and pushed in close to him until her dress rubbed his shirt. He caressed her fingers, one by one; every joint, each crack in the skin, and he circled her wrist to check its thickness, and went back to playing with her fingers.

Olga's skin tingled. She pulled her hand away and turned entirely towards him. Then, slowly and hesitantly, she stretched out her hand to take hold of his neck, and she drew his head toward her.

She was so hot; he kissed her mouth, her forehead, and her nose, and he gently nipped at her earlobe. His breath was tickling her. She kissed him back, drew her fingers along the parts of his face and neck, and moved down along the folds of his stomach. He pulled her to him until all of him was leaning against her, and she fell back into the bedspread and the Jaffa down comforters Sarah had given to them. They both shivered from the chill of the comforters, and Yehoshua matched his body to Olga's and tried to avoid touching the bedspread but rather to absorb into himself the warmth of the body bursting out towards him through the felt of the thin dress. Olga wrapped him with her hands and stroked his body, with her fingers fluttering the entire length of his spine until she managed to move them stealthily below his belt and went on stroking and going lower between the two humps of his body, feeling his quivering with pleasure. She went on caressing him for some time, and finally, she pulled his shirt below the belt and let him lift himself up and undo the buttons of her dress. Slowly, oh so slowly, he opened them, and his hands went searching, touching her nipples, pulling away and then making circles and again caressing, and Olga trembled from his touch. She waited for the next contact, and her entire body tensed and contracted, desiring his closeness. Yehoshua took hold of her breast, his entire body afire, and when he could no longer wait, he gently rolled on top of her lowered his pants. Olga lifted her hands over her head, and she was ready for him; she hinted to Yehoshua to help her take off her dress. Her ample figure and her fullness intoxicated him, and for a moment, his hand fumbled in the folds of her dress. Then, he kicked the bedspread and knocked it off the bed, and together they were swallowed up by the thick quilts. Yehoshua came to her and could no longer distinguish between the softness of the quilts and the heat of Olga's body. The scents of the wildflowers and the fresh wood engulfed them and carried them away, and Olga was with Yehoshua and he with her, and he was part of her, and his movements matched hers; they were alone, only the two of them ...

Sarah and Yehuda Leib, along with the girls, left the colony immediately after the dedication of the well. Only Tanhum remained to help Mendel and Yaakov. Tanhum convinced his parents with the argument that now that Olga had taken Yehoshua with her, the brothers would need another hand at night to share guarding the vineyard and the orchard. The parents laughed, enjoying the younger son's wisdom, left him with his brothers, and went home without him.

Yehoshua began to prepare a new field for planting, without any partners, only for Olga and himself. Olga helped to remove the stones, pull the wooden plow, and make the furrows in the compact soil. They bent forward over the moist clods the plow had turned over—she, to look at the earthworms making way for themselves, and he, to breathe in her scent and to feel her warmth. At midday, they would straighten up and step over to the edge of the field and sit close to each other on a gray stone, looking at the foot of the hill and seeing the Arab village, its women and children, and wondering as they always did—where are the men?

The festivities in the colony ended, and life was restored to routine. With the arrival of summer, the days began to grow longer, and the heat overwhelmed the fields. At daybreak, the farmers went out to their plots to make use of the few cool hours of the morning and came back when the sun stood high in the sky, to take refuge from its searing heat in their homes of clay and wood.

Everyone would gather in the community cabin at sundown to jabber and argue about Gedera. On those stiflingly hot summer nights, the farmers spoke mainly about the Arabs of Qatara, the quarrels over trespassing, and the *fellahin* who raided the farmers' fields, especially when the fruit was ripe. On those nights of idleness, a simple conversation was enough to make tempers flare.

Everything began when a few families from the village at the foot of the hill came to Zuckerman's house and demanded to see the *kushan* (title deed) and his signature on the deed.

The sale had been made without their agreement, they claimed. Salim A'wad, the wealthy landowner, had signed a contract and had treated the joint lands of the *fellahin* as an entire village, as if it were his.

"Masha'a!" they called to Zuckerman. "Cancel the contract, mark the lands, and divide them anew—which parcels belong to Qatara and which to Gedera," they demanded of him.

The farmers did not have the contract at hand, since the Hovevei Zion Committee had made the deal and then turned the land over to the Gedera people. Because of that, Zuckerman asked for the help of Pines, and Pines, sure of his success, traveled to Jaffa to speak with Committee member Yehoshua Barzilai. But the Committee refused to negotiate with the *fellahin* and argued that in any event, Jaffa was far from Gedera, so the farmers would have to conduct their quarrels without him. Pines, who prior to his setting out had promised all of them to conduct matters and succeed as well, returned to the colony dejected and ashamed. He gave Barzilai's answer to Zuckerman. When he saw how heartsick Zuckerman was, he tried to calm him down. "Since the debate over the land of Palestine will take a long time, and since at the end of the summer, the farmers, as well as the *fellahin,* will need to be busy preparing the fields for winter, the village Arabs will not have spare time for disputes."

Pines certainly tried to quiet things down, but the *fellahin* kept going up to the fields and standing at the border made by the removed rocks, and the farmers continued turning their backs to them, and scorning any attempt to present maps or show them documents. They ignored the lawyers who came on behalf of the villagers and refused to go to the Turkish court until a new division of the land would be made. Many families in the colony did not know exactly what the issue was and were not familiar with the details of Ottoman law, but from lack of action, they joined the debate with great fervor. Whoever was able expressed his opinion and raised his voice. That summer, they all agreed that from now on, Pines would be the settlement's official spokesman and Lolik his assistant. That's how the old quarrel was forgotten.

By virtue of his brawn and height, Lolik became the accompanying, threatening shadow. When the Arabs saw him from a distance, they would start running and flee as fast as they could. And just like in the days of Rishon Lezion, Lolik was again dubbed "the giant," and Fanny liked this term, even to the point where often the nickname "Lolik" would be exchanged for "the giant." The Gedera children imitated Fanny's voice and took delight in scaring each other by calling out, "The giant is coming! The Giant is coming."

Shimshon Belkind tried to lower the flame of Lolik's enthusiasm and would occasionally remind him of the event of their expulsion from Rishon Lezion. There, too, the rebellion had begun over a heated debate and the schism between the associations as well as quarrels among the farmers.

"Pines is like Ossowetzky," he tried to convince him. "So why should you be dragged after him?"

But Lolik paid no heed to what his friend was saying and was swept away with the great honor and awe his image bestowed on him, and he enjoyed the admiration young and old felt for him. The slander spread about Pines was of no interest to him as long as the farmers turned their heads after him as he walked by, and the *fellahin* would see his figure roaming the fields.

At first, Yehoshua and Olga did not get involved in the quarrels in Gedera. Instead, they removed the stones from their plot, finished their planting, and waited for the seedlings to sprout. When the others were leaving their fields because of the burning sun, they continued to look for a hideaway in the shadow of the hill overlooking the Arab village and drew the serenity into themselves. If they only could, they would have sat for hours and days steeped in their solitude and happy for every moment they could be by themselves. But their calm did not last long, and the raging debates and quarrels broke into their refuge.

A few days before Passover eve, Husseini Bek came on horseback to the colony with all the young men of the Arab village Qatara following him. The group entered the colony with screams and yells, panicking everyone in the houses and yards or on the pathways, making them come out and assemble along the single street and watch as they came in.

In the entire region of the low hills, they spoke of Husseini Bek and his noble horse. He was a young, brazen Arab, and he had earned his reputation because of the black horse on which he would ride, seated on a saddle with red fringes at the ends of which were tied short daggers and pistols. Behind each of these pistols and every dagger was a story or a victory or a robbery, and Husseini Bek made it clear that he never used the same gun or dagger more than once— and there were a great many of them.

The villagers halted at the entrance to the yard of the community cabin and bunched together in one group, while Husseini Bek continued riding up to the door of the building. He did not get down from his horse, but sat and played with the saddle's tassels. Then, after reviewing his soldiers and those gathered next to the fence, he called out to Pines in a booming voice, "I have come to dispute the lands stretching down the slope of the hill. Therefore, I am holding a court order forbidding Gedera members from entering the plots. Come out, Mr. Pines. Come out to receive the order."

Silence prevailed in the yard. Quite some time passed, and finally, Pines came out of the cabin. The young Arab did not dismount from his horse and did not look directly at Pines but only started his shouts anew, "Until no legal decision will be reached about the disputed land, it will not belong to the *fellahin* of Qatara nor to the Jews of Gedera." The rider ended his speech and did not wait for Pines's response; he only threw the order at his feet, whipped his horse, and galloped the length of the street, creating clouds of dust. He did not stop near the farmers nor next to the *fellahin* still waiting for him at the entrance to the yard. When the dust cleared, the *fellahin* were seen running after him down the slope, and the horse in a dust cluster, going far beyond Qatara into the fields of Duran.

The evening discussion now became an acrimonious debate. Almost every day, policemen were sent from Jaffa. They sniffed around the colony, measuring and checking their paces, across the width and length of the fields — not only on the slope, but also on the shoulders of the hill.

Lolik loved the tumult stirred by the lands the same way he was enamored of the fear and curiosity that surfaced among the surveyor as well as the *fellahin* who came near the fields and tried to force the farmers to flee. The importance that had come to him, the respect and awe turned his mind topsy-turvy. He withdrew from his family—except for Fanny, who was as dazed as he—and the three families no longer visited each other. Yaakov, Mendel, and Tanhum worked on a joint tract, Meir and Shifra raised Sonia and helped Shimshon with his attempts to grow different kinds of vegetables in the small plot next to the house. Olga and Yehoshua were not seen at all out and about in the colony.

Lolik and Fanny paid no attention to the change in the family's attitude toward them, since they were so involved with themselves. Shifra said the day would come when Lolik would wake up, and once his eyes were opened, his fall would follow. But, in the meantime, Lolik had earned a worthy reputation, and on the hills around Gedera, everyone was talking about the "giant."

One day, Pines and Lolik went to Rishon Lezion to meet the chief clerk and manager on behalf of the Baron—Mr. Adolph Bloch. As usual, Lolik did not know the purpose of their going— Pines made the announcement, so he went. Happily, he combed his hair and told Fanny about the honor that was his—to accompany Pines to meet the Baron's representative. Fanny did not like hearing this: Why suddenly to Rishon Lezion? So, she tried to stop Lolik from going, but she was too late. Lolik was already washed and primped, and his horse's mane had been combed. Yet, she looked for a way to delay his setting out and said to him, "For quite a while now, I have not gone up the hill to see how the olive saplings are doing. Perhaps the soil needs to be turned, or pruning needs to be done, as well as whitewashing the trunks against insects."

Lolik laughed at her ignorance. "In summer, it is forbidden to turn the soil. The little moisture must be kept in the land. Pruning and whitewashing can be done in the evening." When he saw her disappointed face, he added, trying to convince her, "What's this nonsense? Why should I delay my going? Bloch is a new manager. Rishon Lezion has become a different colony, and its farmers have long forgotten the rebels and those who refused to sign."

The uprightness of his sitting in the saddle and the child's joy in him angered Fanny a bit, but she couldn't change anything, so she cast away her fears and waved him goodbye.

A few days later, the colony found out that the Baron had agreed to Bloch's intercession and allotted money to give to the *fellahin* and to solve the dispute between the members of Gedera and the Arabs of Qatara. Gedera rejoiced. Most farmers were sure that all their problems had been solved forever, since the Baron was willing to take the colony under his aegis and care for its affairs. One of them hung a placard at the entrance to the settlement with the writing in large letters, "Long Live the Baron." In contrast, others prepared a list of demands and were thoroughly convinced that a clerk-adviser would soon be sent to them, as had happened in Rishon Lezion and Ekron. The entire colony awoke from the summer doldrums.

The joy in Gedera resulted in Lolik being forgotten. People acclaimed Pines for his success in getting the Baron to join in with attenuating the suffering of Gedera, and Lolik, being a rebel against the Baron, could not, therefore, be a party to the cheering. And the more people ignored him, the more Lolik became aware and finally understood what was lurking behind Pines's "intentions." He understood, and he was frightened: Gedera had given in to the Baron, and the days of Rishon Lezion were returning but in a new format—Pines wanted to be a clerk and a manager and did not suffice with the support of Hovevei Zion. The clearer things became, the more alarmed Lolik became by Pines's actions and the fawning to him and Bloch, and all the eminence that had surrounded him in recent months dispersed as if it had never been. He began to be introverted and wanted to be swallowed up by the earth.

In the evening, the delegation of farmers, led by Pines, went to hand over the bundle of money to Husseini Bek. After that, Lolik visited Yehoshua and Olga in their remote cabin.

He found them deeply involved in doing little things: Olga was sewing a new garment, and Yehoshua was fixing the broken handle of a hoe. Lolik envied them and continued to stand for a long while on their threshold, with bowed back and silent. Only after a few minutes went by did, they remember their friend and invited him to come in and sit with them. Yehoshua tried to get Lolik to grin and reminded him of the forgotten jam and the harvest in Yehuda Leib's vineyard, but Lolik did not smile. Instead, he sat on the wooden bed and told them about the bribery payment that had been given to Husseini Bek.

When Yehoshua heard the story about the money, he could not restrain himself, and a curse escaped him. "I will go to Pines's house," he announced. "Perhaps it is still possible to delay him."

Olga's gaze dashed from her spouse to her brother-in-law, and she was sorry Lolik had come to them. That minute she knew that the barrier of calm and solitude that had surrounded them had been breached, and who knew when it would be rebuilt. Lolik noticed her anguish and understood how he had hurt her, but he found no words of consolation and sat down beside her to hug her shoulder. It was hard for her to be next to him, so she moved a bit away, with her pursed lips revealing her state of mind.

Yehoshua went out into the night and tromped on the colony's pathway. This wasn't a boulevard, nor a lane with cypresses growing all along it, and the man walking on the path did not understand what he had to do with the small settlement, what connection did he have to its problems. So, when he approached the elongated cabin, he slowed his pace. Then, he gathered his courage, and without knocking on the door or asking for permission, he went into Pines' house. Pines stood near a bowl with a towel thrown over his shoulder and held a pitcher from which he sprinkled water on his face and neck. Yehoshua came closer to him, grasped his shoulders, and forced the man, who was shorter than he, to turn his face toward him.

That man next to the bowl was frightened and dropped the towel. Since the wedding, he had barely seen Yehoshua, who lived at the other end of the settlement and was deeply involved in working his plot. The colony farmers said that he was not used to a settled life. He would stay for a few months in his home and then become fed up with the calm and wander afar. Pines had no interest in Yehoshua, except for his stories about Olga and Yehoshua Barzilai. Also, from time to time, he remembered the letters addressed to him appearing in the newspapers. He had nothing to do with the couple living on the outskirts of the settlement and did not think about them. But now, Yehoshua Hankin had come into his house without permission and stood opposite him, and he was frightening and threatening with the beard adorning his face.

"You are an idiot, and all your farmers are fools," began Yehoshua, and in the stillness of the room, his words resounded like the striking of a hammer. "You don't understand what the colony's farmers want, and they do not realize your ambition. You are seeking authority, the greatness of managers. But on whose account? The farmers were barely eking out a living. You received money from the Baron's clerk to expand the plots, yet you preferred to give it to the Arabs, although you are not familiar with his ways, nor even the intentions of his sponsors. The soil is worked by *fellahin*, who lease it for three years. Then, they abandon it and go lease another plot. The legal owners sit in the big cities—in Beirut and Damascus—and don't know what is happening to the land, and if they only could, they would be happy to get rid of it. The land in Gedera was purchased at full price. Did you check with the owners? Did you read the sales contract? What did you do besides panic at the threats of Husseini Bek and go to plead with Bloch to ask him for money to use as a bribe for the *fellahin*?

"Go back to Qatara, and see how Husseini Bek is laughing at you. He received money from the '*yahud*,' but what did he give in return? A verbal statement, a promise that the *fellahin* will retract their suit. But tomorrow, they will forget their promise. They were given money, and they have big eyes. A month will pass, two months will go by, and they will renew it. The *fellahin* are better than you at knowing Turkish law and its nature. They know well that the wheels of justice grind slowly ..."

Pines found it hard to stop Yehoshua's torrent of words, while Yehoshua himself did not understand the source of the wellspring from which he found the courage to burst out and not let the person he was facing stop him.

Pines's hands trembled, and his knees were knocking. Then he said hoarsely, "Go, leave my house. You don't belong in Gedera." Yehoshua fearlessly laughed in his face even though he knew that he had just acquired an enemy, so he left the room quietly closing the door—not slamming it as had been expected.

After this encounter, something changed in Yehoshua. Now, he knew for sure that one day he would have to leave Gedera, and this realization made him happy in a way, awakening an expectation as well as disquiet. Suddenly, his nights were very long and sleepless. Olga would wake up in the middle of the night and see him lying in his bed with his open eyes staring at the wood ceiling. She tried to get him to talk and asked a lot of questions, but Yehoshua stayed silent and did not find words to express his feelings to her. He clung steadfastly to his silence; the nights grew long, and Olga stopped asking. None of those visiting their house noticed what was going on inside Yehoshua, but it was enough for Olga to spend time near him when they worked in the field and to see his eyes looking beyond the Arab village, going far away over the flat clay roofs and staring at the tremendous spaces to understand that it would not be long before he would leave her; he would follow his other love.

And the final days of the summer came—the barley was harvested, the vineyard pruned, and everyone waited for the new planting. Between the sowing of the summer and that of the winter, Yehoshua returned to his riding. At first, he went only a distance of one day from the colony, satisfied by the land stretching between Rishon Lezion and Gedera. With sunset, he would return, and Olga would see his shining eyes with their distant gaze, and his shoulders expanded and drawn up straight from breathing the air of the fields. She would welcome him at the entrance to the cabin and pick stalks of straw and thorns off him, and he would tell her about his ride, the scenes, and the people, and she would keep still, feeling his distancing himself from her though she would not stop him. After that, his riding became more frequent and more prolonged, until there were entire evenings in which Olga remained alone. She immersed herself in the housework in the small cabin, uprooting unkempt weeds that grew in the yard, and in attempts to grow the tender citrus saplings that Mendel had given her.

On the long, lonely evenings, Olga would go to the community cabin and teach a few members of Gedera to read from the books she had brought with her that until then had been buried in the box standing in her house. The first few times she went to the joint cabin, she had not felt comfortable with the looks shot at her. After that, she shut her eyes and closed her ears to Fanny's questions, and waited for Yehoshua's return—if not tonight, then tomorrow … and when her spouse would come back to her, his stories would fill them both and drive away the memories of the loneliness and the dull evenings without him.

In those weeks of summer's end, suddenly, there was a call for Olga's expertise. Fox's wife was about to give birth, and since Fanny had spoken about Olga's profession, the colony decided not to bring a midwife from Jaffa. But, increasingly, people in the small settlement began to seek her advice, so much so that she became an expert on women's issues and her loneliness abated somewhat. On several occasions, it happened that Yehoshua returned from his travels, after not finding her in the cabin, went from house to house, knocking on doors until he could see her—sitting next to the bed of the expectant mother. He would wait for her until she finished her work, and the two of them would walk along the narrow path, with him telling her about the expanses stretching outside the colony and about the beauty of the land, gushing springs, and limestone cliffs descending to the sea. But Olga again was not listening to him, only trudging alongside him, with a fleeting glance at his face and then moving on, distancing itself from him. Now, they needed each other less and less. He felt her remoteness, and though he did not understand, he also did not try to fathom its meaning.

In the colony, they became used to seeing Olga by herself. There were already occasions when a messenger came to the house on the edges of the settlement and asked only about Olga, not even mentioning Yehoshua's name. Lolik stayed away from the house of Yehoshua and Olga, Mendel and Yaakov took upon themselves the care of the orchard without having previously spoken with their brother about it. They came and pruned and deepened the tree wells; Olga saw and kept quiet. Once, when Tanhum came to her and asked her for money to buy seeds for barley and lupine, she handed him her purse and told him to take as much as he needed and took no further interest in this. She withdrew not only from Yehoshua but also from the land belonging to the two of them and from the cabin Yehoshua had built for her. She no longer cared about the vegetable garden and did not sew a new loop when the old one tore and the curtain fell from the window.

The autumn holidays passed; the days grew shorter, and the first winter clouds covered the sky. One day, at the beginning of October, Yehoshua returned to his cabin early, and as usual of late, he did not find Olga there. At first, he waited for her, but then fell asleep, and when he awoke at midnight and did not find her next to him, he became frightened. Thoughts ran through his mind, and the more he reflected, the more his fears grew. "She has left me, gone far away, and won't come back." Deciding suddenly, as if seized with delirium, he burst outside. He ran on the colony's path, looking for her between the houses, awakening those sleeping, not even caring about a baby who was frightened by his banging on the door of her house. The farmers offered sleepy shrugs to his questions, and for the first time after quite a while, he paid attention to the pitying, mocking glances of Sverdlov and his wife, as well as the malicious joy the old lady in Zuckerman's house had demonstrated toward him. Yehoshua was panic-stricken. Now, he was sure something terrible had happened to Olga, and the farmers were refusing to let him know, so he began racing down the street, calling her name through the entrances to the homes and the windows. Zuckerman came out of his house and tried to grab the edge of his coat to put a halt to his running, but Yehoshua would not stop. He pushed away the farmer and went on dashing, his eyes afire and his hair disheveled. Finally, the shouts of Lolik, who had been summoned from his bed and was running after him on the pathways of the colony, penetrated his mind. "Are you crazy? Olga is at the Fox's, busy taking care of the newborn."

Yehoshua slowed down, and Lolik caught up with him and only then realized how afraid he was of losing her. When Yehoshua entered the Fox home, Olga did not turn around to look at him, and he just stood on the threshold, refusing to take the glass of water offered him, and waited for her to finish her work. Once she was done, the two of them walked on the street together, with him holding her elbow and saying to her all in one breath, without letting her stop him, "Come with me tomorrow. We will go out of Gedera, and I'll show you other sights."

Olga wanted to refuse but said nothing, only hastening her steps.

"Wait," he asked her. She could no longer avoid looking toward him or miss his terror and the sadness swamping his eyes. She slowed her pace and finally stopped, turning to face Yehoshua. And when he stood close to her, she smelled the bouquet of the earth mingled with the scent of his body, and she could not stop herself. For the first time in many days, she reached out, and her finger dove into his wild-growing hair and stroked his deep-set eyes. She came close to him. Her body touched him, and his arms embraced her. She nodded her head and whispered to him, "I will ride with you. I will follow you to the ends of the fields," but she did not tell him what she felt and did not reveal her great pain to him.

While the colony still slumbered, Yehoshua and Olga left their home, and when Yehoshua was surprised by the holiday garb she was wearing, the woman laughed and told him, "I am leaving Gedera. I'm finished with the weekdays and my workaday world."

All the sadness she had borne in the recent summer weeks and months had disappeared in a flash. She sat next to him on the wagon and drew into herself the views and the air of the fields and repeatedly said to Yehoshua, "I am sponging up into myself the scenes and the air you have not been willing to share with me for a long time now."

Yehoshua looked toward her and heard her prattling; he put his head in her lap like a child caught being naughty and kept his peace. Then he showed her the prickly pear cactus plants and their ripening fruit, the acacia drying out, and the eyeful of bare land. He pointed out the birds' nests and the dry water channel all along which the deep-rooted oleander flourished. When they descended into a crevice, pleasant coolness washed over them, and Yehoshua halted the mule, jumped off the wagon, and extended his sturdy hands to take her down and set her in the shade of a limestone rock. He took off his shirt and spread it on the hard ground; when she sat on it, he handed her a clod of searing soil, but she just pushed his hand away.

"What should I do with it," she asked. "It's not clods of earth I need. I need a husband who will return at nightfall and share my bed with me."

"I will share it with you," he promised. "When summer ends, I will relax."

She smiled at him and was quiet, but a moment later, she added, "After the summer will come the wintertime, and I will be left with my loneliness."

Yehoshua put a finger to her lips to stave off her speech, but she held it, refusing to take it out of her mouth. Yehoshua tickled her ribs, and she bounced until she laughed out loud and released his finger. He ran a finger down her face and on her neck, putting her face close to his until her eyes seemed to join into one, and he said to her, murmuring, "I won't leave you; I'll always come back."

Olga looked at him with a jaundiced eye. She did not believe him. When Yehoshua saw her expression, he quickly added, "Let's go. I will take you to the lands of Satariya to meet the old sheikh. He has taken a new wife, many years younger than he. He married her only after his first had only given him daughters. Now his second wife is pregnant, and for a few days now, she has been bleeding and burning up with a fever, and the old man stares at her, believing that the heavens are punishing him because girls weren't enough for him, and he wanted boys, too."

Olga heard but did not answer, and she was angry deep within that he had not revealed to her the purpose of their joint trip. In her innocence, she had believed that her spouse had wanted to take her with him to compensate her for her many days of loneliness. Yehoshua noticed her disappointment and tried to comfort her, "I didn't do what I did intentionally. The old man and his wife are part of my experience, part of the space that spreads beyond the fences of the colony, and I just wanted to share it with you, to show you."

Olga didn't know whether to believe him and preferred to be quiet. Then, she stood up, straightened her clothes, and climbed again into the wagon. The two continued to move on in heavy silence, with the yellow of the fields and the black of the soil burning their eyes.

The cart jostled, and Olga's body bumped into Yehoshua, and he again could no longer hold back and said to her, with a quavering voice, "It's good you came."

She remembered her anger and did not reply. Her body stiffened and drew away from him, taking care not to fall and holding on to the seat with all her might. Again, they rode without uttering a word, and her tired body relaxed. Since she could no longer ignore his closeness and the smell of his body, she again let her body fall toward him. Yehoshua let go of the reins, and the horse continued to gallop, for it knew the way well and did not need a driver. Close to noontime, the wagon reached a group of black tents made of hair. "This is the tent encampment of the Bedouins of the Bani Satarya tribe," explained Yehoshua. "They leased the land of Duran, sent the goats to graze, and also buried their dead in the ground, and now they treat the tract as if it were theirs, and they are not willing to abandon it and graze their herds elsewhere."

Olga heard what he was saying, but she could not distinguish one piece of land from another and did not understand the Bedouins' problem; she only thought once more about the sheikh and his young wife.

Drawing Away

The leveled path led the wagon into the encampment. The horse slowed its pace and finally stopped next to a fence made of rolling tumbleweed that surrounded a large tent. Yehoshua jumped down from the wagon and tied his horse to a pole stuck in the ground. Then he put out his hand to help Olga alight. Olga gave him her hand, and holding the edges of her dress, she jumped and stood beside him. He asked her to wait for him. He walked toward the tent and lifted the blanket that covered the opening. Then, in Arabic, which she didn't know, Yehoshua called into the tent. In response, a Bedouin woman wrapped from head to toe came out with heavy, sparkling gold bracelets, inlaid with small stones/gems, tinkling on her hands. The woman was not young and reminded Olga of the old hag who had prevented her from helping the woman in labor in Qatara, and she unintentionally recoiled from her spot near the wagon.

Yehoshua greeted the old woman, and she re-entered the tent; a short while later, the old sheikh came out. He was indeed old—entirely bent over, a white beard adorning his face, and a gnarled stick supporting him when he took his prolonged, plodding steps. The elderly man approached Yehoshua, and at that, Olga also came near.

Yehoshua hinted to her to stop, but she did understand the motion. Yehoshua excused himself from the sheikh and hurried over to her, standing opposite her and putting both his hands on her shoulders to hold her back, "Here, a woman does not sit in the company of men," he said.

"But it is acceptable for a woman to give birth to men," Olga grumbled in anger but was immediately sorry for what she had said. Yehoshua said nothing and returned to the old man, with only his gaze full of pain seeming to ask what had happened to the two of them, why had they grown so far from each other.

Olga sat where she had been standing; she felt the hard clods pricking her body, and she looked deeply at Yehoshua and the old man in conversation, sitting near the entrance to the tent. "Probably because of me, he refused the invitation to go into the tent," she thought and was even more rueful of what she had just said. Then she looked at the woman, and inadvertently she spun around the ring she wore on her finger. She had waited so long for the ring, and now that it had been given to her, a rift had been created. Which of them was guilty? Neither she nor he. The difficulties of this hot country and the land with its troubles—all of them were guilty. If they could only distance themselves from the land, to hide from it, she would take Yehoshua and flee. But Yehoshua was tied to it with strong bonds, and she would not run away by herself. Moreover, she loved him fiercely. She knew every mole and every crevice in his body, and she knew that she had to concede and share him with his other love.

While she was sitting there in reverie, the old woman offered steaming tea to Yehoshua and the old man and then approached Olga and sat down a short distance from her. Time passed, and Olga got up to stretch her legs, which had fallen asleep as she sat uncomfortably on the ground. The sheikh and Yehoshua saw her getting up and watched her with their eyes. After she had walked a short distance away, the sheikh hinted to the old woman with a hand movement. She went toward Olga and motioned her to follow her to the small tent attached to the big one. Olga was a bit scared, since her memories of the Arab peasant women were quite harsh. She turned her head toward Yehoshua and asked with her glance for his agreement. He nodded to her, and she accompanied the woman, for there was nothing else to do.

When she entered the tent, it was as if she were blind. She tried to have her eyes trace the strip of light full of dust motes that penetrated through the opening until her eyes adjusted to the dark. Finally, she could make out a pile of pillows placed in one corner and rugs and blankets rolled up in another, along with a few bundles scattered here and there. She was familiar with the arrangement of the tent. If she hadn't known she was in a Bedouin tent, she would have thought she was again in the houses of Qatara. The only thing she could do was try to find a moving bundle among those strewn around. A choking cough and oppressive signs revealed it, and Olga was frightened and stood where she was, trembling.

Once she had overcome her memories, especially her fears, she approached and saw a young woman lying there, with her pretty face uncovered. Beads of sweat covered the young woman's high forehead dotted all over in blue, marking the old man's possession. Burning black eyes followed the movement of this foreign woman. Olga looked at the pile of blankets covering the girl and breathed in the smell of the coals wafting from them. Then she bent down at the girl's feet and watched her body moving under the blankets, rising and sinking, rising and sinking.

Aside from the two women, no one else was in the tent. The old woman had also disappeared. Olga relaxed and put her hand in the pocket of her dress and took out a handkerchief to wipe the sweat of the woman about to give birth. The girl did not object, and Olga continued to wipe, pat, and calm her down. The motions of her body almost ceased. The girl had probably fallen asleep. Olga got up and went to the tent entrance; she called for Yehoshua to bring her a bowl of water and a few items she needed. Yehoshua hastened to do what she asked, asked no questions, and was mainly pleased by her tone in which he recognized action and determination. For a minute, Olga was surprised by his willingness to fulfill her request without asking or being surprised by her actions. But thinking about the girl waiting for her in the tent overrode her musings.

Once Olga had what she had asked for, she went back inside the tent. This time, too, the darkness affected her eyes, but she already knew where the bundles were located, and she stepped surefootedly. There was no one to stand in her way and prevent her from revealing her expertise; no one to delay her or send her out and then say to her—you're a stranger, you don't belong. This was her place, and this was her job, and Olga knew it well.

One by one, she took the blankets off the girl so she could adjust to the cold in the tent, and she looked at the squirming in the thick dress. This was the body of a very young woman, practically a child, a body not yet mature enough yet already having a child growing in it. She did not know if the girl would hold on and withstand the labor pains; she also did not know if the baby was doing well or if its lungs were developed enough to weather the birth. After some hesitation, she lifted the girl's dress and touched her stomach; there were no objections since the stranger's circular, caressing movements calmed her. Olga felt the fetus's movement and noticed it was big for the girl's dimensions and would have difficulty passing through the birth canal. Given its size, the time had come for the baby to be born. But the opening was too small, and the mother-to-be's contractions were not powerful enough.

Olga put her hand inside, and the girl tensed, her body becoming rigid. Olga pressed more, and the young woman rose toward her and grabbed onto her, groaning in pain and panic. Then, slowly, Olga released her hands. She took hold of the girl's shoulders and laid her back down on the bed. Then, she wrapped the blankets tightly around her and left the tent to call for the old woman to come to help her.

The older woman was waiting at the tent entrance, ready to go in, as if she knew she would be needed; on her head, she bore a tin full of steaming water. She trod after Olga and put the tin container near the woman in labor. Then she put in Olga's hand a small saucer containing a calming potion and sat herself down some distance from the girl; her eyes were constantly trying to follow the midwife's swift movements. Olga patted the stomach covered with blankets in circular motions and gave the girl the potion without thinking about its content. Then she turned to the old woman and nodded her head in thanks and waited, knowing that the contracts would come soon.

The woman about to give birth took quiet breaths, and Olga thought about the old sheikh, as well as Yehoshua, so many years younger than he. She wondered about her actions in the tent and the very fact that she was delivering a child for the old man, with no one knowing if he would live a long time and be able to carry the child and go with him to graze the goats. She didn't have a long time to think about all this—the girl's contractions became more frequent, so Olga called for the old woman to come near and showed her how to hold the young woman so her movements would not harm the newborn. The old woman ignored Olga's instructions and held her elbows in a vise-like grip, but the girl tried to break free since she was now fully awake, no longer under the influence of the potion.

The old woman's gaze was locked on the girl, holding her fast, and for a moment, Olga wondered if the older woman was jealous of the younger. The girl's contractions increased, and she bit her lips to stifle the screams of pain waiting to leave her mouth. Yet, finally, she was unable to stop them, and heartbreaking shrieks broke through. Olga hastened to pile bundles under the feet of the woman in labor to raise them, and a minute later, she heard a shout.

With her fingers, Olga felt the head crowning, and with her other hand, she pressed the girl's stomach. The young woman cried out and bent over; again, Olga pressed, and again a scream rang out, and then silence—the girl had fainted. Olga was frightened and tried to pull the head and realized her hands were trembling; she sent a look to the old woman asking for help. The old lady let go of her hold on the girl and struck her face over and over until she opened her eyes and began to push again, and Olga felt the pain cutting through her.

Olga pulled, the girl writhed, and the old woman held on, her veins protruding from the effort. Then one long scream was heard, and everything was over. The baby was in Olga's hands, wrapped in the umbilical cord, wrinkled, and covered in bits of placenta. The old woman bent over the girl and wiped her damp face.

Olga gave the newborn a shake, and when he let out his first cry, she cut the remainder of the umbilical cord and presented the infant to the old woman. She took him from her hands to clean and then handed him over to the old sheikh to receive his blessing. The Russian woman looked into the woman's eyes and saw a gentleness that had not been there before. The old lady did not notice Olga looking and turned to the young woman to check her temperature and to examine her tearing, as if she no longer relied on the foreigner. The young Bedouin woman lay quietly, not yet feeling the after-birth pains awaiting her; she was elated from the liberation and wonders of her first delivery, and Olga's eyes filled with tears from the excitement. The old woman re-entered the tent, placed the swaddled newborn near the girl, and also set down a bowl of water to wash her. The girl no longer looked at Olga, nor did she feel the old woman's actions, for she was busy with her child; Olga left the tent. For some reason, she was unstable on her legs, and the light outside hurt her eyes.

Olga wanted to cry, and dots danced before her eyes. She closed her eyelashes as tightly as she could, and when she opened her eyes, she saw Yehoshua standing opposite her, putting out his hands to steady her. She lifted her eyes skyward and saw the sun at the edges of the heavens, and when she shifted her eyes toward her husband, she saw his gaze yearning for her. She went close to him, forgetting her anger of the morning, and leaned on him with all her might. He held her and almost lifted her up, and helped her climb onto the wagon. The old sheikh came toward them and looked at Olga, and without removing his gaze from her, presented Yehoshua with a bag of coins. Yehoshua refused to take them, and the old man blessed him heartily.

As they drew away from the tent encampment, Yehoshua translated the sheikh's blessings for Olga, "You will have many sons, he said." But Olga no longer heard—she was fast asleep. Yehoshua didn't wake her. Only once they ascended the hill and Yehoshua saw the houses of Gedera standing above them, with the huts of Qatara spread beneath them, did he touch her shoulder and whisper in her ear, "We're home." Then he went on and hesitantly told her, "From the old man, I learned who the owner of the land, Duran is." She didn't understand the connection between that and the birth, and she didn't worry about it; she wanted only one thing—to get to bed and go on sleeping, feeling Yehoshua at her side.

⤏

The summer passed. The wheat yield gathered from the Gedera fields was meager; the *fellahin* from Qatara and Mesmîyeh sent the goats and camels to the farmers' fields, and the farmers would go down to the villagers and threaten them with fines and suits. Still, the *fellahin* only laughed in their faces.

Yehoshua continued to ride in the fields. He drew further and further away from the colony, so the work in the field and orchard rested solidly on the shoulders of Mendel and Yaakov. Tanhum returned to Jaffa to help in Yehuda Leib's store. Olga became closer to her family, learned to accept Yehoshua's riding off, and patiently waited for the day he would stop wandering.

Meir was happy with his returning daughter, who was joining the family, and he still dreamed of the day when grandchildren would scurry around him, and his sons and sons-in-law would accompany him to morning prayers. When she shared his hopes with Shifra, she would nod her head and cast pitiful glances at her daughter sitting next to her, her eyes staring at the doorway. More than anyone else, Sonia was overjoyed with her older sister and trailed her like a shadow. In the year since Olga had left home in favor of Yehoshua's cabin, Sonia had grown up and become a young lady. There were no other small youngsters in the house, and Meir and Shifra continued to see her as a child. Now that Olga had returned, their attention was divided between the two, and their concern for the eldest made things easier for Sonia. She learned from her sister how to prepare medicines, take care of the ill, embroider small stitches on fabric, and go through Russian books from among those Olga had brought from Petersburg or had wound up in the settlement with no one interested in them.

Since Olga had returned, Fanny and Lolik now often visited Shimshon Belkind's house. However, since the Husseini Bek incident, Lolik had not become involved again in public issues and stayed away from Pines. If they did meet, they didn't look at each other, but rather pointedly ignored one another.

Right after the break with Pines, Lolik sank into depression. Fanny was sure they would have to journey to Sofia to dip in the hot pools until the day Lolik appeared in the doorway of their house and called Fanny in his booming voice to receive a guest. When Fanny came out to greet him, she saw behind Lolik's broad back a gnome-like figure staring at the ground.

"This is Rozman," announced Lolik. "The new worker," he explained, needed no further elaboration.

From the minute he became friendly with Rozman, Lolik's melancholy was forgotten, and he was infused with the joy of youth. Lolik's devotion to Rozman and Rozman's dependence on Lolik was known to everyone in the small colony. The two were seen together everywhere: one tall and upright— "the Giant"— and the other, pudgy, with thinning hair and glued to his fear, silent, his eyes always darting around like a caged animal looking for a way to escape his capture. In the settlement, he was dubbed "the servant of Don Quixote," and the farmers laughed when seeing the duo and told many stories about them.

Lolik had found Rozman wandering in the field one day, so he liked to tell. When Rozman suddenly saw a giant stepping toward him, he became alarmed and hid behind a rock. The giant came, lifted him up as if he were a grain of wheat, and asked him where he was headed. The small man choked on his tongue from fright, and Lolik, who thought he was mute, decided to take him on, bring him to Fanny, and use him to help in the orchard. The man was silent for a few days, until he was served boiling soup and his squawks and squeal belied him. Lolik was sorry to hear the worker had been afraid, so he adopted him as a friend.

Whoever didn't like this story would tell that Rozman belonged to the group of builders and masons who wandered about in Jerusalem, living as a unit, with ten people sharing the income earned by one laborer. One time, Rozman rebelled and asked to keep one Egyptian piastre coin rather than putting it into the collective pot. The other group members banished him, so he wandered among the new Jewish settlements. He was thrown out of every place he landed, until he reached the fields of Gedera that pleased him. Rozman sat on the rock for a day, or two days, waiting for the farmers so he could offer himself as a laborer. The farmers didn't come, and he went on sitting in the fields whose sheaves had been harvested in the spring. That's why Lolik found him hungry and frightened and took him home. Since Fanny had dreamed, when young, of joining the band of masons in Jerusalem, she admired the new worker and agreed with Lolik to hire him. She announced to everyone that he no longer needed her, and now he had someone to take care of the essential work and do his bidding. It was just lucky he didn't also ask to share her bed. She said everything with a smile, since she understood that Rozman was replacing Yosef, and she preferred him over Pines.

The *fellahin* in the fields continued to refrain from meeting Lolik, and their fear increased their hatred. They mocked the dumpy worker who accompanied him and waited for a chance when he would be alone when they could injure him—after all, harming him would be like hurting the giant.

The colony's children exploited the name given to Lolik for their own purposes. On many an occasion, when one of the children would see the *fellahin* raiding the fields from afar, he would hold back from running to the settlement to call for help. Instead, he would yell, "The Giant is coming! The Giant is coming!" and the peasants would flee, prodding the animals spreading out on the fields with sticks that had a nail at their end, and scramble in panic on the slope of the hill to hide among the houses of Qatara.

One day Rozman set out by himself in Lolik's wagon to bring sand and limestone for building a stable in Shimshon Belkin's yard. As he passed by the ridge separating the plain from the coast, two members of the Bnei Qatara Bedouin tribe attacked him, hitting and injuring him, and tossing him to the side of the road, while taking the cart and the horses. He walked along crying, not from pain but from shame. When he reached the colony, he did not go to his room at the edge of the yard, nor to Lolik's house, but sat down on a stone next to the fence.

Since the laborer had been gone for many hours and had not returned, a worried Lolik went out to search for him and found him sitting on the rock, his eyes filled with tears. Lolik set himself down at the foot of the rock and tried to get him to talk. Between groan and sigh, Rozman told him how he had been hurt. Lolik took the worker into his house and asked Fanny to bandage his wounds, while he put on boots and set out into the night. He went by himself, not asking assistance from anyone, afraid of nobody. The closer he came to the Arab village and Husseini Bek's house, the stronger his anger grew, and the sharper became the picture of Rozman sitting on the rock and crying.

Lolik entered Husseini Bek's house without waiting to be asked in, and he strode directly to his bedroom. Husseini Bek was already asleep, with his red-fringed saddle next to him; his snores jiggled his mustache. Lolik grabbed him by his galabia and stood him near the door, pushing his back to the wall. The sleepy Husseini Bek did not understand what "the Giant" wanted from him. Lolik's thundering voice and his piercing questions immediately made Bek fully awake. They were alone in the room, and Husseini Bek had no choice but to go along with Lolik and show him the dwelling of the Ajouri—a bandit on the roads who had established a clan in Qatara after his previous tribe had threatened him with a blood feud.

Lolik left Husseini Bek and went to the Ajouri's stable, where he did find his two horses standing next to others of superior stock. First, he released his horses and the others— those not belonging to him. Next, he took Ajouri's horses with him and tied them to the door handle of the Ajouri's house. Then, after examining the strength of the knot, burst into the house.

No one stopped Lolik. He marched through many rooms, shocked old men, women, and children right out of their beds, and came to the last room, where he found the robber sleeping. Lolik stood in the doorway, his dimensions filling it, and called out toward the bed, "Get up! Your time has come." The Ajouri tried to lift himself up and reach for the pistol lying on the chair next to the bed, but Lolik was too fast for him and grabbed his throat, his voice booming at him, and brought him out of the room. The thief was as tall and robust as Lolik, but now he just crumbled and did not resist.

Lolik put him up on one of the horses and tied his hands to the saddle, and the small caravan returned to Gedera. When they reached the colony, Lolik left the bound robber in the stable among piles of straw and went to call Zuckerman and Sverdlov.

Until the return of "the Giant," the young lads made sure to spread around the colony the news of Rozman's being hurt and of Lolik's going to the Arab village. All the farmers waited to see what would happen, and when they heard that the Ajouri was in the stable, they went to see the robber's shame. Rozman strutted like a peacock about among the gathering. Already having forgotten his shyness, and particularly his wound and his crying, Rozman repeatedly told all of them the story of how the Ajouri had been caught. Now, it was his turn to be the hero of the day. He was the one who had told Lolik to go nab the Ajouri. He was the one who had stood staunchly in the face of the gang of robbers and made sure to identify them and show his boss where the tracks led.

At midnight, Zuckerman left the colony and rode to call the Turkish soldiers stationed in the police camp in Ramla. He would never give up, and his revenge against Lolik and the settlement's farmers would be harsh.

No one saw Zuckerman leave, and everyone continued to crowd around the stable, looking at the Ajouri. Opinions were divided among the group: one section, gathered around Pines, was angry about what Lolik had done and claimed the man had taken the law into his own hands—Husseini Bek would not overlook this and would embroil all the people of Gedera in deep trouble, and just at the time when they had come to live peaceably with their neighbors. However, the other group, which had collected around Lolik and Rozman, praised them for their actions and claimed they had acted properly again. To stand idly by was difficult. Whoever found himself there had to choose a side and join one group or the other. And the clamor there was deafening.

Olga left the cabin to see the reason for all the noise, and she followed the voices to Fanny and Lolik's yard. She was taken aback by the crowd and was afraid something might happen to her sister and brother-in-law, knowing well his hot temper. Then, she noticed the two groups of farmers and the stormy debate. She heard the story of the Ajouri's capture spreading from one person to the next, and when she realized their hatred and fear, she was even more frightened. The situation was dire—the time of the Rishon Lezion rebellion had not been long ago. And Yehoshua? He would hear about all of this, and he would quickly pick up and flee the storm. Pines would not keep still; this she knew. He would say they are all cronies, all of them rebels and partners from the days of Rishon Lezion, and if Lolik was found guilty, then Yehoshua and all the Belkind family would be too. If she only knew how, she could stop the surging wave threatening to drown her. Olga left the mob and ran to their cabin as if chased by a demon.

An hour after Zuckerman left to call the soldiers, the people of Qatara showed up in Gedera, men, and women, with clubs and torches in hand and curses in their mouths. They surrounded the settlement and planned to break into the stable and free the Ajouri. Some of them moved close to the yard and yelled at those gathered, "The Giant, where is the Giant? Let him come out to us and show us his strength." Then they fled in mock panic to their band.

Olga did not find Yehoshua in the cabin. Sverdlov was ahead of her and went to look for him in the fields; when he found him, he asked him to be the spokesman for the people of Gedera. Out of all the people in the colony, he was the only one fluent in the *fellahin's* language. In his wanderings, he learned the difference between the Arabic of the lowlands and that of the mountainous regions, and he was well versed in their law and way of life. Since she didn't want to be alone, Olga went back the way she had come and, from afar, heard mocking calls and booming laughter. Olga did not know what this meant, but she felt it could not be good. She crossed the entrance gate and joined her parents, who had gathered in Shimshon's house. She watched Yehoshua approach Lolik and stood with him shoulder to shoulder through the gate posts. He was not as tall as Lolik, but his upright stance and broad chest attested sufficiently to his strength.

The *fellahin* looked at the two young men standing in the stable entrance, moved restlessly, whispered, and finally became quiet. Yehoshua looked at them, afraid to take his gaze away from them, and muttered into his beard a message for Lolik, "Let the Ajouri go. Why provoke a quarrel?"

"It's too late," replied Lolik. "Zuckerman has gone to call the soldiers. In a little while, they would come, and in the meantime, Pines is collecting his lackeys and is ready to hand me over to the police, instead of the Ajouri."

Yehoshua laughed, looking at his friend from top to bottom and wondering how Pines planned to arrest him. Then, he told him to stay put and tromped toward the Qatara group, while speaking to them in their language to calm them down.

Silence enveloped them all, and Yehoshua went toward them until he was swallowed up into their group and began talking with them. Later, he told Olga with a smile that their version was completely different than Rozman's. First, according to them, Rozman went through a field of lupine belonging to one of the old *fellahin* and trampled young plants that had just sprouted. Then, when the old man approached him and asked him to leave the field, Rozman laughed heartily and pulled a pistol out of his pocket and threatened him, saying that the land belonged to the Gedera people, and they could do whatever they want with it. The *fellah*, frightened by the gun, hurried to the village to call for help. And who should he meet but the Ajouri, his relative, the brute who cast fear on all.

The Ajouri, being just as much a hothead as that laborer, hurried to take his horse and ride after the Jew, and he found him in the field, leaning over among the clods, and he was sure that he was continuing to stomp on the seedlings. A stampeding horse came from behind. The spray of earth sent up by its hooves scared the laborer and prompted him to point his gun at the rider. The horseman immediately galloped and knocked him down among the plants, taking the gun from him, as well as the horses, so he would not be able to chase him. He intended to return them to the colony in the evening and only wanted to teach "the Giant" and the worker a lesson. But before he could do so, "the Giant" acted.

When the *fellahin* told their stories to Yehoshua, each one jumping into the others' words, the anger melted a bit, and the mood became calmer. Next, from afar, the observers saw the peasants tapping Yehoshua on the shoulder, and their mutterings sounded to them like the buzz of the wind among the stalks of grain. Some called mockingly to Olga to come close and see her husband standing among the group of villagers, fitting right in. Olga shuddered, and some farmers giggled and laughed. Fox, who stood near her, yelled toward Yehoshua, "*Fellah!*" His bellow set off another round of giggling among those standing there. All their fury and all the tensions of the past night were washed away with the laughter. Pines, who did not like Yehoshua and especially had not forgotten Loliks's anger and Yehoshua's accusations, raised his voice, so his words rang out in the yard: "Not a simple peasant, wallowing in the dust of the floor in the Bedouin tents. Let him go and join them and leave the colony alone."

Olga tried to scream, to use her voice to overcome the mockery and giggles, and tell Yehoshua to leave the *fellahin* and go back to the circle of farmers. She did not want to be alone, so frightened. But Yehoshua heard neither her nor the farmers' sniggers. Quite some time passed, and movement was apparent among the *fellahin*. Their rows split apart, and they let Yehoshua out of their circle.

Yehoshua returned to the farmers with deeply focused eyes and glances toward Pines; he said, "This whole business can be settled with a balanced tone."

Total silence reigned among the farmers, and because they did not respond, Yehoshua went on and explained what he meant. "We don't need Turkish soldiers. The *fellahin* will return to their village. They are ready for a *sulha*. The Ajouri and Rozman will meet; they will come to terms between them, and the whole matter will be forgotten."

Someone quietly repeated Yehoshua's words and added to them scornfully, "They will meet, and the Arab will pull out a knife, and tomorrow he will return and take over the land, but this time there won't be any worker to stop him."

This statement incited his listeners, and the farmers belonging to Pines's group, who only a short while ago had been blaming the uproar on Lolik and Rozman, woke up and now began changing, "We'll teach the Arabs of Qatara a lesson, once and for all."

An immediate response came. Someone shouted, "No one will dare to raise a hand against a Jewish worker." The gathering agreed with the call and answered it with, "*Allehum*! Let's get them."

Pines himself felt they had gone too far and tried to calm down the farmers and scatter them to make them reasonable once again. But no one listened to him; none of them wanted an apology.

Pines stayed outside the circle at one end of the yard, and Yehoshua was at the other end, with derision in his eyes: "You wanted to turn them against me, but it turned out that they became over-excited and out of control." Then he turned away, intending to collect Olga. They did not need him here any longer, not to translate nor take out their anger on him. He was an outsider, not part of their group.

Olga hesitated. She did not know if she should stay next to her parents and support Fanny or go with her husband and separate him from the events of Gedera and its people. She scanned the faces in the yard and saw the farmers crowded together shouting, including Lolik and Rozman with them, and she looked at the *fellahin* standing as a group and waiting for the Turks to release their leader—and in the end, she went with her husband. The two walked in silence, which brought them closer but not calmer.

At first light, the soldiers came. The *fellahin*, weary from the hubbub of the night, had already scattered a few hours earlier, while the farmers had shut themselves up in their houses. The soldiers stayed only a few minutes in Lolik's house to gather testimony from him and Rozman and then took the Ajouri with them and left the colony.

On the surface, the quarrel between the two camps was forgotten, and everyone continued to talk about the bravery of Lolik and Rozman. Still, unease settled throughout the colony and caused a schism in it. Pines and his gang stayed away from the Belkind family house. The *fellahin* were standing at the edges of the fields, checking who comes and goes, as if waiting for a moment of weakness so they could rush into the field and forcibly take what they deserved, according to them.

The autumn arrived, bringing nights that continually row longer. Every day Yehoshua's detachment from the colony increased, and Olga withered, her face turning gray. And then came the events of the *shmita* Sabbatical year that displaced the stories about Rozman the worker, and about Lolik's bravery and sent them into oblivion, at least for a short time.

🙠

The rabbis declared the year 1888/1889 a *shmita*, Sabbatical, year in which the land must lie fallow, and in Gedera, some followed the dictate, but others didn't. Fox and Zuckerman observed it, while Lolik and the Belkind family did not. Pines did demand that everyone carry out the summer planting and refrain from doing so in for the winter, but the families that were not following *shmita* refused to obey this order and argued against it that the development of Eretz Israel took precedence over the *shmita* year. In the winter season, they planted citrus seedlings, special species brought from California, and watched over their taking root in the heavy soil at the foot of the hill. Since they did not want to leave bare soil between the seedlings, they planted barley and hoped to buy fertilizer for the young cuttings when selling it.

When Pines heard about what the Hankin brothers had done, he came to Yehoshua one evening and called out, "Revolutionary, watch over your brothers. They're your responsibility." Since Yehoshua didn't answer, Pines became even angrier. His face turned red, and he screamed, "Wissotsky, a member of the Hovevei Zion committee, gave the tract in Gedera to you and not to your brothers."

Yehoshua maintained his silence, only pulling out from his sleeve a proclamation sent to the Gedera farmers from Odessa, and he waved it in front of Pines. The message was that Hovevei Zion opposed *shmita* and supported those refusing to let the land lie fallow. Pines turned his back on him and left, slamming the door to look for the farmers supporting him and *shmita* to rile them against those refusing to participate in it.

The days of splinter associations had arrived in Gedera, like the ones Rishon Lezion had suffered. Most of the farmers took a stand against those refusing to observe *shmita* and now clung to Lolik's story to make them leave Gedera quickly. Lolik, who had tried to avoid any argument at the beginning of the year, became enmeshed in it. "I will do what I want with my land," he boiled over, raising his voice. "No one will tell me to leave the land fallow or to harvest fruit and plant."

Every morning he would go out to the field defiantly with Rozman, his horse galloping and his whistling being heard. Both of them would first work the land and gather the crop; then, they would march alongside the cart loaded with implements or hay, jumping and skipping between the potholes.

Shimshon Belkind also did not let his land lie fallow, but he did so modestly, as did Yaakov and Mendel, who continued to check their plantings and prayed for rain to increase their barley.

Yehoshua also continued to act as usual. He divided his time between working his plot and riding off into the wide spaces, far away from the looks of the farmers and the pettiness of the colony. The more time passed, and the more the arguments increased, the longer his stays outside of Gedera became, and he was in no hurry to return. Olga felt the happenings in Gedera were passing him by, and he was not part of them. Even when she showed him someone wrote the word "Revolutionary" with coal on their cabin walls, he did not respond. They called him that so many times that the nickname stuck, so it would have been better for him to stay. Despite his silence and his distance from her, Olga sensed

Yehoshua was only waiting patiently for the last push that would send them both away from the settlement.

That year Fanny grew thicker and was about to give birth in the fall. Olga became closer to Fanny, but Yehoshua didn't see and didn't feel the change happening to his wife. At first, she waited longingly for his return and counted the days, and when he was back, she would sit with him and share his stories. She could pronounce the names of the tracts, as well as the names of the Bedouin tribes, and link the names to sights. For her, Kurnub and Amara were places of splendor that drew Yehoshua to them as if by magic strands, and she could not compete with them. But as the *shmita* year drew on, and the non-planting farmers were ferociously jealous of Yaakov's and Mendel's orchards, Yehoshua showed no interest and did not look. The names slipped away from her. Once again, she was no longer a partner in Yehoshua's adventures, and she stopped counting the days.

Fanny's idiosyncrasies took up all of Olga's time, so she ignored the cabin, and couch grass filled her vegetable garden. She no longer went out to sit on the hillside facing Qatara and did not watch the Arab peasant women. She had no interest in them. She was only involved with Fanny. Any change in Fanny was as if it had happened to her, too: in the middle of the night, the two would make pancakes, pickle olives and make slits in them, and dip hot bread in oil and lick their fingers. Fanny ate a lot, and Olga looked at her a lot, and if she asked for more, Olga gave her plate to her, too.

In the Belkind family home, they felt the change taking place in Olga. Meir noticed the pallor spreading on his daughter's face and saw her becoming ever thinner, while Shifra tried to slip food from her plate to Olga's, but she, in turn, gave her food to Fanny, whose pregnancy increased her appetite.

Fierce rains had begun to fall, and Meir and Shifra hoped they would bring Yehoshua home, and Olga would go back to living in her cabin. But Yehoshua did not return often. Even when they told him that his farm had enjoyed a good year, he didn't change his habits. Instead, he would tell those congratulating him about it, "I didn't do it. Mendel and Yaakov did. I have no part in the good yield."

Standing like an island amid the desolation of the fields was the Hankin family plot. At a time when the others had let their land lie fallow, the sesame in the Hankin tract was burgeoning with seed, the barley bent down from the weight of the grain; farmers' envy was rife—and Yehoshua didn't feel a thing.

In the same way he had no interest in his farm, he didn't see its blooming. He also didn't see his wife's distress, neither her wanness nor withering. He was only occupied with himself, his riding, his other love that relaxed him and gave him peace. For a long time, he sat with the peasants in their huts and went off to the desert, staying in Bedouin tents, learning their ways, and enthusiastically drinking in their tales. They told of the land, its errant ways and treachery, its heat, and its vigor; the stories became such a part of him that he no longer remembered whether he had heard them or imagined them.

When the torrents of rain began, the soil flowed into the channel, and water filled the wadis; the Bedouins moved southward to the steppes of Jericho to seek shelter in the protection of the cliffs, and Yehoshua decided to go back home.

Something he could not explain pulled him back to the hill and the small settlement. Whether it was the cold night, the waterlogged fields, or yearnings for Olga—he did not know. One night, he left the Bedouin encampment traveling north towards the plain and the hills. As if possessed by a demon, he spurred his horse on, stopping only to water it and let it chomp on some hay. He rode on like this for four days with scarcely a break; he didn't feel tired, hungry, or thirsty and paid no attention to the rain that drenched him to the marrow. Neither the muddy roads nor the howling wind could deter him. Finally, on the fourth night, he reached the colony, with his shirt sticking to his skin and his eyes red—and he found the door to his cabin locked tight.

Yehoshua encircled the house and saw that the windows were locked. He looked for the paths in the vegetable garden and didn't find them, seeing only waterlogged, rapacious weeds. He went out the gate and saw its broken axis. Yehoshua knocked on Mendel's door, but when there was no reply, he banged on it so hard the walls trembled. Finally, the door opened, and when Mendel saw his brother's stooping figure, he was alarmed. He looked insane to him: his eyes were burning, red and protruding, his hair was long and unkempt, and he was muttering, "Olga. Maybe you've seen Olga?"

Mendel tried to take him into the house, but Yehoshua stood rooted and mumbled his question again.

"She left the cabin," Mendel told him. "She couldn't wait anymore. Then, one day, she fell, anemic and weak, so Shifra took her in."

Yehoshua did not wait to hear the end and began dashing among the drops, yelling, with the rain swallowing his cries, "Olga! Olga!" He slipped in the mud, pulled himself up, and continued to run until he reached Shimshon Belkind's house and burst in, without considering the late hour or the sleeping people. His screams frightened the people out of their beds. "Olga! Where's Olga?"

Shifra tried to calm him down, "She's only sleeping. Come tomorrow." But Yehoshua didn't heed her words, and his cries pierced the walls. Fanny came out from her room, obviously pregnant, and Yehoshua looked at her and stared at d her stomach. Did they want to drive him crazy?

Yehoshua sat down in the corner and buried his head in both hands, without crying out again, only mumbling, "Olga, Olga," and after quite a time, lifted his head and saw all of them frightened, standing a bit away from him, and behind them all also her. She stood barefoot, wearing a white nightgown; her face was ashen, and her hair tumbled over her shoulders. She seemed to him far away and unattainable. He hurriedly rose and sought to feel her touch, but the people held themselves as a wall between him and her. Yehoshua went back to his corner and put up his hand to pull out his hair and tear his collar in mourning, since he was sure she was a ghost and no longer his.

Then he heard her voice above him, close by, "I'm here. I didn't leave."

He raised his eyes to her and then looked around him and saw that the others had left the room. He looked at her again and finally stood up, went to her, and lifted her with his two hands, feeling how light she was.

"I was ill," she whispered to him. "I lay in bed for many days; I was sucked into oblivion, and nothing could stop me. I cried out to you, but you didn't hear. I begged for your return, and no one could tell me where you were."

Yehoshua felt her trembling and wanted to cover her, but his coat was wet. He pulled her to him and tried to share his warmth with her, but his body was cold. Yehoshua placed her on the pillows lying next to the oven, sat next to her, and did not stop looking at her, fearing that the nightmare would return. Tears filled her eyes, and she clutched Yehoshua's arms; he wiped the tears away with his rough-skinned hand. Releasing her grasp, he went and brought a blanket to cover her. When her whimpering stopped, he picked her up and went out into the rainy night, to their cabin. All the way to their home, he whispered in her ear to make her forget the drops and the cold. "Tomorrow, we will set out," he told her. "We will go far away. We will leave Gedera and go to Jaffa."

She tried to cover his mouth with her hand, and he kissed her fingers, continuing to talk through them, "We'll join Sarah and Yehudah Leib. I will stay far away from the land and be a stay-at-home parent. And you will be mine, belonging only to me."

She gave a childish laugh and knew he wouldn't keep his promise, but at that moment, she didn't care. A feeling of partnership came to her, and then—after such a long time—she understood the secret. Without the land, her husband could not exist, and she could not exist without him, so from now on, they would be three.

With a slight push, Yehoshua opened the door, remembering their wedding day when she was so heavy. Then he put her into bed, lit the oil lamp near their bed, and lay down beside her in his wet clothes, continuing to talk to her and making plans as far away from Gedera as possible. But while he spoke, Olga fell asleep, and a short time later, he, too, slumbered.

In the morning, Yehoshua informed Mendel and Yaakov about their leaving. Then, he called for Zuckerman to act as his witness when he signed in his presence that he was relinquishing his plot and transferring it to his two brothers. After that, Olga took leave from her family. Her saying goodbye to Fanny was especially difficult, and she promised to come back to her when it was her time to give birth and make sure to deliver her baby. Fanny nodded and tried to hide the tears welling in her eyes. She did not fear for the baby, but for her sister and her great love. Mainly she was frightened by Olga's blindness—Yehoshua was not destined to be a stay-at-home father, and Olga would not succeed in keeping him with her.

A few hours later, Olga and Yehoshua got on the wagon—the one that had brought Yehoshua Leib Hankin to Rishon Lezion and Yehoshua to Gedera—and with a wave, they left the colony. The horses galloped, and Olga looked forward, not turning again to the people waving goodbye, and she overlooked the Arab village spread on the slope. She saw only Yehoshua's straight, broad back while the spaces shrank. She was no longer cowed by the earth, and she knew she was following her husband.

12. Jaffa, 1918 • Source: 'The Zalmania' Photo Shop.

13. Jaffa in the 1930s • Source: Qurt Tuchler Private Archive.

Jaffa, 1889/90

Yehuda Leib Hankin's house stood on the street going down to the port. A two-story building—not the fanciest but also not the worst. They lived on the upper floor and conducted their business on the ground floor. Camels carried the paper-wrapped rolls of fabric from the boats anchored in the port to the store's door, and Tanhum would accompany the old camel driver and help him make the camels kneel down. Then they would unload the rolls resting on the camels' humps. When that job was done, and all the rolls were arranged in the warehouse, Tanhum would climb up on one of the camels and parade with the caravan in the streets of the city. Whoever saw the joy of the young man sitting on the camel's hump, with his head in the clouds, could not but help smile. Tanhum would look down from above to the pavement of the narrow lanes and the people scurrying in them and imagine himself as a pedestrian passing through the streets of Beirut and Damascus or as a pot-bellied merchant; his hands on his sash, glancing at the merchandise spilling out from the small stores onto the sidewalks.

Yehuda Leib promised him that when he would be older, he would take him along to examine merchandise in other cities: in Jerusalem or Gaza, and maybe even cities abroad. In the meantime, Tanhum continued to sit on the camel's back and drink, and he let go of the memory of his old love for Rishon Lezion and the heavy earth mixed with sand on the hill of Gedera.

In the first days after the family's arrival in Jaffa, Tanhum never stopped talking about Rishon Lezion. At night, he would hallucinate and call out his friends' names and scream the names of his older brothers. Tanhum did not like the narrowness of Jaffa nor its sounds and aromas. He closed his nose off to the odor of the nargila smoke mixed with the smell of the fabric and spices, and he would flee to the port and stand on the dock, looking at the large ships anchored beyond the breakwater. He would breathe in the saltiness of the water, absorb the sight of the fish arranged in piles, and search for a way to get onto one of the boats and escape. Sometimes, he ran in the alleys and looked for the diligence or the Jaffa carriage that went to Rishon Lezion, and he yearned to get on it and settle himself among the goods and the people and return with them to the colony.

Yehuda Leib saw his son's longings and took him with him to teach him something about the textile business, and slowly Rishon Lezion was forgotten and replaced by visions of the big cities.

Tanhum became quite an expert in textiles and could finger them to determine their quality, sort them, and decide which fabric was suitable for clothing, which for linens, and which was strong enough to be used for upholstering furniture. He learned all of this in preparation for the day when he would become a great merchant—as Yehuda Leib had promised him.

As for Sarah, the move yielded no crises. She wanted to come to Jaffa and was pleased that Yehuda Leib had agreed to this without any effort on her part. From the day they arrived, she fell in love with the lanes, the houses, and the aromas. They came in the Jaffa wagon loaded with their belongings from Rishon Lezion; the girls and Tanhum sat on the bundles and seemed taken aback by the views along the way and the tumult of the crowded city, while she remained calm. That same day, they moved into the house on Port Street.

The house was readied in advance for the Hankin family by Elazar Rokach, and he even gave Yehuda Leib a bundle of money to open the store. Elazar Rokach was an important functionary in Jaffa, so many people tried to become close to him. Owing to that, he was able to find a house and store for the Hankins at a price equal to that of the land in Rishon Lezion. The wives of the notables in the Jaffa community repeatedly mentioned to Sarah that it was a great privilege to be supported by the Rokach family. And, in truth, without their help, they would have procured neither the house nor the store. The housing shortage among the Jews of Jaffa was unbearable, and the Arabs exploited the situation by raising prices and people could not afford to pay.

With some of the money Rokach had lent them, Sara added to the Rishon Lezion furniture some new pieces from Jaffa. A year later, most of the Rishon Lezion furnishings were gone from their home, and she could be proud of the elegance of the Jaffa furniture. Yehoshua's prophecy had come to pass so fast that Sarah found it difficult to believe that this was really happening. Sarah became one of the respected ladies of the town.

A few months went by, and the merchandise in Yehuda Leib's store had become known throughout all of Jaffa. Wives of high officials, wives of consuls, and wives of owners of large estates would visit the store, check what was new there, and chatter with Sarah about clothing and coffee. So as not to reveal her ignorance, she would only nod her head. But she quickly learned to imitate their clothing style and manner of speaking, and became one of them.

In that first year, Sarah gained weight. Her face became round, and her hips widened. She became an expert not only on clothing but also on matters of cooking. Yehoshua's wedding in Gedera had convinced her more thoroughly that she didn't belong in the colony and wasn't intended for life on a farm, so her stay in Jaffa was not temporary, but permanent resettlement. Of course, Yehuda Leib yearned for the soil, but his wife found ways to make him forget it— offering the different kinds of spices Jaffa was able to provide for her dishes helped her with that. In Gedera, she never stopped declaring in front of the farmers and women that from now on, she was a Jaffa woman, and she confessed her hatred for the mud gathered at the entrances to the houses and for the tabun oven smoke that filled the yards and stuck to the farm women's clothes. Sarah greatly enjoyed Yehuda Leib's copper oven but bought her as soon as he had repaid his debt to Rokach. She would scrub it and polish it until she could see her face in it, and it was flat and concave, like the plate overflowing with sweets always resting on the French wardrobe.

In December, Yehoshua and Olga joined them, and Sarah was sure that all her wishes were coming true. She believed that Mendel and Yaakov would also come, and her household would grow ever larger, with all of them gathered under one roof. Of course, when she first saw Olga, she was shocked, but she quickly recovered and put her trust in the bounty of Jaffa and the quality of her cooking, so she now hunted for spices and types of food to restore her daughter-in-law's health and turn her into a Jaffa lady in every way.

Sarah didn't ask Yehoshua questions, but only sent him to the barber at the corner for a shave and trim and then sent him to the tailor who had sewn Yehuda Leib's suits. Next, they cleared out a room that had been used for storing unsorted goods in the house on Port Street for Yehoshua and his wife. The goods were then transferred to a small room in the store. In the room for the couple, they spread out a carpet that had been imported specially from Persia. They installed a Damascus bed and wardrobes from France.

Unlike Sarah, Yehuda Leib did ask questions. He didn't understand what the link between Yehoshua and Jaffa was. He was even more astonished that Yehoshua did not go out with his wife to walk about the city to become familiar with its nooks and crannies on their first day there. Instead, Yehoshua sought to learn the store's procedures: how they examine the merchandise coming from the ships, register the inventory, and negotiate with merchants and buyers. Yehuda Leib did not refuse to teach him the rules of commerce, but he didn't take his eyes off his son when he worked and wondered when the explosion would come.

He didn't believe that Yehoshua would ever turn into a textile merchant trussed up in a suit buttoned up to the top, standing for hours behind a counter, dealing with minor matters and the complaints of women who didn't know what they wanted.

To the surprise of everyone, Yehoshua became steeped in the workings of the store and desperately tried to banish from his heart remembrances of the land and open spaces, and he tried with all his might to be a good husband to Olga and to stay in one place. Only in the evenings, after they had closed the store and Olga would join Sarah's kitchen or go to her meetings with the august women of Jaffa, would Yehoshua then go along with Tanhum down to the port. Tanhum would show him the ships afloat in the distance, unable to anchor in the shallow port. At the same time, Yehoshua would gaze at the strongly rolling waves breaking on the stones of the dock and remember the wind blowing in the sabra fields nudging the tops of the stalks and shaking them in wave after wave.

Olga drew close to Sarah and learned from her to love Jaffa. She changed the style of her dresses and rolled her braids in the manner of the urban women; she spent a lot of time with the Rokach family and became friends with the family's daughters. Together with them, she wandered the lanes of Jaffa, looking for medicinal plants, and she learned new medical methods she was not familiar with or of which she had not heard. With the help of the Rokach family, she came to know Doctor Stein and joined his office. The elderly physician was happy to have her help and taught her every medical innovation he was aware of and had absorbed.

Coming to Dr. Stein's clinic were Jewish women and the wives of wealthy Christians and Muslims who lived in Jaffa and conducted their businesses from there. Olga began to be the midwife for these women and learned how to treat various and strange gynecological diseases. Her pleasant manner, her stories about Petersburg and the atmosphere of Gedera, and her soft hands attracted many patients to the office. Dr. Stein was pleased about each one and was even happier about the money Olga's patients brought in, so he let Olga run his affairs, and he often went out to sit among the other notables in the coffee house, shooting dice.

From those patients, Olga absorbed all the "news" of Jaffa and could take part in all the discussions among the distinguished. She learned from the women who owned property and land, who had gone bankrupt, and who later flourished and became wealthy. One time, while sitting with Yehoshua in their room and drinking hot water with lemon peel together, she told him some of the stories from the office and added perhaps jokingly, "My information is of great value. If only there were a crafty agent who knew how to exploit my expertise, we would become rich."

But the man seated opposite her didn't laugh. She kept on nattering in the hope she could make him smile, but he just became more serious and couldn't sit still. She didn't know what had happened to him nor why he had shut her out; she became frightened and changed the subject.

Jaffa was clamorous with long-term residents and newcomers, and on many an occasion, it happened that Olga was walking in the lanes, certain of her solitude, and someone came toward her and greeted her. "A small place," Olga would say, "but I was lonelier in Rishon Lezion and Gedera."

And that was how she encountered Yehoshua Barzilai.

The first time she avoided meeting him. She saw him approaching her at the lit end of the lane, while she was still not visible, hidden in the shadows. She halted and slipped into a courtyard surrounded by a stone fence to escape and avoid memories of Rishon Lezion. The second time she could not flee, because he came to the clinic seeking advice from the doctor. Dr. Stein was not in, and she was by herself. He saw her and became excited; he recalled the young woman who had sat next to him at the youth meetings in Petersburg.

He invited her to visit him, together with Yehoshua, he said, but Olga declined for fear of the meeting and Yehoshua's reactions.

When they happened to meet again, she simply nodded her head in greeting and said a few words, giving him what he had come for and sending him away. Barzilai couldn't understand her evasive behavior and blamed everything on the saga of the Rishon Lezion rebellion.

Life in Jaffa began to make a visible impression on Olga. Her cheeks were again rosy, the ladylike manners she had brought with her from Russia were applied again, and her vitality was catching.

༄

Two months after Yehoshua and Olga had arrived in Jaffa, Olga was called to return to Gedera. Fanny was about to give birth. Yehoshua refused to go with her, so she took Rivka and Haya, Yehoshua's older sisters. Rivka was excited about the trip, and Olga remembered the looks Zuckerman had sent her way during their wedding. She brought along Haya because she helped her with everything, and she was not needed in the store.

They set out in the morning. First, they rode to Rishon Lezion in the Jaffa diligence and from there traveled on in the cart of a farmer who used to bring various kinds of merchandise along with seeds and tools—everything a small place needed. Olga enjoyed the ride. She liked showing the girls the Bedouins' tents on the Duran expanse and telling them the story of birth she had attended. She took delight in explaining the blossoming of the sabras and the spiny fruit among the drooping leaves, as well as pointing out the stream beds, calling them by name. She showed them the wide spaces reaching the low hills and the sea glinting between the outcroppings of the kurkar rocks. She was no longer afraid of the soil churning between the wagon's wheels—it was far away from her— and she now belonged to Jaffa, and Yehoshua was staying with her. When the wagon cut through the houses of the Arab village of Qatara, the girls wanted to hear the story of Lolik's bravery, but she put them off and preferred to point to the peasant women carrying jugs on their heads without losing a drop of water. The farmer pushed the horses to go faster, and the wagon left the village and began climbing the hill. Now, each one of them was lost in her own musings; they no longer looked back. One thought about a farmer she had met a long time ago, the other, about her sister and her parents, while small Haya feared the task of midwife that had been thrust on her.

In Gedera, everyone was happy they had come. Only two months had gone by, and all of them seemed so different to her. Shifra and Meir looked older and Fanny heavier; Yaakov spoke about the possibility of buying passage on a ship and setting sail for Australia, while Mendel looked for buyers for the plot in Gedera so he could join the family in Jaffa. The citrus seedlings had failed, burned from over-fertilization, or perhaps because of rain that had not come in time. Yaakov said that the curse of Pines was affecting the orchard, since he wanted to drive them out of the colony, so he spoke evil about their site. But the reality was different—the small settlement diminished Mendel's horizons, and Yaakov detested the brown tone of Gedera and the ceaselessly exposed, shadowless land.

From all the bustle around her, Fanny had become spoiled, and all day long, she was awash in her fears, while Olga would only smile and bring up memories with her sister of the early months of her pregnancy, without mentioning her own illness and Yehoshua's distancing himself from her at that time.

A bed was arranged in Fanny and Israel's bedroom for Olga, and Israel was moved to a different room. Rivka and Haya were housed in the home of Shimshon Belkind. However, Israel did not refuse to give up his bed. He was even more afraid for the baby than Fanny and was willing to do whatever they told him, if it was only something to help his wife. From the time Olga arrived in Gedera and catered to Fanny, Lolik didn't know what to do with himself. At first, he just got in everyone's way, and they claimed he was bothering them.

Then, he tried to be out of the house in the daytime, only sneaking back into their shared room at night, walking on tiptoes not to awaken Olga. He would move a stool to sit next to his wife's bed. He loved to look at her and put his hand on her stomach, searching for her pulse and that of the baby; when he finally felt a movement, he was silently elated and would relax in his seat.

Lolik wanted a son he could ride with, take to the fields, and teach him, as he had shown Rozman, how to plow and how to run off black goats. Fanny spoke about girls and how she wanted to deck out a daughter in dresses and ribbons and teach her to cook many dishes.

Since he loved Fanny and did not want to argue with her, Lolik did not share his thoughts with her. Fanny was beautiful in her pregnancy; her face had become rounder, and her skin was as smooth as that of the baby she was carrying. Were it not for her wriggling here and there in her bed seeking a comfortable position, and if he had not been afraid of waking Olga and being caught in his weakness, he would have gone on sitting there all night. In the end, he would get up and leave the room, returning to the corner allotted him where he walked to and fro in its confines, finding no rest for himself until he would again go out into the night and join Rozman. They would sit together in the cabin near the stable, tell each other stories about colonies, officials, and disputes, and then take swigs from a bottle of undiluted wine. And Lolik would forget he was a family man.

For four days, Olga slept in Fanny's room, and on the morning of the fifth, Avshalom was born. She didn't even manage to ask Rivka and Haya for help, since the water broke and the delivery was fast; the contractions were short, and with two pushes, the baby was out. Meir ran to call for Lolik and found him in the hut with Rozman, weaving drunkenly. He dragged him home and doused him with a bucket of cold water, and when Lolik sobered up and understood that Fanny had given birth to a boy, he didn't comb his hair or change his wet shirt. He only put his shirttail into his pants and ran, bursting with joy, from Meir's house to his home, yelling to the empty street, "A son. I have a son."

When Olga presented the baby to him, his enthusiasm evaporated, and he was afraid to hold the newborn—he looked so small to him. What if he fell? And what if his clumsy hands should scratch him? Olga urged him to take the baby and giggled at his apprehension. Lolik was embarrassed and finally took the child, as if it were an etrog whose *pitom* at its end should not be touched but only petted and carried on a bed of soft cotton wool. He looked at the baby's wrinkled face and told Fanny, "He looks like you."

Fanny smiled at him and replied, "No, he looks like you. He will be as big as you, and people will call him 'the Giant.'"

He grinned at her, and suddenly felt so very small. He sat next to her on the bed and couldn't take his eyes off the baby. Fanny caressed his head ever so carefully, and then she put her hand out to rub her husband's head; she glowed with joy.

Olga left them in their happiness and returned their room to them. At first, she had intended to stay only a few days after the birth to take care of Fanny and teach her how to deal with the baby, but in the end, they stayed ten days—Rivka asked her to let them stay a bit longer. When the two were completely alone, Rivka revealed her love for Shlomo Zuckerman. Yes, she said he was older than she was, but he was so stable and knew what he wanted. Olga saw Rivka's shining eyes as she spoke and promised to stay with her, as well as to speak highly of him to Yehoshua Leib and Sarah. When Olga asked her if Zuckerman was aware of her feelings, Rivka smiled and said, "He really knows, but he's tongue-tied."

At night, when everyone was asleep, Olga would lie in her bed awake, hearing the baby's wailing and thinking about Rivka and her budding love. If the infant continued crying, she would quickly sit up and place herself at the end of the bed, putting her ear to the thin wall to be certain that Fanny had gotten up to offer him a breast. Only after hearing the creaking of Fanny and Lolik's bed and the baby's burps would she lie down again and try to fall asleep, but it eluded her.

The ten days she had promised Rivka passed, and Olga and the two younger daughters who were with her were ready to leave. But just the day before the three women were supposed to leave Gedera, the Belkind brother Israel arrived in the colony.

While in Jaffa, Israel, Belkind heard that his sister had given birth to a boy, and he hurried to congratulate her. Olga was happy he had come, since she hadn't seen him for a long time. Of course, Israel Belkind had settled in Jaffa, but he hadn't met his sister there. He was full of ideas and was busy with meetings with the important people toward making them a reality. In particular, he spoke about a school in which Hebrew would be the primary language and not German or French. Now, he met Olga in Gedera. He could hardly believe what he saw. She had changed so much. In Rishon Lezion, she had been a young woman from Petersburg, fighting bravely and not afraid to express her thoughts.

Now, all her vitality was gone, and she was scrawny, her Jaffa clothes just hanging on her. Her mouth was framed by wrinkles of suffering, and her eyes, set deep in their sockets, stared at him with a hooded look. But then, she slowly opened up to him, and once she did, she began telling him things and didn't stop speaking. She talked about Jaffa, its lanes, the port, and the ships. She described the colors of the city and the smells of the spices to him. And he told her about his wanderings among the colonies and of his dream to set up a school for Jewish children. "In it, they will learn to tell the difference between a barley seed and an oat seed," he explained to her. "There, they will learn to hoe and to hold a pitchfork, and they will read and speak Hebrew."

For Avshalom, Israel had brought a small sword resting in a silver scabbard and put it at the head of the cradle. He kissed his younger sister, Fanny, and whispered to her, "When he grows up, I will teach him to ride and to use the sword, and I will take him with me on my roaming."

Fanny laughed at him, and picking up the sword, she asked him to put it on the high shelf in the cabinet, "We'll wait until he grows up," she said, and then hung a fisheye with a blue bead in it over the bed, adding, "This will be enough for him in the meantime."

The next day, Olga and the two sisters left the settlement, and Israel Belkind accompanied them for a distance; then, their ways parted.

⸎

Spring came, and now Meir, Shifra, and Sonia were also living in Jaffa. After the birth of Avshalom and Israel's short visit, as well as Olga's stories about the good points of Jaffa, Meir realized that his big dream of gathering the family around him in one of the Judean colonies was not going to be realized. Fanny was busy with the baby, and Shimshon was working his fields. But for Meir and Shifra, there was nothing to keep them busy. Moreover, Sonia had grown up and begun to talk about her interest in traveling to study far from home. All of this made it easier for them to decide to follow the path of Yehuda Leib and Sarah and return to living the big city life.

The change of location was not difficult, and very quickly, the family became accustomed to life in Jaffa. In April, Israel Belkind joined the household and decided to establish a school in Jaffa for the Jews' children.

Israel's decision came at the right time. A month after the Belkind family's arrival in Jaffa, new notions were spreading through the city, and the idea of a school meshed very well with them. The Jews of Jaffa, Ashkenazim, and Sephardim founded a community committee for themselves. They were proud of it, stressing each word in its name, "The Committee of the Heads and Leaders of the Holy City of Jaffa, May it be firmly established." The Jews stood on street corners and spoke about the new committee, praising its name. They discussed what the committee should do and to what end their donations should be earmarked. Since all of them were activists and each had his own opinion, these talks went on into the evenings, with people sitting in the yards, standing in the synagogues, and walking in the narrow lanes.

All of Jaffa was abuzz with the Committee, and Israel Belkind could not help but hear the conversations. He felt that there would be no school if he did not persist now and convince people to invest in his idea. So Israel went from one friend to another to persuade him, and if the person said, "I haven't made up my mind," he would not let him be but came back to him. He even named his idea, Kiryat Sefer. In Jaffa, they were already saying that the young Belkind's frequent visits to the Committee members had finally yielded the hoped-for results, and they had gone along with him and established a school for the Jews' children.

The entire Belkind family thought about the idea of the school and nurtured it, and the most ardent supporter of it was the father, Meir. For years the connection between the father and son had been broken. Israel shared no common ground with Meir. When he visited the family in Rishon Lezion or Gedera, he had come either to see his brothers and sisters or to calm his mother

Shifra and show her he was still alive, but not to spend time with his father. They were so very different. Meir, who wanted to see his sons and daughters around him, continuing his path, did not understand the restlessness that afflicted his son. Now, suddenly, they found each other. The idea of the school had united them and gave them a common language.

Meir and Israel didn't stop talking and interrupting each other, making plan upon plan, and considering calculations; their enthusiasm just increased immensely. They worked out how many hours of religious studies there would be and how many for secular studies, whether the languages of study would be French and Hebrew or Hebrew and Turkish. And who would learn arithmetic, and who Land of Israel studies? Or would it be necessary to teach history or to suffice with studying the nature of man? Shifra, too, was swept up with the passion of the idea, and while father and son were making their lists, she collected different kinds of seeds and sorted them, putting them in jars and writing on their labels everything a child had to know about that seed.

Once the program was ready, Israel, Meir, and Olga went to the Committee and presented their plan to them. Within a week, two rooms were located, albeit small ones, but Israel saw them as a palace, and the Kiryat Sefer school opened.

Olga donated all the books she had brought with her from Petersburg to the school. Yehuda Leib built a cupboard divided into sections, while Sarah wrote the names of the subjects according to which the books were arranged. Once the rooms were organized, the pupils began to come. At first, there were just a few; children whose parents were not afraid to send them to learn the Hebrew language and the names of kinds of seeds and plants. However, even this number was enough for Shifra to fill a large cooking pot and send Sonia there with it every day at noon. Shifra would cook in the morning and stuff into the big pot whatever she had at hand at that time, and Sonia would take hold of the two pot handles and carry it in the street. The aromas from the pot drew some of the poor of Jaffa after them, and they would follow the young woman to see where she was taking it.

The youngsters of Kiryat Sefer, whose stomachs growled the same time every day, would hurry out to meet her and push away the poor. Then, they would go up the steps, with Sonia in the middle and the small children in front of and behind her, afraid she might dribble a drop of food on the floor. Once inside the room, Sonia would put the pot in the middle. Israel would take a serving spoon and divide the meal: first, he gave it out to the children, and from the remainder, he would pour some out for himself and for Meir, as well as for the poor, who were standing at the entrance to the room and peeking, without daring to enter. At the end of the meal, the pupils were thrilled. The poor were rubbing their stomachs, and Sonia would hurry to go back home, skipping lightly with the empty pot.

It was not only the establishment of the Community Committee and the Jewish school that brought about great changes in Jaffa. In addition, the new Jewish immigrants who had come from Moscow after the expulsion edict had been declared contributed to the difference. A few of them were wealthy Jews laden with money for whom the country was but a stopover, and a few were beggars lacking everything. The people of means deposited their money with the real estate agents to buy land for them and hurried to leave on the next ship. The poor stayed and became a burden to the Committee and filled the Soup Kitchens. The Jewish women of Jaffa were pleased about the poor and competed among themselves as to whose apron had more stains. These ladies would accidentally, on purpose, forget to take off their aprons and tip-tap their way from the Committee office to the Soup Kitchen and from the Soup Kitchen to their homes. In Jaffa, everybody saw them so busily engaged.

Not all the poor rushed to the Soup Kitchens. Some were embarrassed to beg or ask for a bowl of soup without paying. They usually wore a sandwich board announcing their skills. At first glance, all the poster boards were very different: one was written in flowing handwriting, another with choppy letters. This one tried his hand at Hebrew, and that one held fast with Russian. But, when people came close to read the messages, they realized they all shared the same skill — they were all laborers; a sixteen-year-old youth, a laborer; a Jew with earlocks, a laborer; an elderly seventy-year-old, leaning on a cane—a laborer. They were willing to do any kind of work, and only once they had begun a job were they happy to accept a plate of food.

In Yehuda Leib's house, they spoke a lot about Russians who had just come to Palestine after the expulsion; they did not talk about cooking but rather about land issues. The first to speak about this was Sarah Hankin. Since she visited wealthy families in Jaffa and was poised to hear anything new, she related one day, when Yehoshua and Yehuda Leib were busy sorting merchandise that had just been brought to the store, that in the Rokach family's home, they only talked about real estate brokerage and were looking for lands to sell to the wealthy people from Moscow as well as to provide employment for all those workers thronging the streets of Jaffa. While talking, she reminded them that most of the customers coming to the store were effendis who owned large holdings, and what was good for the Rokach family was good for the Hankin family too. Sarah went on and told of the great demand for apartments and houses in Jaffa and of exploitation by the homeowners.

After Sarah left to put the younger girls to bed, Yehoshua, his eyes gleaming, approached his father and said, "Let's create a fund of public money for public needs. With this money, we'll buy land, a huge amount of land, and we'll give it to the public—some will buy it, while others will work the land, and everyone will benefit."

Yehuda Leib listened to his son and saw the glow in his eyes and the change in his demeanor from the minute he began talking about the land, but he asked him to wait and consult others.

Yehoshua shook his head and replied to his father, "There's no time. The land is burning beneath the pavement of Jaffa. Why delay? We'll call the fund 'Keren Kayemet,' a perpetual fund, and we'll put into effect an old idea that was around during our stay in Rishon Lezion, and the fund will last forever …"

Yehuda Leib tried to distract him and dampen his enthusiasm, but Yehoshua paid no attention to his hints and went on with his outpouring, "We'll show them, all those apartment speculators whose potbellies swell larger day by day and whose number of coat pockets grows bigger and bigger. We'll go and speak to the large-estate owning effendis who come to buy the finest textiles in the store, and everyone will gain: the Jews looking for land to build a house, the wealthy who want a foothold in Palestine, and the landowners whose land is not worked." Yehoshua stopped for a moment to stare at Yehuda Leib, as if he had had a passing thought and wondered whether or not to share it with his father. Then he continued, with a more confident voice, and it seemed to Yehuda Leib that his son had already decided and was not waiting for his answer, "I will go and speak with the Christian Arab whose wife frequently visits our store and Olga knows her well. This Christian owns the lands of Duran, areas that stretch from south of Rishon Lezion up to the Gedera land …"

Without him noticing it, Yehuda Leib approached his son and grabbed him by the shoulders, and gave him a good shake, "Wake up from your hallucinations.

Land in Palestine isn't sold only with words. You need a plan. You need money, lots of money."

Yehoshua came to and stopped talking, since he knew his father would not understand him and would not want to listen to his love stories. And what would he say to him? That his other love was abandoned, forgotten, with no one standing up to take care of her?! He receded into his shell and left Yehuda Leib alone; he went out into the lanes of Jaffa to calm down.

Yehoshua returned to the room he shared with Olga and found her awake very late at night. She had been waiting for him anxiously and only relaxed when he came in. From Sarah, she had heard about the discussion in the store. What Yehoshua had said didn't surprise her. She expected that, although she didn't know precisely when her husband would wake up and make his father party to his dream nor when he would talk to her openly about his other love. But, instead, Yehoshua sat beside her, with the dewdrops scattered in his beard. She pressed against him and tried to turn his face toward her, but his gaze was far distant from her. He again mentioned to her the issue of "the fund" and the name of the Christian, but he also asked for her help and wasn't aware of her silence. Olga knew that Yehoshua's days in the store were numbered, and she looked closely at every curl of hair and every crack in his skin, as if she wanted to keep deep within herself every detail of his appearance as much as she could. But Yehoshua kept describing the possibilities hidden in the buying and selling land in Palestine to her, but he didn't read her thoughts. He was blind, so very blind.

After things had quieted down and Sarah told again of the Rokach family's successes in acquiring land in Palestine, Yehuda Leib was no longer afraid of the idea of "the fund." He had fleshed it out with his friends and sought advice. Yehoshua didn't push to set up the fund quickly, though, in a roundabout way, he did show his great expertise to those asking him and inquiring about the idea. He knew the names of the owners and the names of the lands. He could tell the difference between *ziburit,* marginal land, and idit, the best soil, as well as how to estimate the price of a dunam and solve complex problems presented by Ottoman law. So, without realizing it and without their taking a unanimous decision, he became the chief spokesman for matters of "the fund."

It was impossible not to see the change in Yehoshua, and since people had a short memory, they did not link the days of his becoming estranged from Gedera to his time in Jaffa. On the contrary, they praised his knowledge and consulted him. His excitement was infectious. Only Olga remembered and was aware of his secret, and in her innermost being, she hoped that the days of Gedera would not return and he would not go back to his long riding trips.

There was reason for Olga to worry. Yehoshua's spending time in the port lessened, while his riding outside of Jaffa kept on increasing. Each evening, he would return to her and tell her about the price of land and Jewish tillers of the soil who were willing to plow even the rocks. Then he would go on and say that if he were able: he would acquire land and give it to the abject poor who swelled the streets of Jaffa so they could work it and make it productive. Once he finished talking about the type of soil and telling her his plans, he would also speak to her of other things that only the two of them knew; about the newborn she had delivered for the sheikh of the Duran lands and about the sheikh's already having married a third wife, who was also scheduled to give birth soon. He also talked about the Qatara Arabs and about Husseini Bek, who had fled to Damascus and no longer spread his terror on the roads. Sabra fruits and limestone soil were also discussed, as was someone named Eisenberg, who knew every path and byway and who went barefoot winter and summer, with the bottoms of his feet already like soles of shoes.

One day, among all the stories, he deftly inserted the topic of the "Valley of the Roses" tract. This was not the first time Olga had heard about the farm in Wadi Hanin that in Jaffa was mockingly called "Valley of the Thorns," and she had never taken the time to ask what was the point of the discussion. But when he told her about the eccentric Jew who was willing to swap a wealthy estate in Russia for rocky land in Eretz Israel, a certain German fellow had worked but not been able to tame. He also described the Jew's new wife—Feygele—Olga could not contain her curiosity and pleaded with him to take her along on one of his rides and stop on the way, so they would meet the eccentrics and take a look at the tract.

Yehoshua was happy to see Olga was interested in his doings. He believed what he wanted to: now she wanted to share his experiences, and she was no longer afraid to see him riding to the lands and being far away from her for so many days. He promised to take her with him, and at the end of September, he kept his promise.

‹❦›

They rose early in the morning, and while Olga was readying a food basket for them with sesame-covered rolls, Yehoshua went to fetch two horses, one of his own and the other belonging to the owners of the stables located at the port. The streets of Jaffa were empty, and the stores had not yet opened, so no one noticed them. The horses plodded slowly in the lanes, and neither Olga nor Yehoshua hurried them up. They passed the Turkish water fountain for travelers, a sabil standing on the main road, and the gates of Mikveh Israel, and they passed by the houses of Kfar Azur, and from there, turned to a narrow lane meandering between the fields.

Despite the early hour, the hot wind mussed Olga's hair, and she felt the touch of the high, yellowing weeds and the stings from the nettles. But when she saw her husband riding in front of her, and the flaps of his student coat flying, she forgot the heat and wondered about herself and about him: a year had passed since she had left Jaffa for Avshalom's birth, and all that time she had been bound in dresses whose laces tied in the back and worn high shoes, stepping so very carefully, while Yehoshua had been forced to work at selling in the store. Now, he had finally returned to his riding, and she did not know whether to be angry, give up, or be happy and accept him as he was. However, when he turned his head back toward her to see if she was riding behind him, she saw the passion surging through him, his eyes sparkling, and preferred not to think but to spur her horse on with her heels in order to catch up with him.

Olga laughed toward Yehoshua with her voice full of joy, so as to hide her thoughts, and she passed him by, galloping on quite a bit ahead of him. They entered fields marked by fences of sabras, and they skirted the homes of Rishon Lezion, scarcely glancing at it to see if something had changed in the colony. Since the rebellion, Yehoshua seldom visited Rishon Lezion. The farmers didn't care for him, and the Gedera stories didn't bolster their friendliness. If he happened to encounter someone from Rishon Lezion in Jaffa, he would turn his face away and go on walking. More than once, he had heard whispering behind his back, "Revolutionary," or noticed a farmer spitting three times, "Tfu, tfu, tfu," but he didn't stop to respond. Olga, too, had no reason to visit Rishon Lezion, for none of her family remained in the settlement, and the Jaffa school and Dr. Stein's clinic kept her more than busy. Besides all that, no one asked her to come to Rishon Lezion to help with births.

The horses crossed the young vineyards, planted with grapevines arranged in neat rows, their branches hanging and their grapes small; they were suitable only for wine but not for eating, and they were intended for the winery of Rishon Lezion. Olga felt thirsty and was reminded of Yehuda Leib's vineyard, so she asked to stop there and rest a bit. She called out to Yehoshua, but with his back to her, he only said, "Look, we're approaching the Duran land. We don't have a long way to go."

Olga was sorry that he was not party to her memories, and she continued to ride behind him. Now, they had left the vineyards and were riding on rock-laden cracked earth. The horses stumbled and slowed the place of their plodding; the sun had begun to climb in the sky and was burning over their heads. They entered an orchard whose trees were short, with unripe fruit hanging on their branches. At the side of the path crossing the orchard, hung an arrow-shaped sign on which, written in charcoal in clumsy handwriting, was "The Reuven Estate."

Owing to the low trees, they could not go on riding and had to alight and pull the horses by the halter's lead rope. The way was narrow, and Yehoshua walked ahead, striding confidently as if he were in the Jaffa lanes. Olga marched on and sighed, complaining about the mosquitos buzzing around and annoying the horse.

When they finally emerged from the orchard, Olga could see an elongated building with low huts attached to it. The wall's mortar was peeling, and the broken seashells dotting the kurkar building blocks twinkled in the sun. Thorny rose bushes in full bloom climbed the peeling walls, but they could not hide their ugliness. A field of wild herbs, dill, and thorn bushes had penetrated among the rose bushes and blocked the path leading to the house.

Yehoshua noticed neither the roses nor the thorns and stomped on the weeds as he walked to the house like someone familiar with it. Sticking up from the earth near the door were a few iron stakes, and he tied his horse to one of them, intending to go into the building. Then, suddenly, he remembered Olga. When he turned around, he saw her standing at the border between the orchard and the wild herbs. She was peering at the rose bushes as if hypnotized. Yehoshua motioned to her to come closer, but she didn't see his signs and went on staring in front of her. Yehoshua let go of the rope in his hand and walked toward her, taking the bridle lead from her hand and hugging her, whispering to her, "Good people live in the house. Come, I'll introduce you."

"I'm not afraid," she replied. "But you said, 'Men are living in the house,'" that is, people, and the woman is, of course, beautiful, while the ugliness outside is overwhelming."

Yehoshua laughed and pulled her to him, "Yes, people live in the house. Don't be scared. They'll be pleased to meet you."

They entered the house, and Olga's eyes adjusted to its dimness bit by bit. Straw mats were spread on the floor, and pillows embroidered with small cross-stitch flowers were strewn about them. The group of young people sat on the mats, some with crossed legs and others with their knees drawn up to their chins; they looked unabashedly at Olga and were surprised by a woman joining their gang.

Yehoshua introduced each of the youths to her, one by one, saying what their name was and where they came from; he explained to her, "Each of them is from the unemployed thronging Jaffa. They live in the mud huts abutting the house. They joined Lerer's farm to help and also to work their own plots."

Olga scanned the faces of the people, but she couldn't remember who was who, since they all looked so alike. Only one of them was different. Yehoshua saw her staring at the young fellow and said to her, "Please meet Aharon Eisenberg."

Olga remembered the name and noticed that he was barefoot, his clothes were unraveling, and wisps of oats were caught in his hair.

"He has no woman to care for him," she thought to herself. In appearance, he reminded her of Yehoshua, being around the same age and having a beard like his, but he was thinner. When she looked at him, she reminded herself of what her husband had told her about the worker walking about with him in the Duran lands, who was an expert on types of soil and plants, and the hiding places of the rock hyrax and the deer, and where the water pools, and where good, edible wild grapes grow. But she had imagined an eccentric elder among the hills, like in the stories about the biblical prophets, but now a slight grin lifted the corners of her mouth.

Yehoshua saw her stifled grin, so he, too, smiled at her in return. She was embarrassed that she had been caught and sought the eyes of the head of the household; he was sitting on a rocking chair outside the circle of the youth.

A thick beard adorned the face of Reuven Lerer, and he wore a holiday *kapote* even though it was just an ordinary day. He smoked a wooden pipe and remained silent, while his gaze wandered around the room and took in the entire group. From his garb and the seat he was sitting on, one could tell he was from Odessa, thought Olga. And this old gentleman, it was as if he had read your thoughts and nodded to her in greeting. When Yehoshua saw this signal of greeting and the comfortable stance of his wife, he knew she had found her place and did not need his attention, so he went and sat among the group of young people, and they accepted him into it and forgot Olga was even there.

Since Olga had not been invited to sit with them, she approached the rocking chair, pulled out a pillow, and sat next to the old man, hoping that he would take the step to speak to her. In her mind, she even prepared a subject for discussion: When did he come to Eretz Israel, and why at such an advanced age? But the man never moved his gaze down to her but continued to look straight at the young people. She sat for a few moments more and then rose and went to look for the woman, the one people had said was pretty.

She went from room to room—they were all simple ones with bare floors and beds made up with only a sheet and a pillow. In some, there was a wooden crate that served as a stool as well as a table, while in others, books were piled next to tools, both types of items looking very used. She went into the hallway and saw a door that differed from the others; its wood had been planed and polished with oil that shined, while on the door was a wooden sign on which was drawn a rural woman holding a yoke and two pails and under that was a greeting in Russian. Olga could not withstand her curiosity and gently pushed the door, which opened effortlessly.

The room contained a double bed. The window frame was decorated with a starched, smoothly ironed white curtain, whose edges were embroidered with the same stitches that decorated the pillows. The curtain fluttered in the wind and alternately covered and exposed pictures hanging on the wall near the window frame. One picture showed a shepherd playing a shepherd's pipe as his flock lay at his feet, while seen in the distance were snowy mountain tops. Olga smiled to herself: the shepherd wore the peasant clothes of Palestine, while the mountains belonged to a different world—an atmosphere not found in Wadi Hanin but was only the fancy of dreaming people. Beneath the landscape picture, she saw a photograph of a family sitting posed for a photographer: the bearded grandfather was sitting in the middle; next to him was a woman with a double chin, whose solemn gaze projected forward; around them were children and grandchildren holding the backs of the chairs. Behind the entire group, hanging on the wall, was a picture of an old woman who seemed to be looking at those sitting, as if checking to make sure each had found his place. It seemed to Olga that the woman's eyes followed her wherever she went. She was ashamed of her nosiness and rushed to go out and look for the exit to the yard. Next to the room, she had just left was a large kitchen with a door at its corner. Olga turned that way and went out to the sun.

The back yard was so very different from the front: no thorns nor weeds were evident, but rather flowerbeds of aromatic Syrian Jasmine bushes and trimmed roses, a passionflower vine clinging to the wall of the house with a hummingbird flying among its flowers, and low myrtles, whose white blossoms attracted the bees. There, between the flowerbeds and the bushes, she saw a woman. She was leaning over, with her back to Olga, and she was weeding the threatening wild couch grass. She was a small woman whose gathered hair was hidden under a broad-brimmed hat protecting her from the sun. Olga bent over at her side and uprooted the weed as she did, but she really very much wanted to lift up her head and look at the face in the shadow beneath the hat and see the woman everyone said was beautiful.

The two worked together at the same pace and didn't greet each other or introduce themselves, as if they had already known each other for a long time. They opened up to each other and did not need official acquaintanceship to tell stories of Petersburg and then stories about Odessa; they both smiled at the Rishon Lezion events and the tumult of Jaffa. They stretched their backs and looked at one another from time to time. Reuven Lerer's wife was really beautiful. Her eyes were large and full of joy. Untamable curls that poked out from under the hat fell across her forehead. Her skin was clear and her cheeks red, and it was as if an artist had held a paintbrush and drawn on her small face points of color and lines of shading under her long lashes.

Quite a while had passed since Olga had come out to the yard. At the side of the path stood a pile of weeds drying in the sun, and sweat poured down both their faces, leaving a salty taste in their mouths. One of the laborers came out of the building and called them to come join those sitting in the cabin since stomachs were rumbling and time had come for the midday meal. They both laughed at the helplessness of the men and went into the house.

The large room had emptied out, with only Mr. Lerer, Yehoshua, and Aharon Eisenberg remaining. Olga did not stay with them but went to the kitchen to help Lerer's wife prepare lunch. The woman cooked meager food, but she served it on porcelain plates with a light blue rim. The men remaining in the room went to wash their hands before eating and came back to sit upright on the chairs, taking care to keep their elbows off the table. They went on sitting like that until Lerer pulled off a piece of the pita, hot from the *tabun*, and dipped it in a bowl, recited grace, and took a bit, with oil dripping on his chin. The others did the same and no longer sat so stiffly but relaxed and open with each other. They spoke about the Germans avidly stalking the lands around Lerer's farm with their eyes and about the land of nearby Duran and about its owner, who was looking for buyers and wanted to sell it as a single unit.

The name of the landowner—Bustros Roq—came up repeatedly in the discussion and was familiar to Olga, for all Jaffa recognized him. He was a very wealthy Christian Arab and frequently visited the business establishments of Jews in Jaffa, among them Yehuda Leib's store. He used to come there accompanied by two donkeys and his wife—he would ride, while the woman would carry a baby on her back and march alongside a donkey. When this small group was wending its way through the Jaffa streets, youths would run ahead of it to see where they were heading and dash to Yehuda Leib's store to let him know of the arrival of the rich man and, by so doing, gain a few Turkish medjidiye. Yehuda Leib loved giving generously, to demonstrate his success, straighten out his clothes, and stand at the door of his store to welcome clients. Sarah would hurry to spread out on the counter rolls of new textiles, kinds of Saponaria soaps, and polishes, then warn her daughters to behave properly and ask them to also call Olga.

The Christian Arab and his wife would come into the store, choose whatever the woman wanted, and load it all on their donkeys. When they were finished with everything involving money, they would sit in two groups: Yehuda Leib and the landowner; the woman with Sarah and Olga. The wife was interested in receiving advice about women's matters, while the landowner sought the friendship of the storeowner, Yehuda Leib, and asked him about the Jewish merchants.

"You are crafty merchants," he loved to say to Yehuda Leib. "You know how to bargain and not give in." When he once heard Sarah call Yehuda Leib "Diadka," he broke out laughing and rolled the name on his tongue; since then, he had dubbed him "Hawadja Diadka" and considered that a special privilege.

Now Olga looked at her husband, surprised by his expertise about Bustros Roq's property. Then, deep in thought, she remembered that about a week after the discussion about the "Fund," the Arab had visited the store. He had come without his wife, so he bought nothing and didn't need her advice.

They sat him down in the covered small room at the side of the store, and Yehuda Leib took a break from all his work and sat with him, out of sight of those coming and going.

The small chamber was used for those deals that shouldn't be made public, and it became a place of refuge to avoid the bustle of the store. At that discussion, she reminded herself, Yehoshua had been present, and since she was used to his silences, she didn't pester him with her questions, and the meeting had escaped her memory. Now, she recalled it, and as it popped up, she remembered the figure of Bustros Roq, who got up to leave the little room, shaking its owner's hand and stepping out of there confidently. Also coming to mind was that she had glanced at Yehoshua and saw heavy sweat on his forehead, so she had gone to him and put out her hand to check for a fever, but he had said to her, "It's nothing. A bit of excitement that'll be gone by tomorrow."

She listened closely, and a shiver ran up her spine, and she did not know if she trembled from the cold or, perhaps, from the unceasing involvement with land. If only a few days earlier, she had convinced herself that Yehoshua was hers and the land would not best her, and she had thought she was a partner to his secret. She now realized that he had revealed a bit to her but had concealed much more. He had hidden from her his intention to buy the Duran spread. She looked at those sitting around the table, and they seemed so far away: a barefoot young man, an eccentric old man, and a dreaming husband.

Olga looked toward the homemaker, Lerer's young wife, and found her sitting calmly, expressing no connection at all to the issues discussed at the table. She didn't want to be like her, to live isolated on a rose farm and see thorns invading the plants. She wanted a husband nearby who would share her bed and know all the small details about her life. The group continued to talk about the size of the Duran land and the possibilities for settling on it; they calculated the number of colonies that could be set up on it, the type of soil, and so on. The noon hour was long past, the room had become shadow-filled, and Lerer's wife went to light the oil lamp. Olga sat silently with a distant look on her face.

Moving her chair from its place, distracted those sitting around from their discussion, and Yehoshua looked at Olga and only now understood she was insulted. He tried to catch her glance and draw her attention to him, but she turned her eyes away from him. He quickly got up and went to her seat; he stood behind her back and, putting his hand on her shoulder, whispered to her, "Let's go."

She felt the warmth of his breath on her neck and trembled, hurrying to rise. Her love outweighed her anger. What good was it to harbor grudges and put on a sour face and make Yehoshua pay close attention to his actions and wonder why she was angry. It was best for her to accept the situation, take him as he was, and restrain herself. She forced herself to smile. She said goodbye to the woman with an invitation to come to the store in Jaffa and with a promise to show her all the wonders of the city. The lady smiled at her and said nothing was as wonderful as the vegetables in her garden, and nothing could match the peace of the farm. Olga could only look at her enviously.

Olga and Yehoshua left the cabin and hurried to set off riding on their way so as to manage to reach Jaffa before nightfall. They rode quickly. Olga was quiet, and Yehoshua tried to overtake her; at wide spots, he would ride by her side and try to make her speak. Slowly, her anger abated, and she understood that it was not called for and that she had to accept all the blame on herself, on the jealousy and self-pity in which she sometimes found it comfortable to wrap herself. Olga slowed her riding pace and listened to Yehoshua when he told her that he wanted to purchase the Duran land from Bustros Roq and then look for buyers among the Jews who were coming to look for land in Jaffa. She paid attention to his words and asked why he wanted to deal with something so much greater than his ability. Wasn't he talking about a large piece of land for which a great deal of money was needed? From where would they take the necessary funds?

"I will take it from the 'Fund,'" he replied. "A lot of money has already been collected, three thousand French francs. From this sum, it will be possible to give a down payment to the landowner."

Olga remained silent and was uncertain about going on and expressing her doubts.

Yehoshua did not like her keeping quiet and pulled on the reins to hold back the horse. "Are you angry?"

"No," she answered. "I'm afraid to air what I'm thinking."

He asked her to share her fears with him, so she gently said to him, "The 'Fund" is closed in a French bank, and only Yehuda Leib has the right to open the account. And what if he refuses? Or, what if he says 'the time's not right yet'?"

Yehoshua released the reins and broke into roaring laughter in the evening darkness. "Everyone knows the 'Fund' has one purpose: to buy for the public. So, I need to find a wide public. And Jaffa is teeming with a public seeking land."

Olga looked skeptically toward Yehoshua, but his shining eyes were stronger than she and quashed all her other questions.

The two continued to ride, and Olga knew that Yehoshua had begun to tread a new path, and all she could do was follow him, for better or for worse. Disappointment would come, and there would also be high points, and when he would be up, she would be happy with him, and when he would stumble and fall, she would fall with him. She could not change him. Yehoshua roared ahead, and when she called to him to slow down, he already did not hear her—the evening wind carried.

᠁

The following weeks Yehoshua spent in Jaffa, but not alone. Aharon Eisenberg frequently visited the store and spent time in Yehoshua and Olga's room as well as eating with them. Bustros Roq also came, though always by himself. The three of them, sometimes joined by Yehuda Leib, would cloister themselves in the small room for hours on end, and Sarah would come with a full tray and return with it empty, over and over.

In Jaffa, rumors began spreading, one on the heels of the others, and Olga heard more details from the women who came to the doctor's office than from her husband or Aharon. At first, they told her a Jew had bought a large amount of land near Rishon Lezion; then, someone said that the buyer was one of the rebels the Baron had expelled from Rishon Lezion. But when they finally dared to mention her husband's name, they added in one breath, as if by the way, "They say it's all wasteland." And whoever was unashamed, or who wanted to mock her, asked in feigned innocence, "From where will he find the money?" Then, to test her response, they asked again, "The *'Keren Kayemet'* is intended only for the public, right?" Of course, Olga answered neither the slanderers nor the dissemblers. Instead, she preferred to hurry home after work and join Yehoshua and Aharon at the table to see their enthusiasm and, in that way, banish her fears.

But not everyone in Jaffa was satisfied with asking questions and talking behind Yehoshua's back. On the contrary, some were fiercely jealous—how dare he go and negotiate with such a large landowner like Bustros Roq. "How can it be that such a young man as he is involved in major issues?" the Jaffa functionaries pondered, "How did he manage to capture the heart of the Christian Arab? And he's so inexperienced!"

Especially envious of him were the real estate agents and land speculators, who tried to win over the wealthy Russians who made a one-day stop in Jaffa and turned over to them bundles of money to buy land for them. All those agents dealt with small plots of little value, and now a nobody comes along, a mere stripling, and he had already managed to acquire a huge tract. And more than anyone else, Yehiel Michael Pines was jealous of him.

Pines had come to Jaffa a year after Olga and Yehoshua had arrived there. He had left Gedera when he realized the farmers didn't need his advice and preferred to act as they wished or in line with the Baron's commands. The *shmita* year had been most troublesome for him. The high bureaucracy wrote letters and complained that he had acted erroneously and should not have imposed letting the land lie fallow, creating disputes with the laborers and the farmers. His actions were detailed in the press, and loads of explanations were given for them. Alongside the lengthy correspondence between him and the officials, statements were given by neighbors who knew what he was cooking up and what his wife was cooking for Sabbath dinner.

He did not forget Yehoshua's behavior and did not forgive him. He considered him and Israel Feinberg as the cause for his decline. But Israel continued to live in Gedera, while Pines now found himself in Jaffa, and Yehoshua's success was a thorn in his heart.

When he came to Jaffa, he was sure the Hovevei Zion Committee would find him a fitting position—perhaps on the Jaffa Committee along with Yehoshua Barzilai. But that didn't happen, and he refused to accept the simple title of "secretary" alone. He searched for something to occupy himself and very quickly discovered the gold mine of wealthy Jews passing through Jaffa on their way to America and believing that nothing was safer or earning better profits than investing in land in Palestine. It was actually easy to convince them to leave money with him to buy land, but he ran into difficulties locating land for the money.

Purchasing land in Palestine was difficult, not only for Pines but also for many others involved in brokerage like he was. And even harsher was the envy of one who actually managed to find land. So Yehoshua, in their eyes, was "the young Hankin," barely an unweaned youth and already a success. Pines looked for a way to invalidate the buying of the Duran lands and tried with all his might to mock and debase Yehoshua and ruin his reputation. He made sure to spread old, almost forgotten, stories of Rishon Lezion and Gedera. There was a smidgen of truth in them, but they were mostly exaggerations and myths. Spreading rumors and talking wasn't enough for him. He also wrote in the newspapers, and all of Jaffa was busy with the Duran land, Yehoshua Hankin, and Yehiel Pines.

The Jaffa Jews were divided between supporters of Pines and supporters of Hankin, and the arguments about the Duran lands overflowed into bigger disputes. No undivided family was to be found in the city. Handbills were distributed everywhere that called for the Hovevei Zion (The Lovers of Zion) Committee and its activists to institute supervision over buying and selling land and not let every "youth" treat the land as his own. In the synagogue, people stood next to the pulpit and demanded to increase the buying and selling. At Yehuda Leib's store, Tanhum gathered a bunch of lads around him, and together they called for freedom in buying, without limitations and without determining everything in advance. In the newspaper *HaMelitz,* someone suggested establishing a company for acquiring land, a company for improving it, and a third company to look for buyers; immediately after that, drawings popped up on the walls of the Jewish houses showing intermediaries: an intermediary for land, an intermediary for land improvement, and an intermediary for buying, which became disreputable terms and were mocked; and Jaffa was engulfed in a great tizzy.

Olga and her brother Israel took part in the debates, mainly to enhance Yehoshua's reputation, defend his honor, and maintain his dignity. Unintentionally, they caused the store's business to flourish. Israel—whenever he was not occupied with his school or had decided that no lesson could equal spending time in Yehuda Leib's store to see the faces of the Jaffa residents— he would come to the doorway of the textile shop, with a bunch of small children following him, and would speak loudly with Olga. People would gather around him and around his pupils, patting their soft curls and listening to his speeches, and incidentally, go into the store and poke through its merchandise. Olga would stand by the counter and calculate aloud the cost of a dunam of land and what was the cost of a meter of fabric, comparing the two and showing anyone interested just how cheap the textiles were in the store of Yehuda Leib and Sarah.

Sarah sat in a corner of the store, listening and keeping still, waiting for the moment when everything would be back to normal: peace and quiet would return to the store, and the people coming to it would only want to buy textiles and not snatch words and sentences to be later handed over brazenly from Yehuda Leib's store to Pines' land panderers.

Yehoshua was not part of what was going on in the shop. He was afraid of Pines, the functionaries, and anyone with ready cash. He knew that Pines was more familiar than he with association leaders arriving in Palestine to look for land. Pines was right. He was still "a kid," "the young Hankin," and who saw young people such as he getting involved in deals too big for them? Pines' name was known to every farmer in the colonies. The pages of the newspapers bore it, and letters sent from Palestine were signed by him. His decision about the *shmita* year had been read by all. Everyone was aware of his activities in Gedera. What did a young merchant like Yehoshua have to offer? Yes, he had acquired the land, but he did not know how to sell it, or make its quality known, or how to enhance his own name. Hankin looked for ways to reach Pines and ask his forgiveness. He did not want to fight with him; he wanted his help.

"Palestine is large and has enough room for many land agents," Yehoshua used to say to himself. Sometimes he thought about suggesting that Pines share with him future land that would be acquired and proposed he himself should learn from those more expert than he methods for buying and selling land.

He told no one about his quandaries, not even Olga. He was sure that when others found out, they would not hold back from mocking him over his weakness. One evening he screwed up his courage and went out. This was after they had closed the store, recited the evening prayer, finished eating, and gone to their own homes to get ready for a good night's sleep. The alleys were empty, and he trod downcast, steeped in his thoughts. He thrust his fingernails into his palms to feel the pain, but not to change his mind. When he reached Pines' house, he stood for several minutes at the threshold and finally rang the bell. He waited for a bit, but no one responded. He rang another time, but again, no one opened up. He put his ear against the door and could hear voices. He pushed his ear as close to the door as he could and caught his name. He heard it mentioned a few times, each one accompanied by giggles and words of scorn. He did not ring again; he just walked away. He felt his body straightening up, and confidence filled him: Pines will realize that it is not a "lad" who is dealing with the land, not the "young Yehoshua," but "Yehoshua, the land dealer."

୶

On the third day of Hanukkah, Yehoshua rose early and rode to the Duran lands. He left at dawn and returned after the fourth candle had been lit in the evening.

When he entered Yehuda Leib's home, he found his parents sitting comfortably and competing against the girls and Tanhum in a game of spinning paper dreidels. His father raised his head toward him, sending an inquisitive look. Yehoshua did not glance at him but went in search of Olga. Rivka, the youngest, pointed toward the kitchen, "She's making latkes. All evening she kept some for you, but you didn't come. We couldn't help ourselves, and we ate all of them. She certainly heard the sound of your boots and went to fry others." Yehoshua blushed and went to the kitchen, but the smell of the latkes didn't attract him; he wanted to share his big secret. He found his wife standing next to a copper bowl with bubbling hot oil. She was scraping remnants of a batter made from flour and water and tossing them into the boiling pot. He approached her and with a quick move, grabbed her waist and raised her up, twirling around with her again and again. His eyes told her everything; she didn't have to ask: Yehoshua had completed the acquisition of the Duran lands and had also signed the contract. The Christian Arab had finally agreed. She wanted to say out loud that she already knew, but Yehoshua had covered her mouth and murmured into her ear, "I will tell you later, only you and me. The matter is still being kept secret, and letting it out early is not allowed if one side should change its mind, and I would be in trouble."

Impatiently, Yehoshua helped Olga take off her apron. Olga took his hand and pulled him out of the kitchen. Then, from behind her shoulder, she blurted, "Good night," and hurried to their room, to become a party to his secret and a partner to his love.

Her flood of questions burst out in their room, and Yehoshua answered them one by one: yes, he had bought the land. He had bought it for 11 francs per dunam. He had shaken hands with Bustros Roq, and Aharon Eisenberg had been the witness. They had already been to the Turkish notary in Ramleh, and the Christian Arab had promised to clear out the *fellahin* and move them to other land. Moreover, he had promised to act to obtain individual ownership of the land—to divide it into parcels— not to leave Yehoshua with a passel of problems.

"He acted this way out of pity," Olga interrupted his flow of answers. "He saw you as a young lad and did not want to spoil your first purchase. Or, perhaps he liked you? After all, you're the son of a merchant, and your wife is a midwife."

Yehoshua laughed in her direction and paced the room, but the room was too small to contain his joy. "He did not see me as a lad, but as one understanding and expert in land deals."

Then they were quiet. Olga wanted to ask from where they would take the money, but she was afraid she might ruin his happiness. Yehoshua stopped going to and fro and stood before her, and as if reading her thoughts, he said to her, "The money will come from a rich merchant. He lent his money to me, and I made a down payment to the Christian Arab. The remainder of the sum and the return of the loan will be paid by those buying the land. The merchant gave me a three-month extension to return the money, and in three months, the land of Duran will be sold."

His eyes were flashing, and his voice grew stronger. He did not see Olga, and it was if he had been seized in a frenzy. He glanced past her and focused on a far spot on the wall, "I will divide the land into parcels, and the 'newcomers' overflowing Jaffa will buy the land. They and the associations sought land and merchants who want to make deals and earn a profit. A large colony will be built there, and it will border Lerer's property, and bring the land of Gedera close to it. Everyone will stand in line, the Jaffa people and the traders. Everyone will want my land."

Olga remained quiet, and his enthusiasm did not infect her. She wanted to reveal her fears to him, to open his eyes. But he didn't see, on account of how invested he was in his secret. But to her, the secret was like a spider spinning a web, entrapping Yehoshua and taking him far away from her. This time the land had beaten her; it was stronger than she and had carried her husband away for a long time.

The Hanukkah festival passed, and Yehoshua's secret had not yet been revealed in Jaffa. In the Old City, people continued to bet over who would be the agent for the Duran lands. But any secret, from the minute more than two know about it, cannot be kept for long, and in a short time, that secret was revealed.

1890—Acquiring the Duran Lands

Yehiel Michel Pines had no interest in giving in easily to the young Hankin, so one day, he invited to his home a few of the Jaffa functionaries, some of the most important ones. He sent a letter by messenger to Lerer's farm to summon Aharon Eisenberg. Aharon, to whom the letter was complimentary, was excited by the possibility of meeting public figures and other significant people of Jaffa, so he set out for Pines' house. Even though he knew his going there would appear in the newspapers, he went barefoot, as he usually did, his head uncovered, his clothes worn out, and his coat completely threadbare.

In Pines' house, all the important guests were waiting for his arrival, all of them portly and dressed to the nines in their long coats and praising a brimmed hat. "This was sewn in France, and it was made especially for the Jews supported by Emperor Franz Josef." When Aharon saw them sitting there haughtily and heard their conversation, he looked at his clothes and regretted having given in to his weakness in accepting the invitation.

When he entered Pines' house, all of them were already seated, and they scrutinized him as he came in. Someone made place for him and invited him to sit. If he had been thinking about turning around and leaving, it was too late now. He sat on the edge of his chair, thinking maybe he'd have a chance to leave soon, and Pines, seeing his confusion, smiled and called to those sitting in the room to be quiet and listen to what he had to say. The stuffed shirts stopped chattering and stared at Aharon and Pines. Aharon felt that everyone, except for him, knew what this was about, and he leaned back in the chair without moving the rest of his body and sat in even more "edgy" than before.

"Kid," Pines called out to him, "only a kid and already an expert who deals in big business. You have joined one of the Hankin family, and together with him, you want to buy land. I'm speaking the truth, aren't I?"

He finished and scanned the faces of those present, and then again, let his glance linger on Aharon. He waited a moment and then raised his voice and said in a confident tone, "You have made a bad choice. You did not look around you. You did not ask who is qualified to be a purveyor of land and who is not. The first one who came and gave you an offer, you went along with him. What do you have to do with this reckless fellow—Yehoshua Hankin? Everyone knows he is not a big expert in land; all his skill relies on incitement to rebellion. While you are still a boy who does everything people tell you, and you do not know how to tell the difference between good and bad. Why do you need all of this? Go to those who are better than he, to the ones Palestine recognizes for their value and relies on their every word. I will give you a lot of money, to make up for your loss, and you will go to Bustros Roq and tell him that Pines is better than Yehoshua Hankin, understands the value of the land, and has no one who can compete with him in land negotiations."

Aharon listened to him but did not reply, even though his eyes grew wide, showing his suspicions and revealing his thoughts.

Pines kept on orating and trying to convince himself and his listeners with his passion, "There is a name for the young Hankin, 'radical,' and who will go to buy land from someone who does not manage to put down roots in one place, and the land expels him from its midst? And rumors accompany the nicknames …." He lowered his voice and looked to see the reactions of his audience.

Pines went too far, but he was not sorry. The eyes of those present were wide open, and their mouths gaped; they were curious to know what those rumors were. He didn't have to raise his voice and try to overcome the noise in the room. The pause he was making grew longer and picqued the listeners' curiosity to the limit. Then, he whispered quietly, as if sharing a secret with his guests, "He doesn't stay much at home and distances himself from his wife. In private chambers, people tell that he roams like a poor wanderer among the tents of Ishmael and stays in the villages of the *fellahin*, preferring the carpet to the bed in his home on Port Street. They speak of his great love, greater than for the woman to whom he gave a ring."

Aharon's fingers began to sweat, and he wiped them on his ragged clothes, afraid of leaving moist stripes on his pants. His entire body shivered, and his feet trembled, and he wanted to cry out to Pines, clear Yehoshua's name, shatter the room's silence, and declare loudly, "Nonsense! Pure lies! The land was given to Yehoshua, and Bustros Roq's choice is not bad at all. He chose, and he knew who he was choosing, the best among you. You said love, and you did not know his love …."

But the cry was stuck in his throat and not thrown into the room. He was still perched on the edge of his chair, waiting for them to leave him alone. He could not stand up for Yehoshua; he was weak, so very weak.

Pines saw Aharon's silence and noticed how tensely he sat, while the others had begun whispering among themselves and churning the "rumor." Pines did not approach him; he enjoyed torturing him. He went to other parts of the room to talk with the different functionaries about the matters of the associations that were coming to Palestine and about his many transactions. From time to time, he would steal a glance at Aharon to see how the muttering around him and the praise being showered on the host were influencing him. But Aharon didn't hear a thing, neither the words of contempt nor those of praise, and he thought only about one thing: how to find a way to escape from the house, from the group of hacks sitting around him and following his every move and expression. He saw this group as a conspiracy of ravens sitting around a wounded animal, waiting for a moment of weakness to attack it and tear off pieces of it.

Time crawled, and Aharon thought that night must have fallen. But just then, everyone was called to the next room to go to a table laden with refreshments. Aharon rose with the other guests, but he did not go to the table but went instead toward the street door. And Pines, who never took his eyes off Aharon, immediately understood his young guest's intention and followed him. When Aharon was about to put his hand on the doorknob, Pines called to him, "Why hurry, young man? We still have a long evening coming."

Aharon reacted with the words rushing out of his mouth, "It's a long way to Lerer's farm, and riding at night is dangerous." Hesitantly, he raised his eyes and saw the gloating in Pines' own. Right then, his wrath exploded; all those words he had taken in when seated on the edge of the chair burst out now and were hurled like rocks towards Pines, "Other deals are waiting for me; deals with people better than you. They won't laugh at me or Yehoshua. Time will come, and Yehoshua will be greater than you. Then, everyone will talk about him and his deeds, while you will be forgotten." With the words still in the air, Aharon opened the door and rushed out into the lane without bothering to close it, and his words were still ringing in his ears and echoing after him.

As he looked for Port Street and Yehuda Leib's textile store, Aharon ran, battered by the Jaffa lanes, stepping on small stones and sliding on remnants of peels. He had to see Yehoshua and convince him to publicly declare that he had actually shaken hands with Bustros Roq and struck a deal with him. The time had come to negotiate with buyers who wanted to acquire for themselves a piece of property in Palestine. There was no reason for this matter to be top secret. It had to be announced out loud so that the slanderers would have to hold their tongues.

It was a long way from Pines' house to Yehuda Leib's store, or perhaps it just seemed so to Aharon. And while he was running among the lanes, the young man tried to shake off the evening's events, and the doubts Pines wanted to instill in him. He asked himself if in Duran there would also be lanes or whether they would build houses along boulevards… and without noticing it, he had gone past the store and had to go back to it.

Aharon went into the textile shop and inquired about Yehoshua. They told him, "He's out, but he'll be back," so he asked to wait for him. They motioned to him to sit on a stool standing toward the back of the store–a Damascus stool of the kind found in many a farmer's home in the Jewish colonies. They must have brought it with them from Rishon Lezion, he thought, as he sat down on it. He bent his knees and leaned his elbows on them, holding his head up with his hands, and looked around in the dimness of the store. He saw Sarah rolling up textiles. She was a stout woman marked by her satisfaction with the business, but her motions were quick and uniform, despite her heavy appearance. She reminded him of Yehoshua. For her, too, every single movement was intentional; none were unnecessary. She did everything quickly and rhythmically. She rolled the material, straightened it, pulled the edges of the roll, and rolled it again, straightening a seam, and smoothing the fabric until a perfectly taut roll was leaning against the wall.

Aharon thought about the three months remaining until Yehoshua had to find the money and repay the merchant from Beirut the money for the loan, as well as hand over the interest. He counted the days and the Sabbaths and added in the holidays, and all that time, only one idea kept on repeating in his head: to declare, they must … his eyelids grew heavy, and he no longer saw the activity in the store and did not hear the customers' request nor Sarah's replies. He fell asleep and had no idea when Olga came to the store and found him leaning on his knees and giving her a fright. Sarah had no answers to her questions. Aharon didn't feel it when she covered him with a blanket to warm him up and make his rest more pleasant, nor did he notice when she sat down opposite him, waiting for the minute he would wake up.

Night came. They lit oil lamps in the store and were waiting for Yehoshua to come so they could close the store. As usual for him at that time, he was late. Seeing how peaceful Aharon was, Olga stepped out into the lane to wait for her husband. She wanted to be the first to see him, to capture his glance, share with him this one moment that was theirs alone, and then he would go and pay attention to Aharon and to the news he had brought with him about the land.

The dark had become denser, so Olga wrapped herself in her shawl and tried to tear away the veil of the night. Finally, she heard bootsteps and knew Yehoshua was back. She closed the door to the shop and leaned against the pillar of the threshold, where she met him. He kissed her mouth and wanted to lift her up and hold her close, but Olga pushed him away and stepped back a little until she could check him from top to bottom and keep his image for herself. Then she did come close to him and let him hug her, his arms engulfing and warming her. Quite a while passed until she remembered the man sitting on the stool, snoring lightly; then, she opened the door for Yehoshua and pointed to the storeroom. Yehoshua left her and rushed to Aharon, wondering why he had come at such a late hour and had stayed in the store; he was also afraid of the harsh report he was liable to hear.

Yehoshua gently touched Aharon's shoulder, and in response, he jumped up as if bitten by a scorpion, and while still sleepy and not realizing what he was saying, blurted, "Pines is giving up …"

Yehoshua shook him, and Aharon looked at him; for a minute, he did not know where he was and whether he was hallucinating.

Slowly, he came fully awake and was happy to realize where he was and took hold of Yehoshua. Sarah set a pot of water on the sizzling coals and went to bring rolls, the kind they bake down the street and prepare for early morning. Olga continued to stand in the threshold of the store, waiting for Yehoshua's call to join them in the small room. But Yehoshua never invited her. He was busy with Aharon and the news he had brought with him, and there was no room for her in those affairs.

Yehoshua, who saw Aharon's powerful emotions, did not rush him and waited for the right words that would come once he had put his thoughts in order. In the meantime, Sarah returned and offered them tea and rolls.

Aharon sipped his drink, and the hot tea defrosted him and unfettered his tongue. Between sips, he told Yehoshua about his visit to Pines' house, but the events of the evening no longer seemed so terrifying. The tea's warmth and Yehoshua's companionship calmed him, and he considered his words. He spoke moderately and waited for Yehoshua's reaction. Yehoshua listened and looked at his fingernails and saw the wisps of chaff and the mud that had collected beneath them—no matter how hard he tried, he could not get rid of that dirt. Even the nail brush Olga had given him didn't help. His craft made it obvious, and once he reconciled himself to the dirt, he was happy about it. He even dared to show it and spread his hands on his knees as if declaring: I am a man of the soil.

He was steeped in his thoughts, with Aharon's voice serving as a backdrop for them. When Aharon finished his story, Yehoshua turned to look at him, and after a moment's silence, he continued where Aharon had left off, in the same tone and same voice, as if it were one long sentence, without a pause, "Let's make this public: in Jaffa, the colonies, and the other Holy Cities, and on Purim, we will divide the land into plots." Then he moved his chair close to Eisenberg's until they were shoulder to shoulder, and he said to him, almost whispering, "We will create gardens, we'll build houses. We will establish a settlement that is not dependent on barons, and the soil will be covered, not exposed. It won't be embarrassed by its aridness nor cry out in its nakedness.

As if a sign had been given, the two rose together and burst out laughing in relief from having been released from the burden of secrecy and silence. They left the small room and took hold of Olga, one on each side, and danced with her between the rolls and piles of fabrics, and she was swept up in their joy and was happy with them, despite her having been insulted. Hearing the noise, Yehuda Leib and Sarah went into the store, followed by Tanhum and the younger daughters. For a moment, the three were quiet. But then, they all began to talk at once, interrupting each other and trying to overwhelm the newcomers with their secret by releasing the words they had been forbidden to use for so long. From the abundance of words and sentences, those who had entered the store began to take in bits and pieces, "three months," "Duran land," "Keren Kayemet." Finally, Yehuda Leib quieted them down and tried to make logical sense of what was going on. In turn, the three of them told him, each one adding to what had been said: Bustros Roq was willing to sell the land to Yehoshua; Yehoshua had pledged to find buyers and to pay the full price within three months; the interest he had managed to set was not high, and Pines was trying to thwart all of this.

When the flow of words was stanched, and the three were breathless, Yehuda Leib turned to his son and asked in all seriousness, "And if buyers don't come and three months go by? Who will guarantee the loan?"

For a moment, Yehoshua was quiet; he took hold of Olga's hand and played with her fingers to give him time to organize his statement properly so it would not trip him up. "I will find guarantors," he told his father. "Perhaps among the wealthy who are coming to Jaffa and looking for a safe way to invest their money. I thought about turning to the Jaffa Committee to guarantee the loan."

Yehuda Leib stood facing his son, sending him a look that penetrated straight through him, and said, "Why should you look among strangers? We will mortgage the store and the house, and with that, we will be your guarantee."

Yehoshua shivered at hearing this and sought Olga's eyes to get her approval. For a second, he was not sure about what he was doing, and what if he didn't succeed? What if he should flounder? He wouldn't fail alone; he would drag them all after him.

Olga wouldn't look at him and refused to be party to his decision. Yehuda Leib urged his son to decide quickly. And Yehoshua saw how his arms were outstretched, wanting to hug him as he had done when Yehoshua was still a small child at the time he had taken him to ride with him among the estates in Kremenchug.

Yehoshua was neither a child nor a lad, as they wanted to dub him in the newspapers. He was a head taller than his father and had to make decisions without consultation and without the support of others. He did not understand Olga's distance—perhaps her fears were unbearable.

Yehoshua saw his son's eyes swirling and didn't understand the reason for his hesitation, but deep inside, he was happy that the decision had not been a hasty one. To reinforce his earlier statement, he told him, "I wanted to redeem the land in Rishon Lezion, but they didn't let me. They took it away from me by force. Now, you again want to redeem land, would I prevent you?" Yehoshua looked again at Aharon and saw that everyone's eyes reflected their excitement. Only Olga still refused to look at him. He went to her and grasped her shoulder, saying to her in a quiet voice, not caring about the others in the room, "You chose me, and you chose the land. I can't do without it or without you."

Olga lifted her eyes and saw his pain. She motioned to him with her head, while Yehoshua turned his gaze to his father and nodded to him in agreement.

❧

The following day all Jaffa was abuzz with the sale of the Duran land to Yehoshua Hankin, and people stressed the fact Bustros Roq supported the young land agent and had not turned to an experienced functionary expert in land issues. From the morning, the entrance to the store had been thronged by many people, who asked about the price of a plot in the Duran land and about the quality of the soil. There were different kinds of skeptics who wanted to know if a benefactor had helped promote the sale, or might it be that Yehoshua had bought it with his own money. Some among the crowd were simply trying to find out whether Yehoshua was as young as Pines had publicized in the newspaper.

Yehoshua wasn't in the store, and Israel Belkind had given the small children a day off from school and come to help and answer all the questions. Olga and Sarah stayed with him and were assisted by the older daughters of Sarah and Yehuda Leib. They had plenty of work, but they paid attention to the questions of those coming to the store. At the same time, they wondered if they were on the verge of success.

Sarah was afraid of success and tried to play it down as much as she could, so as to not detract from her good fate, while Olga wanted to enjoy as much of it as possible. Yehuda Leib mingled with the crowd at the store's entrance and strutted about like a well-dressed peacock. He spoke a bit with those coming in and going out, standing ever straighter.

The bustle of selling the Duran land continued in the store in the following days. Yehuda Leib kept on coming dressed in his holiday finery and muttering to those entering and leaving that his son's deals were enhancing his business.

At that pleasurable time, Yehuda Leib took time off himself from his work and often went to the new synagogue built by the elderly Chelouche in the new Jewish neighborhood of Neve Tzedek. Yehuda Leib would come for the morning, afternoon, and evening services, and missed no fast or New Month prayer. He stood at the entrance to the synagogue and welcomed people coming in. This way, he gained respect and became accepted at the tables of the leading functionaries in the city.

Among those frequenting that synagogue was Yehiel Pines. The gossipers said that it was only because of him that Yehuda Leib had altered his habits and go as far as the synagogue in Neve Tzedek.

Yehuda Leib loved to listen to the conversations behind his back and take pleasure in the looks from Pines imbued with insult and full of rage and helplessness. Yehuda Leib would greet him, ask how he was, and follow him about, while the official would turn his back on him, his shoulders trembling.

All the ado about Duran didn't affect Yehoshua. He was occupied with preparing the land for its division among future buyers and locating nearby landowners in order to have them sign regarding the borders to forestall later problems. What had happened in Gedera had left a scar, and he did not want to encounter once again neighbors screaming about thievery and claiming that the plots belonged to them. He had plenty of work to do, so he stayed to sleep in Aharon Eisenberg's room on the Lerer farm. There, he acted like the bachelor laborers, sitting with them nights, drinking liquor, and speaking about Olga as if she weren't his wife but rather a lover who comes to satisfy the whims of a young man for one night and then disappears in the morning. He would rise early and go out with Aharon to work the land and forget the rowdiness of the night; he wanted to surprise Olga with all his wondrous deeds.

☙

Purim was approaching, and they had promised to divide the land on that day. Yehoshua and Aharon treated the Duran land as if they were caring for a bride: on rainless days, the two of them would go out to it and furrow it with a wooden plow, turning over the soil. Then, one of them would go over it with by hand with a harrow and crumble the clods, while the other would rake and even out the soil in circles around the well standing in the center of the tract. They lopped off the tops of mounds of earth and dragged the soil to open pits; they removed the heavy rocks and placed them near the well to serve as benches. Though on rainy days, they would both stay in the cabin and plan what different kinds of jam and drinks the women would prepare. Other times, they would draw in the dust of the flooring of the entire tract, dividing it into sections— square plots, as well as plots that could not be square, because of a corner or a small hill on them. They included paths and boulevards, a piece of land intended for a synagogue and a *mikveh,* along with a distant field designated for a cemetery.

Yehoshua would return to Jaffa only on Fridays, go to the textile store on Port Street, and climb to his and Olga's room on the second floor. When he spent time with her and with the other family members, he couldn't stop envying Aharon, who continued to stay near the Duran land and could go to it whenever he wanted but still not go beyond the Sabbath limit. Olga felt the restlessness surging through him when he was with her though she did not want to make things easier for him, just the opposite. She niggled at him with petty requests and a raft of questions;

she wanted to keep him near her and extend his stay. But he—early every Sunday morning, even before she awoke, would climb on his horse and gallop toward the wide-open spaces of Duran. Purim was only a few days away.

Purim, 1890

At the beginning of March, Yehoshua urged Olga to come with him to visit the Duran lands, ahead of all the others, so that he could show her its wonderful qualities. With scads of excuses, Olga refused. She had a lot to work to do, she told him, since the purchase of the tract had become public, many people were asking for details, and Yehuda Leib was only involved in talking about it, while her brother Israel was running up and back between the school and the store and adding even more chatter. Nevertheless, she was not willing to admit that she was afraid to go with him and see his success, to see the victory of the land.

Once she refused him, he stopped imploring her, and his involvement with Duran made him forget his desire to have her join him and share his love with her. He was so busy that he did not see that, as had happened in Gedera, Olga's face was growing grayer. Her eyes were sunken, and she became thinner; she was no longer interested in the store or the ups and downs occurring in Jaffa. All of her actions were mechanical: upon rising in the morning, she forgot to comb her hair, left her cup of coffee half full on the table, and rushed to the doctor's office, listening but not hearing what people said to her—so it was every day. Sometimes, while walking in the city's lanes, her husband's name played in her head, Yehoshua, Yehoshua, and she would imagine him walking by her side and asking her again to come and share his experience with him. She agreed, riding together with him and forgetting her sorrow. But Purim was approaching, and Yehoshua's visits home grew shorter, and all of her hinting was of no use. He was distant from her, very distant.

Now, Yehoshua would visit Jaffa once in two weeks to stay for Friday and Saturday. He did not come for Olga but for the purchases he had to make in the city or to solve some issue with the Turkish notary. He would sit with the family around the table, though his eyes did not take in his wife. He would tell stories about the land, and Yehuda Leib would thirstily drink in every word and ask him to repeat them so he could boast about the stories in the synagogue, and Tanhum would hang on to the back of the chair and ask to hear more and more. Olga would sit opposite her husband, not taking her eyes off him and trying to gain his attention, even just a short glance, and pleading with her looks for him to consider her, for him to be hers—even for one evening. But Yehoshua would keep his tales flowing and not think at all about her pain.

Not only was Olga trying to draw his attention, his mother, too, attempted to make him realize that the time had come to make his stays longer and concentrate on his own personal interests and not only on his land. But Yehoshua would dismiss her, murmuring into his beard, "After Purim," and become engrossed once again in telling his stories and his strong desire to return to the Duran land. Then, in the heart of night, when he would finally go up to his room, he would fall asleep in his clothes and not know when Olga joined him nor when she covered up with the same blanket, taking care not to touch him so as not to disturb his sleep.

Purim time was coming closer. Now, Yehoshua could not even take Fridays off and stopped coming to Jaffa. He only sent regards with laborers who went to the city to buy necessities.

During those weeks before the holiday, Olga began going to fortune-tellers and asking about offspring. She did not go alone. Her sister Sonia went along with her, first in mockery and as a joke, but then out of a growing fear for her sister. Olga did not stop with the seers in Jaffa but proceeded as far as Nablus, Jerusalem, and Hebron, and from each, she came away with different methods: a few taught her to rub her body with ointments and herbal mixtures; others recommended hanging garlic and onions in her room; some said to drink a wormwood concoction consisting of turbid water mixed with chaff and ash take from Rachel's Tomb; still other suggested to go about with a red thread tied to her wrist. Olga did everything she was told to—and unabashedly walked about the Jaffa streets in full view of everyone with the red thread tied to her arm.

During the week, she went to sleep early and evaded the questions of Sarah and the younger daughters who wanted to help her. She wanted neither their pity nor their involvement. She did not want to see their looks watching her every move. She preferred her bed to their company, even despite her fear of the long nights, in which she would turn over again and again on the bed in her loneliness and toss Yehoshua's pillow on the floor so as not to remember the indentation his head made in it. Then she would curl up in the big quilt they had received for their wedding. She would imagine and dream about a grain of soil growing and swelling and engulfing her until it filled the room, reaching into every corner and leaving nothing of her except one open, searching eye. The dream repeated itself every night, and sometimes it seemed to her that her holding onto the dream was greater than her fears. For some reason, she yearned for it, waited for it, and for the deep sleep that followed it, but there was nothing in either the hallucination or in the slumber to make her forget Yehoshua.

On the days that she didn't go to seek salvation from the women who read coffee grinds or cards or looked in crystal balls, she would make things hard for herself and work like a madwoman in the elderly doctor's office and in the store. She would visit ill women in all parts of Jaffa, and even in the sheikh's tents at the edge of the desert, riding in the Jaffa stagecoach.

Doctor Stein saw the bags under her eyes and her scrawniness as well as her gray face losing its vitality, and he tried to speak with her. But, when he explained to her that her situation was the result of pressure and fatigue and that the more she would work and travel, the more she would harm herself, it made no impression on her.

He said she and her husband were going through a difficult time and that she had to understand that it was imperative that Yehoshua not fail. He cajoled her with more words intended to encourage her and increase her stamina. She would laugh and mock his worrying about Yehoshua. One time, she told him bluntly, "Yehoshua needs the land and doesn't need a wife. If the land knew how to give birth, he would call me to help with the delivery. That's what I was meant for. But the land belongs only to him, and he doesn't want to share me with his other love."

The aged doctor trembled and suddenly understood her pain, and her fierce desire to have a child of her own became clear to him—something to hold on to and to be helped by, so as to keep Yehoshua near her. Now he could see the connection between all her visits to the soothsayers and witches, her lengthy silences, and the frenzy of work she had sunk into. The doctor wanted to comfort her and share with her what he had learned from life over the years. Once, when they were near the door to the clinic and about to take leave from each other at the end of a workday, he said to her, "If your husband doesn't spend time with you, how will you get pregnant?"

Olga was taken aback when she understood that her secret had been revealed. She ignored him and fled into the alley. The next day, she loaded herself with even more work. The doctor did not give up and spoke again about this issue and suggested she go to a different physician, more expert than he on barrenness. He mentioned a doctor who had recently come to Jaffa from Jerusalem and had a reputation for being very knowledgeable about the most recent advances. He found the name and address and gave them to Olga. But Olga did not reach out to take the note, and Stein just kept it, thinking she might change her mind.

When Olga's situation worsened, Dr. Stein went to the home of Meir Belkind and asked to speak with Sonia; he gave her the address of the new doctor. Sonia became very worried and took the advice he gave her and went to meet the new doctor, feeling the news would be bad. When she stood near the physician's door and saw the burnished copper sign bearing the name "Doctor Masie," her heart sank, and she did not know what she would say, in whose name she had come. Overcoming her great hesitation, she knocked firmly on the door.

Neither advice nor cure for Olga developed from that meeting, but Sonia's friendship and closeness with the doctor certainly grew. Sonia began to work for him and hoped that Olga would stop with her fads. She didn't have time now to keep an eye on her sister; she could only bring her a pile of booklets and studies on medical issues—maybe that would be enough for Olga.

Sonia was wrong. Olga needed no one, and since Sonia was not with her to calm her down, she became ever more involved with issues about her body. The closer Purim came, the more crowded the dresser became with jars of soapwort solution imported from the Orient and small bowls of medicinal herbs, whose wonderful aromas filled the room. The smell became part of her hallucination; Olga continued to toss and turn in bed, beat the earth, crumbling its clods to fine dust, and that speck of soil grew, swelled, and tossed dust into her open eye, and again Olga did not know if this was a dream or reality.

The day before the Fast of Esther, Yehoshua returned to Jaffa. This was not a Friday but just a most ordinary Monday. Jaffa hummed with the daily bustle: people ran in the streets and went down to the port and came up from it; porters carried wood beams; merchants hawked their wares; and the Jewish exiles from Moscow, noticeable by their unfamiliar clothing, went from one businessman to the next trying to decide where to invest their money. Yehoshua had forgotten how Jaffa looked when it wasn't Friday or Saturday and hurried to the store to meet his wife. Olga wasn't there; he found only Tanhum and Rivka, while the others had scattered with different tasks. Rivka told him that everyone would be back in the evening and tried to understand the reason for his unexpected arrival. She wanted to ask, but his coolness discouraged her, so she decided to keep quiet and leave priority to Olga.

Yehoshua went up to his room and looked for his Sabbath finery and his holiday hat, finding them in the wardrobe folded just so. Then, he dressed, polished the buttons of his coat, wiped off his boots, and went into the lane. First, he went to the Germans in the "German Colony" near the houses of Neve Tzedek and rented wagons from them. The Germans promised him to have them ready on Purim morning and agreed to add pillows, at no extra cost, to make the trip more comfortable for the riders. From there, he went to the port and ordered the diligence that went to Rishon Lezion, Ekron, and the other new moshavot. After finishing with travel arrangements, he headed for the small print shop to have them prepare small notes giving the place and time, along with a map sketching the way between Jaffa and the Duran land. When he had finished his tasks, he returned to the store, but Olga still wasn't there.

Yehoshua drifted between the counter and the storage room. He scrutinized buyers coming into the store to finish their last-minute purchases before the holiday. They asked for different kinds of colored ribbons, rummaged through the straw basket crammed with cheap metal decorations, and the Purim rattles set out in a bowl. Since there were only a few people, they did not need his help. So, he went up to his room to wait for Olga and think about the last few minor things he still had to do. He lay down on the bed and covered himself with the thick quilt and saw in his mind's eye a caravan of wagons, one stagecoach, and walkers, all on the same path. He tried to count them in his imagination

His eyelids grew heavy, and he fell into a deep sleep. He did not hear the crier going through the streets, announcing the end of the fast and the start of the festival: he did not hear the whoops of the children nor smell the aroma of the delights baking in the ovens, and he did not hear Olga coming in.

When she returned, Sarah informed her of her husband's arrival, so Olga rushed upstairs to meet him. She saw him sleeping in his clothes, sat down beside him on the bed, and looked at him. She noticed his gauntness and said to herself that the earth had consumed him, and the sun had scorched his face. If he would only stay by her side, she would take care of him and fuss over him like a baby, like the child she so fiercely wanted to have. She patted the stubble of his beard, straightened the creases in his pants, pulled off his boots, and arranged them neatly near the side of the bed, careful to make no noise. Then, she lay down next to him, leaning on her side; she looked at the lines of his face, the blotches from the sun, and the singed hair at the edges of his beard. As usual, she stretched out her hand and used her fingers to smoothen his broad forehead and swept down to his sunken eyes and proud nose. She stopped above his lips, not touching them. She wondered when she would tell him of her trouble. After Purim, she told herself, after the division of the land. For a moment, her dark thoughts surfaced again—and what if the sale will fail and they won't find buyers? She dispatched these musings and snuggled next to him. Then, adjusting her body to his, and fell asleep. She slept without imagining things. A heavy, comfortable, dreamless slumber came upon her, with the warmth of her husband engulfing her, and he smiled in his sleep, seeing caravan upon caravan proceeding to his lands. They lay together, close to one another, forgetting the preparations for the next day and the joy of the holiday, only the two of them by themselves, in their room.

Rays of sun skipped about the floor, full of dust motes. Purim morning— Yehoshua rose first and found his wife curled up at the end of the bed, not to take up too much space, still wearing her clothes.

"She didn't want to wake me up," he thought to himself and covered her with the comforter, tucking it in on both sides. Then, he wrote a note and put it on his pillow, moving it near hers, so she would see it as soon as she opened her eyes. "Wear elegant clothes," he wrote, "so everyone will know who my wife is, and I will be proud of you and proud of my tract. I will wait for you next to the well at the center of the tract so that my eyes will be aimed at you and not at the crowds coming with you."

Then, he washed his face and rushed to ride again to the Duran lands. Strands of black clouds collected at the edges of the sky, and a cold wind blew.

He hoped that the storm clouds would turn into cirrus clouds during the day, and the afternoon heat would overcome the cold. Yehoshua leaned on the horse's back and felt the wind cutting through his lungs, so he galloped faster and went further away from Jaffa toward the horizons of Duran.

❦

The lane turning from Port Street to Yehuda Leib's house began to fill up in the late morning. First, the wagons halted; then, the people came squeezing between the wheels and the horses, climbing up and catching places for themselves and others. A few put down bundles to save their place. They then alighted from the vehicles to go meet acquaintances and see who was coming and whether that included the Jaffa functionaries and the important residents. Finally, a few spread out kerchiefs and sat down, but then got up and left the wagons.

The wagons filled up quickly with bundles and kerchiefs, and people filled the space around them. Among them were penniless laborers, children in costume, woman showing off their dresses and eyeing the clothing of the other ladies, pot-bellied hacks who wore one coat on top of another—a winter one and a spring one. Pines was there, too, along with a group of functionaries, but they all sat in their own carriage, higher than all others. Pines' eyes darted about and counted those present. The more people came, and the greater the crowding, the more yellow his face became, and he lifted up the collar of his coat.

An hour went by. People climbed into the wagons and the diligence and prepared to set out. The bundles were placed between their feet or pushed to the ends of the wagon to make more space for other people who shoved each other. Sitting in the first wagon was the Belkind family with other Jaffa people. Israel sat on the coachman's seat, ready to show the way to the driver of the horses.

Sitting in the stagecoach were the associates of Yehoshua and Eisenberg, with Yehuda Leib leading them. The other wagons held the Jaffa riders, and last came Pines' carriage. Olga sat with the Hankin family, wearing festive clothing, as Yehoshua had asked. She rode silently, looking at the black clouds filling the sky. Sarah smiled and tried to be encouraging, and Rivka stuck close to her because of the cold. Olga drew a bit away as if asking to be alone and to prevent the noise of the wagon from reaching her—and she did not look toward Sarah.

Israel called to the horses, and the wagons set out with the screeching of the wheels on the paved streets and with the ringing of the reins and the shafts. But just as the wagons began to move, the first raindrops started to come down.

The Jaffa crowd sitting in the wagons murmured the Traveler's Prayer and broke out in song. The women competed to prove whose voice would be loudest and wanted all of Jaffa to be aware of their setting out and hearing it, and the children waved their Purim rattles. Then, to the sound of the singing, the shrieking of the wheels, the whistles of the wagon drivers, and the children's merriment, the horses galloped and left the Jaffa lanes. They were swallowed up on dirt roads, among the thorns and thistles just at the start of their ripening, as well as green oat florets.

The wagons passed by sand dunes and plodded through the brown soil; they quickly left behind the gates of Mikveh Israel and the boulevard of palms and turned onto paths that took them far away from the noise and bustle of the city. The people became quiet. The Jaffa homes could no longer be seen, and there was no one to sing to. The sky alternately became dark or clear, and the wagon riders were busy spreading out a covering over their heads for catching raindrops or removing them, as necessary when the sun's rays shone through until they saw the first houses of Rishon Lezion.

They made their first stop in the colony. It was not every day that such a large group came from Jaffa, and many knew each other, for Jews always know other Jews. So, a few of the travelers got off and visited their acquaintances to give out "Mishlo'ach Manot," gift food portions for Purim that they had carried with them and to receive portions and put them in their bundle. A few remained seated in the wagon to nibble at food and look from the heights of the wagon at what was going on in the courtyard and boulevard that wended its way to the top of the hill, with trees standing on both sides of it that were beautifully trimmed.

Olga stayed seated and noticed that the bougainvillea no longer climbed the trees, and their purple color no long struck the eye. She looked for Yehuda Leib's house and the barn that had become the winery. Someone had put up a high fence, and nothing could be seen behind it. She wanted to go and peep between the slits, but she was too weak to get up, so she just sat in place, with her ears ringing with the voices of the rebellion and Hanukkah songs.

Her brother Israel's call roused her. She straightened her back and looked at the people rushing to return to the wagons and grab their spots. They set out again, and this time, too, Pines' carriage was the last, with those sitting in it silently and scrutinizing every step and clod bringing them closer to the Duran lands. After they passed through a field of lupine and one of sesame, they entered the land of Wadi Hanin—the land of Reuven Lehrer—and encircled the orchard, and halted near the bushes climbing and clinging to the walls of the house. The impatient children jumped down from the wagons, but those in the know said, "We're not there yet."

The raindrops thickened and beat lightly on the coverings spread over the wagons. The women did not alight for fear of ruining their hairdos and clothing and satisfied themselves by calling to the children not to wander too far. Since they did not want to be considered annoying, their calls grew weaker and were swallowed among the drops. Mr. Lehrer came out of his house, along with a few of his workers who lived with him, and he waved in welcome to the visitors and was sorry when Israel yelled to the tots to go back and climb aboard the wagons. When those who had walked about to stretch their legs came back and gathered together, Olga descended from the Yehuda Leib family wagon and climbed onto Israel's. Israel was pleased she had come, and he went up and sat down next to her; Olga waved her hand to Lehrer. Now that she sat higher up with her brother and was far away from the looks of Sarah and the girls, she felt more comfortable and safer. She leaned on her brother's shoulder, and the more the clouds dispersed and moved apart, revealing the blue sky, the more her lungs expanded and her eyes opened, and she was ready to call out her husband's name to the universe and the expanses and to announce, "I'm coming! I'm coming!"

Olga knew the way. She was familiar with every bump and bush, each pothole and each scarp, and her flood of words burst forth like crashing waves. She told Israel about Reuven Lehrer's beautiful wife, about the sheikh and the birth of his son, about the Bnei Qatara and the sabra fruits ripening after the blossoming of the purple, orange, and red flowers. At times, she would straighten up in her seat and try to stand up and embrace the land with her eyes, and inadvertently, she would put her hands out to show the land her victory: she was going to her husband.

She asked Israel to make the horses go faster, and he, sensing her excitement and enthusiasm, urged them on. After their wagon sped up, the others increased their pace as well, for fear of lagging behind and getting lost.

The caravan crossed the sabra field, turned into the plain, and then passed low, black hair tents scattered around like the goats who lay dispersed in a field at rest time.

Olga was the first to see the well, its cover, its dome, and the figure standing over it, waving to her with a hat and an open mouth, yelling something she couldn't understand. After her, Israel noticed the figure and pulled on the reins, the horses slowing their march. The wagons, the stagecoach, and the carriage neared each other, practically bumping into one another, and arranged themselves in one long line. Olga jumped down from the wagon while it was still rolling and began to run, drawn by Yehoshua's unheard calls. She tucked the hems of her dress into her belt and didn't feel the mud spraying abut, nor the drops spattering her face, and she did not see the figure standing atop the dome.

When she reached the well and halted at its foot, she reached out for Yehoshua, while he stretched out his hands and lifted her. Now, both stood on the top and surveyed the expanses of land that abutted the cloud-covered peaks, with the wind buffeting them and their tears stinging their eyes. They did not see the wagons nearing the well nor the people alighting from them and crowding together next to the stone wall, lifting their eyes up to the peak and wondering where they were and about the two standing above. They did not pay attention to the diligence or to Pines' carriage that halted at a distance and did not dare come too close.

Aharon was the first to break the silence. He approached the circle of people and called for the crowd to follow him. Obediently, they did what he asked and clustered around him, trying to take in his words while attempting to hide from the wind at the same time. Aharon explained to them what the borders of the estate were and, with his toes, drew the streets and boulevards and squares and, within the squares, houses with tile roofs and groves and orchards. Then, they followed after him and went around the tract until they stopped next to broad wooden beams laden with many kinds of sweets and liquor. The people ate the food offered on the plates and raised their glasses, and only when the plates and glasses were empty did they remember the frigid air and their distance from any inhabited place and wrapped themselves in their scarves. Women were sorry they had dressed lightly and sought refuge from the cold. Now, they are recalled that they had come here to watch the division of the land into plots and not to stand about with an empty glass in hand. Women yelled out, looking for their children; men looked towards the setting sun and began to fidget restlessly in place.

And just at that moment, the air was pierced with the cry, "Rehovot! They'll call the tract of land Rehovot!"

Everyone stopped what they were doing and turned toward the source of the shout. They saw Aharon Eisenberg standing on the dome next to Yehoshua and Olga, waving with the scroll he was holding, "Measure with your feet, take broad steps, choose a plot. This is a sales contract. Yehoshua Hankin bought the land. See the expanses around you and look at the man. He is a great man, and his deeds are great."

The people were not inspired by his enthusiasm and excitement and did not know what he wanted, for most of them had come out of curiosity and not to buy land. Who would go settle on the rocky ground between fences of sabras?

Aaron saw the look on their faces and was unwilling to give in to their fear. He jumped down from the dome, grabbed a bearded Torah scholar by hand, and pulled him after him, capering and dancing in front of the crowd. But they simply stood still. Aharon took hold of a child's hand and of a young man, joined them, and pulled them after him; slowly, a chain of men formed, and at its side was a line of women. The chains turned into circles that came, touched each other, and drew away from one another, touching and pulling away.

The tempo of the dancing grew faster and faster, whether from the cold or from Aharon's calls, and the fears began to fade away.

Three people stayed far away from the circles and did not take part in the dancing or the tumult: Yehoshua and Olga, who still stood on the dome of the well and looked at each other, and Mister Pines, who sat in the carriage with his eyes cast down to its wooden floor, turned away from the merriment.

14. Olga and the Whip on her rides to help with the birth of Bedouin children, 1890
Source: Central Zionist Archives

Purim was over. Yehoshua went back to working in the store, or rather, he went back to spending time in the store, waiting for buyers to come and purchase plots of the Duran land. But Jaffa was silent, and no longer spoke about Duran. Other things arose to engage them: the matters of the associations and merchants and the wealthy, and the quarrels between the Sephardim and the Ashkenazim. The days grew longer, Yehoshua's face paled, while Olga's became pink, and she gained some weight and became stronger.

Non-stop talking overwhelmed her. She stopped visiting the fortune-tellers and the soothsayers. She threw away the medicinal herbs and hid the jars containing ointments. Her husband sat with her, and the Duran land was far away, but in the same way that he did not see the pallor of her face at other times, she did not see his sadness at this time.

Yehoshua began to worry. His father took off his holiday finery—he no longer needed it, since he had stopped going to the Chelouche synagogue in Neve Tzedek and preferred the small prayer hall next to Israel Belkind's school. He did not berate his son and did not say a word to him—he simply didn't speak. Rather, his eyes betrayed his thoughts, and Yehoshua could not look directly at him.

Winter passed into spring, and in Jaffa, people began to take their down comforters out to the streets, hang carpets on the stone fences and paint the entrances to the stores blue and green to protect against the evil eye. And when the pleasant smells from the orchards surrounding Jaffa wafted through the air, Yehoshua left the store's counter and began to go down to the harbor. Again, he took Tanhum with him, like in the days before the land deals, and together they looked at the "newcomers" arriving in the port, hoping to see a rich person and find a way to convince him to purchase the Duran lands. But unfortunately, he was feverish, hallucinating, and in the store, they said, "spring fever," but Olga knew—it was land fever. And the more he went down to the harbor, the more infected he became with the idea of the "wealthy man."

Sitting at the table in Yehuda Leib's house, he would calculate the wealth of the Muscovites, and if Olga would tell him, "Not all of them are rich," he denied her statement and repeated, "Very, very wealthy."

He asked Yehuda Leib to tell him about the large estates once again, the farms he had leased and made sure to harvest the barley, wheat, and potatoes. Time after time, he said that if he would find a rich man, he would suggest to him to act like in Russia: to buy large estates where laborers would work and build a colony adjacent to it.

Olga refused to listen to Yehuda Leib's stories and repeatedly claimed, "This is all nonsense, megalomania. What rich man would agree to put money into such an uncharted venture?" Yehoshua made himself deaf to her arguments and climbed up to their room later and later; he increasingly wrapped himself up in his quilt on one side of the bed and refused to feel his wife's yearning body.

One day, Tanhum brought Yaakov Karlinsky to Yehuda Leib's home. He was a wealthy nineteen-year-old lad with a babyface, only a bit bigger than Tanhum, who lived in Nadarzyn near Warsaw. Yaakov tried to hide his origin and his being extremely rich. Still, with their special sense, the beggars felt that a prize had fallen into their hands and were drawn to him. That was how Tanhum found him—trapped in an alley, not far from Port Street, with one beggar pulling his coat and begging, and not letting go, and another beggar, a lame one, blocking his way and waving his cane, threatening him. The young fellow did not understand what the beggars were saying, was disgusted by them, and covered his face with his hands, exposing his gold watch. Just when the beggar stretched out his hand to snatch it, and the lame one readied his cane to hit him and knock him down, Tanhum happened upon them in that alley and drove the beggars away from there; then, he invited Karlinsky to his father's house.

It was a Friday when Karlinsky came to Yehuda Leib's home. The first to see him and welcome him happily was Olga, since, by his accent and his clothes, he reminded her of other places and stirred memories and yearnings. So, Olga sat next to him and asked him a great many questions in his own language, and the boy enjoyed the attention he was given. The other family members saw him as a wanderer sampling the atmosphere of a new country and becoming excited by everything, so they paid slight attention to him. Even Yehoshua did not devote too much of his time to him and sat at the corner of the table, talking about the ships arriving from Moscow and Warsaw and about the best time to go down to the harbor to look at them. He was not envious of his wife and did not feel her enthusiasm, while the young man, after the fourth shot glass of liquor, began to speak and tell the story of his life, with his voice carrying in the room.

The young fellow was not used to drinking, and stories that were supposed to be kept secret made their way around the room. Those present halted their other talks and gathered round him and Olga. Yehoshua snapped his eyes open, as if waking from a long winter's hibernation, and followed the discussion. Then, he left his seat and moved toward his wife, standing behind her and rubbing her neck in circles. Olga enjoyed his touch as she conversed with the guests and the very fact that he addressed his questions to her and that the others were paying attention.

Karlinsky related that his father had died and left him a large amount of money, and that his uncle, who had become his guardian, had sent him abroad to test his ability to conduct business and support himself.

He had given him a year, and when it was over, he had to return to Nadarzyn and present himself to him. If found worthy, he would inherit his father's wealth and do with it as he please. If the conclusion was that he had no business sense, the large amount of money would go to charitable works, with only a scant amount going to Yaakov to support himself. The young Karlinsky was worried about the assignment and about the test, but he had no choice, so he had left Warsaw and gone to Paris.

He liked the city, but he did not know how to open a business there. The language and the currency—everything was different from Nadarzyn—so he packed his bags and traveled on to Italy. There he met two swindlers who proposed opening a joint business dealing with pelts. They went to a bank, and he was supposed to sign and guarantee all their actions. When the clerk realized his confusion, he took him aside and warned him not to act rashly. The boy was frightened and left there by a back door, went down to the port, and embarked on a ship sailing to Greece. He spent two days on the dock of the Piraeus port and going from bar to bar, drinking and getting to know the pleasures of life. On the evening of the second day, he was sitting with a glass of wine in hand and a pretty girl at his side and heard about a ship headed for Palestine and recalled his father's stories about the Holy Land. So, he joined the ship to sail there to see if things were really happening in Palestine, as he had heard. After a lengthy voyage on stormy seas, he finally reached Jaffa, intending to stay for a few days and then to travel by wagon to Jerusalem—maybe he would find a rambler who would be willing to take him to the Judean Desert because he had a strong urge to float on the Dead Sea. Perhaps after that, he would come across a camel caravan going to Egypt and spend a few days in Alexandria.

Yaakov went on and on, and the family members began to leave the table. At first, his stories interested them, but then they shook their heads and muttered to themselves, "A boy who has a windfall and does not know what to do with it. How unfair that is!" Only Olga continued to sit next to him, with Yehoshua standing behind the backrest of her chair. Yaakov went on chattering the prattles of youth and paid no attention to his meager audience nor to the wee hour.

Then, when Olga yawned, the young fellow got up on shaky legs and looked for his coat to go to his hotel room. But even before he took one step, he stumbled and fell back onto his seat. He apologized to Olga and tried to rise again, and this time Yehoshua gave him a hand.

The entire evening, Yehoshua had kept still, and the young man had not even noticed he was there, though now he looked at him and asked him his name, and from the look on his face, one could tell that he was sorry to hear that the woman sitting next to him was married. But Yehoshua did not see his expression, since he was deep in thought and then suggested the fellow stay overnight with them. Then, as if caught in a misdeed, the youth blushed, refused the hand offered him and sat down again.

"You have a nice wife," he noted.

Yehoshua did not hear those words, since he expected to hear something else, and again urged the young man to stay. This time the fellow agreed, but Olga felt uncomfortable—where to offer him a bed—their room was so small? She looked at her husband, trying to unravel his thoughts, and saw his eyes were shining, passing by her but not even seeing her. She was frightened, since she knew that he would not be staying in the store much longer, and his nights with her were also few, and she had hoped to become pregnant before he went off again.

Olga offered the guest a mattress in the tiny kitchen and went to their room. Yehoshua took the young man, sat him down in a chair, and poured him a cup of tea, while for himself, he prepared boiling water with lemon peel floating in it. The fellow sobered up slowly and began to recall the events of the evening. Yehoshua brought his chair close to the visitor's and sat so close their knees touched. Then he told him about the bureaucracy in Palestine and about the time of the rebellion in Rishon Lezion. He discussed with him the rulers' decrees and the pressure of the apartment owners, about the expulsion from Moscow, and ways to make money. He described the pain of the earth sprouting thistles and also of the wonders of the Duran land. The young man began to be engaged with the man with the long hair and deep-set eyes, and his own eyes grew wider from what he was hearing. In his imagination, he saw the picture depicted for him: caravans making their way on the paths out of Jaffa toward Duran, with people plowing on the sides of the road and shepherds with their flocks scattered on the hill. When dawn broke, Karlinsky asked Yehoshua to take him to the Duran tract, but even before he finished making his request, he stretched out his legs and fell asleep on the spot. Yehoshua looked at him and saw a child's smile spread on his face and heard his gentle breathing; he took off his tattered student coat, covered the fellow with it, and left him to go up to his room.

Even though the house was still, Olga did not manage to fall asleep, and deeply afraid, she lay in her bed and waited for Yehoshua. She heard the rustling from the kitchen and then heard the creaking of the door as Yehoshua came into their room. From the corner of her eye, she saw him pull off his boots and lay down in his clothes next to her; she felt his movements from under her quilt. She snuggled next to him, trying to put an end to his distance from her. While still settling in, he breathed in her scents and glided over her shivering skin, making her tremble. When he moved her hair away from her ear and whispered to her, "I found buyers for the Duran land," she knew this night was different. Her quivering grew stronger, and she drew her body a bit away from him, but he didn't want her pulling away and drew her to him, clasping her waist fiercely, and she wanted him with all her being. He caressed her and calmed her down; slowly, her trembling ceased, and she responded to him. At first, hesitantly, but then she was swept away with her love and released her pain for a while.

Yaakov Karlinsky wrote a long letter to his guardian and showed it to Olga. She laughed at his description of the beauty of Palestine as could be drawn from his letter, to the words that belonged to Yehoshua and not to a youth. In his letter, he related that the conditions in the country were good and that it was possible to make easy profit in buying and selling land. He already had a plan for commercial investment: to buy a large tract and divide it into plots. He even implied that he had been offered a tract and thought of turning to wealthy people in Europe to invest in it. They would not have to pledge to immigrate to Palestine but would hand the plots over for cultivation by laborers who were crowding the streets of the cities, and they, because they were paupers, would agree to work for meager wages.

He asked Olga's advice and added to the letter that he had heard that it was worthwhile growing grapes and almonds in Palestine. The workers would plant and till, and once the orchard was productive, the owner of the plot would come and enjoy the results of the harvest. They could invest the profits from the orchard in factories, banks, hotels …. The plan amused Olga. For some reason, when these statements came from the young man, they sounded different from when Yehoshua offered them. She was willing to forgive the youth and smile when hearing his fancies and dreams, since his words could not harm her. But when she spoke with Yehoshua about land and settling it, she would become tense and apprehensive. She wanted to ask Yehoshua many questions, though she didn't dare pour her heart out to him and the silences increasingly weighed her down, but she did ask Karlinsky, and she also responded and was considered thoroughly knowledgeable by him.

Karlinsky waited for an answer, and in the meantime, became a close friend of Yehuda Leib's family. He went along with Yehoshua on his trips to Reuven Lehrer's farm and to his meetings with Eisenberg; he tried to walk around barefoot but only hurt his feet; he also bought Arab garb, an abaya, and an aqel, to protect himself from the sun and to look like the easterners he had seen in drawn in travel books. His face turned red from the sun, and his skin cracked, but he did not manage to become suntanned, and he remained a foreign figure. He had forgotten his wish to go to Jerusalem and to float on the Dead Sea, and he wasted a lot of money. In Jaffa, a rumor quickly spread about Karlinsky's wealth, and people began to talk about him respectfully. Since he had become friendly with Olga, people asked her to help make a match. Since she didn't, the busybodies began to whisper behind his back—he was in love with Olga, and Yehoshua didn't notice. Karlinsky didn't hear the gossip, but it most certainly reached Olga and the other family members as well.

Sonia, who had begun to work at Doctor Masie's, reported that women coming to the office prattled that Karlinsky was Olga's lover and that was no wonder, since she had preferred a young man over more mature suitors and married him, but that "youth" was away from home and involved in other things. There were no children to keep him connected to his home and his wife. So why shouldn't she seek consolation with other young fellows?

Olga dismissed the matter, claiming that they were only gossipers aimed at muddying her name and her husband's as well, but even so, she began to be circumspect about her meetings with Karlinsky.

Karlinsky, in contrast, did indeed love Olga's company, but he was not attracted to her but rather to her husband. After the first evening when he realized that Olga was married and after he got to know her husband well, Olga was the link connecting him to Yehoshua. From her, he learned about Yehoshua's habits and deeds and tried to imitate him as much as possible. When he had had enough with the kaffiyeh and the aqel, he came across an old student coat in the used clothes market, let his hair grow long like Yehoshua's, and learned how to raise his eyebrows the way Yehoshua did.

The hoped-for letter from Nadarzyn did not arrive; Olga became accustomed to the whispers; Karlinsky became used to Jaffa, and Yehoshua still hoped. On one of the last days of cleaning before Passover, the letter with the reply came from Warsaw. Tanhum, who had brought Karlinsky to Yehoshua, also brought the letter. As usual, he went down to the port to see the approaching ships, and since he always followed the same path, he made it a habit to bring the letters from the post office. When he saw the stamps and the foreign address, he began to run and look for Karlinsky. He didn't find him at the hotel, so he hurried to Olga. Perhaps he was spending time with her. Karlinsky was not there, but Olga was, and she took the envelope from his hand and read the address in Russian aloud. Tanhum realized her excitement and asked where the fellow was. She replied that Karlinksy had gone with Yehoshua to her brother Israel's school. Tanhum left the letter with her and dashed away to bring them.

When he reached the school, he found the three of them in the center of a group of wee ones—Israel holding a jar of seeds in his hand, Yehoshua teaching them the names of the seeds, with Karlinsky breaking his teeth over the Hebrew names and the children laughing at his unclear language. Tanhum impatiently entered the circle and informed Yehoshua about the letter. Yehoshua stopped him in mid-sentence and looked for words to tell Yaakov, and when he couldn't find them, pulled his coat and took him out of the circle, instructing him to go with him.

The three went down to the lane, and while running, Yehoshua told him of the letter waiting for them in the store. The spring heat worked its magic, and they began sweating, and as they ran, they took off their upper layers and let their hair and coat wings flap in the air. Looking like a group of madmen to the passersby—the two bearded fellows and the youth ran through the alleyways—and everyone made way for them, avoiding bumping into them. When they reached the entrance to the store, they squeezed in, breathing heavily, their lungs about to burst. After they calmed down a bit, Karlinsky was handed the letter by Olga and with apologetic eyes, went to sequester himself in the small room at the store's end.

Tanhum wanted to follow after him, but Yehoshua held him back, saying, "Leave him alone. Let him get the first taste of Warsaw. The letter is all his, and we are just waiting for his decision."

Olga, who sensed his effort to hide his fears, looked up and went to him to reinforce him. While Tanhum, who didn't know how to understand Yehoshua's calm, burst out, "Your entire future is in the letter, and you're quiet?" But Yehoshua only held Olga's hand, crushing her fingers to the point of pain.

Nightfall came, and Yaakov was still little in the small chamber. The impatient Tanhum, who paced the store like a caged lion and took merchandise off the shelves and put it down, and then did it again and looked at it, went out to the lane but immediately came back, asking, "Nu?"

Finally, they saw Karlinsky coming out of the small room. Tanhum ran toward him, but Yaakov Karlinsky ignored him and turned to Yehoshua and stood opposite him, while Olga saw that his youthful expression was gone and was now replaced by a feeling of power and maturity.

"I am ready for business," said the young man, addressing only Yehoshua, as if no one else were present. "You will buy the Duran land, the money will be paid in full and Yehuda Leib's property will be released and not serve as a guarantee for your acquisitions." He was quiet for a moment, then took one more step toward the bearded man and added, "I am also great, like you. You bring the land, and I will bring the plot owners, and in Jaffa and Warsaw and Nadarzyn, they will say—Yehoshua Hankin conducts business with Yaakov Karlinsky." The fellow came even closer and handed him the letter as if seeking to prove what he had said, with tears of excitement running down his face. Yehoshua turned his face away from him, trying to conceal his zeal. However, Olga saw, and at that second, all memories of the aggravation she had undergone and all her hopes for a child of her own were forgotten. She was familiar with his weakness. She knew the power of the land and prayed with all her might for his success. She did not want to see him fall again and be dragged down to the bottom of the pit.

Passover ended, and Karlinsky returned to Warsaw to take care of his business and found a company for buying the plots of Duran. A month after he left Eretz Israel, a letter came from him, informing them he had found "a match," a young Enlightened woman. They had even managed to establish an association named "Menuchah ve-Nachalah" (Rest and State), which had already sent emissaries on their way to Palestine to move matters along and fulfill his promise to Yehoshua. These representatives should be arriving in a few weeks.

Above the entrance to his store, Yehuda Leib had hung a sign, "Yehoshua Hankin, Land Agent—Selling and Buying." Inside the store, the small chamber had been assigned to Yehoshua's business with the hope that he would be kept very busy with it. Olga had sprinkled a cup of rice on the room's threshold as a good luck charm for many buyers, and without anyone seeing, she sprinkled a few grains on herself—a charm for sons. Summer had broken out in the Jaffa lanes. People came into the store to ask about land. Yehoshua promised each one that he would ask for information and inquire about their request after the Warsaw emissaries had arrived.

In July, the representatives of "Menuchah ve-Nachalah" reached Jaffa: Yaakov BroideBroide and Eliahu Lewin-Epstein. As soon as they had disembarked, they immediately headed for Yehuda Leib's store to look for Yehoshua and give him the letter handed to them by Yaakov Karlinsky.

The lumbering BroideBroide entered first, and while still filling the doorway with his body, he decreed, "I have bought the leadership of the Menuchah ve-Nachalah society." To prove that, he showed those present in the store a certificate of confirmation stating that BroideBroide had bought five plots.

Then he looked over the people there and announced that he was seeking the land agent—Yehoshua Hankin.

Sarah pointed out Yehoshua to him with a nod, and when Broide turned to face him and saw who they were speaking about, he muttered to him, "But you're just a boy! How will you know how to deal with such serious things? Where is your father?" adding to himself, "This must be a mistake, and Karlinsky meant the father, not the son."

Broide looked at Yehoshua again and was not sorry for what he had said; then, he went to the counter to examine the fabrics. Broide's entrance had hidden the approach of the other emissary. Only once Broide had gone a bit away toward the counter where Eliahu Epstein revealed—a thin young man with eyes reflecting a good heart. Epstein walked toward Yehoshua like someone asking forgiveness for the rude behavior of his associate and offered his hand to Yehoshua, "I've heard a lot about you. Karlinsky never stops praising you." Then, he told him about their plan to visit Jaffa and the colonies and learn about transactions and the ways to invest in Eretz Israel and examine the quality of the Duran soil to know how to advise the association members in Warsaw. Once they have finished their inquiries and examinations, they will come to Yehoshua with their answer as to what they will advise the society members in Warsaw.

Yehoshua heard but didn't understand; hadn't he already concluded with Karlinsky about the sale of the land? And, what was the meaning of the examination and analysis? Yehoshua became frightened and felt doubts creeping in. He had been sure that everything had been settled, and now it was all open again, and there was no agreement, for Broide considered him a "child" unfit for business. Yehoshua glanced at Epstein, whose kind eyes reassured him. He looked at Broide, and the contempt and mockery in his eyes filled his heart with dread. Yehoshua kept still since he was dependent upon them and their decision, and until he could write to Karlinsky to clarify the issue of the emissaries and then receive a response, quite a while would go by. Better to wait patiently and to see how things would turn out.

The emissaries spent a few days in Jaffa before Yehoshua rented a carriage and took them to the Duran land. Olga joined them. She was not thrilled by the delay and shared Yehoshua's fears. On the way, they visited Rishon Lezion. Yehoshua stayed in the vehicle, and Olga accompanied the association representatives and showed them the Administration Center, the winery, and the farmers' yards. With his eyes, Broide estimated the value of the houses and calculated the cost of putting up the fences and the silos, and came to conclusions about the other colonies by considering Rishon Lezion. He told Olga that founding a colony in Palestine was an expensive undertaking and had to be reconsidered. But Olga did not tell this to Yehoshua. Next, they stopped in Wadi Hanin, at Reuven Lehrer's farm, and Broide did not hide his disgust from the weeds growing along the walls, while Epstein was thrilled by the display of growing roses and was enthusiastic about the beautiful woman from Odessa. When they reached the well on the Duran tract, Yehoshua alighted with them and waited silently for the emissaries' reaction. Epstein separated himself from them and went to walk around the borders of the tract; he picked sabras and returned with thorns sticking out of his hands. He stretched his hand out to Olga so she could remove them and gave her a happy smile. "The parcel is very nice. The expanses are beautiful. What fruit is in my hand?" Broide, contrarily, did not move from his place near the well wall and surveyed the site by looking, making his calculations, and murmuring into his trimmed beard without even looking at Yehoshua.

When they returned to Jaffa, Yehoshua urged them to make their decision. Epstein clapped his hands like a small child, and Broide made him stop with a flick of his hands, saying, "Some questions remain unanswered. I haven't decided yet. But, when I do make up my mind, I'll let you know."

The emissaries got off near the hotel where they were staying, while Yehoshua and Olga continued home and returned to the carriage, with anxiety gnawing at their hearts.

Days passed, and Broide's answer did not arrive. In Jaffa, people began to be familiar with the two of them and laughed at Yehoshua, "Those two have loads of time. Nothing is urgent. Until Broide examines every inch of the soil, he won't give his agreement. He's a 'businessman' and has the soul of a 'haggler.'"

Actually, the two often walked about the lanes of Jaffa, examining and scrutinizing every possible facet. In fact, Broide was the one doing the looking, and Epstein dragged after him. It was strange to see the two of them together: Broide marching along swiftly, passing everyone and never turning his head, but yelling from time to time, "Eliyahu!" to check that Epstein was still near him. Epstein would increase his pace to catch up to him and hear what he was saying. Broide would examine merchandise the stores offered, and Epstein would stand in the alley, give a coin to a beggar, and ask questions as his reward. He wanted to know about tombs of the saints in Eretz Israel, about its places and its rivers, but the answers were never enough.

After the joking came the seriousness. Jews began to come to Yehuda Leib's store to discuss the petty issues of Jaffa. Still, occasionally they would sneak in the names of Broide and Epstein: Look, one of them has approached Pines and sits on the same bench with him in the synagogue, and they drink coffee together, while the other went away from Jaffa. Eliyahu Epstein located a donkey and joined a group of Hasidim who were traipsing between Safed and Mount Meron to visit the graves of the 'Tzaddikim,' righteous Jewish figures. When Yehoshua and Olga heard these things, they trembled even more. But instead of pushing them apart and each one shutting out the other, they held on to each other in search of consolation.

At first, Olga was astonished by the fear bringing them closer and told her sister about her hesitations. "This is not the usual way," she said, "a couple is supposed to be together for good and bad, but with us, only the bad brings us closer."

Sonia tried to calm her down, thinking that perhaps the time had come when Yehoshua would concentrate on his own household. But Olga laughed and abandoned all thought of an infant and a home of their own. She did not like the feeling of fear and helplessness, but Yehoshua's situation was worse than hers, and she saw comfort and dependence and a strong connection in that.

When she thought his pain had become unbearable, she sat down and wrote a letter to Karlinsky, but Yehoshua didn't know.

The summer of 1890 was not only the season of the Duran land. That summer, masses of Jews came to Jaffa, all of them looking for a way to become established in Eretz Israel. Not only did the exiles from Moscow come and not only rich Jews stopping in Jaffa when heading to America, and not even laborers looking for salvation for themselves and for the new teachings spreading around the world. Representatives of Russian associations arrived, as did Jews bringing along families, all of them prompted by the rumor that in Eretz Israel, it was possible to make a lot of money. They would leave the boats that took them from the ship to the port and trod on the Jaffa sidewalks, wearing layers of coats so as not to have to carry them by hand and holding the many bundles that held all their worldly goods.

Every Sunday, a wagon full of those families would set out from the Turkish post office and turn north toward the river of Nahal Uja or go southward to the dunes of Nabi Rubin. In the evening, it would return with the families who got out and rushed to stand in line in the Soup Kitchen, where they debated whether it was worthwhile investing their money in the land they had just visited or to wait for a better deal. While they were eating the steaming stew, they would check the pockets of their coats stuffed with money to make sure it was still there. The Jaffa traders would hear of their hesitations; in the meantime, the price of a dunam rose, and land speculators burgeoned like mushrooms after the rain.

Even Broide joined in the tumult of the newcomers and became involved and investigated the value of the Duran land in comparison with the others. From Pines, he learned the Turkish laws and accompanied him when he negotiated with people looking for a plot, and he heard from him what a lout and ignoramus "the young Hankin" was about land matters. Broide, who didn't realize the venom in those words, was influenced by them and his contempt for Yehoshua only grew.

Yehoshua ignored the crowds filling the streets of Jaffa and did not feel the rush for land that gripped all of them and continued to wait for the reply from the "Menuchah ve-Nachalah" emissaries. Olga, in contrast, was aware of the passion igniting the newcomers when they spoke about land. She saw that love in their covetous eyes and among the traders lurking on the street corners, offering one square foot in the city and a dunam in a rural area at rock bottom prices. She could not bear to listen to them. They would come to the clinic and ask for a pill against malaria or headaches and stomach aches but were unwilling to stay in the clinic to rest and get better, lest they miss any new kernel of information about any tract and not be among those haggling over it.

They reminded her of a brood of hens, standing around a basket full of wheat kernels, each one pecking the feathers of the other and grabbing a wheat berry and then spitting it back into the container. The basket stays full, but the fighting over it just grows worse. She told this to Yehoshua and asked him to go to Broide to get a straight answer from him, but if Broide refused to respond, she suggested that he threaten him that he would find other buyers for the Duran land. Yehoshua did not listen to her, not wanting to press the issue. He repressed the frenzy enveloping Jaffa, and his ear was only tuned to listen to the bits of information telling about the growing friendship between Broide and Pines.

In the afternoon of the Tenth of Av, one day after the commemoration of the mourning and destruction of the Jewish Temple, Broide came to Yehuda Leib's store to inform them of his decision. Eliahu Epstein did not come with him. He was in Galilee or maybe in Jericho—no one knew where he was.

Yehoshua waited in the store, whether he felt he would come or because he had nothing else to do. He sat hunched over on the board, staring at one point. Then, when Broide came in, Yehoshua jumped up, combed through his beard with his fingers, straightened his clothes that had become wrinkled from sitting, and called to Sarah to serve steaming coffee in a glass cup. Next, he invited him into the small room, moved a chair toward him, and watched his Adam's apple rising and falling as he drank. And when Broide finished, he slapped his cup down on the table, and words began to pour hastily out of his mouth in a rush, so Yehoshua had no chance to respond. He had received a letter from Karlinsky. The young man was asking to conclude the matters of the "Menuchah ve-Nachalah" association, and that being the case, Broide would expedite his decision and announce the purchase of all of the Duran lands.

Yehoshua took a deep breath, and Broide kept on speaking: the land would be divided into two. One part would be handed over to the society members, and the other would be sold legally to whoever would meet the price. The profits would be shared by the association members and used to develop all the plots.

Yehoshua began to be suspicious. These things sounded to him too good to be true, and something in Broide's tone didn't seem right to him. He surveyed the speaker opposite him with a furrowed brow and thought he could discern a flickering smile at the corner of his mouth. Now, Broide raised his voice, "The association pledges to make all its payments on time; Karlinsky will be the guarantor for the members and the payments in the presence of "the young Hankin."

"But listen, my friend," and Yehoshua realized what was about to hit him. "Listen to the conditions I am making. Karlinsky is a baby and doesn't understand business, so he left the decision up to me. You're too young to be a land dealer. In Jaffa, they call you "a revolutionary," inciting others to rebel. Land agents whispered to me that you don't stand by your word. But I'll ignore what they said, if you prove to me that they are wrong. Instead, prepare a proper, legal purchase contract, get a kushan for each plot separately, make the Arab neighbors who border the Duran lands sign so they won't come with claims, and you will obtain building permits from the sultan. If you do all this, the deal will stand; if you leave out one issue—everything is null and void."

Broide finished and sat comfortably in his chair, with his folds of fat dripping on the sides and his small eyes laughing in contempt and waiting for Yehoshua's response.

Yehoshua was still. He took in the words slowly, and on his fingers, hiding behind his back, he counted off Broide's demands one by one. Sweat began to accumulate between his fingers, and he was afraid to open his mouth in case his voice would reveal his dread. Perhaps, he hadn't understood the representative's message, since everyone knew it was impossible to go to the Turkish land office and demand a kushan from a Turkish clerk, and register Turkish land in the name of a Jewish Russian subject.

He saw the sardonic grin on Broide's face and understood well that his intention was to make Yehoshua fail. He was very familiar with the limits of Turkish law, preventing sale of land to a Jew who was not a Turkish subject. He had spent the past few weeks with Pines and saw how negotiations over land were carried out. If he told him to register the entire tract on the name of a single Jew who was an Ottoman subject, he would find a way. But Broide insisted on registering each one separately. Yehoshua had already forgiven him for the nickname he had stuck him with, since he knew Pines well and the bad advice lurking behind his demands, but how could he meet them all?

Now, his entire body was dripping with sweat; it flowed under his armpits, and the yoke of his collar and was absorbed in the rough material. His rage began to collect in his innards, and he felt the words choking him and ready to explode and hit Broide. He dug his fingernails into his palm, feeling the pain, and pulled himself together. His words came out broken and stammering.

Broide cupped his ear and motioned to him to raise his voice. Yehoshua spoke louder and slowly, "I will get a kushan. For now, one kushan for the whole property. I will find a Turkish subject in whose name the land will be registered, and at the right time, the division will be made, and each parcel registered separately. I'll also try to get building permits, God willing." He paused and saw how the man opposite him was running out of patience and hurried to add, "In Palestine, things are done differently. It takes time. Until you don't pay the price of the land, we won't be able to get things going. Pay the price. I will repay my debt and be able to take a new loan and deal with the other permits."

Broide set his legs down and stood up defiantly, saying loudly, "You are a really young fellow, a boy who doesn't understand business. Who will be willing to put his money in such a flighty risk and receive a plot not registered in his name? My friend Pines was right. No one should do business with you. He warned me about you, but I didn't listen." He was quiet for a minute, looked over his notes about what he had said, and went on. Out of respect for Karlinsky, I will give you an extension to obtain the kushans in the name of the Russian members of the association, as well as permits for the houses. If you don't get them—I will look elsewhere for land. From the day I arrived in Jaffa, thronging my door from early morning are many speculators who have earmarked land." He looked at Yehoshua's drooping shoulders and moved to stand opposite him to catch his glance and see his pain, "Why do you need all this? Take care of your household, of your wife. I have heard she longs for children, but how will there be any if you keep running around to see pieces of land? Having offspring is an important commandment. Without it, we won't be about to fulfill any other, not even that of settling the country."

Yehoshua's hands turned into fists; his eyes gave off sparks, and his body tensed. How could he dare talk down to him? What's the connection between Duran and Olga? An old reprobate! A fat merchant! Yet, his hands remained clenched, and he uttered quietly, "Give me the extension, and I will try to meet your conditions."

Broide left the small chamber without turning to face Yehoshua, without saying goodbye, and without thanking him for the coffee, only muttering behind his back, "Only ten days will I wait."

Yehoshua followed him, his head spinning and his knees atremble. His fury overpowered his sight, and he noticed neither Sarah, his mother, nor his sisters, and he left the store with tears welling in his eyes—and he was not embarrassed by them. He just called out to the interior of the store to tell Olga that he had gone to look for Aharon Eisenberg at the Lehrer farm or perhaps on the Duran tract.

He was not sure they had heard him or if they would pass on his message, but he went out into Port Street and from there to the yard where he kept his horse. He had had enough of the depressed moods reigning in Jaffa and of its honorable traders, who pretend to understand the issue of land when they actually know nothing.

They trust their money and don't understand that it is losing its value; they are convinced that the land will wait for them forever, and all they need to do is only to reach out and grab it. The land won't wait; the land rush will grow, and they will fall in their panic and be ready to gobble up each other. He predicted bad times and did not know how to help himself and sell the Duran land.

Moving swiftly and without thinking, he barely put on his horse's bridle and saddle and galloped off towards the exit from the city. He bypassed the houses of Jaffa, the new neighborhoods, and the fence of the crowded cemetery, with his eyes not taking in anything and him feeling nothing, not guiding the horse that knew the way and didn't need him.

Near twilight, the horse traversed the sabra fence and the orchard in the Valley of the Roses and halted next to Lehrer's house. Yehoshua saw a few workers burning thorns and preparing ashes to improve the soil. He asked after Mr. Lehrer and was told he had gone to Rishon Lezion. He inquired about Eisenberg, and they said he had gone to wander about the fields. Yehoshua turned his horse toward the beaten path leading to the Duran lands, and his riding calmed him down, so his thoughts began to take orderly shape.

He found Aharon stretched out next to the well among the clods of dry earth and the brambles, with shepherd's needles blossoms caught in his hair. He lay there enjoying the earth, near the well's wall, and letting the setting sun's rays caress him. He smiled at Yehoshua's dismal appearance.

"It's been quite a while since you came here. Has the land been sold?" he asked.

Yehoshua nodded his head, bent down near him, closed his eyes, and listened to the sounds of the earth.

The sun set; an evening breeze made its way among the clods, sending up chaff and scattering heads of old-man-in-the-Spring, and Yehoshua told Aharon about the Pines'advice to Broide.

Aharon roared in laughter and declared out loud, "We'll reject his advice. We'll show him that we are better than he is. We'll teach him a lesson and prove who understands land matters. The land gives love back to whoever becomes familiar with it and knows its ups and downs and not to someone to is out to exploit it. He will not best you. He won't win out over the second Yehoshua!" But Yehoshua wondered how he had known the nickname used only by Olga.

He spent that night next to the well on Duran land. The darkness was their blanket, and the warmth of the summer night gently stroked them. That's how the two of them talked to each other, clinging to the earth. At sunrise, Yehoshua left the well and mounted his horse, having made a firm decision. Aharon remained among the clods of earth to protect the land and wait for Yehoshua.

As evening settled, he entered Jaffa and rode toward the Christian neighborhood, to the home of the Russian consul. The aroma of a meat dish and bread tantalized him, and he was aware of his hunger and was sorry for his appearance. He should have stopped at home to change clothes and brush his hair, he thought, but he was in such a hurry to put his decision into action he had no patience to delay at all. Now, he didn't want them to consider him young and inexperienced, but it was too late to change his mind.

The servant who answered the clanging doorbell asked him what he wanted, and Yehoshua answered in fluent Russian that he wished to see the consul. From his tone of voice, the servant understood that he had come for an urgent matter and left him in the entranceway as he hurried to call his distinguished boss. Yehoshua buttoned the last button of his coat sleeve to hide his tattered cuffs. He bent over and put a finger in his spittle to use it to clean off his boots, but his hands became dirty, and he had no handkerchief to clean them off.

The servant returned and asked him to come to the table to join the consul. Yehoshua entered the great hall, adorned with consular symbols and flags of the different districts; displayed on one wall was the flag of the Ottoman Empire, while on the opposite one—the flag of the Russian Empire. At the center of the room stood a long table with only one person seated at its head. He was a squat man, reeking of importance, whose long, curly mustache was waxed at both ends. The consul looked Yehoshua up and down and ordered him to sit down opposite him, at the other end of the table.

Yehoshua took a seat at the table and was served bread and the evening dish. Despite his great hunger, he did not want to seem avid for food, so he nibbled slowly, even though it was hard for him to hold back.

The consul finished his meal before Yehoshua, wiped his mustache, and folded his napkin, and Yehoshua, even though he was not full, did likewise and folded his arms against his chest. After the table had been cleared and cleaned, the consul motioned to Yehoshua to speak. At first, his words were hesitant, but after a few moments, his voice grew stronger, and he forgot where he was and who was sitting opposite him. He told him the story of the Duran lands and went on to say that he had found a group of people, all of whom were Russian subjects, willing to buy the land. But their nationality worked against them, and the Turks would not let them register the land in their name. However, if the consul would be willing to act as a guarantor for the Russians, the Turks would agree to the registration of the land in the name of the foreign subjects. Yehoshua continued, saying, "The brokerage fee, I will share with you—I will give you twelve thousand gold francs—and you will receive not only money but gain great honor."

Yehoshua's voice trembled, and he was frightened by his own words, but he could not take them back. His statement had been made *and it hung in the air. The consul was quiet and continued to scrutinize Yehoshua. With his hands on the table, he played with the gold rings adorning his fingers.

The silence grew. Yehoshua tried to convince himself that he had acted properly, for he surely knew how much the Russian Empire wanted to acquire a foothold in the Ottoman Empire. The consul would certainly want the glory and the money he would gain by buying land in Eretz Israel and turning it into Russian property.

The man had still not opened his mouth, and Yehoshua began to fear that he had gone too far with his words. Now, he was at the consul's mercy, and if he wanted, he could turn Yehoshua over to the Turkish police, and they would accuse him of treason.

The trepidation that had seized him increased; his hands trembled, and he had to hold on to something stable, but the table was completely bare. So Yehoshua took hold of the tablecloth and folded its edges, and then he heard the consul speak, "I will sign. I will provide the necessary guarantee, and I will see to it that every kushan will be signed and registered in the name of a Russian subject."

As an issue of honor, he did not mention the matter of the money, but Yehoshua had obliged himself and had to stand by his word. Yehoshua took leave of the consul and went out into the night, feeling depressed and sordid. "Speculator! Speculator!" he muttered to himself as if demonized as he mounted his horse and rode to the backyard. But even as he rode, he sought to find solace, for he had found buyers and saved Yehuda Leib's property and not failed in the land deal. Time would come, and his acquisitions would increase, and this act of deception would be forgotten, and the bribe money given for the signature would no longer be remembered.

As he went up the steps to his room, he was already busy thinking of the Arabs of Qubeiba, Zarnuqah, Mesmîyeh, and Satriya, whose lands bordered those of Duran, and on ways to convince them to sign on the maps and on an agreement of the borders of the tracts. He knew he would need a lot more gold francs, as well as have to find new land to sell to others to use the money to pay his debts. But in those moments, he wanted Olga to hear her voice and obtain her agreement to his actions.

He found the room empty, the bed made, and a note on his pillow, "I don't know when I'll be back from the doctor's office. I am going to Vladimir Tyomkin's house. I was invited to a party, and if you want, change your coat, put on ironed clothes, and join me."

The Engineer Tyomkin

Olga called him Vladimir, while the others called him the engineer Tyomkin— all according to how close they were and how much they dared. He had arrived in Jerusalem during the uproar and confusion about the Duran land episode. He had come and led the "Executive Committee of Hovevei Zion in Jaffa," alongside Pines and Isaac Ben-Tovim, to reduce the pandemonium for land that had spread in Eretz Israel, to organize land acquisitions under a single roof, and to cool down the panicky rush to buy.

Olga remembered the stormy meetings of the Bilu movement members in Petersburg, which she attended with her brother Israel and her sister Fanny. The purpose of the meeting was to discuss the forms of agricultural settlement that should be established in Eretz Israel. The other young people took part in the tempestuous debates and called for abnegating private will in favor of the will of the public. They spoke about the "Great Vision," while she sat quietly, giving off an air that relayed that she did not believe in what she was hearing. One time, Tyomkin asked her to sit with him in a small café, and he asked her why she attended the meetings? She laughed and blushed at having been caught out.

"Because it's interesting," she replied. But he didn't understand, and she had to explain what she meant. "They are children. Dreamers and visionaries. The arguments seem to me to be like a theater performance in which the actors believe every word uttered in it because that is how the show succeeds."

Tyomkin enjoyed hearing her clarifications and was ensnared by her eyes hidden under her heavy eyebrows. From then on, they often spoke and met, expanding the time they spent together. After that, Tyomkin left Petersburg, and when he returned, the Bilu members had already gone to Eretz Israel, and Olga had disappeared.

At one of his first meetings with Pines and Ben Tovim, Tyomkin mentioned the Bilu members along with the name of Olga Belkind and saw how Pines's face soured, and he knitted his eyebrows.

"She belongs to the Hankins," he spit out toward him, and Tyomkin did not understand what was wrong with being part of the Hankins, since he had not met them nor the other residents of Jaffa yet.

The venom in Pines's voice angered him. But when a few weeks had passed by, and he had been introduced to the ways of the city and the vicissitudes of its people, he took notice that the newspapers mentioned "the young Hankin" and Pines quite a bit and that their names were linked to the issue of the Duran land. From the papers, he learned that Olga had married "the young Hankin," and he also understood from them the meaning of the hatred obvious in Pines's voice.

Olga was happy to meet Tyomkin. The Petersburg stories served her as an anchor to grab onto at this time when everything raged around her and Yehoshua was distancing himself from her. She often went to his house to join in the parties held in the large hall and to mingle with the bureaucrats and other Jaffa residents.

Now, she began to change her habits and dress differently; in Yehuda Leib's store, she spoke a lot about the dishes served in Vladimir Tyomkin's home and about her conversations with the women of the big world. She would wait for statements by Pines, who frequented Tyomkin's home, mocking him and adding from time to time, "He is so different from Vladimir!"

In the store, they enjoyed Olga's stories and mentioned, as if by the way, "The head of the committee likes her," and Sarah repeatedly muttered to herself, with everyone hearing, "See the rosiness in her cheeks. See her success among others..."

Sarah's words were aimed at her son, and Yehoshua heard but did not let them know. Instead, he ignored them, while saying to himself, "They're speaking now the same way they talked about Yehoshua Barzilai and Aharon Eisenberg. They are all jealous of him, and when the Duran deals are finished, the whispers will melt away," but he didn't know how long those negotiations would take.

᳁

When Yehoshua now stood next to the bed, and the white of the consul-signed paper merged with the white of the quilt cover, it seemed to him that the circles of Duran were reaching completion, and he could take time to deal with his own family unit. It was no longer necessary to pretend that his wife's matters were not his and that he was not a member of her circle of friends. He reread the letter and was still wrestling with himself over whether to go after Olga and see her in the company of strangers. He was somewhat afraid of meeting with the high official and tried to put off going to her.

After some hesitation, he washed his face, put on clean clothes, combed his hair, and lay down on the bed—for just a few minutes.

The cold wakened him. It had begun to get dark outside, and he remembered Olga's note—who knew if she was still in Tyomkin's house. He made himself get up, smoothed his wrinkled clothes, washed the sleepy seeds from his eyes, and went out to the shadowy street.

While walking about in the darkness, Jaffa looked different to him, strange. Suddenly, it seemed as if Port Street was filled with new stores—all of them with Jewish owners—and next to them stood many beggars, who were also Jews, and all were yelling, "Charity!" "Charity will save you from death!" From there, he turned to the street of the Turkish regime officials that separated the Christian neighborhood from the Arab one and saw large, stone houses standing the length of it; he stopped next to one that was more lit than the others.

The door was ajar, and voices spilled into the street. He stood on the threshold and was uncertain whether to announce his arrival or just push the door to enter. For a moment, he reminded himself of Hanukkah eve in 1886 when he went to ask for Olga's hand—and it seemed such a long time ago to him.

When he finally entered, he saw people scattered around the hall in groups, a few of them standing and a number sitting, all of them dressed in finery even though it was a weekday. Dangling from the ceiling were brass oil lamps, and the flames of the wick cast spots of capering light on the tables covered with tatted tablecloths and laden with trays of sweet rolls. Yehoshua felt uncomfortable and was sorry he had agreed to Olga's request. Didn't he want her for himself? But the hall was large, and the people crowding it were so very strange to him.

Yehoshua looked around insecurely, seeking his wife's eye, and he saw her standing in the middle of a group with a red-headed man slightly older than she standing next to her. He held himself upright and surveyed his guests. The head of the house, Yehoshua guessed to himself; this was the man his mother wanted to warn him about, the chairman of the new committee. Yehoshua looked at his own old-fashioned clothing and his dusty boots; he took a step back, hoping to sneak away and disappear with no one noticing, but Olga saw him and realized his intention, so she rushed out of the center of the circle toward him like a young woman happy to greet the one she loves and wanting to take glory in his affection. She ran to him joyfully, forgetting his remoteness and his leaving just yesterday. The confused Yehoshua stood there with thoughts running through his mind: What should he say to her? How will he tell her about his despicable act: the 12,000 gold francs he had promised to the consul. That makes him a speculator like all the others—for a moment, he forgot where he was, and all his senses blurred. Only Olga's calling out brought him back to the large hall. "Vladimir, this is Yehoshua, the Second Yehoshua!"

Olga pulled him after her and presented him to those around her, proudly telling all of them about his expertise in land deals and his involvement in selling the Duran land. Slowly, the group around the two grew, and one after the other, they shot questions to him, and more than all of them, Tyomkin asked him many questions. As for Olga, who was close to both the one asking and the one answering, she drew herself up, and her eyes were shining: wasn't she the wife of the acquirer of the lands of Duran, the wife of Yehoshua Hankin?

The hall began to empty out at a late hour, with only the close friends remaining, sitting at the room's edges and talking among themselves. Olga spoke with Tyomkin while Yehoshua kept quiet, trying to catch Olga's attention so they could leave. At first, she did not notice his inquisitive glances, but after a while, his piercing looks made her uncomfortable, and she turned to face her husband and understood his impatience and saw the nervous drumming of his fingers. She wanted to toy with him a bit and ignore his expression, but he didn't let up and finally stood up, and Olga realized she had overdone it and rose, ready to leave with him. She said goodbye to those lingering, and the two of them went out to the street and strode between the new houses. She offered him her hand and intertwined her fingers with his, and Yehoshua began to speak and tell her, in brief, the story of his profiteering and of his promise to the Russian consul.

When she heard his words, she stood stock still, trying to look at his expression and see if he really meant what he said, but Yehoshua evaded her look, and only his so very tired voice was heard. Olga felt weakness rolling through her, and she didn't know whether to be critical of him or to encourage and support him. Somehow, he didn't look the same to her, different; he didn't belong to her. She tried to pull her hand away from his, but he held on tightly and wouldn't let her go.

After they reached their room, Olga went to steep some tea for herself and prepare for Yehoshua a glass of boiling water with a slice of lemon—as he liked it—and to think over what he had told her in the meantime. Until the coals were burning bright and the water bubbling, she washed her face and spread all over herself one of the lotions she had been given in Jerusalem to increase her husband's desire. She looked in the mirror and again did not know what she wanted. She moved her hand over and face and bosom, while thinking: the body of a young woman without the wrinkles after giving birth, firm breasts longing to be caressed, to feel a suckling mouth. She was frightened by her thoughts and pulled her hand away, hurrying to go check if the water had boiled.

When she entered the room, she found Yehoshua sitting on the edge of the bed, staring toward the doorway, waiting for her to come in. He put his hands out toward her, and she set the tray on the floor and stepped close to him. She wasn't thinking anymore, not about French francs nor about Duran. It was not even about her wish to become pregnant. She yearned only for his touch, and every caress and every stroke thrilled her with supreme pleasure.

In the third week of July, Yehoshua, Eisenberg, Broide, and Epstein were summoned to the Turkish governor's mansion to sign in his presence the deed of transfer for the Duran lands. Two days later, Broide and Epstein left Eretz Israel.

Epstein promised to return and left in tears over the scenery and people he had come to know, while Broide didn't say goodbye to anyone.

Everyone felt the storm around the Duran land had abated and that Yehoshua would return to the store to help with the sales rush towards the High Holidays as well as to look after his own interests. If a fresh proposal for buying new land would arise, so be it; he would act as he had concerning the Duran lands. But if there were no such offer, Yehoshua would be a textile merchant like his father. Beside Olga, no one else knew about his agreement with the Russian consul.

🙠

The Jewish New Year, Rosh Hashanah, passed; the Ten Days of Repentance were counted; and the more settled Jews looked for ways to invite beggars to their homes for a meal as dictated by a commandment as an expression of charity, so their iniquities would be forgiven. The mornings saw the streets filled with early risers, and in the evenings—with groups that stood at street corners and talked about their deeds during the past year. No one spoke about trade in land nor argued about the price of a dunam—everything was pushed off until after the holidays.

But then, two days before the pre-Yom Kippur meal, Bloch, the Baron's official located in Rishon Lezion, showed up at Yehuda Leib's store. He arrived early in the morning, causing Sarah, who was alone there, to think she was about to start the day with a good sale. She did not recognize him. Bloch had come to manage Rishon Lezion after the rebellion, and Sarah had not gone back to visit the colony.

"What would you like," she asked, and when he didn't answer, she thought that he had still not made up his mind, so she bombarded him with questions and advice, "Perhaps, sir, you need memorial candles? We have received new ones that are guaranteed to burn the entire day. Or, maybe, you need rolls of material for making sheets? Excellent merchandise arrived just this week."

But the man maintained his silence, and she gave up on him, turning to other tasks behind the counter, lifting her head to look at him from time to time, and wondering about his reticence. She forgot about him completely until a nearby voice, actually right over her, asked her, "Where is the young Hankin?"

Sarah was taken aback at hearing the voice and the question. What's the connection between him and Yehoshua? But she told him she would go to call her son and climbed to the second story.

When she described the man's appearance to Olga and Yehoshua, neither knew who he was. Yehoshua put on his student's coat, ran his fingers through his beard, and put a few drops of water on his hair to make it easier to comb; then he went down to the store. He did not rush to get there because he had a bad feeling about this. He paused at the entrance to the store, his eyes looking around to see what was going on in it. When he saw the man standing next to the counter, with his chin leaning on one hand and wearing a coat too heavy for summer's end, he identified him immediately—Bloch from Rishon Lezion, an official of the Baron's who was considered a cut above the others. He went in, and without shaking hands or greeting him, motioned to follow him into the small room that served as an office. The man trailed after Yehoshua, and without an invitation, sat himself down on a settee that was too small for his dimensions. His host remained standing and looking at him while Bloch's eyes darted restlessly here and there in such great contrast to his heavy, relaxed body.

Bloch was the first to speak, with his booming voice, all the while his eyes refraining from looking at Yehoshua. "Cancel the deal with the 'Menuchah ve-Nachalah' association and don't sell the Duran land. The Baron wants the land for himself, and his wish takes precedence over theirs, and a transaction with him is more reliable than one with Jews from Warsaw. If the 'Menuchah ve-Nachalah' association members are serious about their decision to settle and become farmers, the Baron will allow them to do so and will also support them. But they have to know they will not be independent farmers but working under the patronage of the Baron and operating in line with the advice of his administrators."

When he finished speaking, Bloch took out from his upper jacket a long envelope, closed with a seal, with three words in gold displayed on it: Edmond de Rothschild.

Yehoshua hesitated before taking the envelope, but his curiosity won out, and with a trembling hand, he reached out for it and hurried to open it, but he saw neither words nor a signature but only numbers: Twenty thousand gold French francs, the entire sum he had pledged to the Russian consul, all the payment for the bank loan and interest in Beirut, with enough left over to start new transactions.

The document seared his fingers, and Yehoshua hastily tried to get rid of it and hand it back to Bloch. But the official did not put out his hand to take the envelope, and he focused his eyes on his host. Yehoshua just stood there with his hand in the air and muttered unclearly, "What does the Baron have to do with the Duran land? Of course, it is good land, but there is a great deal like it in Eretz Israel, and with this money he can acquire a very large amount of land."

Loch laughed and made himself comfortable in his chair, stretching his legs out and putting his hands in his belt, "You really are just a kid. It's not for nothing that they call you "the young Hankin." Think a bit—is there room for another colony that does not belong to the Baron between Ekron and Rishon Lezion! Its new farmers will give up one by one. Better ones than they tried to hold on without support and failed."

"And perhaps they'll succeed?" Yehoshua interrupted him and continued, "And maybe they will conduct their affairs wisely and learn from the failure of their predecessors and plant orchards rather than not deal with dried out field crops, so they will increase their income and live the way they were accustomed to in their former places?"

"They won't succeed," replied Bloch. "Not a chance."

"They will make it," Yehoshua repeated, adding, "they will prove their understanding." Now his voice did not tremble, and his back straightened; he approached Bloch's settee and stood over him.

"It is forbidden for them to succeed," Bloch declared, and his eyes darted around again. "It is unacceptable for the supported colonies to see the flourishing of a settlement that is not supported, forbidden!"

"Why is it forbidden?" Yehoshua asked in a quiet, calm tone.

Bloch began to wriggle on the settle, and sweat broke out on his forehead. He wanted to search his pocket for a handkerchief to wipe it off, but he could not reach into his trouser pocket because he was sitting so low. Finally, he rose, took out the cloth, dried his face, folded the handkerchief, and put it back in his pocket. He turned his face away from Yehoshua, who saw that his back was trembling. Then, he pivoted again, stared at the wall behind Yehoshua, and told him, "Take your contract and cover all your debts. The Russian consul is not tight-lipped. He has spoken about your agreement with him. And if he has told the Baron, he will certainly tell others as well. So, if you're not acting for yourself, think about the farmers. They are all familiar with the Baron's power, and you yourself know what sums are needed to maintain a colony in Eretz Israel. How long with the members of "Menuchah ve-Nachalah" be able to sustain a settlement by themselves? They will need a director, physician, teacher, gardener, and an agronomist to teach them, let alone budget for a storehouse and a mikvah. The list is long, and many are the needs of Jews, especially Warsaw Jews used to a life of luxury." Bloch's voice grew hoarse, and he mumbled something else and then stopped talking.

Yehoshua's eyes were locked on Bloch's until the man had to look straight into them. His final words had turned everything topsy-turvy and revealed this functionary in all his conniving. Yehoshua remembered rumors about money belonging to a private person in Rishon Lezion that he had pocketed instead of them reaching the farmers' fields. He smiled to himself and winked at the man standing before him, "I know very well what the budget of a colony should include, and I'm well aware that there's no need for all the services you mentioned, and especially not for officials. They're not talking about me nor about my agreement with the consul. They're talking about bureaucrats like you—the ones who inflate the budget to the Baron and don't give the farmers what they're supposed to but put the money in their own pockets."

Since he took heart and saw how the big man was caving in, his voice now became even stronger, "You're worried about your own skin, in case the Baron will find out that it is possible to firmly establish a colony on a lower budget than the one you have declared and to attain economic independence without a system of administrators and other flatterers. You are trembling, lest the Baron ask questions and raise doubts about the way your administrators operate."

Bloch lowered his eyes, and Yehoshua knew he had found his weak point. "And perhaps it was not the Baron who sent you to me? Maybe you did this behind his back to push me away from the Duran matter, so you could go to the Baron yourself and say to him, 'I have increased your honor. I managed to acquire the Duran land and set up a new colony that will be added to the list of settlements supported by you.'" What do you think? Maybe it'd be worthwhile checking the signature on the document another time?"

Bloch moved backward, and Yehoshua followed him, with his hand still holding the document and proffering it. Bloch halted and snatched the document, leaving the small room with a slam of the door, his hurried steps echoing on the tiles of the lane. Yehoshua left the room and went into the store; he saw Sarah and Olga, who had heard the conversation escaping the small room, standing and fearing for him. Moving toward them, glowing with pleasure and smiling, he grabbed hold of his wife's waist and lifted her up, and all of his discomfort over the agreement with the consul vanished in an instant. He was sure of his actions and knew he had succeeded in his transaction and that the Duran land would bring in its wake other deals and that a great deal of land would be redeemed, a very great amount of land.

❧

Life in Jaffa continued to flow. After the holidays, the Belkind and Hankin families expanded: Mendel and Yaakov left Gedera: Yaakov journeyed to Australia, while Mendel came to live with his father and mother. Fanny, Lolik, and Avshalom also arrived. Replacing the stories about the Duran land were those about their leaving Gedera that spread throughout all the colonies and cities in Eretz Israel.

At the end of July, Israel Rozman was shot, that same worker who had come to live in the Feinberg family farmyard and had become like a brother to Lolik. While guarding the colony's granary, he had been attacked, and the story of his killing took on many versions. And no one knew which was the truth: A few people said he had been murdered by Qatara Arabs who had not forgotten the Ajouri incident; others related that he had been shot by mistake and that the bullet had actually been aimed at Lolik; still more reported that the guard accompanying him had heard noises on the other side of the fence and was sure that robbers were trying to get into the granary, so he did not hesitate and shot, hitting Rozman in the temple. Whatever which way, the colony was astir and shaken up after midnight. First, they heard the shot, then the sounds of the tins tied to the rope around the granary to warn if strangers were approaching.

Upon hearing the blast, the colony quaked, and everyone went outside to see what had happened. Farmers grabbed a pitchfork, hoe, or cudgel, while the woman took hold of each other, and all of them scanned the fences and looked for tracks leading to the Arab village of Qatara. Since they were stepping in the same places, they could not locate anything arousing suspicion of the Arabs, but they did find Rozman lying wounded next to the fence. The farmers brought him to Lolik's yard and began arguing about who could have been responsible.

But Lolik didn't hear what they were saying. He called Fanny and asked her to sit next to the wounded man, while he saddled the horse and galloped into the night.

What happened to Lolik was gathered from rumors and from the Turkish policemen. First, Lolik dashed to Ekron and alerted the local doctor, and then he continued to the Arab village—Qatara—where he went from house to house and fence to fence, looking for a horse that still had foam on its lips, wet nostrils, and the sheen of sweat on its coat. Wherever he entered, he mercilessly woke the family members, dug among the bridles and plow shafts, with the *fellahin* following after him, not daring to stop him and calling out after him, "the Giant," "the Giant." He finally found one saddled horse with foam still noticeable on its lips. He took the animal and its owner to the police station in Ramla. That Arab was associated with Ajouri and, like him, collected pistols and daggers. Of course, the tent dwellers and residents of the huts talked about robberies and looting he carried out from time to time, but aside from the pistols and daggers, no one had seen him involved in such things.

The policemen regarded Lolik's burning eyes and the Arab's terrified look, but they did not investigate and did not inquire and simply threw the Arab into the jail pit—until the trial.

He returned to Gedera to sit next to Rozman's bed. The doctor said he would last for a few days, but Rozman held on for a week, the whole time constantly his body convulsing. At the end of the week, the twisting stopped, and they dug a grave in the Gedera colony. Two days later, the Arab was released, since no proof had been found that he was actually Rozman's murderer.

But Lolik did not give up. He returned to Qatara, grabbed the Arab, and dragged him to Ramleh again. This time he did not ride alone—a group of young cronies of Ajouri followed behind him. When the policemen saw the furious looks of the Shabab (youngsters) from Qatara and Lolik's frenzy, they refused to accept this Gederah fellow's version. Lolik returned alone, and like someone possessed by madness, he ventured among the farmers' homes, calling them to come and take revenge on the Arabs of Qatara. But they didn't join him and strove to distance themselves from quarrels and fights. Lolik was angry at them and was ready to strike them, but they just yelled out to him, "Lunatic."

In the evening, a few members of the colonies gathered outside Lolik's yard but did not dare enter; they demanded that he leave the settlement. The first night he ignored them; the second night, someone threw a rock wrapped in paper and broke the window. Slanderously, someone had written, "Leave, go away, you murderer," and Fanny and Israel left.

Fanny handed over their plot to Zuckerman and packed a few belongings. The family arrived in Jaffa in a small wagon hitched to one horse.

Jaffa, 1891

Yehoshua was correct. The Duran transaction brought new offers and negotiations to his door. All of the Duran land was sold; Yehoshua covered his debt to the Beirut bank and paid the Russian consul what he had promised him. Bloch's threat faded away—no one in Jaffa cared about the sudden wealth of the consul. Now, Yehoshua was a frequent visitor to the home of Bustros Roq as well as to that of Vladimir Tyomkin, while Olga respected him and his success. At that time, Olga left her work at the clinic and joined that of a young doctor. Dr. Stein had become hard of hearing, and his hands began to tremble, so he suggested she find a different physician to assist. Sonia agreed with the elderly man and turned to a new doctor to employ her sister, and he was happy to do so.

15. The "Khan" in Hedera 1891 • Source: Hedera Archive.

2 HÉDÉRA - Orphelins juifs des pogroms ukrainiens au travail

16. Hedera 1891 • Source: Hedera Archive.

17. Hedera River 1891• Source: Hedera Archive.

18. Hedera Forest 1891 • Source: Hedera Archive.

Before she started working, she underwent a series of examinations with him, and she was told that her tubes were blocked and no one could tell if she would ever have children. To her surprise, she did not take the news hysterically, since she had sensed that all her attempts to give birth would be of no avail. To be sure, the doctor did calm her down and told her about innovative experiments and about advances in medicine, but she hushed him and put an end to the discussion, "Until they will find a solution, I will become even older." Olga steeped herself in her clinic work and kept at bay any thought about children and about her husband, more than a decade younger than she; he was full of vitality and could have many offspring.

In Jaffa, the deluge continued of wealthy people and emissaries of associations looking for land, as well as penniless beggars and laborers knocking on doors asking for any kind of work, anything to avoid living on charity. Many required the services of the doctor, and he needed Olga's expertise; the matter of her barrenness was not mentioned again.

In Tyomkin's house, great and secret issues were dealt with. They told that the American president had turned to the Sublime Porte and asked to settle one million Jews throughout the Ottoman Empire. The Committee's income increased daily—any place where Jews were found, associations were established. All were seeking property in the Holy Land, and all were willing to pay a great deal of money to the Committee and to the land agents working with it.

To the Hankin family, so it seemed, a life of comfort had arrived. Olga would return at night bone-tired to her second-story room and wait for her husband. He would come and tell her of other places and land ready to be redeemed. She heard–not heard what he was saying, whether owing to fatigue or because she was bothered by the question of when she would find the right time to tell him about her barrenness. The nights passed, and that discussion was postponed over and over, and the thought of children he might have been banished to oblivion. Yehoshua paid no attention to her ongoing quiet, all his involvement in land deals. On those evenings, Olga was not jealous of the land; she just saw it as merchandise for the businessman who studied it to consider its price.

Once, when she was sitting at the table, Olga smiled and said to Yehoshua, "The land acts like an unfaithful woman—she'll promise one person and make eyes at another and go with whoever pays a higher price."

Yehoshua laughed, adding, "Land is treacherous, but not you—you are always with me."

Her heart clenched, and she made a firm decision to tell him very soon.

Then, the wintry days arrived, and Yehoshua and Olga's visits to the Tyomkin home declined; few customers came to the store, and even people seeking land did not come by. The rain and mud deterred people from dealing with land, and everyone waited for the spring.

One evening, Yehoshua and Olga extended their silent stay in the small kitchen near their room. Olga did not enjoy the lengthy quietude that reminded her of other long silences and of the remoteness from Yehoshua—and she feared a return to that situation. So, she moved her chair close to her husband's and patted his veiny fingers, and saw the smile shining in his eyes. Hence, she told him about the Russian mother-to-be who had fled in advanced pregnancy after the great expulsion from Moscow, and she and her husband were staying with Dr. Masie and had no place to go. But Yehoshua didn't listen to her story, and when he started to speak, it was about other things, so she did not go on talking.

"Will you come with me tomorrow," he asked suddenly.

Olga kept quiet. "He didn't hear a word I said," she thought to herself, looking at him and trying to understand him

Yehoshua repeated his question.

"But it's winter now, and the roads are muddy," was her evasive answer.

He paid no attention to her response, but declared, "Tomorrow you will ride with me, and I will show you new things. I am carrying a secret that is burning in my bones, and I won't be able to keep it to myself. So share it with me."

For a moment, she was taken aback; she scrutinized his face that was so familiar to her. She rose and stood near him, and he took her hand and pulled her toward him, setting her on his knees and whispering, "Mine, mine." She saw him as a toddler who had revealed his mischievous deeds and was relieved. Olga tucked her hand into his shirt, petted his body, and wound his chest hair around her finger, while he passionately pressed her to him, stood her up, and took her to their room. For a moment, she tried to hold him back, to pour her heart out to him and scream into his ears, "You will never have children. You will only have the land. And when you understand that, will you go on saying, "Mine, mine?"

but no shriek burst out of her mouth, and she stifled her pain as usual and gave herself over to his caresses.

Olga woke at the break of dawn. Yehoshua still slept, so she covered him and went to put on her riding clothes and pack a bundle for the way. When she finished, it was time to wake him. Yehoshua refused to give up his sleep, so she tickled his ribs and trailed her fingers all along his body. The man jumped up, filled with pleasure, and opened his sleepy-seed–filled eyes until he saw her figure standing next to him. He closed his eyes again and pulled her toward him, wanting to go on dozing. Finally, she gave in and lay down on him fully dressed, his heat engulfing her, and she said to herself, "Just for a minute." The minute stretched until the first rays of the sun burst in full force and prompted both of them to rise. Olga threw the blanket off Yehoshua, and he pretended to be angry, saying, "What a filly! Just a hint of the open spaces, and she loses patience." She was elated and forgot that she had wanted to tell him yesterday about her barrenness. She went to prepare a quick breakfast and get them on their way.

No one saw them leaving. Jaffa was still fast asleep, and except for a homeless beggar who had staked out the street corner, the lane was empty. The morning was chilly and dense clouds were coming in from the west promising rain. The two rode swiftly, and soon the homes of Jaffa disappeared. They traversed the orchards surrounding the city from the north, went over the new stone bridge across the Uja stream, and did not stop at the Sheikh Munis village. They galloped into the swamp trails and found a way among the tall reeds.

Yehoshua, who knew where to find the solid ground, galloped ahead, with Olga following r him exactly in his wake. They bypassed sorghum fields, entered meager orchards, and swept into mounds of dunes surrounded by kurkar cliffs. Yehoshua showed her the limits of the wandering of the Abu Kishk tribe and pointed out the expanse of the Jalil lands and that of al-Kharm, and Olga looked for hints to distinguish between their land and that of others, but it all looked the same to her: sand and sand and sand …

The wind became fierce and brought menacing, dark clouds. Yehoshua spurred his horse on and leaned over its back to protect himself from the wind, and Olga did the same.

Rain began to fall, and the drops grew stronger, lashing at their backs and stinging their faces. Olga called to Yehoshua to stop. He didn't hear her but turned his face to her from time to time and motioned with his hand—just a minute. But the minute grew longer, and the rider ahead of her disappeared from view and could be seen again. Finally, she found him standing next to his horse near a ruined dwelling supported by a cliff. The horse's snorting was swallowed up in the sound of the crashing waves of the violent sea that sounded so near. Olga dismounted and looked for shelter.

Yehoshua pointed out to her the dome surrounded by the sycamore trees, making a canopy over it, and whose exposed roots had become intertwined, forming crooked arches. They headed there, and Yehoshua took the horses and tied them to the stone fence near the hovel. Then, he said to his wife, "The tomb of Sheikh Sidna Ali. We will wait until the storm weakens and then be on our way." While she was still amazed at the scope of his knowledge, Yehoshua disappeared from view, and she remained alone.

She circled the dome and pressed close to the tomb's walls to protect herself from the raindrops; she also scanned the stones. At the bottom of the wall were large, planed stones and above them a row of smaller, chiseled ones and a row of heaped kurkar stones. She reminded herself of her brother Israel's explanations about the different stones making up the walls and the turrets and the other ruins in Eretz Israel, which serve as testimony to the periods of the rulers and caliphs who destroyed and built at the same time. She smiled to herself—she could stand near the stones and create stories out of them, forgetting the raindrops and her missing husband. She turned around and looked for a place to sit and rest her bone-weary body after the riding.

Suddenly, she felt eyes staring at her and following her. Frightened, she looked around her and saw no one. In a panic, she sought Yehoshua and ran in the rain back to where they had tied the horses, yelling, "Yehoshua, Yehoshua!"

She found him standing next to the opening of the ruin with an old Arab at his side, the two of them speaking to each other. The Arab's eyes darted about repeatedly and went back and forth between Yehoshua and her again and again. Olga was embarrassed by her panicked running, the hysteria of frightened women, and since she did not want to be caught out in her weakness, she turned to go, but Yehoshua called to her, wondering about her panting. She did not tell him but only said she was tired from the journey.

Yehoshua showed her a corner within the hovel, where sacks were stacked one over the others. Meanwhile, the old Arab went a bit away from them and stood under the dense sycamore tree and fingered his prayer beads.

As a smile spread over his face, Yehoshua explained to her, "This is the guard of the holy gravesite. He is not used to riding women coming to the tomb. He thinks you are a marvel or perhaps a hallucination."

Olga laughed in relief, put her hand to the braid wound on top of her head, pulled out the pin holding it, and let her plait fall to her shoulder. Yehoshua reached out to lightly touch her hair but immediately remembered the Arab watching them and took his hand back and stuffed it in his pocket. He spread out a sack for her and went back to the Arab. Olga added a few more sacks to make her stay more pleasant, sat herself down, and wrapped her feet in another bag. She then looked at the Arab and Yehoshua sitting bent over and leaning toward each other at some distance from her, while she was not part of their actions nor their conversation.

From time to time, the Arab pointed to the dunes and drew with his fingers in the moist sand, and Yehoshua followed his finger with shining eyes. Then the Arab went and fetched a jug of steaming coffee and poured some into a small clay cup for Yehoshua, who took it and got up and brought it to Olga and then went back to the Arab and took some for himself.

Olga gulped it quickly. The coffee's warmth and sweetness suffused her body. She leaned on the stone wall and felt the bumpy surface, so she wrapped herself in the scarf and tightened the sack around her. The salty sea wind licked her face, and she heard the hum of the waves; she felt her eyelids getting heavy.

When Yehoshua came to wake her up, she saw the sun hanging low at the edge of the horizon. The Arab was again nowhere to be seen, and Yehoshua helped her up, straightened the horse's saddle, and supported her as she mounted her ride. They did not speak; Olga was still steeped in her nap, and Yehoshua was deep in thought.

They rode a short while toward the north, and then Yehoshua pulled the halter and changed direction. Anxious about the approaching evening, Olga wanted to tell him about her fears, but then thought better about it and decided to trust her husband. They were by themselves in the endless, dry expanses of sand, surrounded by bird tracks left in the sand, dry broom bushes, and tree trunks, scattered all around, whose roots had blackened from moisture.

Now the two neared the sea and saw a wooden dock and fishing boats tied to it from afar. Olga looked at Yehoshua questioningly, and he read her thoughts and replied, "Umm Khalid," and he showed her the thick branches lashed to each other and concealed in the sand. "In the summer, the *fellahin* load watermelons on them and float them toward the ma'onot, large sailboats heading for Egypt."

Olga was sure Yehoshua was making fun of her because everything looked so desolate, and the sea was so tempestuous. But Yehoshua spoke again, "This is a good port. A fishing colony could be built next to it."

"Fishermen!" she laughed. "Jews are good at business, not fishing."

But he stood his ground. "You'll see," he said. "The day will come when I will buy the dunes and build you a house on a high hill, and you will sit in the window and gaze at the sea."

"You're crazy," she giggled again and prodded her horse to gallop faster.

They turned away from the shore and crossed kurkar ridges to the swamps and the thick reeds. The thundering of the horses drove away from the wintering storks and herons who had planned to spend the night. The flapping of their wings alarmed Olga; she trembled and wanted to be close to Yehoshua, but again, he went ahead of her, breaking a path for them among the reeds.

The ground became solid and the galloping less urgent, and Olga became aware of black tents scattered among the rolling tumbleweed. Olga turned her horse toward them, since almost all her trips with Yehoshua ended near the Bedouin tents, but to her astonishment, Yehoshua bypassed the encampment and called to her to hurry up. "These are tents of the Abu Kishk tribe, and they will not be pleased with strangers arriving at sunset." She was a bit angry—once more, he was hiding his intentions from her. He spoke little and barely explained.

After a short ride, other tents, larger and more numerous than the previous one, came into view, and they were surrounded by dry palm trunks. In the yards stood mounds of goat droppings, and crowded within them were flocks of camels and sheep. "Bnei Wadi al-Hawarith," Yehoshua answered before being asked, even before she turned her head toward him. "Robbers," he went on explaining. "The entire valley is afraid of them, and no one dares to open his mouth and complain."

She had not realized they had reached the valley—they had been riding the whole time on a plain—and in response to her question about where they were precisely, he smiled happily at her ignorance, aching to reply and break the silence.

"For over an hour, we have been riding on the land of Antoine Bishara Tayyan, that same Maronite who lives on Christians Street in Jaffa and whose house is surrounded by high walls."

Olga knew who he was talking about but didn't want to ask, both because she was a bit angry that he had hidden their destination from her as well as because she was tired from the journey and hoped to stop between the tents.

Since she didn't respond, Yehoshua thought she needed further explanation, so he said, "the Bnei Hawarith (Bedouin tribe) are sitting on the Maronite land and guard it against trespassers. This is good soil, and many tribes would like to work it and reduce it strip by stip. One day, I will go to the Maronite and convince him to sell the land to me. I will approach him when I am a large land agent and am selling throughout Palestine."

Olga was taken back by his bragging. But he went on weaving his plans. "I will go to him when I finish another purchase, larger than the acquisition of Duran." Suddenly, he sobered up when he realized he had revealed his secret and that it was his wife he was speaking with and not just to himself.

"To see the land was why you took me along," she finally muttered in an angry tone. "And I, in all innocence, thought you had a different secret."

Yehoshua did not understand her fury, since she knew him better than he knew himself. "Do you remember the ride we made when we went to the sabra fields to see the Duran land? Then you wanted me to share my love with you, and now I wanted to do the same," he told her, pausing and looking at her. Olga's face softened, so Yehoshua went on talking as if wanting to hurry before her expression would change. "It was not the Maronite's land I wanted to show you but another tract. It's not far from here. The day will come when it will be the turn of the Wadi Hawarith land (Emeq Hefer) and the Umm Khalid land." Now, he spoke gently, without boasting, and he aimed his words only at her.

Night fell. They stopped and let the horses rest, and in the meantime, Yehoshua took two white scarves out of his pocket and tied them to the horses' necks. When he finished, they both mounted the horses to continue their way. The darkness engulfed Olga, and she saw nothing but the flash of white of the scarf showing her the galloping of Yehoshua's horse. She again prodded her horse to go faster and came close to Yehoshua's ride, yelling into the night, "Where are you taking me? I've seen more than enough land for one day."

"You didn't see the main thing, my big secret! We are riding to the land of Khudeira."

He had just mentioned a new name, and she couldn't fathom how Khudeira. (Hadera) differed from Wadi Hawarith (Hefer Valley) or from Jalil. Names, all of them names of lands, all of the names of other loves.

"I've had enough of new names. Let's find us a place to spend the night," she yelled.

"We'll stay at the home of the effendi who holds the Khudeira land," his voice sounding very close to her ear. "They are waiting for our arrival. The way took longer than expected. So please be patient, for only a little while."

His voice was comforting and calming, and she was again happy to be riding alongside him. She imagined that she put her head on his chest and heard the beating of his heart; the two of them were far from Jaffa and the sounds of the store that slid through the crack in their clay floor. A cold wind struck her face, so Olga covered her face with her scarf, leaving only a small opening for her eyes, in the fashion of the Arab women, to see the white handkerchief tied to Yehoshua's horse's neck. Yehoshua spurred his horse on and did not forget to occasionally turn his head to check for Olga's scarf. The horses galloped, and the raindrops lashed them fiercely; the road seemed endless. When, in the darkness, she could make out the silhouette of a long building, Olga thought that the gloom was playing tricks on her. But as the horses drew nearer to it and Yehoshua dismounted and offered a hand to Olga, she knew that they had reached her husband's target.

The structure in Khudeira was similar to a khan and was surrounded by a wall of stones. Rising over its threshold was a large arch above, which was a tall wall whose end could not be seen. Behind the arch, Olga could make out a heavy iron gate, and she wondered how old the stones were. The strong pounding of Yehoshua on the iron gate drew her out of her thoughts, but no one came to open it. Yehoshua moved a bit away from the gate and shouted in Arabic, but the stormy night swallowed his cry. He drew Olga to the gate so she could stand near the wall and avoid the wind and rain while he went to bring a heavy stick. He hit the gate again, bent down to the keyhole and called out, until, at last the lock creaked and the gate opened.

A lad came toward them, walking barefoot like someone not affected by the cold and rain, and Yehoshua handed him the halter. The fellow showed them the way to the central hall, while he disappeared into the pitch dark.

Like two vagabonds trembling from cold and fatigue, they pushed their way in and were received at the entrance by a white-robed, old man whose eyes were blinking and did not look directly at them. He sat them down on pillows near the oven, but the heavy stench of the animal dung that engulfed them made Olga dizzy. She leaned against the wall and did not want to straighten up again. A few minutes later, they were brought a copper bowl containing rice pottage and pieces of meat, and a large, thin pita to roll the dish in. Olga took a taste from her fingertip and did not want more. Her eyes closed and she desired only sleep.

Olga did not know how long she slumbered, but her head was no longer dizzy when she woke up, and the smells did not seem so heavy. She was hungry, but the food in the bowl was cold. When she searched for Yehoshua and did not find him next to her, her eyes darted to the corners of the hall, which was a large room supported by four arches. There were no pictures in it, and no decorations save for one inscription in Arabic that was chiseled about the entry's lintel.

Standing in one corner was a large oven used for cooking and heating. Pillows were scattered near the oven, and next to them, low tables resting on three legs. Only one man was in the hall—an outsized effendi whose heavy body was sunk into a pillow and whose white robe covered his rolls of fat. The man looked at her, and his scrutinization that took in her every move and flutter made her uncomfortable. Olga looked away from him and continued to seek Yehoshua. When she didn't find him, she looked again that the food near her hand and finally broke off a part of the tasteless pita. The piece stuck in her throat, and she started coughing again. Luckily, she heard Yehoshua's footsteps behind her, and she felt his hand slapping her back and calming her down.

"They want to meet you," he said. "Come with me."

She knew full well who wanted to be introduced to her, since the hall was empty except for the effendi. She smoothed her hair with her hand and got up and adjusted her clothing. When she put out a hand for support from her husband, Yehoshua moved back. But she was not insulted, since he had already told her that the Arabs were not used to seeing a woman dressed in men's clothing. She stood up straight and walked slowly after him to annoy him.

When she approached the table, Yehoshua introduced him: "The effendi Salim Khoury."

She greeted him with a nod of her head and debated whether to offer a hand, so as to add to their anger, but she held back and sat a bit behind them.

The two men spoke French between themselves, and she could only catch a few of their words. They spoke about the sizable distance of the building from the main road and about the tribes of Wadi Hawarith and the brigands of Abu Kishk; they talked of the riders' courage and the reeds used as a hiding place for the murderers who fled into them for fear of blood libel.

The effendi told of a beautiful daughter of a sheikh who had run away to follow her love. One day, her horse had returned to the encampment with only its saddle on its back, and since then, on full moon nights, wails were heard among the reeds, and a white figure was seen hovering. There were men who had gone seeking that image, but they had disappeared in the swamps, and no one ever saw them again.

Olga's eyes had shut again while listening to the monotonic voice, but she wanted to fight against sleep, so as not to lose the main thread of their discussion and to finally discover the meaning of Yehoshua's secret.

She awoke in a panic, being certain she had slept for hours. But when she saw Yehoshua and the effendi still talking, she calmed down. Now, they spoke Arabic, and again, she could not put together their discussion. However, she did notice Yehoshua's shining eyes and knew that they were in the middle of negotiations about the land.

Yehoshua saw her neither in her sleep nor when she arose. The effendi's words drew him like magic strands, and the mesh of the land was wound around him, becoming ever tighter. Olga shuddered. She thought about interrupting their talk and cutting off the streaming discussion, so as to draw her husband's attention to her. But the effendi had greater influence than she. She sought a way to break the magic bonds, and the idea came to her to clap.

The two turned to gawk at her—one with fury and the other in astonishment. She pointed to her mouth, outlined the shape of a cup with her fingers, and made signs of drinking. The effendi broke the silence first, nodded toward her, and also clapped, but his was strong and heard throughout the hall. Upon hearing the thwack, the lad came to them, one hand bearing a copper tray overloaded with cakes dipped in sugar water and the other, a pitcher of water. He first served the woman and then the men. The effendi took from the tray and stuffed his mouth with sugar-laden cake. Neither Olga nor Yehoshua took cake. When she saw that the effendi's mouth was busy with chewing, and there was no chance of his speaking in the next few minutes, she let out a rush of words that no one could cut off. She muttered in Russian and saw Yehoshua's face turn yellow in fury over her harm to the host's honor and for speaking a language he did not understand.

Olga was not hurt by his anger, especially when she saw the smile to her on the effendi's face in response to her mischievousness. He patted the pillow and shifted his position, relaxing, and turning his face to her to catch her words. He gave her his permission to speak but had no idea what she was talking about.

"With whose money will you buy it?" she asked. "You won't be able to mortgage Yehuda Leib's textile store any more. He won't let you. The land is larger than your dimensions, too big. Learn to be satisfied with the Duran land and with lots around Jaffa. Why do you need the Khudeira land? Why should you want to buy swamps and reeds?"

Yehoshua wasn't used to hearing any opposition from Olga about his actions—maybe she was right? Perhaps there was no need for such wild dreams and to look for deals so far from Jaffa?

Olga saw how the gleam had vanished from his eyes and how a veil of sadness was spreading in them, but she upheld her notions. Here, she had an opportunity to expose her pain and suffering because of a competitor that had captured Yehoshua's fancy—the land.

The effendi continued smiling, waiting for the moment her explosion of words would finish, and her anger would abate. Then he could bring the land agent back to him. And he was right. Olga finished speaking and was now left empty. She straightened her legs and put out a hand to take cake, but the effendi was quicker and offered her the tray a smile as if forgiving her for her misdeed. Olga knew she had been caught, lowered her eyes, and felt the crumbs of the cake stuck in her mouth, refusing to be swallowed.

The three sat and kept quiet Yehoshua looked up and back from the effendi to his wife and did not understand the closeness that had formed between them. He had been sure the Arab would be angry, and here he was, smiling at his wife.

Yehoshua turned to his wife and muttered, whispering in Russian, "I was at the Hovevei Zion Committee office in Jaffa before riding out to the land of Khudeira. Vladimir Tyomkin, the head of the committee, showed me a long list of buyers that included 50 families organized in three associations looking for real estate. He promised to act as a guarantor for the families, sign in their stead, and pledge that their payments would be on time. Everyone wants land, as you know ..." He stood up to stretch his legs that had gotten stiff after the crouched sitting, and he went on trying to convince her, "It's good land. Choice soil. Better than the land of Duran and three times larger. If I cannot redeem the land, the small speculators will come and tear it into tiny pieces and not redeem it. They will speculate with the land and wait for prices to rise; they will not live on it nor improve it. They will not build colonies on it." A pleading tone was discernible in his voice, but Olga did not give in easily.

"The Khudeira land is huge," she said. "What's so bad if others will speculate with it? You'll have time for me, and you will be at our house, and we won't have to use the second story over the store that does not allow us any privacy. You don't know how much I suffer. The pain of others doesn't reach you."

Now Olga was scared by her own audacity and tried to turn the conversation away from personal matters. "In Jaffa, they call after you 'speculant.' Pines and Herzenstein tell about the large sum of money you made from selling the Duran lands. Now they will hear about the Khudeira land and spread even more vicious stories. Not one member of an association will be interested in your plots."

But Yehoshua heard well what she wanted to hide. He heard and was frightened. He came close to her without thinking about the effendi and grasped her shoulders, feeling her trembling. Then, in an undertone, he told her about the events occurring in Eretz Israel that she did not know about, while his eyes revealed his love for her and his desire to be alone with her, along with his sorrow that this was not possible.

Olga felt uneasy and cast her eyes down, refusing to look at him. She knew that if she did so, she would soften and not think logically. Yehoshua understood her fear but did not give in, taking hold of her chin and turning her face to him, until she had no choice but to raise her eyes and pay attention. "And a new pasha has been assigned over Palestine, and he is not lenient. He doesn't like what the Jews are doing and is only waiting for the chance to impose his decrees. He delays land transfers and wants to shutter the gates to Jewish immigration. And you want me to sit idly by? No, not me! I will buy land as long as they let me. You know me better than the mother who bore me, and why do you say I am unfeeling about pain? And that I don't see your suffering? Or I don't see the pain of the land? I am aware of both of them, and they gnaw at my heart day and night and never let up."

Yehoshua took his hand away and went back to sit on the pillow opposite the effendi, while Olga stayed in her place and turned her eyes away, not wanting them to see the tears pooling at the corners of her eyes. Once again, he had linked her pain with that of the land and didn't differentiate between the two.

All that time, the effendi sat comfortably in his place and shot a mocking glance at the obsequiousness of the land agent to his wife. Yehoshua read his look but didn't pay attention to it—he had come to negotiate with him, to finish the matter. He wanted to share the signing of the contract with Olga and looked again at her, waiting for a signal from her. A long moment passed, but finally, Olga opened her arms wide and whispered helplessly, "Buy, do whatever you want. I will be with you for good or for bad."

☙

Negotiations were short. As a down payment, Yehoshua gave the effendi all the profits from the Duran land. After that, the lad came and brought a silver tray with paper, and a nib pen dipped in ink, and both signed the contract. For some time, they continued with small talk, but finally, the effendi rose, took leave of both of them, wrapped his cloak around himself, and left with measured gait, leaving behind unbearable confusion. Yehoshua got up and stretched out a hand to Olga to support her as she stood up, but she didn't want his hand. They waited for the young fellow to come to lead them to the room assigned them for their overnight stay, and they followed him.

The room was located over the stables. On its creaking, wooden floor, whose boards had not been polished for a long time now, was a large straw-filled mattress covered with rough fabric. Yehoshua and Olga lay down fully dressed, but the straw poked out and pricked them. Sleep was still far off, but they remained quiet, each sunk in their own thoughts.

After their hurtful conversation in the large hall, Olga was determined to tell him all about her visits to the sorceresses and the doctors and reveal to him the painful truth and declare out loud, "I am barren." Doing so would uproot the pain and the false hope she had been holding in, but now she felt distanced from him and did not know how to open her heartstrings and tell her husband. As long as she had not revealed the truth, it seemed as if it was not cold fact. She was again overwhelmed with jealousy for the land and recalled how she had yearned all day for his caresses. But he, his thoughts were not aimed at her. Now, they were laying side by side, back-to-back, like two strangers. Tears burst out and wet the straw pillow, and once more, she could not stop the agony that filled her completely.

Yehoshua heard and could not withstand her sobbing, so he pivoted over to her side and pulled her to him, hugging her and curling up along with her body. Then, he gently touched her face and wiped away the tears, and when she turned her face to him, he kissed her wet cheeks and tasted the saltiness of the teardrops. Yehoshua rolled her over him and clung to her more tightly, while his hand rubbed her back with long strokes. Olga sat atop him and split her legs, holding fast with her thighs to the sides of his body. Her weeping stopped, and only moisture glittered on her face in the moonlight stealing in through the cracks in the roof. She leaned toward him, and he felt her nipples beneath her blouse, barely touching his body. His hand slipped between the blouse buttons, and he continued caressing her body. Her skin quivered, and she leaned into him, seeking his warmth and desiring his touch. She opened the buttons of his shirt and those of her blouse, and moved toward him until their bodies touched, all of him in her, all of her in him.

When they were finished, they lay side by side, touching, belonging, and she told him what she had not been able to express before, and the more the words flowed, the more her distress lifted.

"They say I am barren," she whispered. "Some women want to irritate me and never stop saying to me, with a nod, "May you soon have children." Others say nothing, but you can see the pity in their eyes. But more difficult for me than what the women say are the words I heard from Dr. Masie. He declared that my body will not absorb your seed and not give you fruit. The land is what will give you productivity, and on it, you will leave your impression."

Yehoshua remained silent. Olga knew the message had been given, and he was now digesting it, so she waited for his response. But Yehoshua did not speak and held her closely to him; only after quite a while did he say to her, "I am your child; why would you want others?"

"You are my husband," she laughed, feeling relieved. "And I wanted both a husband and a child. I wanted a husband who would lay by my side and a child to cradle in my arms. So, if you are running about among the tracts of land and are not with me, at least I would rock my son in the cradle and take comfort from him."

"I don't want children," he replied. "They would compete with me for your love."

She laughed again, "For sure, you won't have children. You will have land. An enormous amount of land. And I will learn to live with your other love, with jealousy ..."

"You are beautiful in your envy," he quieted her. "You are all mine, and nothing separates us." She moved close to him and matched the folds of her body to his, and finally, fell asleep. This time, her slumber was relaxing and peaceful as it had not been for a long time.

But Yehoshua did not manage to sleep; he only lay there staring at the woman at his side. His fingers wove the ends of her hair and then undid them, and he knew they would not talk about this again.

Land, Land, Land

Olga was right. The land was like a wild beast, with a forked tongue and elusive, playing hide and seek with all its suitors, and the more they pursued it, the more wily it became, and the more they desired it, the more it laughed at their misery. The Khudeira land was a great challenge to obtain. It was more difficult than the

Duran land, more quick-witted and tantalizing than it, and three associations entered the chase: Riga, Kovno, and Vilna, and together they all made a laughingstock of Yehoshua.

During the winter, the emissaries of the associations came to the Jaffa Committee, and Vladimir Tyomkin sent them to Yehoshua. He promised and carried out his pledge. On Hanukkah, Yehoshua rode with them to the dunes, with the rain pelting them and the wind buffeting them. Since Yehoshua did not want to make things difficult for them, he took them to the top of the kurkar hill, and from there, they looked out at the expanses of land. He pointed out to them the good soil, the swamps, and the estate villa (that looked like a wayside inn—khan—so it was dubbed the "khan") and praised everything highly and asked them to close their eyes and use their imagination to see scenes of the future. They wanted neither words nor dreams; they requested to walk the length and breadth of the land and turn over every rock on it. Yehoshua did not like this group of functionaries who wanted to check if the land was good and see whether it was possible to exploit every inch of it. He didn't say anything and agreed to do whatever they asked—he had no choice, for all his money had been given to the effendi and he needed bundles of money to go on and promote other acquisitions. So, he went with them a few times during Hanukkah and in January and February, and they still delayed their answer.

The Abu Kishk and Wadi Hawarith tribes began to mock the sight of the riders visiting the land once a week. The effendi Salim Khoury began to become impatient while Yehoshua went on leading them from corner to corner and keeping quiet. One night they stayed over in the manor house, and Yehoshua was late in getting to the large hall. He sat near the oven, wrapped up in himself, with his eyes fixed on the jumping flames. He heard steps approaching, and when he turned to look at the source, he saw Khoury entering the hall and sitting down as usual on the embroidered pillows. The obese man gave a sign to the serving boy to come close to him and bring him his nargila (water pipe for smoking) and steaming coffee; then, he whispered something to him, and the lad turned to Yehoshua, saying, "The effendi is calling you."

Yehoshua knew—Salim Khoury was not the bearer of glad tidings. He was beckoning to him to discuss the contract and the delayed payments. For several minutes, the two sat without uttering a word while looking at each other, then they began with small talk, and only after they had drunk a second cup of coffee did the effendi ask him what was going on with the agreement.

"Jaffa speculators have turned to me," he told Yehoshua, in measured tones. "They want the land. They promised a great deal of money, much more than what was agreed on in the contract between you and me. But we have shaken hands, so I will not go back on my word. The time has come to finish the purchase."

"I will conclude it soon," Yehoshua promised him, although he was not certain he could stand by his promise.

The effendi, who sensed Yehoshua's hesitation and his unsteady voice, added, "Show your seriousness to me, prove that you are really a great land agent with whom it is worthwhile negotiating."

Yehoshua did not know what to say and furiously tried to think of a way out, and then suddenly blurted out, "I will buy land and register it in my name, and I will be a partner to the acquisition by the associations. The Jews will see my agreement with you, and they will say, 'The agent bought. That's a sign that the land is good and one can make a profit with it.'"

"And money for the purchase, where will you take it from," wondered the effendi.

"From the broker's fees the associations owe me."

The effendi nodded his head and then became silent. Then he showed Yehoshua that their discussion was over, called his lad, gathered his wide robe and left.

In the morning, before the representatives had woken up, Yehoshua chose a plot of land for himself that began at the bottom of the dunes and ended near the sea. By the afternoon, he showed his selection to the emissaries. Now, they no longer hesitated and were ready to sign the agreement with him, transferring the land from the effendi to the societies. They returned to Jaffa and promised to fulfill their part of the agreement immediately after the Turkish land office registration was completed.

Yehoshua did not tell Olga about his new purchase but waited for the agent's fees promised to him. He secretly hoped that the emissaries would not learn from the acquisition of the Duran lands and ask, as had Broide, to register each plot separately in the name of a foreign citizen, but he was wrong. Instead, these representatives demanded to register each plot in the name of the owners, and to note in huge letters on each land certificate next to the name: "A Russian bought this land." But that was not enough for them; they insisted on receiving at the time of purchase also the building permits as well as the listing of the borders and the drainage of the swamp water and its diversion into canals—and all of this was made Yehoshua's responsibility.

The list of demands was long, and the outlays needed were beyond the capability of a land agent just starting out, and beyond all that was the debt for the land Yehoshua had bought for himself. To Yehoshua, it seemed that the Duran episode had returned with greater force and with larger dimensions, and again he refrained from looking straight at his wife. But Olga did not need explanations, since the gossip offered by the wives of the functionaries brought the news to her, and along with the chatter, the estrangement of Yehoshua from the store and from the room on the second story grew greater.

At the time of the arguments over the Khudeira land, Yehoshua became close to Tyomkin and relied on him, hoping he would rescue him from the demands of the associations' emissaries. His connection to Tyomkin differed from Olga's closeness to the Committee chairman. She used to visit when the house was abuzz with people, while Yehoshua came when everyone else had left. If at first, he called him "the engineer," now he called him "Vladimir," who would respond with a smile, "the young Yehoshua." Olga stopped going to Tyomkin's parties and devoted herself entirely to obstetrics, traveling a lot in the doctor's wagon to attend births throughout the desert for the wives of shaykhs and the wives of effendis; she went as far as Nablus and Hebron. She delivered the babies of Muslims, Christians, and Jews, and when she had finished her work, she would return at night to the room above the store and collapse with fatigue.

Yehoshua became the Committee's chief land agent. He was pleased by the new title that had been given to him, "The Primary Land Agent of the Hovevei Zion Committee," and he had already heard people were prattling behind his back and calling him "Tyomkin's boy," "Baron Rothschild's competitor," and "the one who wants to buy all the land of Eretz Israel from the sea to the river." He enjoyed hearing the undertones and sharing them with Tyomkin, as well as planning ways to concentrate the buying and selling of all the lands in the hands of the Committee. He firmly believed that the closer he would become to the chairman of the Committee, the more the land issues of Khudeira would be solved. But this belief blinded him and influenced his other actions. He would sit with Tyomkin and mock the attempts by others to acquire land and tell him again about the purchase of the Duran land and boast about the expanses of Khudeira. The two would share a bottle of wine from the Bordeaux vineyards and staggered as they jabbered until the wee hours of the night.

Enemies began to pop up against Tyomkin, and the more Yehoshua stayed with him, the more they too became his enemies. Included among these foes were old ones as well, chief among them being Yehiel Michael Pines, the number two man on the Committee after Tyomkin. Pines harbored the insult he had received from Yehoshua and was waiting for his downfall; his growing closeness with Tyomkin enraged him further. To him, it seemed as if the two had conspired against him, and he took every move by Tyomkin as instigated by Yehoshua. Now, added to all the murmurings of the emissaries from Riga, Kovno, and Vilna were the hateful remarks by Pines and the other land brokers, and they increasingly fomented Jaffa and presented Yehoshua as growing ever closer to Tyomkin.

A month after the associations' emissaries agreed to buy the Khudeira land, they asked for Yehoshua to accompany them one last time to the lands for the signing of the conditions in the "khan" in the presence of the effendi. Then they would no longer bother each other. At first, Yehoshua refused to ride with them, since he had an inkling that their real aim was to rescind their commitment and remind him of their requests, since everyone clearly knew he would not be able to meet the expenses they were demanding.

"Let's call for an arbitrator," he responded to their invitation, "and he will decide between us. In Eretz Israel, it unheard of that the costs of drainage and leveling the land will be borne by the broker, moreover on a single agent."

But Tyomkin, who knew of their approach, convinced him to go with them and promised to ride with him and even made it obligatory for them to pay the brokerage fees to Yehoshua at the end of the trip.

Everyone would calm down, he explained to Yehoshua, and a compromise would be reached and the expenses divided. Seeing no alternative, Yehoshua gave in to him, since his debt was mushrooming and the effendi was about to withdraw from the deal. The very idea of getting far away from Jaffa in Tyomkin's company attracted him.

In the evening, he told Olga about their trip and tried to convince her to go with them.

"The three of us will ride," he implored her. "We will escape the commotion of the city, and at the end of the journey, the purchase of the Khudeira land will be completed, and you will be part of the seeing things finished."

But Olga refused to go, since she sensed that the agreement between him and the effendi to which she had been a witness would not be met, and she did not want to see Yehoshua's new failure.

With a forced smile, she told him, "Your riding is better than mine. Your friendship is better without me. I will wait for you and fend off the evil whisperings running around Jaffa."

In early morning, the group of emissaries set out, with two riding in front, going some distance further than the others and galloping joyously in each other's company. It was a sun-washed day with a slight breeze swaying the bushes. At evening, the group climbed the hill and entered the manor house, which looked like a khan, that rose up from and dominated the lands of Khudeira. Next to the heavy wooden gate, the effendi waited for them, wrapped as usual in his wide abaye, standing with his legs slightly apart, his hands concealed within the folds of his cloak, and a smile on his face. After the group had made itself comfortable in one of the large rooms, the effendi joined them and clapped to call the serving lad to offer the guests the rice and meat. The hall was empty, the smell of mold rising from the kurkar stones, the hot stew, and the ease of the Arab cast a sense of serenity on the emissaries, and they felt that the effendi held a genial opinion of them and would prefer to side with them and not Yehoshua.

Yehoshua sensed this, quaked, and sought Tyomkin's support. But the Committee official was busy with the stew, the rolling of the pita, and filling it with rice and pieces of lamb.

While some emissaries were tasting the sweet cakes and sipping coffee, others were again detailing their demands to the effendi—to register Russian citizens on the kushan and to see to the building permits, determine the borders, and drain the swamp. The effendi nodded his head in agreement to every translated word, since the requests seemed absolutely logical to him, and he even laughed toward the translator and said that had he known that it was possible to turn swampland into rich soil, he would have raised its price and maybe think twice whether it was worthwhile selling it. The representatives did not understand his language, but Yehoshua did—the only one to do so.

"An agent does not have to take care of the building permits, and I already said that in our oral agreement," Yehoshua dared to say and interrupted the sounds of chewing.

"You did it for Duran," the representatives told him, "Do it for us, too."

He sorely remembered the Duran episode and was in no need of a reminder from them. The net that had closed around him contained the incident surrounding the purchase, and now the strings of another net were tightening around him—the acquisition of the Khudeira land. But this time, he would not let them trap him. He grew angrier and burst out to the group, "I will not sell! I will find buyers with fewer demands than you."

The effendi smirked his familiar, venomous-tinged smile, bent down toward the translator, and asked for explanations. After listening, he gathered the edges of his white jalabiya, lifted himself up from his pillow, and directed his speech toward Yehoshua, "Of course, there is an agreement between you and Salim Khoury, but you are not meeting the terms, and the obligation of the seller is no longer valid. If you will not sell the land in line with the demands of the buyers—the owner of the land will find other agents. As I already pointed out to you, many like you are knocking at my door."

The whole time, Tyomkin sat quietly and didn't interfere with the discussion. When he finished chewing the meat that he was not used to and had also dipped his fingers in lemon water, he slid his pillow out of the circle and waited to see how things would develop. The effendi's support of the emissaries astonished him and even made him bitter. But Yehoshua's fury made him fearful, because from the way he was sitting, it looked as if he would get up and strike the effendi and the group of representatives at any moment.

Tyomkin rose and stood next to the translator and cut him off mid-sentence. "You are all blind," he called. "Marching in the dark and not seeing the upheavals in the Turkish regime. The Turks hate the Russians and won't allow registration of the name of a Russian citizen on land that was Turkish. Write only a name, without citizenship. Plain names," he declared. Then, he turned to the effendi and measured his words, one by one, "The emissaries are represented by the Committee, and the Committee has only one land broker, Mr. Hankin. That means I will cancel the entire deal if you refuse to honor the agreement."

The translator himself was frightened from what he had translated and sat right down, fearing the effendi's reaction, but Salim Khoury was silent.

The emissaries, after whispering among themselves, finally agreed to the word "plain," but they did not concede about the building permits nor on the fences or the stone bridge or the water channel draining floodwaters. Tyomkin continued to argue with them and agreed to some of their demands, but others, he refused.

The entire time, Yehoshua just continued to sit in his place and did not become involved. To him, the representatives, including Tyomkin, looking like a bunch of haggling women in the market, who fearfully hop around like a cackling, plucking feathers and checking meat, raising and lowering prices. Suddenly, weakness assailed him. Olga's words buzzed around in his brain, bothering and burning him. The land was bigger than he was, bigger … the hall's walls were spinning around, and faces became blurred. His hand found something stable to hold onto but bumped into the tray of rice and dragged it, and again he remembered nothing.

When he came to, he found himself lying on pillows, with a frightened Tyomkin at his side and the emissaries leaning over to see what had happened. He pulled on Tyomkin's coat lapel until their eyes focused on each other and whispered to him, "Sign in my name. I'll do whatever you say. This is all too much for me." Then, he closed his eyes again.

The emissaries were actually about to sign before evening, and Tyomkin was ready to sign next to the broker's name, leaving space for Yehoshua's signature. After a short discussion, it was decided the money the associations owed Mr. Hankin would be turned over to Tyomkin for safekeeping, until the agent fulfilled his obligations. Furthermore, Tyomkin would allot some of the brokerage fees to Salim Khoury in exchange for the land that Yehoshua had bought at the dunes. The remainder would be divided into three equal payments Yehoshua would receive after completing each stage as described in the agreement. The Riga representatives did not suffice with all this but demanded that Tyomkin be a guarantor for Yehoshua. The Committee chairman agreed to that without hesitation, and when he added his name to the proper places in the agreement, he refrained from looking at Yehoshua.

Now, it seemed as if those present were satisfied. Vladimir was the first to rise and used his arms to support his friend and invited him to walk with him. Yehoshua was dragged after him and tried to hold himself erect and not lean on his comrade; he asked to go up to his room, seclude himself there, and not see the faces standing in the hall.

Near the doorway, a cry from Shecktzer, the Riga emissary who was the youngest of them all, halted them, "I will not sign. I will first see the entire tract and measure every step. In Jaffa, people said the broker took land for himself. But what if he took the good land and left us the worst?"

Yehoshua was furious. They did not rely on him; they were behaving like Broide, wanting to make him fail and watch his ruin. He overcame his weakness and turned toward them, and with a measured gait, returned to the pile of pillows and yelled, "Russian, plain Russians! Without any identity and without character, and without a spine. Go back to Kovno and Riga. There they buy land by the pound. They get the feel of it and examine it. And if they like it—they take it; if not—they toss it away. You sought to redeem land, to fulfill the commandment to settle the land. Now, I see all of this was simply empty words. Leave, go back to your places. I've had enough of you and your demands. I will find better people than you, Ottoman citizens and not just plain citizens."

He threw to the floor the page of the contract resting on the tray, and when he straightened up to leave and cast them a penetrating glance, he noticed their astonishment. He took a few steps toward the door, and Tyomkin, who was rooted to his spot near the threshold, came toward him to hold him back and grabbed him by the shoulders, yelling at him furiously and ignoring the people around him, "No! I won't let you ruin all my efforts. This time you have gone too far." Then he dragged Yehoshua back to the group and said in his name, "In the morning, all of us will ride. We will measure the length and width of the tract, and you will see Mr. Hankin's tract and judge for yourselves."

The men did not argue, and the smile disappeared from Salim Khoury's face. Then, very quietly, each one went to his own room, with only Yehoshua and Tyomkin remaining in the hall. Yehoshua's legs were leaden, and he couldn't move from where he was. He did not know whether to be furious or get up and flee. Weakness again overwhelmed him, and his legs trembled. Vladimir, who saw his stumbling, approached him and, brooking no refusal, took him by the arm and brought him over to the oven in the corner of the room. Once they had sat down, Tyomkin called the serving boy to bring them a bottle of warm liquor, and he poured for both of them. The two quickly finished off one bottle and asked for another. The wine went to their heads, and they forgot about the anger and insult, which were replaced by the laughter and glee of drunks.

Yehoshua mocked the emissaries and imitated the way they spoke, while Tyomkin repeated after him, "Russians, Russians!" And Yehoshua responded, "Plain, plain!" Hours passed, the bottles piled up, and the two of them did not notice that they had shifted to speaking about Olga. Tyomkin told Yehoshua about his meetings with her in Petersburg and added, "She was different. Different from the other young women. A pretty girl with many suitors. At the Biluim meetings, they whispered about a great lover she had, an army man. But she rebuffed him and emigrated to Eretz Israel." Yehoshua smiled and tapped his friend's shoulder, mumbling her name, and in his insobriety, he mixed up the letters, so he repeated it, saying, "But now she is mine, my Olga."

"If she weren't yours," Vladimir tapped him back, "I would go on being interested in her and convince her to follow me."

Yehoshua poured another shot of drink, lifted it toward the ceiling, and declared, "Since Olga's mine, be interested in this," and he gave it to his friend.

Slowly, the two ceased chattering and sat mutely. Yehoshua lowered his head onto his arms, stared at the bottle and the remaining liquor, and remembered the thick braid wound around the head of the woman waiting for him in their room in Jaffa. He wanted to take her in his hands and took hold of the bottle; he pulled himself together and was sorry they had spoken about his wife. If it weren't for the fumes of liquor that swathed both of them, he would have told Tyomkin about his dream of building a summer home for Olga on the edge of the Khudeira tract. He would describe to him the port and the watermelon patches and the sailboats gliding during the summer months, reaching both Jaffa and Egypt. But the two were drunk and couldn't get the words out straight, so he said, "Let's go up to the room. It's already late, and you promised in my name to ride tomorrow and to show the emissaries the entire Khudeira property from one end to the other.

They rose and staggered, leaning on each other, and while holding the walls for support, they looked for their room, and when they didn't find it, they made horrendous racket until the servant lad came and showed them to their room on the second floor that faced the courtyard of the "khan."

Yehoshua slumbered a dreamless sleep, dead to the world. When he woke up, he saw he had slept in his clothes and didn't remember where he was, but his headache and the shifting floor reminded him of the bottles of liquor that had piled up on the tray. A mix of voices penetrated into the room and was probably what had woken him. He approached the vaulted window, turned the knob, and bent over the railing.

A company of mounted Turkish gendarmes filled the courtyard. The soldiers sat and polished their rifles and curled their mustaches, and he didn't understand what they were doing in the "khan," so he decided to go down to the yard to see why they had come. From one casual conversation to another, he understood that a serious dispute had broken out among the Wadi Hawarith tribes, and a call had been sent to the soldiers stationed in Caesarea for fear of a blood feud between clans. But until the troops had arrived, the number of victims slain had reached a few dozen. The soldiers were divided—a few of them looked for the avengers among the reeds and the swamps, while others were sent to the courtyard of the effendi's house to change horses and to rest. They talked about an engagement meal and about the daughter of Shaykh Abu Rabia who had been promised to the son of Shaykh al Umar, but when they had come to bring the gifts to the bride's family, the girl was nowhere to be found—she had run away with someone else.

Actually, Yehoshua was happy about the arrival of the soldiers. He knew he could not fulfill Tyomkin's promise to ride the length and width of the Khudeira land with the Russians, since the Turks would see the group of Russians and ask questions. What would they say? They're just "plain" Russians? He smiled to himself, forgetting his drunkenness, and went to wake Tyomkin.

He found him sleeping soundly, and neither the rays of the sun nor the bustle in the courtyard had disturbed his rest. Yehoshua tried to wake him gently, and failed. Then he tried to remove his blanket, but Vladimir Tyomkin curled up and brought his knees up to his body, and moaned like a child trembling from cold. Yehoshua went to dip a cloth in the water bowl, came back, and wiped the sleeper's forehead and the rheum from his eyes—to no avail. In the end, he put his mouth near the slumberer's ear and shouted, "The Turks are on you, Tyomkin!" The man jumped up in a panic and called to the person standing over him, "Go, look for the Russians. Warn them not to say a word about the reason for coming to the effendi's house." Then, while still trying to get back to breathing normally, he added, "It's best if they don't say anything so their language will not be identified. Find them other clothes."

Yehoshua broke out in a roaring laugh and asked, "Why warn them? They're just 'plain' fellows. Who cares about the likes of them?" But he did go and called out gaily as he walked through the arched corridor, "Plain, p-l-ain."

He found only a few Russians. Most of them had scattered—a few rose early to pray; a few went up the high dunes to scan the panorama of sea and land, while others had circled the "khan" and examined its stones and layers. Only at about noon did he manage to gather them in one corner of the stables, far from the main courtyard, and order them to mount their horses and to ride quickly back to Jaffa. But the men refused to do so and ignored his explanations about the danger posed to them by the Turkish soldiers.

"You promised," they told him. "You promised, but your word is worthless." Someone dared to call out after him, "Little speculator!" But Yehoshua ignored their insults and continued to prod them to leave. Shecktzer, the leader of the dissidents, collected the emissaries around him, and now they looked to Yehoshua like a conspiracy of black ravens fixing their evil eyes on him.

Tyomkin was not in the courtyard, and while still waiting for him, Yehoshua tried to threaten them, "I will ride by myself, while you remain in the estate's yard and, in Russian, explain to the soldiers why you are staying in it. You will be pretty good company for each other. In any event, they don't understand your language, and you don't understand theirs. Anyway, who are you? They will ask. Russians? And you will answer, plain, just plain fellow."

Shecktzer broke away from the group and left the courtyard, but Yehoshua paid him no mind and began readying his horse to set out. A minute later, the young emissary returned, accompanied by Tyomkin. When he saw Yehoshua's inquisitive expression, he explained, "I went to speak with the company commander. Robbers are on the way. Murders are wandering among the swamps, so I asked for an escort."

"You asked for an escort? An escort for who? What for?" wondered Yehoshua.

"An escort for the emissaries and for you," he replied. "After you left the room, I considered what to say to the soldiers, and I looked for reasons for us staying in the "khan." Then, a brainstorm hit me, to say we are pilgrims, visiting the tombs of saints, moving about between Jaffa, Jerusalem, and Nazareth. We will ride together, and you will ascend the hill and show the emissaries your land and theirs, and that will have to be enough for them."

Yehoshua saw Shecktzer's brief grin expressing joy at his misfortune and realized that he was alone against all of them, and he cried out angrily, "You are all fools. Not knowing anything about how things are done in Palestine. I will go up the hill and point out the pieces of land, and the Turks will believe whatever I say. Then, about a month later, the surveyors will come, and the land will be in the *tapu* (Tabu) office in the name of plain Russians, and no one will be surprised and connect one story to the other. You are blind. In all innocence, I thought the Committee chairman understood more than the average Russian." He turned his face away and rushed to attach the halter and straighten the bridle, while behind him, he heard Tyomkin approaching him.

"Give in," Tyomkin chided him in harsh tones that he had never heard before. "The emissaries did their part and gave up on examining the entire tract and are satisfied with just taking a sweeping look at it."

"Give in!" Tyomkin repeated when he saw Yehoshua was going to refuse. "I have all the brokerage fees, and if you do not follow my instructions, you won't get the money."

Yehoshua was quiet. He had been humiliated in front of the representatives, and he could only agree to Tyomkin's dictate. He got on his horse and waited for the group to organize their belongings and ride after him. The tumult in the courtyard went on for quite a while, but finally, they set out from there in a long caravan. The leader was Yehoshua, at a distance from the others. Then came Tyomkin, who, from time to time, called to his friend, "Wait. Slow your pace," while in Russian he would growl, "Hurry up. The day is short." Two Turkish soldiers were bringing up the rear, wondering what kind of caravan they were escorting.

Yehoshua rode seething with bitterness, and the faster he galloped, the more his fury grew. He still didn't understand why Tyomkin had taken the emissaries' side; just the day before, the two had made wild merry together and were close to each other, to the point that Yehoshua had told him of his great love for Olga. Better to leave them, he thought. He would go far away and run to the ends of the country and not see their faces nor that of the Committee chairman. He spurred his horse on, and when he heard Tyomkin's cry, he pulled himself together and slowed the pace of his riding. He had given all his money, the Duran funds, to the effendi in exchange for the plot he had bought, and Olga didn't know. He promised her a house on the dunes. He dreamed of plowing a field and of charting paths. Now, they will find out about his huge failure, and everyone will mock him as Olga had said to him: the land is greater than you, too great.

He slowed his riding and waited for Tyomkin and the emissaries. And when they all stood around him, he asked them to accompany him, and they climbed the kurkar cliff. Yehoshua showed them the sand dunes, the sea, and the swamps between them, blue abutting gold. He stretched out his arm and pointed to the dunes of Caesarea and those of Khudeira, including his own piece of land. Once they saw the swap and sand, they did not envy him and turned in the direction of the black tents with flocks of goats grazing on weeds between them. The afternoon sun beat down on their heads, and the emissaries scattered over the hill, examining their plots and arguing among themselves whether it was good soil or poor and how many parts of it to give to the members of the Riga association and how many to the societies of Kovno and Vilna. Yehoshua descended the hill and mounted his horse, refusing to meet Tyomkin's gaze, and waited for the call from the Committee head telling the men to get on their horses and continue riding.

They rode into the swamps, Yehoshua alone at their head, and behind him, a unified group—emissaries who had come to investigate the land of Palestine, the chairman making promises, and two soldiers who scanned their surroundings and cocked their pistols in case a brigand should pop up among the reeds.

Two weeks passed. The Russian emissaries did not call Yehoshua, while he did not go to them, and as far as Tyomkin, it was as if he had been swallowed by the earth.

Yehoshua did not tell Olga what had happened when they had gone to the Khudeira land, and when she asked how Vladimir was doing, he answered, "A plain Russian. Busy with Committee matters, confident of himself and in his expertise in the laws of Palestine and the quality of the land, so he does not need brokers."

Olga realized there was a growing rift between the two of them and thought it stemmed from the visit to the Khudeira dunes. But she did not console him nor try to find out. As was her wont, she remained silent and waited for the end of the entire matter of the purchase, after which would come the calm.

Yehoshua returned to going down to the port, gazing at the ships anchored far from the shore, at the boats sailing into the harbor, unloading Marseilles tiles for building the roofs of the houses in the new colonies, and again going out to the open sea. More than once, he had wished to embark on one of the ships to sail far away from Jaffa and the land, leaving behind its idiosyncrasies. But then he would remember his debt and the mockery of the effendi, as well as Pines lurking around the corner waiting to witness his fall and Olga's words as well, "The land is greater than you are. Too great."

One evening, he had had enough of the ships and of wandering around aimlessly. Disquiet seized him, and he wanted to know where he stood, so he made his way at a late-night hour, when Jaffa was still fast asleep, toward Tyomkin's house.

An old man opened the door, and Yehoshua did not wait for him to announce his arrival to the homeowner, so he hurried up the stairs toward the Committee chair's office. Without knocking, he opened the door wide, but heard the old fellow wheezing on the stairway, yelling, "Wait, Mr. Hankin, the head of the Committee is busy."

Yehoshua blinked when struck by the strong light in the room, and when he got used to it, he saw Tyomkin sitting in his robe at a table loaded with signed letters. The breeze that came in from the open door drew his attention, and he turned to see who had entered. And when he saw Yehoshua, he could not hide his astonishment.

They neither greeted each other, nor apologized. Yehoshua did not wait to be invited in and sit down; he burst in without letting his host utter a word.

"I have heavy debt, but that's not all. I bought a plot in Khudeira to prove my trustworthiness, so they would say I am an honest broker, ready to risk his own money for the nation." For a moment, he cut off his flow of words as if wishing to see the impression they had made, and then he added, with downcast eyes, "But you scorned me and deserted me. I can't look anyone in the eye, and I feel everyone is laughing at me. Help me finish the episode of this piece of land."

Tyomkin was quiet and embarrassed to see the dismal land broker. Since he did not respond, Yehoshua trembled even more and was frightened by the silence, so he spoke slowly, in fragmented sentences, "The Khudeira land has good soil, the best of the best. But you know that the Russians won't buy, and I can't sell, and the speculator will pounce on it and chop it into tiny pieces. The price will soar, and I will be stuck with my debt and the name of a small hustler."

Tyomkin was still quiet, and again, Yehoshua did not understand the meaning of his silence.

"Olga doesn't believe in my ability," he repeated beseechingly. "Just like you, she keeps her peace and does not share my pain. You said on the night we were flying high that if it were not for me, you would be wooing her. Do something for her, if not for me."

Now, Tyomkin raised his hand, attempting to silence Yehoshua and prevent him from saying things he would rue later. Yehoshua swallowed his last word and saw himself as contemptible and fawning, as someone whose honor had been trampled.

The interlocutor sitting opposite him opened his mouth to speak and was chary over which words to use. "I will have you sign when they are not present." He spoke slowly, "And you will promise to obtain the kushan certificates (title deeds) for the land and register each plot with a name but without citizenship. You will obtain building permits, see to the draining of the swamp, and the rest will be done at a later stage, after settlement. Two days after you sign, the whole matter will be over. You will receive your broker's fee, and the emissaries will leave Jaffa, and you can take care of your plot, pay off your debt, and continue with other acquisitions. People have short memories, and they will forget the details and only remember the success in selling and buying a huge tract."

Yehoshua only nodded and didn't make a peep. He saw himself like those Jewish speculators teeming in the streets of Jaffa, forging signatures and inventing names of associations only to enhance their status and building colonies no one had ever heard of and selling land that did not exist. Tyomkin didn't look at him but only thrust a paper at him for his signature. He signed and left there quickly, escaping into the dark, wishing to flee from himself and his humiliation and the deep sense of failure that had attached itself to him and would not let go.

Tyomkin was right. Two days after Yehoshua signed, the emissaries signed the purchase agreement for the bloc of land in the Khudeira tract. Once they had completed the matter, the representatives returned home to Riga, Kovno, and Vilna to prepare the people for immigration to Eretz Israel. After that, all Yehoshua had to do was go to Haifa and register the lands at the Land Office in the name of the Russians—plain people without citizenship— pay a bribe, and see to the permits for building on the land. In response to the clerk's questions about the identity and origin of the people, he said, "Half of them are Turkish, and half will be Turkish," and with the help of such mutterings and a handful of French francs, he eased the wonderings of the clerk.

He acted with no pleasure, without the joy of purchasing, selling, and redeeming. However, he was apprehensive about touching the papers since he considered them cancerous and hurried to hand them over to the Committee chairman, so he wouldn't have to hold them even for a day.

And in his second-story room, he waited for the day on which the Turkish soldiers would knock on his door, accusing him of treason, and sullying his name, "He registers Turkish land and hands it over to Russians in exchange for filthy lucre." They would rip up the property certificates and swing a hammer to remove the sign above the entrance to the store, and Olga would continue to say, "Greater than you, too great."

The days grew longer, and spring burst out again in the lanes of Jaffa, and once more, people took out their carpets and hung them on stone walls. The changing of the seasons went unnoticed by Yehoshua, nor did he register the renewed look of the streets. He would button his coat all the way up and go down to the port to stare at the waves and then return with quick steps to the room over the store, looking back from time to time to see if he was being followed. He didn't hear what people were talking about, or Olga's questions. He was fully drawn into himself, waiting and not knowing whether to expect Turkish soldiers would come to take him; or whether some piece of news would extract him from his sorrow and anger at himself, alongside his weakness, dragging him down ever further.

One morning, an Egyptian dressed in black entered Yehuda Leib's store — one of the Egyptians who had come to work in Jaffa and the new colonies; workers who lived in huts at the edges of the courtyard. They made do with a mere mill and bread and olives, sending the rest of their money to their families in Egypt. The Egyptian had brought a letter written in a foreign language addressed to the young Mr. Hankin. The letter was handed over to Sarah, since no one else was in the store. Sarah signed for the letter and promised to give it to the addressee. However, the smell of the envelope, the whiteness of the paper, and the clear handwriting made her uneasy. Finally, she closed the store and rushed to Dr. Masie's office to turn the letter over to Olga.

The younger woman was surprised by her mother-in-law's panic and promised her she would go to look for Yehoshua. Then she sat Sarah down, finished her work, and then ran to the warehouses in the port. Yehoshua, as usual, was standing on the dock and counting the ships coming and going.

"Yehoshua!" she cried excitedly. "They sent you a letter. It's in French."

Very slowly, he turned to her, without her enthusiasm affecting him. "Sarah said that an Egyptian brought it to the store. And, maybe, it has good news?"

Olga carefully opened the envelope, so as not to tear it or damage the ornate writing at its edges and read out loud, "Antoine Bishara Tayyan asks to meet Mr. Hankin. Would your good self kingly inform him of a proper time for the meeting?"

Olga was frightened, for she remembered their riding together in the sands toward the land of Wadi Hawarith and the Khudeira expanses. Besides that memory, all of Jaffa knew who Antoine Bishara Tayyan was—a very rich man owning a great deal of land. Olga stopped reading and looked at her husband to see his reaction. But Yehoshua seemed so distant that she did not know if he had heard what she had said or not. She continued to read the content to him, but he just stayed silent. Once she realized there was no reason to go on reading, Olga hastened to drag her husband out of there, and the two marched together to the shop. There, among the rolls of textiles and copper bowls loaded with notions, she read the letter to him—for the third time. This time, she saw how his face softened, his eyes refocused, and a gentle smile played at the corners of his mouth.

"Land," he whispered to her, "the expansive, rich land of Wadi Hawarith. Antoine Bishara Tayyan is a rich merchant known everywhere in the Ottoman Empire, and he chose me, the Yehoshua who has been dubbed 'the petty speculator,' to be the broker for his lands. I'll show all of them, the Russian emissaries and Vladimir Tyomkin and Pines, the insidious schemer. I am not a petty scalper, but a great broker." Olga suddenly imagined seeing him taller and more erect and solemnly reinforced him: "Yes, you will be great, the second Yehoshua."

Since she knew French, Olga sat down and jotted down Yehoshua's reply to the letter—in four days he would go to him.

After handing the letter to the messenger, with the two of them remaining in the store as happy as children, he told her, "Wash the white shirt from our wedding time for me. The years have probably left their mark on it."

Olga laughed, hurried to their room, and opened the straw chest, finding his shirt among the pieces of fabric and old clothes. Next, she went down to show him, and when Yehoshua put it on over the blue shirt he was wearing, she counted the stains and murmured, "I'll take them out with salt, dry it over coals, and iron it. You'll go looking like a bridegroom."

Yehoshua grabbed her hips and swung her around in a dance, whispering to her close to her ear, "Like a groom, a groom whose bride is waiting."

On the day of the meeting, Yehoshua put the white shirt on early. Olga stayed home to polish the buttons of his coat, brush his boots, and trim his wild beard, rather than go to work to see her patients. He was restless and was ready to go quite a while before the time of the appointment; he asked her to accompany him to Christians' Street.

Olga was pleased to be asked, put her shawl on her shoulders, and set out, escorting him. As they walked slowly side by side, Olga chattered about her patients and the births, trying to reduce his excitement, and without paying attention, they had neared the Christians' homes.

The Maronite's house was higher than the other Christian homes that rose above the harbor, with a white wall concealing the lower floor so that only the second floor could be seen from the street. A grapevine climbed the wall and hid the gate in it, sending its branches into the lane. Olga stopped next to the gate to hold him back a bit and smoothed his clothes to straighten a wrinkle. "Wait," she whispered. "Be careful in the negotiations. Think before you agree. Don't let the days of Khudeira recur." She saw his smile and his confidence, but even so, she added, "Rumors are rife in Jaffa; behind my back, they are murmuring, 'The wife of a small speculator.'"

Yehoshua stroked her hair and said, "No longer small. Do you remember?"

Then, she heard him laughing, a dry, brittle chortle, a laugh of greatness. Or, perhaps, it only seemed like that to her? She was taken a bit aback and looked him up and down. At that moment, she wanted to go on and tell him about the evil, gossipy, wagging tongues blathering that he had taken for himself a tract in the dunes bordering the estate of Salim Khouri with the very best land, but his overriding self-confidence intimidated her, and she kept her peace. Deep within, she prayed that this transaction would go smoothly and his confidence would be justified. But Yehoshua did not sense her worry and turned to a niche in the wall and rang the small bell; Olga saw an Egyptian wearing black clothes opening the gate and ushering him into the courtyard.

The woman stood for a moment in the shadow of the wall and then turned to the loneliness and self-pity overwhelming her. She took a few steps slowly, her body hunched over and her thoughts harsh: they call her Olga, the wife of Yehoshua Hankin. He had given her a ring and built her a room, but his total love was still uncertain. Then, perhaps, she should leave? She would return to Shimshon's house to live with Meir and Shifra. In any event, they had no children to keep him with her, so her leaving would be easy. But in her heart, she knew that these ideas would never be put into action. Her love for him was too strong; she would hold onto him the way the land grasped him and would not let go.

෴

Summer arrived, and its heat chased people into the shade of the homes and yards. The functionaries of Jaffa and their wives sat in secluded corners, sipping cold tamarind juice and lemonade, while drinking in news about the Empire — a rising ruler and a falling ruler, matters of laws and limitations, and the reputation of Hankin, the land broker, increasingly became part of their conversations.

He was dubbed with a new nickname—"the lad." The first to call him that was Yehiel Michel Pines, who wrote a long article in the newspaper *HaTzefirah* paper entitled, "The Lad and the Buying of Eretz Israel." After it appeared, many Jaffa residents came to Yehuda Leib's store, not to make purchases but only to sniff around and see "the lad" and check if he was really as terrible as Pines had described him. The rumors spread by word of mouth, and as happens with gossip, there was no similarity between it and the newspaper source. People spread stories about the theft of the lands of Khudeira tract; about "the lad" who held kushans and would not let the Russians establish their colony, and even the good soil he took for himself— the delta of the river of El-Hudeira and the port Minat Abu Zabura. And as if that were not enough, he cast a spell on a wealthy land trader, who enabled him to buy the land of Wadi Hawarith and to deal in selling it to others. They even related that "the lad" walked about Jaffa with swollen pockets, unwilling to forgo even a penny or a smidgen of land. He is greedy for money and lusting for land, but even so, he is miserly and goes about in a worn-out coat and untrimmed hair in order not to spend a bit of money or share it with others. One morning, on the store's door, Yehuda Leib found a caricature drawn in charcoal: a naked man with only his long hair covering his private parts and his long fingers extended to grab silver coins strewn about and written beneath his nose in large letters "the lad."

Yehuda Leib saw the drawing and was shocked; he slammed the door and rushed to climb the stairs to the second story to look for his son. He didn't find him, but his daughter-in-law was there, and from the look on his face, red in rage, and his trembling hands and his broken voice, she was frightened and pushed a chair toward him, but he only exploded in a thunderous voice, "Where is my son?"

"In Haifa," she tried to calm him, "he went to register land to designate the borders of the associations in the Khudeira tract."

"And what about the accusers?" he asked. "Can it be that they write things for no reason? Come, I will show you how far things have gone. They have reached my house, the entrance to my gate," he yelled as he pulled her after him on the steps to show her the charcoal drawing.

Tears welled in Olga's eyes. She snatched her arm away from his grasp and hurried to the store, where she took a rag, dipped it in a bowl of water, and then gave it to her father-in-law.

"Clean it!" she screamed in a voice harsh. Then, she dashed up to her room and came back a minute later with a document in her hand. Meanwhile, all the other members of the family came rushing, frightened from hearing the sounds of crying; they were wearing their housecoats and wiping rheum from their eyes. First, Olga waved the document she was holding toward Yehuda Leib. Next, she went from one to the other and read what was written on it, pointing out the clear signatures: the signature of Antoine Bishara Tayyan and the signature of Bustros Roq.

"They signed in golden letters," she shrieked. "The owner of the Duran lands did not hesitate and gave Yehoshua a letter of guarantee along with a loan of five hundred gold francs to use as a down payment for the land of Wadi Hawarith. But unfortunately, he did not determine a date for the repayment; he relied on the person they are calling 'the lad,' and the Maronite signed the document for land transfer to Yehoshua and sufficed with the word of the 'small speculator.' They believe in Yehoshua, but his father and the rest of the family do not have faith in him and prefer to listen to the murmurings of the accusers, and their eyes are glazed over so they can't see things as they are."

Her voice became hoarse, but she knew she could not stop now. She had to let go of everything that had been weighing on her chest and protect Yehoshua, for there was no one else here to stand up for him. She took a deep breath and went on in a whisper, "The transfer of the Khudeira land to the names of the associations has been delayed, but that is not Yehoshua's fault. The emissaries wanted to register citizenship for the land, and Yehoshua stopped them because any knowledgeable person knows the Turkish laws, but they didn't want to hear. Then, they agreed to list in their name without citizenship and went to inspect the land with an escort of soldiers, whom they told they were pilgrims so they wouldn't suspect them. Yet, this was a bad mistake on their part. The soldiers were suspicious of pilgrims who examined the land, turning over every rock and pacing off the length and width of the Palestine land. Now, the Turkish official is investigating and interrogating Yehoshua about who these pilgrims are and who the kushans Yehoshua holds are for. At the same time, the associations are applying pressure and giving Yehoshua's letter of engagement out to whoever wants to look at it, and who signed it? Vladimir Tyomkin. He worked together with them."

For a moment, she halted her flow of words, and then inhaled deeply and scanned the faces of her listeners to see the impact her speech had on them and quickly added in a louder, firm voice, "And who stands behind Tyomkin, mumbling to him what to say and what to do—none other than Pines. The Committee heads and the emissaries are demanding that Yehoshua build a dam on the wadi and dig drainage canals to draw off the water, as well as to set the boundaries of the plots and divide them among the associations. But how can he do all that without kushans and with the money moldering in Tyomkin's pocket 'until Yehoshua will act, until he will fulfill his promise,' but how can he do it?"

Now, Olga collapsed and could not go on speaking, the tears choking her throat. She did not want her weakness to be exposed, so she switched her glance to the entrance, and the morning light that broke through blinded her and increased the flow of tears. She gave the agreement to Sarah and cleared a path for herself to the small room at the end of the store. She heard Tanhum question Mendel, asking about the plot Yehoshua had taken for himself. She could not control herself, and tossed a remark toward him behind her back, in a broken voice, "I do not know what we are talking about, but if he took it, it was by right. The associations owe him money and have not given it to him. They promised a franc per dunam. And he travels all the time from Jaffa to Haifa and between Haifa and Beirut, and he pays bribes to the clerks so he can obtain a kushan and a building permit, and there is nobody to reimburse him. And I am waiting, waiting in my loneliness …"

She entered the little room and lowered the curtain; she sat on the one stool remaining from the Rishon Lezion furniture and sobbed into her hands. She did not believe her own words and was afraid to think. But the thoughts made their way into her brain and pricked like thousands of pins. Perhaps the slanderers were right, and Yehoshua is nothing more than a hell-raiser who chooses to follow his own path without considering others. And if he did take some of the best land for himself, as people are saying, why didn't he tell her and let her in on his secret? She trembled violently and wanted to lean back, but the stool had no backrest.

Yehoshua did not know about Yehuda Leib's explosion or Olga's coming to his defense for a long time. His trip to Haifa took more time than expected; the

Russians and the Turkish rule put many obstacles in the way of transmitting the kushans; the Hawarith lands occupied him, and added to them were new dreams and great imaginings. He did not read the newspapers. He immured himself within a thick wall and did not consider the power of the derogatory remarks.

The summer months passed, and in September, Yehoshua returned to Jaffa. The frenzy of the holidays kept routine matters at bay, and in the store, business was brisk, and they needed Yehoshua to help.

Yehuda Leib did not ask questions about the whisperings and the newspaper articles, but he did distance himself from his son and turned to Tanhum, who had become a young man who knew what he wanted and how to attain it. Tanhum had not forgotten his short stay in Gedera and loved the connection that had been forged between him and Mendel. After Yaakov had left for Australia and Mendel had joined the family in Jaffa, the two spent a great deal of time together, dreaming together, and speaking about a joint plot of land. Mendel continued to read and study about innovations in orchards. He prepared a nursery in the yard behind the store, in which he grafted different kinds of species onto others. He planted seeds in the ground and improved them. He measured and watered the seeds, and every day, he recorded the development of each seedling in his notebook. Tanhum was a partner in these experiments, and when they had time after working in the store, the nursery, and the port, the two sat and discussed Yehoshua's new tracts of land. Yehoshua had promised them a plot without going into great detail. In time, when the hesitations and quarrels about the Khudeira land increased, their idea was pushed off, and only when there began to be signs of a solution for the transfer of the kushans and the division of the plots among the purchasers, did their notion come up again and take shape.

Despite the rumors about a large piece of land reserved for Yehoshua in the Khudeira dunes, no one spoke about this aloud in the home or store. The family members found it difficult to decide whether the rumor was evil, whether it contained a pinch of truth, or might it be that it was entirely true? They expected Yehoshua to clarify the issue for them, but he remained silent. Since he was quiet and had never denied it, Mendel and Tanhum had something to cling to.

The great explosion had intensified suspicions, and Yehoshua's presence in the house during the holidays was accompanied by depressive silence. But the involvement with Tanhum, his adulthood and his wishes, led Yehoshua to shatter his silence, and finally, the story of the tract of the effendi's land was revealed. This is how it happened: between Yom Kippur and Sukkot, Tanhum and Mendel announced that they were going to one of the Baron's colonies to be farmers. This announcement was made to the family when they were about to close the store. Yehuda Leib became angry and told them that even though they had kicked down the family and thrown them out from the barns of Rishon Lezion, his sons now wanted to go back and lick dry hay in that same barn?! But when Mendel answered back that not all of the Baron's colonies were the same, his father cut him off and bellowed, "You have a short memory. I won't let my sons return to serving barons. Do you want a plot? Buy one and work for yourselves, without depending on anyone else and without support."

"I have little means," Mendel replied. "And I don't have the money to buy a plot and transfer ownership or improve the land and for planting and then wait five years until the orchard will bear fruit."

"Go to your brother," Yehuda Leib said mockingly. "He has plenty of lots. Maybe, he will finally conclude the purchase of one of them and give it to his brothers."

And Yehoshua, who was in the store at that time, could no longer hold back and still keep quiet, so he said to them, "I bought."

When all of them were staring at him, he said in a quiet voice, "Of course, a large estate is registered in my name, but it is not the best soil but rather the kind nobody wanted, and it's at the edges of the huge parcel. If they want to, Mendel and Tanhum can work it as much as they want. If they care to—they will plant an orchard and an almond plantation; if they want—they can grow sorghum and barley on it."

The family members stopped what they were doing, and they could not help but recall Olga's forceful outburst that had occurred not so long ago, and their eyes wavered between the husband and his wife. But Yehoshua did not catch their glances. Humiliated and disgraced, he turned to look at his wife, his eyes pleading for her forgiveness for revealing the secret to those visiting the store before he had told it to her. Olga wrenched her face away from him and went out to the street with hurried steps and a trembling back.

Yehoshua delayed no longer to examine the influence his speech had on his listeners; he hurried after his wife and caught the edge of her shawl to hold her back, and even when she tugged hard to make him release it, he did not let go.

"Wait," he asked her. "I bought it because I had no choice, but to save the entire purchase."

But Olga only mumbled, "And I say, it's a rumor. Gossip. But it's all true, and I am a gullible fool. Go, go to the land, go to Khudeira, to Wadi Hawarith, and hide among the Bedouin tents. They understand what you do and welcome you. They don't ask questions."

He expected her forgiveness, her understanding. He was sure his words would be enough for her, for, after all, he had only done what he did to find relief for his distress and prove to her that he was great, the second Yehoshua. That was how she loved him; that was also her term of endearment for him.

Olga noticed the astonishment in his eyes and understood how distant he was from her pain and how deeply he was immersed in his lands. She recalled how she had told him that they would not have children, and he said to her then, "I will be your child." She remembered her accompanying him to his first meeting with Antoine Bishara Tayyan. "I will always be at your side," she had told him, and she had continued to give in and swallow her insult to her and live in the shadow of his purchases. She stopped and, as always, asked herself—why? But when she turned to face him and saw the beseeching in his eyes along with confusion and surprise, she saw him once again as a child who needed her. She said no more and prepared to go back, with him at her side. The two marched close together but not touching each other.

Yehoshua tried to placate her for a few moments and bring a smile to her face. "I'll build you a summer home on the Khudeira land, near the sea, and everyone will envy you. Mendel and Tanhum will plant orchards, olives, and almonds, and they will stretch to the gold of the dunes, meeting the blue of the sea."

Olga found it hard to go on scowling and understood that she would never be able to change him and that she had no choice but to take him as he is. She slowed her pace and rubbed her arm against his. By the time they entered the store, she was no longer wearing her furor on her face, and only Yehoshua's back was more bent.

The fall holidays passed, and in December, the Russians received the kushans for the Khudeira land, and the quarrels between them and the land broker ceased though the associations now became engaged in arguing with each other, each one claiming that the lands of the other society were better than theirs. Initially, they asked Yehoshua to settle their problem, but when he refused, the emissaries once again poured out their anger on him, and they devoted themselves to slandering him in the newspapers as Pines had done earlier. Yehoshua, however, had concluded his dealing with them and had completely washed his hands of them, claiming to Olga that he would never set foot in the colony that was to be established on the new lands.

Now that the lands had been handed over to the members of the associations, Yehuda Leib's family had calmed down. Mendel received a plot on the Khudeira land. He took Tanhum with him, both of them promising to return on Fridays to Jaffa and accompany Yehuda Leib when he went to synagogue and to sit with the family for the Friday evening meal. Olga became immersed in her work and adjusted to her husband's ups and downs, praying within that the episode of the Wadi Hawarith lands would differ from the previous ones.

The Belkind family now dealt with Sonia. The young woman had decided to study medicine and wanted to go to Geneva. When they tried to prevent her from doing so with the argument that the city was big and there was no room in it for Jews, let alone it was no place for women wanting to learn medicine. She laughed in their face and declared she had made up her mind to travel there, and they could no longer stand up against her. Israel was busy with the school and discussed with Meir and Shimshon the decrees about to be announced and the new Turkish ruler. Fanny and Lolik were raising a son and already wanted to leave Jaffa. They had not found their place in Jaffa and did not like the petty functionaries of the big city, the houses standing so close to each other, or the muck and sewage building up in the paved canal passing through the center of the lane. Sarah sorely missed Tanhum. Only Haya remained at home, and she had already reached marriageable age, while her mother felt that old age had crept up on her, and she went less often to the store. And since it is the nature of people to forget the bad and remember only the good, the old newspapers with the slanderous articles were tossed from the house, and Pines' name only came up when Sarah asked Yehuda Leib, "Who did you meet in the Chelouche shul in Neve Zedek?"

It was a very rainy year. The roads filled with puddles, and water flowed between the broken tiles. People shut themselves up in their houses, and there was no one for whom to open the store, and business dwindled. The Jaffa port emptied out, and the fishermen, who were prevented from sailing out by the storms and breakwaters, pulled their boats onto short or tied them down with ropes so they would not be swept into the open sea. Occasionally, the sun broke through for a short time, and the women would hurry to stick their noses out and rush to make their purchases; the storeowners would emerge to conduct business, and the children—to mischievously stomp in the water and spray it about.

During one of those pleasant sunny moments, Feibush Dolnik appeared, filling the doorway to Yehuda Leib's store with his wide body.

Of course, he told everyone that his name was Shimon Dolnik and that the name Feibush was only apt for a small, spoiled child, but nobody in Jaffa called him Shimon, since the name Feibush was a better match for his round shape, his clothing, and his gait.

As soon as he had entered the store, he immediately began to behave like an expert and someone who knows every nook and cranny and each family member. They showed him the little room to host people wanting to deal with land issues. The man hastened to sit himself down on the low stool, took a folded newspaper out of his pocket along with a tin of snuff, and called for Yehuda Leib to sit with him. He spoke unapologetically and unhesitatingly, as if he knew that Yehuda Leib would do his bidding. After sitting opposite him, taking a gulp of steaming coffee and nipping at the rolls Sarah had offered them, he went back to reading aloud, for Yehuda Leib to hear, the article by Pines about "the lad" and the transaction over the Khudeira land.

"I liked the nickname 'the lad.' Is he your son?" he inquired.

Yehuda Leib nodded, so the man went on, saying, "I would like to meet him and conduct business with him. Someone who could withstand an attack by the land speculators and come out of it alive is someone I like. In our world, there is only room for the strong, not the weak frightened by every peep and accusation."

Yehuda Leib was quiet. Of course, Yehoshua was his son, but the Khudeira episode had not flattered him, and he did not want to remember it or talk about it. Yehuda Leib invited him to drink a second cup of coffee and, in the meantime, went to call Olga. When he didn't find her in her room, he asked his daughter Haya to bring her from the doctor's office. He sensed that the issue was important and maybe highly beneficial, and perhaps it would even restore Yehoshua's good name.

When Olga entered the small room, she was surprised by the appearance of the man sitting on the hassock with a newspaper on his knees, the one with the slanderous article. But when he smiled at her, rose to come toward her, and extended his hand, introducing himself, her self-confidence returned. He then repeated what he had said to Yehuda Leib, "It's the 'lad' I wish to meet, your husband. Tell him a good word about me, and I will come back to meet him."

Olga laughed out loud. "He doesn't need my word. When he hears someone inquired about him and his lands, he will come. He would cross the length and width of the country and not give up. The love of a woman he would forgo, a hearty meal he would forget about, but not about a land deal."

The man chuckled loudly, but did not hear the bitterness creeping into her voice. After promising to come the next day, he left the store, leaving behind him the heavy smell of aftershave mixed with the stench of tobacco.

But the man did not come back a day later, as he had indicated, but only four days later, and Yehoshua was already waiting for him at the entrance to the store, watching the lane every day. He asked Olga repeatedly to tell him about the encounter with the businessman. But when he did finally arrive, Yehoshua was not there. Fearing that his anger would grow and that he would pour his wrath on the store customers, he had gone down to the port to look at what was going on there.

The shouts from Haya drew him from his thoughts, "The merchant from Yaketarinoslav is waiting for you in the store with another two people with him, very odd ones, and they asked me to call you."

Yehoshua hurried to run to the story, telling her behind him, "It's not nice to mock businessmen you plan to do deals with in such a way!"

The younger sister dashed after him and, panting, answered back, "Just wait, wait, and you'll see for yourself."

His sister's statement scared him, but he moved even faster, regardless. When he entered the little room, he saw a small, portly man with a pointy beard and restless eyes, trying to take in everything going on around him all at once. A boy of about thirteen, dwarfish like him, was running about the store between the counter and the shelves, examining the textiles and pawing among the notions overflowing from copper bowls and asking incessantly what each thing was used for and of what was it made. It was enough to see his father's satisfaction from hearing the queries to understand the reason for him dragging along his son on his journeys to different places.

When he saw Yehoshua, the man apologized, saying, "My son is almost bar mitzvah age, and I decided to teach him the ways of Eretz Israel and how to conduct negotiations. Who knows, maybe he will be like his father," and he patted the boy's shoulder.

In a corner of the store, stood another escort, a tall, thin bookkeeper-type wearing black clothes and holding a satchel brimming with papers and account books. His small eyes were frozen and his prominent nose quivered and sniffed. Now, Yehoshua understood his sister, "So strange," and it was really difficult not to laugh at the trio's appearance.

In the evening, Yehoshua told Olga about his conversation with Feibush Dolnik. "He wants to buy the Wadi Hawarith land," he related. "He will give a down payment to seal the deal with Antoine Bishara Tayyan. After I obtain ownership, the problem of the *fellahin* squatting on the land will be solved; he will hand over the remainder of the remainder the sum. He did not come in the name of himself but rather on behalf of an entire association, 'Tzemach David' (descendant of David), all of whose members are from Yekaterinoslav. The society members are relying on him to know how to find good soil, and they have given him a great deal of money to use."

"And his demands," wondered Olga, "he will buy without asking for anything?"

"He is not demanding anything!" Yehoshua smiled, "He is willing to buy without quarrels, disputes, and shouting. He is prepared to hand over lots of money without delay."

But Olga was not convinced that things were so simple. When Yehoshua saw her disbelief, he said to her, "Regarding Tuesday, the Bible says twice 'very good.' You will stay with me and be a witness to the signing of the contract." Then, he asked her to share his joy, poured a shot glass of whiskey, raised it toward the oil lamp, and called out, "Mazal tov, mazal tov." Olga preferred to join in his happiness, repel her doubts, and believe Yehoshua would indeed succeed in selling the Wadi Hawarith land as he had pledged to Tayyan. Olga asked him to pour her a shot glass full, and when they finished one, they drank another, and Yehoshua reminded himself of Tyomkin and drinking with him on the effendi's estate many days ago, so far off. For a moment, his face grew dark, but then he saw the ruddiness spreading on Olga's face and heard the words escaping her mouth, "You will be great! You will again be great in the opinion of the Jaffa traders, and there will be many rushing to buy the lands you are dealing in, and all of them will be knocking on the doors of the store." The end of the sentence came out garbled and confused, and the words did not make sense to her. Yehoshua hugged her again and carried her to their bed, and both of them rolled around in their clothes and pushed the quilt to the edge of the bed; they were breathing out the whiskey fumes and tasting drops of it on each other's lips. "Mine, mine," he whispered in her ear; "Mine, the second Yehoshua," she answered him.

On Tuesday, Feibush Dolnik came and signed the purchase agreement for the land of Wadi Hawarith (that is, Emeq Hefer), and after they drank to this and gave Yehoshua a bag of coins, he hastened to go from there to Jericho. "People say the land there is good, and there are many transactions there. My son will learn about the quality of the land and feel it with his hands. He will be a businessman, just like his father."

Panic, 1891

With the end of the Khudeirah land episode and the start of the story of Wadi Hawarith, it was as if old episodes were sealed and new ones opened. The three families that had become linked with each other, first in Rishon Lezion, then in Gedera, and eventually in Jaffa, scattered in every direction and became distant from one another. Mendel was the first to leave, taking Tanhum with him, and they devoted themselves to working Yehoshua Hankin's land that edged the dunes. Every Friday, the two returned to Jaffa, as they had promised Sarah, bringing with them stories of the virgin land. Israel Feinberg waxed enthusiastic from their stories and wanted to return to being "the giant" walking about the fields, with youngsters running after him and mothers warning their toddlers about him if they refused to eat. Fanny agreed to try to go to work the land of

Hadera, in the colony that came into being on the Khudeirah land. "The village air will be good for Avshalom," she convinced herself, "and it is better to leave the sauna of Jaffa and its muggy air." But the two were waiting for the moment when a plot would be ready to accept them, perhaps after the first harvest, after the next Passover, or maybe after Mendel and Tanhum would announce that they had been successful and that the plots on the new land were good.

Israel Belkind's school closed. When not enough pupils were found to fill even one table in the room, its two rooms were turned over to homeless Jewish families, and the books were piled up in one corner of the store. Israel was deeply in debt and was forced to sell his plot in Gedera. He found himself other employment for a few weeks—one time, helping the baker; another time driving the wagon between Jaffa and Rishon Lezion, or arranging merchandise in the pharmacist's store. One day, he went to the doctor's office and waited for Olga's workday to end.

"I've decided to leave," he told her, "to go back to my wandering. They say they're looking for a teacher in Jerusalem at 'La-Torah ve-la-Avodah' school. Maybe they'd agree to hire me. If they refuse, I will go on a walkabout on both sides of the Jordan. A slice of bread and the clothes on my back will be enough for me, and I will breathe the air of open spaces. And when I return, I will sit down and write my book and describe everything I saw and heard."

Olga knew full well that she could not stop him, so she gave him a few pennies and added a Russian ruble, an old coin she had been keeping from long ago.

Shifra and Meir enjoyed the flow of life and the sounds of the city, and they frequently walked about Jaffa and joined in the general chitchat; they argued with Sonia, who was uncompromising and demanded they let her travel overseas to study medicine. Sarah worked in the store, with the two daughters by her side, helping her. They had grown up, and marriage proposals were being discussed. Rivka hinted at her love for Zuckerman, the farmer from Gedera, though Yehuda Leib rebuffed her, saying, "Become a bit more mature, and we'll decide." That winter, the visits to the Chelouche synagogue in Neve Zedek became part of the routine way of life he had adopted for himself: In the morning, he would rise early, pray the morning service, and go back home to eat his breakfast. Then he would make a round of the stores and visit merchants, discussing with all of them the edicts, rulers, and disasters that were on the horizon. But they all only talked, and no one did anything to prepare for the bad times. In the afternoon, he would go for the afternoon prayers and then discuss the same topics with the men in the synagogue. Then, he would enter his shop and share rumors and news with Sarah. After sunset, he would attend the evening service and stay there, to study a page of Talmud as it were, but actually, he was waiting for more Jews to gather so they could exchange news items and look them over from every aspect until they took on a new form.

In Jaffa, everyone became used to the Russians filling the streets, and to the land speculators, the Turkish soldiers, and the price of apartments that rose daily. That made it seem as if the life of the city had become routine. People no longer dealt with Yehoshua. They didn't write about him in the papers or talk on the street corners; they no longer called after him "the lad" and not even "the young Hankin." His hair grew longer, and his curls reached his shoulders; the young children identified him as "the man with the hair." If someone looked for Yehuda Leib's store to inquire about land, the little ones would shake their heads and say, "The land office of the man with the hair is what you want!" Then, they would immediately run and show him. The working of the land increased as did the lands Yehoshua dealt with, to the point that it was difficult to distinguish between their names, so it was enough to use a general term — "the Hankin lands."

Olga also enjoyed the calm and, once again, took an interest in the matters of the Jaffa Committee, attended Tyomkin's parties, and took meticulous care about her clothes and hairstyle. Now, she was "the wife of the land agent Yehoshua Hankin" and repelled the disquiet and disturbing thoughts. Fanny and Avshalom were not with her; Israel was wandering, and she was fully occupied with work and social events. She became a chatterbox, and her relationship with her husband moved along smoothly. But everything was good and beautiful only on the outside. Sarah saw the changes taking place in Yehuda Leib, in her son, and in her daughter-in-law. She longed for the arrival of summer, knowing full well the customs of Palestine—to withdraw from society in the winter and to burst out in full strength with the arrival of the first heat wave about the time of Passover, to be followed by the long summer days.

Sarah was right. The summer arrived, and Jaffa began to boil over. The Jewish residents said it all began because of the petition initiated by the Jaffa Arabs and joined by the Jerusalem Arabs in which they demanded that the Turkish governor stop the immigration of Jews to Eretz Israel and forbid the sale of land to anyone who was not an Ottoman citizen. Uninvolved people, however, ascribed responsibility to a slew of happenings that developed step by step and swept away everything in their path—and were also the cause of that petition. Had it not been for the winter hibernation that had slowed down the rhythm of life, perhaps nothing would have happened, but something did occur, and again it was impossible to halt the course of events.

In the newspapers, Arabs and Jews published hateful articles against each other. In the mosques and synagogues, those coming to pray discussed and repeatedly addressed what was happening in Jaffa. The Russians who had come in the winter began to leave Jaffa—at first, clandestinely, but openly and publicly with the arrival of summer. The Soup Kitchens closed; the wives of the functionaries did not gad about with aprons wrapped around their middles and did not take good care of themselves, since there was no one to make themselves up for. The old-time beggars returned to the lane next to Yehuda Leib's store, and they were satisfied with little, in contrast to their Russian predecessors, and didn't need coins, being happy with a slice of bread and half a bottle of liquor.

Yehuda Leib tried to console those who came to the store and say that the situation was only temporary, but Sarah nodded her head and said, "In Jaffa, they say that Vladimir Tyomkin, the Committee chairman, is about to leave."

"Many winters and summers will pass before the Engineer leaves," replied Yehuda Leib confidently. "He hasn't yet organized enough parties. He is still working with the Associations' money, since he has pledged to buy land for all of them, and until he fulfills his promise, they won't let him be idle," he added. "If I were in my son's place, I would stay in his company and forgive him for every insult and continue to act as the Committee's main land mediator. I raised a proud son," he told Sarah. "He's not a man of compromises."

"It's better that way," Sarah declared. "Better that he leaves Jaffa and takes his wife with him so that they can find peace of mind outside the raging city."

ᗑ

In those summer days, Sarah's wish was filled. To be sure, Olga and Yehoshua did not leave the city and did not build a home of their own, but they envisioned a big, shared dream and erected a wall around themselves and let no one pass through it.

In August, Feibush Dolnik returned to Yekaterinoslav to collect money from the members of the "Tzemach David" society to pay Yehoshua and to conclude the purchase of Wadi Hawarith. Of course, in Hadera, the settlers still threatened to hold a public trial against Yehoshua, but the wheels of Turkish justice ground slowly, and Yehoshua was not afraid of a trial. Now, Yehoshua turned to doing something for his own household. One evening, he held Olga back from going to Vladimir Tyomkin's house, telling her, "The time has come."

After spending time with him for years, Olga identified the sparkle in his eyes and the trembling of his hands attesting to the excitement linked to his second lover. The couple now began to make plans for their dream, which they had begun in their time in Gedera and which had been repressed because of the stress of the times. In those days, when they had planted the olive seedlings on Yehudit Mountain, Yehoshua would tell Olga about *the Valley*. She would sit on the hillside and look at the Arab village and its women, while he would point toward the distant dunes near the sea and show her the peaks of the Judean Mountains. He'd crush gray lumps of soil into dust with his hands and whisper in her ear, "In *the Valley*, the soil is black and fertile, and it is good for wheat and barley. Its clods are rich, and water flows in the springs between the valley and the mountain." Then, he would bend over and insert a support beam for an olive plant that was almost dry and add, "There everything turns green." To her question as to where precisely in *the Valley*, he would stretch out his hand and point, "Beyond the Carmel, at the foot of the Galilee mountains. Bordering Mount Gilboa, it begins at the foot of the Harithiyeh Hills, and is called Jezreel Valley (*Emeq Yizrael*).

"So far," she would say, and he would laugh heartily, with the wind carrying his merriment toward the houses of the village below, "In time, it will be close."

In time, when he drew distant from her and bought the land of Khudeira and negotiated for the land of Wadi Hawarith, Olga knew that he continued to ride beyond the Harithiyeh Hills and would tarry there for many a day. But, as usual, she did not ask nor aggravate him but only waited for his return.

Now came the last days of summer, followed by the winter, and Yehoshua came back to Olga and made her party to his dream. The upheavals in the city of Jaffa thrust her into closeness with Yehoshua, and for the first time, she did not compete with his other love, nor was she even equal to it. But she was her husband's partner in determining the future of the land.

The land of the Jezreel Valley belonged to brothers belonging to the Sursuq family, who were large-scale merchants with worldwide businesses. These very wealthy men, based in Beirut, visited kings and rulers, and everyone wanted their company and needed them. And whoever owed them money and did not have the funds to repay them would compensate them with land instead. Olga had heard these details from Christian women who had accompanied a woman from their family who was about to give birth; when she was acting as a midwife, the women would usually try to forget the pains of the woman giving birth by engaging in idle chatter. They would sit in a circle, with their voices drowning out the sounds of the sighs and the screams of pain. Olga would comfort the women, while at the same time listen to the prattle and later tell it to Yehoshua. The longer the winter nights grew, and the more Yehoshua shared his big dream with her, the more she would add details and enrich his knowledge.

Olga did not let Tyomkin in on their secret. Now, she did not have to, since her husband had returned to her, and she closed her eyes and shut her ears and ignored the fall of the Committee chairman.

After Hanukkah, announcements increasingly appeared in the Jewish newspapers defaming Tyomkin and Ben-Tovim, the two Committee leaders. Their names were no longer preceded by "mister" or "the respectable," and people accused them of being responsible for the exodus of the Russians from the country and said they owed large sums of money to the Associations' leaders. Small land speculators thronged the doors of the Jaffa Committee office, waving signed documents and agreements bearing the names of these two who were the guarantors for the debts of the societies.

No one spoke to Pines, even though he was a member of the Jaffa Committee. People called him "the rabbi" and did not consider him part of the "Committee." Everyone remembered his endeavors for the colonies and did not see him as part of the new leadership that had come to Palestine and did not intend to stay more than a year or two.

And as usual, now too, Jaffa was divided between those in favor of Tyomkin and those who disparaged him, between those seeking solutions for the masses abandoning the city and those who gave advice about what to do against the petition and how to behave toward the Turkish government that tended to justify the Arabs' demands.

Yehoshua and Olga were still far away from all this, cloistered within their walls. Close to Purim, the settling of the Hadera land was completed; all the kushans were obtained, building permits allotted, and the settlers were working apace at erecting their homes. Notices told that the homes would be dedicated on Seder night and the Passover meal would be enjoyed by each family in its new house. However, anger against Yehoshua did not subside, and Mendel and Tanhum's living among them made them even more furious and did not let the Hadera farmers forget. During the winter, the rainwater collected in one big swamp. The farmers remembered the unfulfilled promise to dig drainage canals for them and build a bridge over the stream, and they grew increasingly enraged.

But Hadera was a day away from Jaffa on a fast ride, and the cry of its members did not reach such a distance, not to Jaffa and certainly not to the ears of Yehoshua, who had gone far away from the city, with no one knowing where he was except Olga.

When a letter from Feibush Dolnik arrived at the store telling them he was continuing to raise money for the land of Wadi Hawarith and hoping that by the end of the year, they could come divide the land among the buyers, Olga knew Yehoshua could begin to realize their dream. "Now, it would at least be possible to open a new page and write a single term at its top—*The Valley*. She told her husband, and Yehoshua laughed, adding, "May it be that I will succeed in starting many pages, setting down at the top of each the name of an estate."

19. What started as a dream in 1891 became a reality in 1934. Yehoshua Hankin in Kfar Yehoshua. Behind him a map of the land purchases of Land of Israel and on the right side is Olga Hankin. Source: Central Zionist Archives.

Eight days before the Passover seder, Yehoshua went down to the Jaffa harbor to wait for a boat that would take him to a ship sailing for Beirut. He was about to journey to meet Musa Sursuq, owner of the land of the Jezreel Valley.

He waited alone at the dock. Olga did not want to go through his departure, and the others did not know. He sat on his packet among torn nets, baskets of fish, and coils of rope eroded by sea salt with many traders near him, Christians on their way to celebrate Easter at home, and Muslims laden with merchandise. Some he recognized, while others knew him and nodded in greeting, and he did likewise. Someone tried to start a conversation with him, but he turned away and remained steeped in his musings. He waited like that for a few hours. Then, in the afternoon, a boat came that took them and their bundles to the sea. They stood packed in it, and the boat almost sank to its rim; one Jewish merchant laughed and said, "Let's cast lots among ourselves, and like in the story of Jonah, we will throw one of us into the waters." But the others did not laugh; they only cursed within.

Yehoshua looked for his cabin and learned that his shipmate was a heavy Greek fellow who did not understand his language. He was happy about that since he preferred the silence that would let him think and plan his next moves. Before the boat set sail, Yehoshua went to the deck and sat down on a barrel of smoked fish, which is what he did most of the hours of the trip, sitting on the same spot and watching the lanes of white foam and the flocks of wintering birds that were now returning from the warm lands to their distant homes. Occasionally, they landed on the masts and took off again. First, just one of them, and then the entire flock followed, disappearing among the fluffy clouds.

Whenever Yehoshua spent time on the deck, the ship drawing ever further away from the Jaffa harbor and the houses leaning on one another, he was reminded of his childhood in Kremenchug and wondered what had made him think of it. Was it the light breeze that created ripples in the sea like the breaths of air that had caressed the heads of wheat in the fields of his youth, or perhaps it was the calm of the sea and its distance from Jaffa? His childhood memories pleased him, and he tried to reconstruct them and remember details. He was sorry about the old age that had overtaken Yehuda Leib and about his own maturity. Would that he could stop time and continue to be a small child riding with his father in the fields his father leased.

Yehuda Leib had had a large estate, and the farmers worked the fields he had rented. Yehuda Leib used to ride among the villages, his older sons with him, to teach them something about the rules of working land. Sarah did not like her sons accompanying their father. One time, Yehuda Leib returned from a long ride with Yehoshua reeking of whiskey; Yehuda Leib explained that he had given him a taste because he could not withstand his pleading. Sarah was furious and sent her son to Kharkov to study science and the manners of the rich. Now, Yehoshua reminded himself of his taking leave of his parents and his long train trip while he was still a child. He recalled how he had cried when no one could see him, and he had not wanted the city with its large buildings and carriages; he did not like its sounds nor its smell. He was homesick for the fields, for riding with his father, for the farmers who waved pitchforks in greeting, and the whiskey that burned his insides.

He did study in Kharkov, but he was interested in the revolution. There he began to let his hair grow long and wear a student's coat and march with the others, calling out slogans against the rule of the master and against discrimination. He was caught and thrown into jail together with a band of young people, and instead of lamenting their arrest, they wrote books and protest songs. He did not tell his parents about his detention because he did not want them to worry. But upon his release, he found a letter on his bed and then took the first train to return to his village. When he arrived there, he saw they were all packed and ready to immigrate to Palestine. He did not need much explanation. It took just one look at the empty stable to understand that his father had been deprived of the right to lease fields. So he sold the remaining belongings and hid the money in the linings of coats. Then he asked his three older boys if they would go with him, and when they said yes, they bought tickets and sailed for many days on a ship and then traveled by train and wagon and again sailed until they landed at Jaffa.

In those days, Jaffa was different, and perhaps because he was still a young lad, he saw things other than he perceived them today. They ceaselessly looked at the minarets of the mosques and the closed courtyards, at the women with covered faces and the young women looking through the wooden slats covering the hanging balconies. Despite the dirt and the jumbled houses, Jaffa seemed mysterious and so very different. They stayed in it for a month, until half their money was gone; then, Yehuda Leib hired a wagon, and they went up to Safed.

ⓒ⃗

In Safed, they saw Jews suffering poverty, Jews trying to establish a colony on rocky soil near the village of Jaouni, and they became frightened and wandered to Jerusalem. Yehuda Leib and his family saw tombs of the *tzaddiqim*, saintly Jews, and remnants of stone and walls in the city, but they did not like the quarrels between the Sephardi and Ashkenazi Jews, so they returned to Jaffa. Now, they were almost out of money, prompting Yehuda Leib decided to strike root there.

Yehoshua smiled when he recalled his father's first attempts at being a merchant. Yehuda Leib had not understood the value of merchandise, nor the nature of the Turkish money, so he often fell into a trap and returned to the hotel to tell his adventures. Of course, he failed, but each failure taught him a lesson, and Yehuda Leib always knew how to justify his predicament. Luckily, they met a group of Jews that had organized to buy a tract in the lands of Ein Qara, south of the Jaffa orchards. Even though they did not know the location of the land, Sarah wholeheartedly wanted a plot after she had been disgusted by her husband's failures.

"The time has come to build a home for ourselves," she would tell her older sons. "A house with a yard with space for building a *tabun* and a kitchen where I can knead dough and fill the space with the aroma of baking."

Had they had not gone to Rishon Lezion, they would not have been part of the rebellion and wandered to Gedera, nor would they have returned to Jaffa and set up a fund for buying land. The twists of fate are wondrous—for they had come to Jaffa, left it, and gone back to the spot, with it being right there that Yehuda Leib encountered success. In Rishon Lezion, Yehuda Leib had built a wagon and hitched two camels to it; the vehicle had provided a livelihood until the plot there produced its first fruits. The wagon made the trip from Jaffa to Rishon to the colony at Ein Qara, and when it would enter the Jaffa Gates, the city's small children would march behind it and bombard it with sycamore figs to disturb the camels. Yehuda Leib would pull on the reins and turn the camels' necks toward him and gallop like that through the lanes, with the children running after with great joy. Oftentimes, Yehuda Leib took Mendel and Yehoshua with him, and they would sit in the back and send the children away, enjoying the wild ride.

The days of Rishon Lezion came to mind to Yehoshua, and the smile was wiped from his face. They had been so difficult. For a moment, he was angry at himself that instead of organizing his actions and thinking about what to say to the great merchant, he was busy with flights of imagination. He promised himself he would not dream anymore, so he went down to his cabin to lay down on the pallet and prepare himself for the meeting with Sursuq.

The ship sailed past Acre with the landscape of the plain and that of the kurkar rocks being replaced by views of mountains reaching the sea, and the oaks and cedars on their slopes looked as if they were falling into the pounding waves.

The ship anchored in Beirut port on the morning of the second day of the trip. Beirut was a big city, and its houses climbed the sides of the mountains. The narrow streets went down to the sea and rose up from it, and disappeared into the tangle of narrow lanes and stone walls. Since it was very early and Yehoshua did not want to waste time, he decided to try to move up his arrival at the Christian merchant family. He approached the first store he encountered on his way.

The Sursuq family is rich, he mused, and the local inhabitants are familiar with it.

He saw a butcher shop with the pieces of meat hanging at its front, turning red and attracting flies. Yehoshua entered the dimly lit store, and when he asked the butcher about the Sursuq house, the man took him out into the daylight and pointed out a lane to him, adding, "Lions stand at the entrance to the house, and they have emerald eyes."

The butcher did not stop with this answer and tried to draw Yehoshua into a conversation, but Yehoshua was not interested, said goodbye, and headed up the lane. While marching, he buttoned up his coat, and when he saw his tattered lapels, he felt bad about his miserable appearance. Next to a shop window, he halted and looked at his reflection in it, at his unkempt hair and his unruly beard; he came to a new decision and went back down to the port to look for a barber.

The barber, on whose shop walls posted haphazardly were pictures of naked women, sat him down in a chair and made him wait quite a while. Finally, he made time for him and gave him a wide grin anticipating a lively conversation, as was apparently customary in a barbershop. But Yehoshua kept quiet. When asked why he had such long hair, Yehoshua's curt reply was, "This is the way I have kept it since my student days," and added no more when he saw the astonished look on the barber's face, only smiling into his beard.

When he had finished the haircut, the barber took a bunch of photos of unclad women from his coat pocket and asked, "Maybe my guest would like a young woman? I have many, and they are all beautiful."

Yehoshua laughed, pushed aside his pocket, and got up. "I'll be on my way," he said. "I'm headed for the Sursuq family."

"You're connected to them?" The barber's astonishment changed into admiration. "They're rich, one of the revered families of Beirut," he finished.

"I'm only going to them," snickered Yehoshua.

The surprised barber danced around him, brushing off snippings of hair and accumulations of dust from the way, and then he bent over and polished Yehoshua's boots with the edge of his smock, and while his hands were moving about, he murmured, "Very wealthy, owners of land in Palestine, and they hold passports like others have handfuls of sweets. Maybe you have come to them on a matter of business?" He was not put off by Yehoshua's silence and pushed him again gently into the seat and sprayed him with aftershave.

What should he tell him? That it was a matter of land, thought Yehoshua. But then he would think that he was rich. He put his hand into his pocket, took out a few bishliks, stuffed them into the barber's pocket, and left him mid-sentence. The barber ran after him for a bit to straighten his clothes and shake the dust off them, and as he walked up the mountain, he suddenly remembered his open store and stood stock still, looking at Yehoshua moving further in the distance.

The lane was covered, and the houses touched each other. Behind the walls spread myrtle and jasmine bushes whose flowers filled the cracks in the tiles and whose fragrance permeated and perfumed the entire path. The homes on the narrow street were magnificent. Only toward the end did he see the gate and the open-mouthed lions standing at both its sides. Yehoshua paused at the gate to catch his breath and then approached the lions and examined their eyes. For sure, the eyes were gems, and they didn't look so fierce. He calmed down and stretched out his hand to pet the rounded stone mane, and then went in the entranceway and pulled the bell hanging over the gate. He rang a second time to be sure they had heard him; then, he waited.

An old Arab opened the heavy gate for him and asked for his name. Next, he motioned for him to follow. The old man walked barefoot, and his footfalls went unheard, while the sound of Yehoshua's boots resounded strongly and disturbed the silence of the courtyard.

They were walking in a closed courtyard paved with small stones and surrounded by small rooms shuttered with interwoven wooden slats, such that whoever stood behind the shutters could see a walker in the yard, but anyone in the yard could not see him. A fountain stood at the center of the yard, and its waters fell into a pond, with the drops creating rainbows. From the pond, the water poured into channels that crossed the tiled floor in equal-sized squares and ended in small pits into which the water disappeared, their only traces seen in the rows of myrtles trimmed into triangular and diamond shapes among which bloomed varicolored flowers.

The elderly fellow slowed his pace and then stopped next to an arched opening decorated with curly engravings in the stone interlaced with Arabic letters. His guide disappeared, and Yehoshua remained standing in the large courtyard next to the entrance and stretched tall to see what was hidden behind it. He saw a large hall with a high ceiling in the center of which was a skylight pierced by sunlight forming a circle. Dust motes rose from within the circle on the floor and climbed all along the skylight's beams of light. Yehoshua dared to lean into the room and looked around him.

He saw the merchant smoking an orange- and red-colored hookah on an embroidered pillow, scanning Yehoshua from top to bottom, taking in his every expression and every movement. When their glances met, the businessman motioned to Yehoshua to approach him without his rising and without extending a hand in greeting; he only pointed to a green pillow. Yehoshua sat down and crossed his legs the way this Christian was sitting. Yehoshua examined the man's mien without taking his eyes off him and without revealing his hesitations. Musa Sursuq was a man of large dimensions bearing a double chin that unnecessarily added years to his appearance. He wore a well-tailored suit in the latest European fashion and, from time to time, inhaled from his hookah. His eyes became foggy; he rolled them and closed them, then opened them again; he went back to surveying his guest as if he wanted to test his patience.

Yehoshua's limbs stiffened, but he was afraid to change his position and shatter the calm. His legs fell asleep, but he finally dared to move them a bit. The Christian opened his eyes and moved the bottle away from him; he clapped his hands in an even rhythm as if participating in some ceremony. Two men entered, one carrying a bowl of water along with a steaming towel on his arm, while the other had a bowl of meat in his hand and a pile of pitot on his head. Both went down on their knees, set down the water and the meat, offered the towel, and left, facing the diners and keeping their backs to the door. By some miracle, they did not hit the wall or bump into a cushion or carpet, vanishing through the doorway, their steps unheard. The Christian broke off a piece from a pita, rolled meat in it, and put it in his mouth; then, he dipped his fingers in the water and wiped them on the towel. He again took part of a pita and hinted to Yehoshua to do the same.

Yehoshua ate a bit, while the Christian stuffed his face and chomped on the food, grinding it and chewing it, with his Adam's apple rising with each swallow. When the bowl was empty, the Christian clapped his hands again, but only one lad came this time, cleared off the bowls, set down coffee and a tray of sweets dipped in sugar. Both took a sip, feeling the coffee's warmth suffusing their bodies, remaining silent and continuing to examine each other.

Only after a burp did the Christian begin to talk. At first, he spoke French, and Yehoshua understood only a bit, and then he switched to Arabic, and Yehoshua understood it all. They were a widespread family, he said. A few of the brothers lived in Beirut, others in Alexandria, and one wandered about, returning home once a year. They dealt with commerce, bought land, working it, and selling it at a profit. "And you, what is the connection between you and land?" he suddenly asked.

Yehoshua, unprepared for this direct question, was confused and cast his eyes downward, and because of the look of his tattered coat, he feared that perhaps he was not inspiring respect, and like the others, the merchant saw him as only a "lad."

"I deal in land," he whispered, hurrying to add, "a real estate agent, buying and selling to others."

A smile spread on the trader's face. "Buys and sells, and certainly also measures how much land the Sursuq family has in Palestine." A slight mocking tone could be heard in his voice. "Have you already examined the family lands?"

Yehoshua knew he could not outsmart his interlocutor, for the merchant was clearly aware of why he had come to Beirut, but he did want to prove his greatness to Christian and that he exceeded him on one issue; an issue regarding which even the sharpest trader could not outdo him — his love for the land. Initially, he spoke slowly, then his voice grew stronger, and his words flowed; he forgot who he was speaking to. He related to him the acquisition of the Duran land and that of Khudeira, and he told the story of the Wadi Hawarith lands and reviewed for him the land of Marj Ibn' Amer, which is, of course, the land of the Jezreel Valley bordering the Gilboa Mountains and meeting the Carmel. He talked about the *fellahin*, who sucked out the essence of the land, without improving it, and left at the end of three years of leasing and turned to work another piece of land. Once they are gone, the swamp comes and consumes every good plot, and after the swamp the valley is taken over by desolation and neglect.

The Christian's eyes gleamed, and unintentionally leaned his body toward the narrator and thirstily drank in his words. Yehoshua pulled him toward himself as if by magic ropes. He saw the expanses of the distant land together with him and felt the pain of clods of earth, disintegrating in the summer and becoming doughy lumps of mud in the winter.

"A swamp can be dried, water can be drained, and soil can be improved with fertilizer." Musa Sursuq continued the words of the Jew sitting opposite him, and it seemed as if he was giving voice to Yehoshua's thoughts.

"I will buy the land from you," said Yehoshua. "I will drain it, improve it, and sell it to others. In Palestine, many people who want land knock on doors, willing to pay a great deal of money for it. They will buy the land in the valley and cultivate the fields. The black of the swamps will turn into a green carpet and glorify Sursuq's name. Give me a year, and you won't recognize your land." The Christian sat comfortably on his pillow, the glow disappearing from his eyes. He again became the merchant worrying about his pocket and seeking to become even wealthier.

"I'll sell to you," he declared. "For a price of twenty francs per dunam. You said the soil is good, and many are trying to get it. Let's see. This will be for you, for me, and for the land."

Yehoshua listened but didn't bat an eyelash and didn't reveal his panic at hearing the high price.

"Let's make a deal," he said hoarsely. "I will buy from you the heart of *the Valley*. I will give you two and a half million francs. Give me an extension, and I will find buyers, while you promise not to negotiate with others. We'll complete one transaction and then begin the second. I will buy the Galilee lands from you and the land of the Jidro Valley north of Haifa. They will all be blooming land, and whoever lives on them will say—it is Musa Sursuq's land, and Yehoshua Hankin bought it from him."

"They won't remember my name," laughed the Christian, "and who knows if they will remember yours. They will plow the field and establish new villages, and no one will remember whose the land was."

"They will certainly remember," declared Yehoshua. "People don't easily forget those who are great in property and deeds."

"You're talking like a child," the merchant contradicted him. "A child who hasn't acquired any life experience yet, but so be it. Let's shake on it." He clapped his hands again, and the lad entered the hall once more and stood at the side of those present, waiting for his instructions. The merchant rose and stretched out his hand toward Yehoshua and shook it. He then invited him to stay overnight in his home, since it was late, and the following morning they had to sign a memorandum in front of the clerk. Yehoshua, who was exhausted and who, in any event, had made no arrangements for a place to stay, nodded and accepted the invitation.

The servant lad led him among the rooms of the house, and then they crossed a small courtyard and went up stone steps. The young man opened a heavy door and showed him the prepared bed, the location of the water bowl, and the towel. He tapped lightly on the pillows and folded the blanket, turned, and left with a silent footfall. Yehoshua lay down on the bed in his clothes and shoes, and he fell into a deep slumber quite quickly.

In the middle of the night, he awoke in a panic. He did not remember his nightmare in detail, but one sentence echoed in his mind and made him feel he was suffocating, "I will buy from you the heart of *the Valley*, two and a half million francs."

Where would he take the money from? In Palestine, land buyers were no longer clustering at every street corner. Should he go to Tyomkin? How much would the man help him? Weren't people saying that he was about to go away and leave behind him a passel of problems and unfulfilled promises? He would go to Bustros Roq. No, he owed him five hundred gold French francs that he had borrowed from him for buying the land of Wadi Hawarith, while Feibush Dolnik writes scads of words but does not send one cent.

"Love of the land overwhelmed me," Yehoshua chided himself. "I wanted to aggrandize my name, and I could not reject the temptation. My instinct told me 'Buy,' and I bought illogically."

He waited impatiently for morning to come, but outside, darkness still reigned. "I'll void the purchase," he decided. "I still haven't signed the contract. One can annul a handshake. I will flee before dawn and Musa Sursuq won't see me in my disgrace."

He tried to get up but couldn't. His legs were as heavy as two iron bars. He lay down again on the bed and pulled the blanket over himself, feeling the cold spreading and making his body tremble. He closed his eyes and saw the land approaching him in dancing moves — like a woman wrapped in brown and green dresses, stretching long arms out to him, with the sleeves of her garment flowing over the slopes of the Carmel and the hills of Haritiyeh and *the Valley*, becoming narrower until it disappeared into the sleeve seam, at the spot where the neck area is revealed. He tried to open his eyes but didn't succeed. His eyelids were stuck to each other and boxed him into his hallucination.

When morning broke, he did not sense the light bursting through the window nor the blanket overwarming him. Rapping on the door roused him from the bed, and in panic, he went to the door, wondering for a moment wondered why he could hear the sound of his steps. The servant stood at the doorway with a bowl of steaming water and a clean towel in his hands. He put them down in the room. He took the water bowl and towel from the previous night and left.

Yehoshua straightened his clothes and washed his face, combed his hair, and sat down on the bed, waiting for them to call him. A few minutes later, he heard a weaker knock than the previous one, and in the doorway stood the old man who had shown him to the great hall yesterday. The man motioned to him with his head to follow him; the two descended the stairs and entered the spacious courtyard and from there went into a small chamber overflowing with a mixture of furniture in different styles: a heavy, antique table inlaid with ivory, a Persian rug embroidered with small flowers, three gilded French chairs. This room is supposed to impress important people, Yehoshua thought to himself.

The old man sat him down at a table and signaled him to wait. A few minutes later, Musa Sursuq also entered the room. The servant spread out the agreement for them to see, and Yehoshua put his signature on it; he heard the Christian speaking, but did not remember about what. He sat opposite him, utterly frozen.

⤶

The day Yehoshua returned to Jaffa, the city was in the frenzy of preparing for the Passover seder, since only a few days remained before the holiday. The fragrances of the orchards intermingled with the aromas of the cooking, sheets were spread on fences, and summer-weight clothing hung from store doorways. Yehuda Leib's store was full of people who bought new bedding, tablecloths, and curtains for changing whatever in their homes might have particles of leavened food.

No one waited for him at the port since everyone was busy with work. Yehoshua knew that and did not expect anyone. The first people he saw were Fanny and Avshalom. Fanny stood in the middle of the kitchen, trying to tie packages while the tot crawled among them and pulled on objects, ruining the order his mother had arranged. The toddler saw his uncle, stood up straight, teetered toward him, and clapped his hands. Yehoshua lifted him up high over his head, looked into his eyes, and thought how much they looked like his mother's eyes—winking and laughing—while his nose and mouth were his father's. He tickled him and scrunched up his face and spun him around, and the tot squirmed and tried to get out of his big hands, and one could see he had inherited his father's strength. Yehoshua put him on his shoulders, and the child calmed down, so Yehoshua now switched to talking to Fanny undisturbed.

Fanny explained that she was packing for the trip to Hadera but that it was impossible to get ready with Avshalom, and it looked like this task would not be finished even by next Passover. Both laughed, and the little one did not understand why they were giggling, so he bent down over Yehoshua's head and put his cheeks next to the beard to rub it and draw some attention.

"Where is Olga?" he inquired.

"I thought you would never ask," laughed Fanny. "The Passover efforts have hastened births, and Olga has a lot of work."

"And I thought she would be waiting for me in the store," his face crumpled his face, and he stuck out his bottom lip like a baby.

"Don't cry," Fanny comforted him, laughing. She put out her hand to take Avshalom. "Good boy, Yehoshua," she patted his face, with the tot copying her motions, but she became serious when she saw the gloomy look on Yehoshua's face. "Go. Your wife will be happy to see you," she said. He left, going toward the clinic to find Olga. At first, he ran as if trying to shake off the weight of his thoughts and his exhaustion from his travels, as well as the issue of the two and a half million francs. He would find a way to explain, and she would understand and share his worries. He had found a wise wife. He smiled to himself and inadvertently bumped into a stand full of heaps of fruit, with some of them falling and rolling into the lane. Yehoshua stopped, catching his breath, and helped pick them up and put them back where they belonged. Then he apologized and continued dashing, stopping only when he reached the door to the office.

He was greeted by Fatima, the Arab woman who assisted at births; she told him to sit and wait and that she would notify Olga of his arrival. She went and came back with her hands full of towels and on them a tray with a cup of hot water with a piece of lemon floating in it. He was surprised that she knew what his favorite drink was. She saw his astonishment and winked, "Women understand each other and tell one another the small secrets of the private room."

As he sipped the hot water, he felt the fatigue of his trip overwhelming him, so he sat up straight in his chair to keep himself awake. To pass the time, he took the agreement out of pocket, and he saw for the umpteenth time his name displayed next to that of Sursuq in ornate letters and a firm signature. But his eyes grew heavy, and a light sleep took over, with the contract still resting on his lap.

When Olga came in, he had already closed his eyes. Without him noticing, she stood behind his chair and covered his eyes. Yehoshua felt the smoothness of her skin and the sensation of her long fingers patting his face, so he turned his head to see her and moved his body toward her and put his arms around her waist, and would not let go. She shook him off, "Not here. Fatima is looking."

But he laughed aloud, "She said she knows the small secrets of the private room." But Olga did not give in to him and pulled him out of his chair and into the empty doctor's office. Only then did she turn her body toward him; all of her was his. He took her again by the waist and clasped her to his chest. Both of them were a bit breathless, and he whispered into her ear, "I bought it. I fulfilled my dream. I have acquired the land of the Jezreel Valley."

She caressed his face and curled the ends of his beard around her finger. "Are you comfortable with this purchase?" she asked.

"Why do you ask?" he wondered and asked himself whether his hesitation was written on his face. But she only waited for his answer. He let her go and turned his face to the wall so he would not see her expression when she heard his reply.

"I pledged to buy for two and a half million francs. I could not resist the temptation. I could not let it go."

When the silence grew, he slowly turned to face her and saw her eyes wide open and her forehead wrinkled.

She looked neither angry nor happy, only sober and serious. Finally, she broke the silence, and said to him, "Let's go."

"Where?" he queried.

"To Tyomkin," she answered. "It does no good to think about acts already committed. You promised, and now you have to find the wherewithal to pay. The only one who can support your actions is Vladimir."

"But he's angry," he said, trying to hold her back. "Since we went to the Khudeira land, I have barely seen him. And what can I say to him?"

"I will talk," she smiled, knowing her power over him. "Once, he told me that he would have set his sights on me if it were not for you."

"I won't let him do that," he replied, nodding and still refusing to go.

"You will certainly do so—if it is land that is at stake. Why should you hide the truth? I have accepted the fact that I am barren and have recognized your other love that competes with me every day." She spewed her words in a rush, without letting him hush her.

Yehoshua went toward her and put his hand on her mouth to stop her and to avoid hearing the entire truth. She nipped his palm, so he quickly took it away.

They went out into the lane. Olga trod a bit ahead and dragged her husband behind her. He held her hand and let her pull him, feeling like a lamb being led to slaughter. He did not know whether he did so out of exhaustion or because of his desire to seek a reprieve.

They passed by the Christians' homes and reached a row of new houses facing the sea. Finally, they halted near a large home with which they were so very familiar. Yehoshua stopped behind Olga, hoping that she would go in without him, but she did not give in and pushed him in front of her and rang the bell.

A lad opened the door for them. Olga did not wait for him to lead them but hurried up the stairs, with Yehoshua slowly following and seeking the right words to open the discussion. He recalled the rumors about Tyomkin and what they had written about him. They had called him "troublemaker" and dubbed him "speculator."

And what would he do if what people were saying was true, and Tyomkin was really leaving Palestine? No! These are only rumors. He hurried to calm himself while walking behind his wife.

Without any hesitation, Olga opened the door to the parlor. Tyomkin was not sitting there alone; at the table, next to him, sat Ben-Tovim, while on the other side sat Pines. Olga halted at the entrance and tried to hold her husband back, but she was too late. He had already peeked over her shoulder to see what was going on in the room. Tyomkin saw them and motioned to them to wait in the hallway until the meeting was over. He did not look happy to see them but rather angry that they had dared to come to his house and go into his office without notifying him in advance.

They went out and leaned quietly on the banister, not knowing what to do with themselves. They did not speak to each other, nor did they share glances. Their waiting period grew long, and from the room, they heard muffled, jumbled sounds of an argument. Then, finally, the door opened, and Pines and Ben Tovim came out. Ben Tovim nodded to them in greeting, while Pines ignored them and passed them by with his head held high and his stomach protruding. He looked straight ahead and walked confidently.

Even though his invited visitors had left, Tyomkin did not immediately call them in and let them wait. Both were sure he was doing this on purpose but said nothing to each other. The lad came up the stairs, opened the door, and was swept inside the room. A few minutes later, he came out and told them to enter.

They entered and sat down—Yehoshua on the edge of his seat, Olga erect and quiet. She sat with them only for a short while and then stood up, claiming she had to go out to wash her face, and left the two men alone. Tyomkin did not look at Yehoshua. He pretended to be writing, but his hands were trembling, and the corners of his mouth attested to his great anger. Yehoshua wrung his hands, put them together, placed them on the table, and held them against his chest. He had to be the one to speak first, to give in, even if he had to embarrass himself. So, he spoke quietly with a shaky voice. "I have bought land, a great deal of land."

"Who did you buy it for," Tyomkin attacked him. "Have you finished solving all the problems of the Khudeira tract? Has the Wadi Hawarith land been handed over to the buyers? And what now?"

"For Khudeira, I have turned over the kushans and obtained permits. They have already built houses and are working the land. They are angry at me there, and they'll always be mad at me."

Tyomkin got out of his chair and walked restlessly about the room, from time to time turning his head toward Yehoshua and addressing him with stern words, "You don't learn. You are a 'lad,' dealing with very important issues, covetous of land without thinking of its future."

Yehoshua stopped him and tried to justify his deeds, "I have bought the land of the Valley, from those belonging to the Sursuq family. It is good land, fertile soil, and befitting many associations."

But Tyomkin didn't hear him and went on speaking and creating links between things that are unconnected. "Land, land, you are only obsessed with land. And you, like a blind person, have fallen into the trap it laid for you. You

306   IRIT AMIT COHEN & RUTH KARK

disappeared. You did not come to me for a long time and did not apologize or inquire about how I was doing. In Jaffa, people are spreading slanderous things about me. 'Land robber,' they call me. And you, the lands, have turned your head, and you want to deal with momentous things. Land, land, how much land do the Jews need?"

"Stop," Yehoshua thundered at him. "Pay attention to what you are saying. Once upon a time, we dreamed together. We worked toward great achievements, you and I. Today, you cut yourself off from your dream to settle the country and increase the number of Jews in it. The hateful words have influenced you, too. You know what they said about me, but I did not give up. I held onto the dream, and if I have to let it slip away from between my fingers, it will be because of you." Yehoshua stood and placed himself opposite Tyomkin, putting his hands on his shoulders, and then described the Valley land in an attempt to convince him. He limned its borders for him in words—strips of cultivated soil adorn the wide plains and reach the feet of the mountains. He tried to make him forget Jaffa's sorrows. He wanted to persuade Tyomkin and himself that acquiring land is something good.

Vladimir was enchanted by the spell that fell upon him, and he could not take his gaze away from Yehoshua's shining eyes. For the moment, he forgot the tempestuous sounds and the bad rumors, and the land burning under his feet, but Olga's return to the room carrying a tray brought him back to his senses.

"I will help," said Tyomkin hesitantly and cautiously. "I will look for buyers, and in the meantime, you will get a down payment to give the Sursuq family. Of course, I can't promise, but I will try to help." For a moment, he was quiet and then added quietly, as if speaking to himself, "In remembrance of other times, I will help. Who knows? Maybe this will be my final assistance."

Olga heard what he was saying and was frightened. She stood with her back to both of them and poured tea for the three of them with a trembling hand, and hot water spilled onto the plate with the cookies. Yehoshua paid no attention to the statement; he only raised his cup and took a mouthful of tea, burning his tongue in doing so.

Of course, none of the three revealed what had happened in Tyomkin's house, but somehow word got out, and the rumor about the intention to acquire the land of the large valley spread rapidly. The homes of Jaffa turned white as summer advanced, and the light intensified to the point of a fierce flame. Jaffa began to burn.

Running hither and thither in the narrow streets were the land speculators. Like rats emerging from their holes and feeling the wall of fire, they sell a piece of land, buy another and again make a sale. At first, it seemed like everyone wanted land, and this abundance of buyers made prices rise. Whoever had an empty lot was pleased to watch how its price rocketed skyward more every day. People already spoke at social gatherings focused on land. Someone mentioned available land, and the touts came to look at the merchandise: one named a price, another raised it, a third added to it and brought it higher, until finally, all of them promised to come the next day with a buyer, but they did not come, so the following Sabbath the landowner announced that his plot was for sale and new speculators would come. His wife had already set up a samovar and was serving tea among the squabblers, while wearing her best dress. Only, in the end, the land remained in her husband's possession.

The speculators, too, arrived in Beirut and knocked on the doors of the Sursuq family. They offered him a great deal of money, and he did not withstand the temptation and tore up the contract between him and Yehoshua; the great promise was forgotten.

As always happens, now too, the episode took on a life of its own and grew in size, and many different kinds of stories were spread about it. One of them was published in the pages of *Hamelitz* and was the source for anybody who liked juicy gossip: the young Mr. Hankin's success and his friendship with the Committee chairman, who promised to find buyers for *the Valley* land are what brought about his downfall. Pines could not accept the renewed success of "the lad," so he called Ben-Tovim, who really didn't like Tyomkin, and the two of them had the banker Ratzenstein join them, and together they went to the Armenian Murad, who was deputy consul of Germany. Pines told him about *the Valley* land at the foot of the Gilboa, praised it highly, and went into detail about the possibilities for working the land and raising different types of crops, but one thing he forgot to mention—that the land had been promised to the agent Yehoshua Hankin.

The deputy consul became enthusiastic about the idea of buying a dunam of land at 25 francs and the following morning selling it for 40 francs—as the three of them had promised him and backed up their words with innumerable examples. And the Armenian—who prior to his coming to Palestine had been promised that it was possible to turn its sand into gold, but until now had seen no gold, only sand—jumped on the bandwagon.

The Armenian set sail on a ship for Beirut; on it, he had been allotted no less than three cabins for himself and his cook. In Musa Sursuq's house, he was received with respect and glory, as befit a deputy consul, and when he asked for land, it was impossible to refuse him. In any event, he had offered three times what Mr. Hankin had. Moreover, he had promised to take care of the other family lands in case a Bedouin tribe invaded it, seeking to take possession of it.

Murad spent four days in Beirut, at least that's what was written in the newspapers, and upon his return, already waiting for him in the port were Mr. Pines and Mr. Ratzenstein, pushing each other and asking, "Nu?" He gave them the broad smile of a man who had made an excellent deal and tapped them on their shoulders; then, he hurried on home.

As for Sursuq, whether because he was a businessman and wanted to maintain good relations or whether out of pity, he sent a telegram to Yehoshua informing him of the transaction.

"I did not sign about a sale with the Armenian," Musa Sursuq was quoted in the newspaper. "The contract is still open. If Mr. Hankin can present a more tempting offer than the Armenian, the lands are his." But Yehoshua had nothing to offer. He had no money, and he had not been given a loan. All of them suddenly remembered the Egyptian bank, the threat of a lawsuit against Yehoshua by the Khudeira residents, and the debt that was repaid very late. There was no reason to turn to Yehuda Leib, since the family's entire holdings could not serve as a guarantee for the cost of the land.

Yehoshua journeyed to Beirut and knocked on Sursuq's door, pleading and humiliating himself, to ask for a delay in the agreement with Murad, until he would find money to finance the purchase. He had a dream, a big dream, and it was about to slip between his fingers.

Musa Sursuq found it difficult to see the humiliation of the young land agent and offered him other land. "Not far from Nazareth," he told him, "I own a large tract of land with a khan at its center, and it's close to the Arab village Sejera. If you are not interested in these, I have available other land—I can sell you the land of Jidro Valley, which is the language of the Jews is called Zevulun, and they stretch for Acre to Haifa." Musa Sursuq's offer was very good, but these were not "Emeq" lands, so Yehoshua rebuffed them all.

The Emeq was lost, and just like the purchase of one tract had failed, so did other transactions. A few weeks after the trip to Beirut, a telegram was delivered to the store from Feibush Dolnik, asking to meet him in Constantinople and transfer the contract he held for the Wadi Hawarith land to a third party, Baron Rothschild. Yehoshua knew that any attempt to link the Baron to the Wadi Hawarith arrangement would make him a laughingstock. When the Baron had wanted to buy the Duran land from him, he had refused and not allowed the establishment of even one colony with support money. Now, however, he had to agree to many colonies, and all of them Baron supported. But he had no choice, since his name, his love, and all his property were in danger. Yehoshua had convinced himself to go to Beirut. Perhaps, a solution would be found in any event, and with the Baron's money, the other troubles would be resolved. Again, he did not hesitate, so he packed his belongings and intended to set out for the port. When Yehoshua left his house, he noticed a gendarme standing at the corner of the lane. Yehoshua stepped down the street, with the Turkish policeman openly following him and the tapping of his soles making a rhythmic accompaniment to Yehoshua's fast marching. As Yehoshua was about to climb into a boat to row over to the ship anchored a distance out, the policeman arrested him. Yehoshua struggled against him and hit him, forgetting both his honor and his status. The policeman managed to evade the blows raining on his back and blew his whistle to call for help from a few other policemen and led him to confinement. Had it not been for the fellow making the camel kneel, no one would have known anything about the arrest of "the lad." The young man who worked in the port witnessed the arrest of the *hawaja*, the important land broker, and ran to the store to inform Yehuda Leib. But that was not enough—he hastened to tell the story of the arrest to whoever wanted to listen, and they were many.

Yehoshua's father broke down and did not want to hear about his son's failure. But Sarah and Olga did not give up and asked Tyomkin to intervene. Half-heartedly, he agreed to help. However, he did so only after Olga reminded him of other times and waved newspapers in front of his nose and went on to say, "There will be other days when you, too, will need friends, and what will you do when they turn their backs on you?"

Tyomkin turned to the Turkish governor, and he released Yehoshua though ordering him to stand trial for hitting a policeman and for the attempt to evade paying his debts.

Olga assumed that her husband had calmed down and accommodated to his failure. But Yehoshua was determined to try to run away a second time and clung to the trip to Constantinople like a drowning man clutching at straws. This time he asked for help and did not act alone. He gave his sister Haya a letter for the Egyptian servant in the house of Bustros Roq, and then left through the store's back doorway, dressed in women's clothing and his face veiled in the manner of Arab women, and snuck through the shadows of the houses. The Egyptian waited for him next to the Muslim cemetery, ready to transport him in a small boat hidden among the rocks on the coast. The servant was very familiar with the path between the shoals, and when the boat reached the ship bound for Beirut, he called aloud, and a rope was thrown to him. When Yehoshua was climbing in, wavering between the side of the ship and the sea, he wondered if Bustros Roq was aware of the help his servant had provided him and if he intended to ignore what he had done. When he jumped onto the deck, he was met by a different Egyptian, a relative of the servant, and Yehoshua put several bishliks into his hand, hoping to reward the man for his kindness on another occasion.

The ship's voyage on the sea lasted for several days, and most of the time, Yehoshua slept, eating little and not differentiating between day and night. As he slept, he imagined that Dolnik was waiting to tell him that the Baron wanted the Hawarith land and was willing to finance the purchase and take care of the colonies that would be put up there.

During his stay on the boat, he was helped by a Turkish sailor, who liked Yehoshua's long hair, sunken eyes, and the sadness reflected in them. He would sit next to Yehoshua on a wooden board that served as a bed and looked at his gaunt face, taking care to put some food in his mouth. And Yehoshua, who did not have the wherewithal to shoo him away, would again escape into sleep.

In Constantinople, the sailor helped him to disembark and made sure to tie his bundles well. He also put into his hand a note containing an address. But the minute the ship disappeared, he tore it into pieces, threw them away, and went to wait at the entrance to the hotel, as Feibush Dolnik had told him in a telegram. Yehoshua waited a day, two days, not daring to move from the hotel entry, in case that man should appear. The doorman took pity on him and let him sleep in his bed while he was on duty, and when he would finish his shift, he would awaken Yehoshua, who would then go back to standing at the entrance and waiting. He could not tell one day from the next and did not know how long he had waited. Finally, Dolnik came by himself, without his son. He was still round and nimble, with the eyes of a merchant, darting about restlessly and not looking the person standing in front of him directly in the eye. Dolnik did not see Yehoshua's gauntness nor his wild hair. He only regarded his wrinkled clothes and his worn-out student coat. He told him that an appointment had been made with the Baron's secretary, and perhaps it was better he went alone, since Yehoshua's appearance was not respectable. Yehoshua heard what he said and became furious; his helplessness melted away without a trace. He wanted to grab Dolnik by the scruff of his neck, lift him up, and crush him like a mosquito.

"It's my land as long as you have not paid for it," he cried in pain. "I will go with you to the secretary. You won't act alone!"

He arranged a room for a day with the hotel's doorman; he ate well and made sure to shave properly, trim the ends of his hair, iron his coat, polish his shoes, change his shirt, and despite his fatigue, he straightened his back when he went to the meeting with the secretary. At the entrance to the Athena Hotel, the most luxurious hotel in the city, Dolnik was already waiting for him, looking like a peacock, with a red handkerchief in his jacket pocket and a curled collar peeking out of his coat and encompassing his jowly neck. Next to him, Yehoshua's skinniness was emphasized, and he saw his image reflected in the dozens of mirrors surrounding the immense lobby.

The secretary was already waiting for them in a comfortable armchair, with a long cigar in his mouth and a pile of orderly documents next to him. After they sat down, the secretary asked them polite questions, and tea was served. Yehoshua took a sip and related the story of the purchase of the lands of Wadi Hawarith, pouring out his heart after having kept his silence for a long time. All the time, Dolnik sat and swung his feet, while lightly tapping his fingers on his ironed trousers. The drumming disturbed Yehoshua, though he tried to ignore it and to impassion the secretary with his speech about the sand and the cliffs reaching the water and the Bedouin tents spread out as far as the eye could see. But suddenly, he realized the man was not listening to him but was engaged in dipping one cookie after another in his tea. Dolnik, on his part, was impatient and wanted to leave.

Yehoshua had the feeling the two of them had already decided on the future of the land, and the invitation to Yehoshua had only been made because of his special trip to Constantinople, and because it was customary to do things properly — a meeting is a meeting though it was not important if a word was a word. Yehoshua looked at his full cup of tea and the secretary's empty one with cookie crumbs at the bottom. He also noticed that Feibush Dolnik was already standing, ready to go, while the secretary was waving his handkerchief to clear off the crumbs scattered on his clothes. He could not accept the fact that was quickly becoming more evident, so he pressed, wanting to hear a clear statement, "I came to sign, to change the name of one buyer to that of another and to sign in place of the Baron."

The secretary looked at him with a smile of pity mixed with contempt. "Profiteering is rife in Palestine. Little speculators buy land. They buy and have no one to sell to. They make worthless deals, raise prices, and don't see the decrees about to fall and the fleeing of the masses. The Baron will buy land, but who will he sell it to? It does not befit him to deal with small profiteers in times of crisis and unrest. Things will calm down; prices will stabilize, and then the Baron will consider things again."

The words struck like blows on Yehoshua's ears, and he was sure he was about to faint. One thought repeatedly pounded in his head: Not to fall, not to show the two of them his weakness. He still did not understand why he had been invited to Constantinople. Had the Baron's decision been made just now? Had Feibush Dolnik stirred the pot to bring about his failure? Perhaps, it was his appearance that forced this happening. The Baron never did like him; he knew that. He had long been aware it was so. But such a great man was above such pettiness. He looked for an answer from the other two, but they did not see his glances and only wished to leave. He stood and marched toward the door without turning his head.

"Wait," Dolnik called after him, "we haven't finished. I will take care of collecting the money, but not now. We will write a new agreement and determine new periods for payment. The situation is bad, and people have forgotten their promise to buy land in Palestine. But just wait! Better times will come, and I will buy the land of Wadi Hawarith from you, and maybe by then, land prices will come down, and the seller will not exploit us—neither me nor those who have sent me."

But Yehoshua remained silent and left the hotel's doorway, being swept up and vanishing in the city's lanes. That very day, he went down to the port and waited for the first ship that would bring him back to Jaffa, and when he did return there after a lengthy voyage, he was more stooped and emaciated and ready to be judged for having run away without permission. He only wanted to be left alone, even in a jail cell on the clay of a hardened mud floor.

Feibush Dolnik went back to Yekaterinoslav, and they no longer heard from him. The debt owed to Bishara Tayyan still loomed large, and the leaders of the associations continued to knock on the store's door, shouting, "You promised us land. The 'lad' land agent should fulfill his pledge." The sum of five hundred gold francs also remained, taken to be a debt to Bustros Roq. The debt pursued him like a relentless nightmare, and the Turkish gendarme, who continued to stand at the entrance to the shop, chased him and watched his moves.

Rising on the store's counter was a pile of court orders and newspaper clippings full of slander; Yehoshua became gaunter and moved about like a sleepwalker, indecisively and twitching like a dove with a broken wing. He clung to one person and hoped to be saved by him—Tyomkin, but the fall of the Committee chairman was soon to come. Olga tried with all her might to maintain Yehoshua's humanity and accompanied him wherever he went, refusing pregnant women and urging the gendarme to move a bit away and stand at the corner of another street. She tried to hide newspapers from him, as well as the increasing number of decrees and gateways being shut to Jews—

and with them any chance to find a buyer. Sometimes she would accompany him on his visits to Tyomkin and sit apart from them, watching them wither. One time, the Committee chairman said he had indeed found buyers for Galilee land next to the Arab village of Shajara, and even for land in the Zebulon Valley. So, he suggested that Yehoshua speak again with the Sursuq family and replace the dream of acquiring the Jezreel Valley with dreams of new purchases. But Olga felt contempt for him and knew that these were only empty words and that the Jews were still not coming to buy land. Yehoshua didn't even listen to what Tyomkin said, and his speeches made no impression on him.

Afterward, Yehoshua stopped going to the home of the Committee head and was steeped in his own pain; he even shut down in front of Olga. She, on her part, after a long while of attempting to come close to him, caressing and encouraging, began to distance herself from him and decided to no longer take pity on him and let him pull himself together.

Moreover, since births continued even in distressful times, and since those living in the well houses around Jaffa, and like the tent dwellers, were unaffected by the decrees and didn't sense the Jews' panic, Olga had a great deal of work. Besides this, they needed money to cover Yehoshua's debt and his trials and take care of a few vegetables to prepare hot soup. Seeing to the small issues occupied Olga fully, so she had no time for emotions and pity and waited for her husband to come to his senses and come back to her and be great—the Second Joshua.

In October 1892, the gates of Jaffa were closed to new Jews. After this decree, commercial enterprises were closed, and Sarah Hankin no longer said that it was just a matter of the season, and she knew that Jaffa was beginning to lick its wounds. Boats continued to leave the port full and come back empty. Borrowers went from the house of one land speculator to another to collect their debts, but the touts turned out their pockets to show they were empty.

The Egyptian Bank closed its doors, and then the speculators fled, leaving unpaid debts behind them. They sailed to Beirut and from there scattered all over, so there was no longer anyone who would stand on the street corner and praise the land of Palestine. The Committee chairman left as well. Even though he had promised to return, everyone knew that was just talk. He took one bundle with him and abandoned a house full of objects and instructions for Pines and

Ben Tuvim to sell if someone should come and demand he cover his debt to them. Many did come, but there was not enough in the house to pay all of them, even if they knocked on the door a few times. But when they were turned away with nothing, they left in shame since there was no one before whom they could scream and shout.

Yehoshua wandered in the Jaffa lanes like an abandoned cat, and then he changed his path and went off into the swamps of Hadera. He didn't dare climb the slopes of the Carmel, and his heart did not let him traverse the hills of Harithiyeh, and Sheikh Abreq and stand facing the entrance to *the Valley*. He stayed in the swamps and did not show his face in the colony whose houses had just been completed. In Hadera, they were still angry and continued to threaten him with a lawsuit; they boycotted the plot worked by Mendel and spat aside whenever the name Hankin was mentioned. The dunes at the seashore took him in; Bedouin tribes gave him a place to sleep at night and asked no questions. He went far away from the tumult of the city and the repeated announcement of decrees as well as from the woman he loved; he did not dare to be seen by her when he was so weak and disgraced. He very often trod along the seashore and left his footprints in the wet sand. He repeatedly stood opposite the small watermelon ports at Umm Khalid and Minet Abu Zabura. His heart went out to the ships setting sail in the summer for Egypt and wanted to remain alone on the desolate shore in the winter.

That was how he went about for a long time, emaciated and feverish. One day, he stayed with the Arab guard of the tomb of Sidna Ali, trembling from the cold, and the guard covered him with a camel-hair rug. In the morning, Yehoshua could not manage to get up. The Arab gave him an herbal tea and put him on a donkey—to go back home to Jaffa.

Yehoshua was like an infant who couldn't take a step without support for quite a while. He did not express an opinion when the couple left the room over the store and rented a room for themselves in Ajami, near the doctor's office where Olga worked.

Income from the store was meager, so Sarah decided to sell the second story to merchants so they could open a store there. Perhaps, customers would come to one store and see the other and then enter it as well. Maybe the idea that two stores were housed in the same building would be enough to draw more clients, or so she hoped. In any event, she couldn't help her son, and she did not want to see his decline, day by day, hour by hour; she worried about Yehuda Leib and encouraged Olga in her decision to go and rent lodgings somewhere else.

Olga was steeped in her work. Now, there were no longer family obligations that would steal her time nor joint evening meals—but also no Yehoshua. She had properly done her duty to him as a wife. She cooked a hot meal, prepared a moist towel, put his mail in a pile, and paid his debt bit by bit. The work in the doctor's clinic was not enough for her; she learned to drive a wagon by herself and rented one in the Jaffa port. Every week, she would take along Sonia. The two of them would head south toward the Bedouin tribes, pass by the Rehovot colony, and reach the Sitriya and Zarnuga tribes: Olga delivered babies, and Sonia learned, both of them gleaned gold coins. As a result, Yehoshua's debt grew much smaller. Some of the trials against him were closed, since the plaintiffs had fled; others resulted in light fines, since the qadi took pity on the woman accompanying the accused and paying his fines out of her pocket.

To be sure, there were reasons for this mercy. Yehoshua's silence was part of it. His hair grew, his beard sprouted wildly, and he hid from people. Now, he was called "the crazy one." They did not remember "Yehoshua," not even "agent for land matters"; they found it enough to dub him "the lunatic with the long hair." Children would run after him and pull at the hem of his coat until it tore—whether because they tugged forcefully or because it was old. Olga tried to replace the coat, but he wouldn't let her, and he remained attached to it. After that, he became one of the characters of the Jaffa landscape; the years passed, and he drowned in them, unchanging, as if it had been determined, and so he would always be.

20. Yehoshua and Olga Hankin in Jaffa, 1913 • Source: Central Zionist Archives.

1915

The whistles began to shriek. Officers rose from their seats and tucked their shirts into their tightly closed belts that raised their paunches and passed among the soldiers, kicking rear ends and pointing out with their staffs wrinkled shirts or a cap that was not put on and hitting snapped fingers against the stubble of unshaven beards. Muttering the same sentence over and over, they criticized, "With such dress and such behavior, you are not fit to be soldiers of the Sultan."

The wounded sat up straight in their place. Whoever could sit erect, exploited their injury and, trying to rise above the noise of the whistles, demanded in a loud voice that the lad bring them water so they could wash away the remnants of sleep and the aches and pains from the long journey. Anyone who could not pull themselves up arranged their blanket, tried to comb their hair, and hid sweaty, blood-stained bandages.

Sivas was still far away, tucked among the Taurus Mountains, but now they were nearing Adana. Urban scenes replaced the landscape of the exposed high region: minarets of mosques that perforated the horizon, jumbled houses with unpaved streets running among them, ancient arches and walls, and children waving near the track, screaming, and showing their wares. The train never stopped blowing its horns and often slowed its speed, and every time that happened, it shook those lying down or standing up, making them fall on each other.

Great tumult reigned in the "Aliens" carriages. Whoever was traveling to Constantinople took down bundles and collected them like a hen sitting on eggs gathering her chicks, with her eyes darting all around, lest she forget one. Then, he gathered his packages around him, put his arms around them tightly, and closed the last sacks that had been open during the long ride to show their content. Next to the lavatories, women stood in a long line and tried to put on perfume and beautify themselves and erase the last traces of the journey still visible on them.

At the entrance to the last wagon, the gendarme stretched in place, straightened his rifle, and wiped its barrel with the edge of his clothes so it would shine and look ready for use. Then, he got up and peeked through the widening crack between the door and the lintel and tossed a sentence to those sitting inside the car, "Adana is already not far." But he didn't raise his head to see their reaction and added, as if speaking to himself, "There is a large prison there, and many of the Turkish criminals are held there. You will stay in the jail for two days, waiting for the trucks going to Sivas. You will have two good days there. You will long for them later." And he laughed, making his paunch wriggle like jelly, and rolled his mustache; then he went back to dealing with his rifle and went on talking, each word reverberating well in the wagon, "In Sivas, there is only devastation. Barely a few are lucky enough to get out of Sivas, and they are carried out in a coffin. Most of them are thrown into piles, and no one knows who is buried where." The man so enjoyed his joking that he could not help but share it with others, and he called the serving fellow to bring him coffee and listen to his words of wisdom.

The four sitting in the wagon did not need to prepare for alighting from the train. They were not planning to continue on to Constantinople, so they slept in the same clothes they sat in and left the train in the same clothes they had worn when they got on it. The two women did ask the gendarmes to take them to the toilette so they could wash their faces, but he didn't allow them to go there. "There's a big fuss in it," he told them. "Make do with what's here," sliding toward them the bowl with the hot water brought by the lad.

All four knew he was worrying about himself, lest they try to escape and he would be accused of dereliction of duty. He had already told them that special care had to be taken with anyone who was linked to the name of Hassan Bey, since he had brought them to the train and had even testified against them at the trial, so they bore his mark and weren't regular traitors but dangerous ones. Another time, he informed them that he had been promised a gold medal if he would bring them to the prison gates. Moreover, he would be able to quote statements he had heard from them on the sly about love for Palestine, hatred of Turks, and their wish to obtain land with authorization and with the agreement of the nations to establish a Jewish state. They had provided the words for him; for now, they had nothing to lose, and weren't they being sent to Sivas from which few came out alive?

Israel observed Mania and was amused to see her dealing with Olga's hair. For whom? He thought, in honor of a Turkish prison. He winked to the gendarme, who, like him, was peeking at the two of them combing hair and taking a look at the curls resting on their chests and wound around the comb. The gendarme winked back at the prisoner, and then remembered his duty and turned his face away and continued working on the rifle.

Yehoshua stayed apart from the group. He was immersed in his plans, looking for ways to get out and replace the exile of Sivas with the exile of Bursa, a Turkish city on the shores of the Sea of Marmara, not so far away from Constantinople. He had heard that diplomatic prisoners were concentrated there and kept watch over in case of negotiations. The guard had told them they would spend two days in Adana, and if he only knew how to reach the American envoy sitting in Constantinople, he would ask for his help. The gendarme was right. Two days in Adana wouldn't change anything. They were like a cigarette or a luxurious meal given to a condemned man. They had closed all avenues to salvation, and from Sivas, they would only return on biers — if they came back at all. He leaned his head down, supporting it with his hands, and he looked at unkempt clothes and his unpolished coat buttons and was saddened. Again, he turned his gaze to the woman he loved; perhaps that would comfort him. At least she had come with him and not stayed alone, and she did not let him go through terrible exile and a harsh death by himself.

Olga noticed his looking and pulled her hair out of Mania's hands. She got up and approached Yehoshua's bench. She sat beside him, pushing him a bit to make room for her. He smiled and hugged her thick waist, and whispered into her ear, "Bursa. We will get to Bursa, and there I will find a way to save us all, no matter what."

She nodded her head in mute agreement. And what should she say? There was no consolation. Maybe a sliver of hope?!

Her eyes caressed him. He was fifty-one, and she was older than he, but he had more gray hair than she did, and it was mixed in his thick beard. They had supported each other for thirty years, and their connection was stronger than anything else. There had been days when she had seen his devotion to the land, and she had been jealous of it, until it betrayed him and left him bereft of everything. For such a long time, she had not forgiven its treacherousness; and he had withdrawn from his loving wife and not wanted to make her part of it.

But the woman had seen his fall and had not intervened. She let him hide behind his long hair and escape from the mockery of the children who yelled after him in the streets, "Crazy," "Crazy." She covered all his debts and often traveled to the Bedouins and to the Arabs and had met traders in land among them and heard them mention his name, speaking of him as a legend. But in Jaffa, he was not a legend. He was bearded, silent, and eccentric. But she did not give in and did not take hold of his head to pet it and to console, and she waited for the day he would rise and begin anew. Sarah was angry, and many a time had sent Haya, her daughter, who helped her in the store, to give advice and call him to come home and find a way to deliver him from his sorrow.

But Olga did not let Haya get near him. He would arise by himself, without her support, she convinced herself; he would straighten up any dependence that would drag him down, even to the depths of forgetfulness.

Olga knew people said she was difficult; an evil-hearted old woman, exploiting her success and demonstrating her power over her husband. Sonia reinforced her, and on those days when Olga didn't have the strength to see his pain, Sonia went instead of her to prepare a bowl of soup and sit opposite him to watch him sip it slowly.

Yehoshua felt her scrutinizing gaze, caressed her, and whispered, "My *dyevka*. Olga, the wife of Yehoshua Hankin."

"From the Belkind family," she laughed.

But he shook his head as if refusing to hear this, "No, no, only Olga Hankin."

She nodded her head and replied to him, "Jashiya." But she did not stop with the pet name, saved only for him, and added, "the Second Joshua."

Yehoshua smoothed her wrinkles and patted her haggard hand dotted with age spots. More than once, people had said to him, "Your Olga's too old. She won't have children. Look for someone younger than she." And he answered all of them that he did not need children, and he had no desire for an infant that would suckle at her breast and steal her attention from him. He loved her as she was, all of her; she belonged only to him. A long time passed until he sincerely recognized her love. In the meantime, the years had gone by them, and he had fallen and was in exile within Palestine, and at that time, Olga was far from him and unobtainable. When he finally dared to extend a hand and beg that they should take him out from the lowest depths of a pit, only she stood there, at the edges of the pit, and offered him both hands.

1897

Yehuda Leib passed away the year the First Zionist Congress convened, 1897, and the name of Theodor Herzl was mentioned by everyone, while for Yehoshua Hankin, nothing had changed. A day had passed after the end of the *shiva*, so he went to visit the house near the port.

They called it "the house," because they did not want to give it another name, and they tried to demean it as much as possible. An oil lamp burned day and night over the entranceway, spreading a red glow around it. In daylight, the flame was unseen, and a house of simple kurkar bricks was swallowed up among the other port structures. At night, the light created a moving, fleeting magic circle dancing on the wall. At that time, the warehouses melted away in the dark, and only the house was seen from afar.

Long ago, when he would go down to the port with young Tanhum to watch the ships anchored far out and to dream of distant countries, the lad would stop in amazement and look toward that house and ask innocently who the elegantly dressed woman going into the house were, and what about the men, many of whom he knew, and this house? Yehoshua would pull him away from there, promising him, "In time, you will know!" and his laugh would resound among the warehouses. Tanhum grew up and left Jaffa, joining Mendel to establish a plot in Hadera, and forgot about the house next to the port, but Yehoshua didn't. Now, Yehuda Leib had met every man's fate, and Olga had grown distant and shut herself off from him, so he no longer had to explain his actions to anyone and decided to visit "the house."

As he entered, he saw sailors and Turkish policemen standing in groups. He heard a mix of voices in an unidentified language and smelled heavy scents of perfume and shaving soap, as well as the smell of wine mixed with the smell of the resin of wooden furniture. He became dizzy and already thought about leaving there, but a tumult in the corners of the house attracted him. He went over to it and bumped into drunks and giggling women and a glass rolling on the floor; he joined the group of people crowding around a woman who wiggled her stomach and her butt and shook her breasts, with the bells around her middle tinkling. The men stamped their feet and accompanied the knocking of the bracelets with whistling; they beat on a table and stuffed bills among the golden straps adorning the dancer's body. She slithered among them but refrained from contact, and her audience was excited, so the sound of their stamping rose. The dancer neared the end of the circle and left it dancing as she passed among the tables. Also, those seated tucked bills into her outfit, and she would wiggle her body for them and shake her head so that her red curls would slither down like snakes touching-not-touching her audience. She returned to the corner, approached those standing at the edges, and rubbed Yehoshua's coat.

Yehoshua was frightened by the intoxicating smell and the obscuring of his senses, so he pulled back and did not put a hand in his pocket to take out money and bury it among the straps, but she did not give up and continued to cavort around him. Yehoshua hid his hands, putting them in his sleeves, and stepped back. He saw the expression, perhaps astonishment, perhaps anger, limned on her face, and he lowered his eyes. She danced next to him for a moment longer, but when she did not succeed in breaking his silence, she turned away from him and returned to her stamping, whistling crowd.

Close to dawn, the place emptied out. Only a few remained, including Yehoshua, who sat in his corner and stared at his glass that was still half full. He did not know where he was and what he was doing, and for a minute, it seemed to him that he was still sitting in the Athena Hotel in Constantinople opposite the glass of tea of Rothschild's secretary with the crumbs at its bottom. He did not notice the dancer who came to his table, pulled out a chair, turned it so the backrest faced him, swung one leg over the seat, sat down, and looked at him. He was so disparate from the others who frequented the house: different in his hair, his sunken eyes, his gauntness, the student coat hanging on him, his thunderous silence. She lowered her head and leaned her chin on the backrest, but he did not see her. It was only the cup in front of him that he saw. She put out her hand and moved the cup aside, and he became alert, looking quizzically directly at her. She kept quiet as he did, and then she stood up to go, and he rose as well and went after her.

He did not ask for her name, nor did she ask for his. If he had to address her, he used the term "The Turkish woman." After the first time, he revisited the house in the port many times. At first, he would only come after nightfall, going surreptitiously between the shadows of the warehouses, his hair stuck into his raised coat collar. Later, he was no longer embarrassed and would come in the mornings to drink liquor, forget where he was, and leave there in the afternoons, wandering in his defilement, with the children running after him, calling, "The crazy one," "The crazy one." Their voices pursued him up the street to the house that Olga had rented in the Ajami neighborhood. In the evening, he would return to the port and the Turkish woman, sitting apart from the rowdiness of the place and wait for her to finish her dance and hint to him to follow her.

In the hours between day and night, Yehoshua would go back to his home and enter the room that was his and Olga's, seeing her wrapped in a quilt at the edge of the bed, and he would lie on the other edge in his clothes that reeked of the house in the port. He did not know if she was awake or whether she heard his plodding steps—and he didn't even think about it. He thought of her as an object belonging to the Ajami house and as part of the bitter, weighty memories that he wanted to evade, and he didn't have the strength to take any measures toward change. The abyss drew him ever deeper, and nightmares attacked him, making him tremble in his sleep. But Olga knew and cried into her pillow, waiting for the moment he would return. He had to come on his own accord, without embarrassment, strong, like she knew him to be.

Yehoshua returned to Olga when the Turkish woman went away. One evening she did not dance in the house at the port, and instead, another woman with black curls wriggled more energetically. Hour after hour, he waited for her. Finally, the new day dawned, but he still waited until the owner of the place came to him and told him, "She left. She collected enough money and went back to her old place, where they did not know where she was and didn't ask where her money came from. Now, she has a sufficient dowry in hand to bring an honorable groom to her parents' doorstep."

The words penetrated Yehoshua's awareness, piercing and painful. He rose to flee from there, knocking over his chair and slamming the door. He was frightened by his self-image that was suddenly depicted for him. He ran and climbed the hill, his hair flapping, getting in his eyes. Suddenly, he understood how much he had hurt Olga. His entire body trembled in shame, and he did not know what to say to her or how to ask for her forgiveness.

Yehoshua hoped to find her asleep on her side of the bed and imagined himself hugging her and wrapping her in his arms, but Olga wasn't there. As usual for her at that time, she was busy covering her husband's debts and worrying about rent and basic necessities. He saw an ironed nightshirt at the edge of the bed, a dry towel placed next to a bowl of water and became even more ashamed. He hurried to wash his face, smooth out his old coat, and clean his boots. Then he went out into the lane to look for a barber, and he came to some firm decisions.

When he finished grooming his body and saw his face in the mirror, he calmed down a bit. But, unfortunately, he didn't have a qirsh in his pocket to pay the barber, so he promised to come back early the next morning. The man, who registered his fervor, his gaunt face, and his burning eyes, believed him and even sprinkled a few drops of rosewater on his clothes. From there, Yehoshua walked to Christians St. to knock on the door of Bustros Roq.

The Egyptian, his long-time acquaintance, opened the door and, without asking questions, led him to the large room where the effendi welcomed his visitor. He left him at the doorway and went away, without making a sound, so Yehoshua stood alone and rued his impulsiveness.

Sitting in the room, with crossed legs, was a group of effendis dressed in long galabiyas and smoking nargilehs. Bustros Roq looked at him in surprise and motioned him to come near and sit with them, but Yehoshua felt out of place and nodded his refusal. The effendi clapped his hands, and the Egyptian returned. He approached his master to hear his instructions. Then went toward Yehoshua and took him from there to another, darker room, with many pillows and a copper tray that, as needed, was turned into a table and a large, heavy wood cabinet made of out one block of wood, with incised openwork and slivers of ivory inlaid between them in star shapes. In its upper section were two glass panels behind which one should be able to see wine cups, but the cabinet was empty; it had certainly been purchased in some faraway eastern country to decorate the house and boast of its antiquity and of the homeowners understanding of antiquities. The cupboard was out of place among the colorful pillows and the white and black intertwining floor tiles, a triangle of black tiles within a square of white ones, and in the center of the room, a black square.

Yehoshua sat among the pillows, reminded himself of the vitrine in Fanny and Lolik's house, and wondered about what they were doing. He began to count the floor tiles and test the agility of his memory, arranging in his head times and events that had happened so long ago. He remembered Feibush Dolnik and the episode of the Wadi Hawarith land that was not concluded and the trip to Constantinople and the house of Mousa Sursuq in Beirut, and the dream of the Jezreel Valley that had shattered.

While counting the floor tiles, he thought about the events that had taken place in Jaffa and that he had ignored all the years he had considered himself dead. In Jaffa, they had long forgotten Tyomkin and the craze for land, foreigners had stopped coming, and the Palestine Jews had gone back to dealing only with their own private affairs. Then, there had been the episode of Eliezer Ben Yehuda, who wanted to speak Hebrew and obliged all of them to speak as he did, and the people called him crazy. Then, they talked about a mysterious society, "Bnei Moshe," which every self-important hack wanted to join. But the society did not accept all of them. There were also those that it did take in and a short while later spit out, and that's what had happened to Pines. At first, the "Bnei Moshe" added him to their association and then found out that he did not want to follow their path but only came to spy on them and mock their ideas, so they drove him out. Pines went and collected about him a group of rabbis who opposed the speaking of Hebrew and protested vociferously against anyone who wanted to make it a vernacular and, moreover, sought to change the Jews' way of life and scorned the support for rabbis and *talmidei hakhamim* (Torah scholars). But the esoteric society laughed at the attempt to ruin it and set up a school where they taught in Hebrew and encouraged Ben Yehuda to continue writing in Hebrew and to spread his idea, with Ben Yehuda's newspaper *HaZvi* becoming their mouthpiece.

Pines fought back and informed the Turkish authorities that Ben Yehuda was publishing seditious items in his paper and called for a rebellion against the Turks. He also spread a rumor in Jaffa that the "Bnei Moshe" school was a focus of unrest. So it was that Pines's war against the "Bnei Moshe" became another episode in the battle of the "Old Yishuv" against the "New Yishuv." This great war, which began in Jerusalem, ultimately also made its way down to Jaffa, but Yehoshua was not involved in it, since he was immersed in his own sorrow and did not feel the changes taking place around him; he didn't hear, and he didn't see.

Now, while sitting in the home of Bustros Roq, Yehoshua felt how the lump in his throat was strangling him and wanted to burst out yelling. He tried to withhold himself and stuck his coat lapel into his mouth to stifle the screams. He went back to reconstructing past events, and for some reason, he envisioned the announcement that had been plastered on the walls of the Jaffa houses about a new play called *Zerubabel* that the workers in the Rehovot colony were performing and that had women playing in it. He recalled that the following day, he had found bits of the announcements floating in the refuse in the channel when he went down to the port. At the corner of the lane, he noticed rabbis stamping on their remnants and hanging other notices instead that bewailed wantonness of women. Since he was thinking about the Rehovot settlement, he wondered about what Aharon Eisenberg was doing. He called to mind Olga's story about a Jew names Zalman Levin Epstein and his big plans to establish a winery in Rehovot that would compete with the one in Rishon Lezion. He smiled to himself because he knew that the colony's farmers intended to show those supported by Baron Rothschild that it was possible to tend to vineyards and olive trees with benefactors' money. Right then, he wanted to know if they had built the winery, and who was this Epstein of whom they spoke? His grin was wiped away, his head ached, and he didn't know if this was because of the memories flooding him or because of the drink he had imbibed the day before when he had waited for the Turkish woman.

He did not want to think about her. He wanted to erase the past six years and begin where he had left off. To renew the days of Hawarith and to find out what had happened with the lands of *the Valley*; had the Austrian consul bought them, or had he changed his mind when the panic started and the land had lost its value. He wanted to see Olga's face smiling at him when he presented himself now that he had changed. But he knew deep down he was dreaming, and that Olga would not receive him with a smile dancing in her eyes.

Quite a while passed, and Yehoshua wondered why the effendi had not come in and had left him by himself. When the Egyptian finally entered, holding a jug of coffee and a pitcher of water, he discovered Yehoshua sitting with his head hanging down and his eyes closed. A few drops of water sprinkled on his face woke Yehoshua up, and he jumped up, startled; only when he saw the Egyptian hovering near him and smiling did he calm down. The tall man offered him a bowl of fruit. Yehoshua plucked one grape off a cluster, put it in his mouth, and let the sweetness trickle down his throat; again, he remembered Lolik and Fanny and that time with the jam in Rishon Lezion. His eyelids became heavy once more, and the cluster fell and scattered on the floor, and he slipped into a very deep, nightmare-less sleep the likes of which he had not enjoyed in a very long time.

When Bustros Roq entered the room quite a while later, he found Yehoshua sleeping on the pillows and sat down opposite him, looking at him in his sleep. He saw the wrinkles of sadness carved into his temples and his gaunt cheeks, and he wondered how he had spent the years when the man's name and deeds had been forgotten. He sat there for a long time, scrutinizing, questioning, and waiting for the man to wake up by himself. When the sun began to set, and the Egyptian lit the oil lamp, Yehoshua woke up. Embarrassed by his sleep, Yehoshua apologized for his weakness, but the Christian stopped him, took a pear, wiped it with the edges of his robe, and gave it to Yehoshua. Yehoshua took a bite of it, and juice dribbled out the sides of his mouth; the effendi smiled, and the silence was broken.

Yehoshua began to speak, his words jumbled at times, and when he finished waited for the Christian's reaction. Bustros Roq did not speak much but only took out a bundle of bills of French money, held it out to Yehoshua, and told him to go Yekaterinoslav to meet with Dolnik and find out what had happened to the association that had sought to come to settle the lands of Wadi Hawarith; perhaps he would be able to convince them actually complete the purchase.

Yehoshua hesitated about whether to take the money, but the Christian convinced him. Roq's eyes showed he was like a very wise elder, while Yehoshua was still a young person mulling over his deeds.

Finally, he got up to go and did not look back; he hurried out to the dark lane to go to the room in Ajami. Olga still wasn't there. For a moment, he was sorry, but then he wrote her a note: he was going down to the port to wait for a ship that would take him to Beirut, and from there, he would travel by train to

Constantinople, cross the Black Sea by ship, and from Odessa he was set to sail on the Dnieper to Yekaterinoslav. "Don't come to look for me in the port," he asked. "I have to do this by myself to gather strength and become the Second Joshua once again." As he wrote, his hand trembled, and he imagined himself feeling the heat and the smell of her body, and even though he wanted to write words of love, he could not find them, so he only added at the note's end, "I will return the minute I finish my meetings," and signed his name.

In the wardrobe, he found his shirts arranged one atop the other. He took underwear and toiletries, packed a knapsack, and slipped out, hoping to return as a different person — erect and worthy of again being called by the name he had been awarded, "Mr. Hankin—Agent for Land Matters."

৵

The trip took two weeks. For two weeks, Yehoshua held his peace in his cabin, in railway cars, and at the ends of carts. He hid his eyes and became completely devoted to his pain, but he slowly emptied out, and the closer he came to Yekaterinoslav, the more his despair faded away. On the legs of the journey, he often sketched on the travel tickets and on pieces of travel documents to reconstruct the borders of the land and paths and sand dunes and swampy areas. He found it hard to retrieve them from the depths of forgetfulness, but the drawing encouraged him, so that when he reached Odessa, he already had pockets full of snippets of paper and knew how to plan his moves.

He waited a few days in Odessa, and when he did not locate a ship sailing in the direction of Yekaterinoslav, he decided to rent a wagon and ride to Kherson and from there to ride on a merchant ship on the Dnieper carrying lumber and returning to Yekaterinoslav empty.

Upon arriving in Kherson, he asked where the Jews lived. People showed him a synagogue, and he went there. He sat near the pulpit and looked over those coming in and going out, and when prayers were finished, the beadle invited him to eat and sleep in his house, since he was certain that he was an emissary from Eretz Israel who had come to collect money to support Torah scholars in the study houses in Jerusalem. Of course, Yehoshua seemed strange to him, with his long hair and the lack of *tzitziyot*, ritual fringes, waving above his belt, but the man did not ask questions, and Yehoshua did not tell him the purpose of his trip.

He stayed a few days with them, waiting for the ship, and in the meantime, told the family stories about Eretz Israel. At first, only the family gathered round, but then, every evening neighbors joined them, and the rumor about the emissary spread among the community, so the house was full of people who came every night to see the man's burning eyes and hear his voice who captured their hearts with the bonds of his love. On the fourth evening, Yehoshua dared to ask his host if he had heard of a businessman called Feibush Dolnik and about a society called "Tzemah David." He inquired and then was sorry he had asked, since suddenly the light in the eyes of those sitting in the room turned cold, and one by one, they stood up and left. He did not understand and urged his host to tell him what was the matter, but the man only said, "Asmodeus disguised as a Jew. Satan walking the earth."

The man refused to say more, but Yehoshua could not calm down and turned and tossed on his bed out of fear of the result of his journey. The entire following day, he followed the beadle everywhere and pressed him to answer his question. After all the other family members had gone to sleep, the man detained Yehoshua and invited him to the kitchen. Over a bottle of liquor, he opened up what had been kept inside. First, he went all around the issue and told of the Jewish life before the great expulsion from Moscow, and then about the protection documents from the tsar and about the quota of Jews in each regional city. Yehoshua knew all this but kept quiet, pushing the wine bottle toward the man and pouring some for him, while waiting for the main point. And in the wee hours of the night, when the bottle was empty, the fear of talking about Feibush Dolnik evaporated.

"Not only in Yekaterinoslav do they talk about Dolnik," the host told him. "His name became known even as far away as Poltava on the Vorskla River in Ukraine. He promised everyone land at a bargain price. He praised it highly, and this made the price soar daily. Many saw him as a savior in a time of woe and wanted to buy a section and fulfill the commandment of settling the Holy Land and gain some profit for themselves. Then rumors came from Eretz Israel about new decrees, the prohibition against Jews buying land, and the hatred of the

Turkish sultan for anyone whose name is linked to Russia. Emigrants who moved to Palestine and returned from there told about their misfortunes and about people who had been promised land in the Land of Israel, and they now were destitute, and about the rich businessman who had sold all his property to finance buying land and was left without land and without money. But Feibush Dolnik pretended he didn't hear and continued collecting money, writing documents, and making promises. People believed him and still saw him as a savior. Once, one of the buyers wanted to go to Eretz Israel and see the land on the seashore with his own eyes, but Feibush told him, "Wait until things settle down. I know the value of the land better than you. It's a safe investment. Trust me." Three years passed, and Feibush Dolnik succeeded very well wherever he turned and opened a fur business in Alexandrovsk, as well as a lumber enterprise in Yekaterinoslav. He bought a ship that traveled between Odessa and Kherson, and named it after himself, but as for the land he promised, there was no trace.

But the Jews could no longer sit twiddling their thumbs when they saw great wealth, and simple Jews and members of the association and anyone who had given him his own money came to him, demanding their money, but did not accept his explanations. At first, he tried to convince them that all of his actions had been performed honestly, but later, he stopped and laughed out loud and supplied no answers, only showing them newspapers from Palestine with headlines, such as "The Gates of Palestine Are Closed," "Panic Has Gripped Its Inhabitants," "Money Has Gone Down the Drain," and many others in a similar vein. People could not do anything to him, only look in desperation at this ever-growing wealth and his ill-gotten gains burgeoning. The beadle's story pervaded Yehoshua's body like poison. "I will go look for him," he cried, "to convince him to fulfill his promise." But the beadle only guffawed, since he was too drunk to take his guest's words seriously.

Two days after their talk, a ship was found that went to Yekaterinoslav. Yehoshua embarked on it after taking leave from the beadle, who stood on the shore following him with his eyes, doleful and sharing in his sorrow.

In its hold, the ship held sacks full of grains of wheat and barrels of fish and liquor, and it stopped along the bank to unload merchandise and pick up other goods. In every village, there were wares to sell, and each village needed different items. The captain knew very well what to take and to whom to sell, where the streams were strong, and where he had to move to the middle of the river.

After three days, they reached Yekaterinoslav. Yehoshua found Dolnik's business quite easily, since the passersby pointed proudly at the street on which the rich merchant lived and toward the lumber enterprise that bore his name.

After some hesitation, Yehoshua went into the store. Although, after he was stopped and informed that the boss was busy, they finally let him enter the businessman's office. Next to a heavy table, he met Dolnik. He was much fatter than he had been in their last meeting in Constantinople, and his chin melded with his neck, and his neck was indistinguishable from his shoulders.

Feibush was not happy to see him and, for a moment, his face was clouded, but he recovered quickly and put a forced smile on his face and invited him to come and join him in a meal.

"Mr. Hankin must be tired from the long trip," he said, while Yehoshua felt his anger mushrooming at seeing the abundance in the store. He did not want to sit in the man's company. Rather, he only wanted to clarify the issue and escape from there as fast as he could.

Yehoshua demanded to see the lists of the "Tzemach David" association members, and Dolnik sat on his chair and said—that there was no such association. And when he wanted to see the receipt books, the man showed him scattered pages.

"The others were lost," he smiled. "A long time has passed; six years have gone by since Constantinople. The Baron did not want the land, and I kept my promise to you—I waited for two years. Then, bad news came from Eretz Israel. The money lost its value. The association members stopped paying for the land. After calculating the emissary's expenses and trips up and back, whatever was left in the fund was returned to the investors."

Yehoshua didn't believe what he heard and could not stand his smile or attempt to calm him down. His little eyes, sunken in his fat face, pricked him as he gazed. He did not know what to say and looked for ways to save the land of Wadi Hawarith.

"I will go to the synagogue," he whispered. "We will organize a new association."

Dolnik just laughed in his face. "The Jews of Yekaterinoslav are misers. They tried once and failed. They won't try again."

"It's good land. You saw it yourself! We'll try again." Yehoshua screamed at him, moved close to the counter, and almost grabbed the edge of Dolnik's coat. Then, at the last second, he recoiled and whispered, "The mood has quieted down in Eretz Israel. There is no panic in it anymore."

Dolnik did not utter a word, but his look said it all, "Insane."

21. Yehoshua Hankin and Feibush Dolnik, 1889 • Source: Central Zionist Archive.

That very evening, he embarked on a ship sailing the Dnieper with a cargo of trees for commercial enterprises in Odesa. He was not angry, and he did not weep, but he did not forgive Feibush Dolnik. Instead, he vowed to himself to negotiate for the land of Wadi Hawarith, as well as to find other buyers and to incite the jealousy of the merchant from Yekaterinoslav. Envy would burn in his bones; he decided; it would eat away at his innards and cause him pain, and he would find no relief for a long time. While he, Yehoshua, would publish in the papers and declare his success to the world, seeing to it that the information would reach even beyond the Black Sea. Maybe then, Dolnik would realize what injustice he had done to Yehoshua and to the Jews of Kherson and Odessa and Yekaterinoslav. The more he mulled the idea over, the more he liked it, and he decided to erase the memory of this merchant from his mind and, for now, not to recall his name, not even in his thoughts, until the opportunity for revenge would develop.

The trip from Jaffa to Kherson had taken two weeks, while the sail to Jaffa lasted two weeks and two days. A storm at sea slowed the boat's speed, and Yehoshua spent most of the time in a deep sleep to fill in what he had missed during the years of nightmare-filled slumber.

When he finally arrived, he found Olga waiting for him on the dock. She had been waiting for two days, and she believed she was waiting for the Second Joshua, for her Jashiya. She saw him from afar, plodding slowly on the dock, and she did not know if he had good news—and she really didn't care. She wanted him for herself, without stories about an enemy and without glad tidings. She ran toward him, and Yehoshua stopped, put down his knapsack, opened his arms wide, and waited. When she reached him, she bumped into him with all her body, so he lost his balance and broke out in ringing laughter. He hugged her and lifted her, feeling the rapid beating of her heart as it surged through her body as it met his body. When they had quieted down and begun to march side by side to their room, Olga told him, as if incidentally, "While you were gone, Antoine Bishara Tayyan, the owner of the Hawarith land, passed away."

"The landowner has died, and the deal with Feibush Dolnik has died," he replied in measured tones. "But the land is still ready and waiting."

He saw her face turning toward him in astonishment, so he explained himself, "There are heirs to the landowner of Wadi Hawarith, and it's just a matter of time and a way to convince them. In the end, the son will come to agree, and the land will be put up for sale, and many buyers, many times more wealthy than this merchant who dwells beyond the mountains of darkness, will come and beg for the land."

She tried to inquire with her eyes and understand what he was saying. "Have you given in?" she asked. "Have you given up?"

He smiled and stopped, pulling her to him, "For now, I will be yours. Land matters are of little interest to me. I tried to speed up and change the paths of my fate, and I failed."

Then, he continued to walk, pulling her hand, while she trailed behind, with plodding steps.

Other times will come and different acquisitions," he said, "and everything will take place at its own pace and without trying to force the outcome in a hurry."

Her face withered, and she halted, pulling her hand away from his. "Why did you retreat?" She was angry, "You've fallen enough. The time has come to hasten fate. Help it, and it will help you."

Yehoshua could not hold back the joyous laughter that piqued him. He stopped moving and held his sides, his thin body trembling with excitement. And Olga, who was caught up in his laughter, leaned on him, her body atwitter with happiness.

"You'll still want me to stay by your side," he muttered while chortling. "You will want me to forget the land deals and sit on a chair in the kitchen, waiting for a cup of hot water, and I'll talk about this and that."

"I really will want that," she replied, "but I will want even more from my Yehoshua, the Second Joshua."

"I will be," he said, looking at her. "I will be, until you are satisfied with my greatness."

In their room, he loved her with such a power that she had not known for long. He forgot the Turkish woman and Feibush Dolnik and *the Valley* and the lands of Wadi Hawarith. He took her toward him and caressed every inch of her skin. They hugged and kissed, and he breathed her scent into himself. And she returned his love and rebuffed her innermost thoughts, flitting her fingers over every wrinkle, every raised spot, and every throb full of vitality.

Constantinople, 1915

The train stopped. "Adana," yelled the gendarme. There was no need to shout. The noises of the big city penetrated into the train cars. The doors had not evened opened when the children standing on the platform stuck their heads in through the open windows and held out handfuls of sugared almonds and green pistachio nuts wrapped in paper. Yehoshua wanted to buy from them for Olga so she could savor the taste of a Turkish city, but then he remembered the small amount of money hidden in the lining of his coat and the gendarme getting up from his seat near the door and straightening his uniform as well as lifting his rifle and taking a peek to examine every action and every movement.

The gendarme had indeed woken up and changed the mild manner he had had during the journey; for now, he had an audience: children peeping through the barred window and soldiers standing all along the train platform. Cursing, he urged the lad in charge of the wagon to hurry to brush his coat and polish his boots. When he had finished yelling, he stood in the entryway and blocked it with his entire body, with his back turned to those sitting in the car and his face towards the peepers.

The four of them continued to sit in their wagon, while in the other ones, peasants and soldiers and diplomats jostled each other, waiting for the doors to open so all of them would rush out.

Israel had already told them that until every last passenger had left the train, they would not come to take them, and he added, with a smile, "The Turks love sentimental scenes. They love to extend performances, and they know that the more witnesses there will be, the greater will be the pity and whispers, 'These are going to Sivas. They're dangerous.' That way, the starring role of the main players would grow—the guards, the policemen, and the soldiers."

"At least it's hot in the wagon, and we don't have to wait outside and freeze," Mania responded, and Israel gave her a hug.

The minutes dragged on. People began to leave, and the sounds of their footsteps on the stones of the platform echoed among the wagons. Olga busied herself with their few bundles, piling them up, but then she would scatter them again and keep them close to her feet. Yehoshua sat in his seat, immersed in his thoughts. The gendarme's voice startled him, and he jumped up, frightened for a moment, but then he swallowed his laughter. The gendarme asked him to take care of the wagon until he would go to make inquiries and return. The policeman did not wait for him to say yes but went out and locked the door.

Mania could not stifle her giggling. "Idiot," she burst out. "He leaves the cats to guard the cream and doesn't realize that it is a wooden door. Let's break it and escape."

The four of them continued to sit in their wagon, while in the other ones, peasants, soldiers, and diplomats jostled each other, waiting for the doors to open so all of them would rush out. "To where?" laughed Israel. She stopped talking and snuggled next to him.

It was not to clarify matters that he had gone there but to boast about his function. This was his shining hour. Now all of them would understand the responsibility he had been charged with—to guard "the traitors," a danger to the Empire, and also to take them to the large prison in Adana and from there to Sivas.

While they waited, Mania bandaged her feet which were still swollen from the beatings she had suffered, but at least she could now walk slowly, without the help of others to carry her. Olga looked at Yehoshua and wondered at his serenity, for he was going into his second exile, and it was as if he did not consider that a tragedy and had come to terms with it and taken it as self-understood.

These two exiles were so different from each other. In the first exile, Yehoshua had been exiled within Palestine, and his name had been forgotten for many long years in which he had dealt with minor matters and was the emissary for others, and they took the honor due him for themselves. In the first exile, they forgot his name, made fun of his appearance, and whispered behind his back, "Crazy one." They did not remember his great deeds, his great aspirations, or meetings with the wealthy of the world.

For twenty years, he had remained quiet until they established the new "Office," "The Palestine Office," and alongside it, they established a new "Company," "The Palestine Land Development Company." Now, he was going into the second exile, after he had already been retrieved from his anonymity and everyone mentioned his name, and no one dared to do anything without asking his advice.

Olga thought about the years that had passed so quickly and left her memories. She looked at her husband and saw his temples that were turning white, his heavy hands placed on his knees, and the mud that remained in the cracks in his skin, land that cannot be erased and accompanies his actions wherever he turns. Then she put her hand on her husband's. Feeling her warmth, he turned over his hand and patted hers. He read her thoughts with his eyes and whispered to her, "The Sivas exile will be short. It won't last twenty years."

Autumn, 1898

Palestine had changed, and its people had done so, too. Few in Jaffa remembered Yehoshua Hankin. Of course, they did recognize the eccentric man who helped the aging Sarah Hankin in the textile store on Bustros Street, carrying rolls of textiles on his shoulder and frequently going down to the port, but they did not mention his name. In contrast, Olga's name and that of Rosa and Haya, two young ladies who were growing more beautiful, everyone knew. In the shadow of women lived the former land agent, and he was not hurt by that and had made peace with the idea—he was even happy with it. From his work, the muscles of his hand grew strong, his body filled out, and his skin became tanned, while at the same time, his silence increased, and his hair grew long. Moreover, just like they did not mention his name, they did not cite the name Duran. The colony had already been "Rehovot" for eight years. The houses of the Hadera settlement were already standing on the Christian effendi Selim Khuri land, and the colony had left behind the curse of its swamps.

Fanny and Lolik were now in Rishon Lezion. Avshalom had gained two sisters, and the Belkind family no longer had only one grandchild. Israel Belkind trekked to Galilee and the Dead Sea, and when he was not wandering, he sat and wrote his impressions in books and continued to dream of a school in which all subjects would be taught in Hebrew. Meir Belkind passed away, and Shifra joined the household of her son Shimshon. Sonia studied medicine in Switzerland. Stamps from the faraway country provided a few days' occupation for Shifra's friends. Sonia's mother would receive a letter and gather her companions, who would sit on benches in the enclosed, paved yard, take in the heat of the suns' rays, and chatter about children who had left home and about huge successes in distant places.

In those days, people began to speak about a new association for acquiring land for Jewish settlement. As usual, opinions were divided in Jaffa regarding whether to look favorably on the idea or to fear it. Some considered it as competition to Baron Rothschild and his bureaucrats, with its aim to operate in Palestine in those colonies not supported by the Baron. This new association also had a baron—Baron Hirsch, who had already died and been forgotten, with only the group remaining. This association established colonies for Jews throughout Argentina, Brazil, and Canada, and if it succeeded in those places, so they said, why shouldn't it also do well in Palestine? It had a long name, which was always cited in French, until it was shortened only to its initials, and finally, its truncated name remained, JCA (for Jewish Colonization Association).

JCA's name became attached to that of the "Bnei Moshe" society, and since that group was no longer secret and its founder, Ahad Ha'am, had also been revealed, everyone could talk about them, and its founder could voice his cry in public. Ahad Ha'am railed against the situation of the farmers in the Jewish colonies and belittled the support for them, while encouraging the new association to show interest in the colonies, and perhaps even take some of them under its aegis.

The JCA and the Bnei Moshe society, Herzl, and the Zionist Congress all mixed together in a jumble in people's minds. Everyone talked about them to demonstrate their involvement, but they did not always understand what that meant. In the evening, people would stand in the Jaffa lanes in groups and argue among themselves, while quoting statements by others. One group would call for the building up of Palestine by only the chosen few and distribute manifests containing quotes from Ahad Ha'am, while another would raise their voices and demand a national home in Palestine for the Jewish masses. The children were just as divided among themselves as the adults, struggling to pronounce the word "charter" and poking fun and saying "chosen people" without understanding its meaning. Each one had his own hero that he admired, and if someone was not involved in what was going on, everyone thought him weird and strange.

There were many debates in Sarah Hankin's store, too, especially on Friday afternoons, when Fanny and Lolik's wagon would stop next to the shop, and Tanhum and Mendel would come from Hadera. Then, toward evening, before they went to the synagogue to usher in the Sabbath, some of the Jaffa functionaries would join the Hankin family, identified by rumor as supporters of B'nei Moshe. They would tell each other about their experiences and opinions, with no one listening to what the other was saying, but all enjoying the loud argumentation. Two people stood out in that raucous group, one being a physician who worked in the colonies, Dr. Hillel Yaffe, and the other— an old-timer, who for a number of years had been the head of Hovevei Zion's Jaffa Committee—Mr. Yehoshua Eisenstadt-Barzilai. Both had changed their position and were now challenging the Baron's support and praising the colonies that tried to work and hold on without support.

The Friday discussions reminded the visitors of the days of Rishon Lezion and the arguments about rebelling against the Baron and his officials. Olga loved these meetings, and they excited her, adding variety to the routine of births and the dullness of her life.

Yehoshua perceived these heated discussions as nonsense and meaningless. He always kept to the edges of the group and did not enter into the conversations. He especially laughed to himself over the word repeatedly heard voiced by people, with different variations: "improvement," "JCA makes improvements and gives money as a loan, all in the name of improvement," "there's room for improvement in the colonies," and on and on. Once, in jest, he asked Fanny, what the precise meaning of improvement was, and she shrugged her shoulders to say she did not know exactly. But since he did not want to hurt Olga, realizing how much she waited for Fridays, for the people overcrowding the store, for the joy engulfing everyone, and for the feeling that now they were dealing with major, lofty issues, he preferred to stay away from them. More than once, he had left during the frenzied debate and went into the Jaffa lanes, going alone to the room in Ajami or to the dock in the port, and no one noticed he was no longer there.

‹❧›

One Friday, when Yehoshua had already stood up to leave, he suddenly saw a stranger who attracted his attention. The man had come to the store with his brother-in-law, the colonies' doctor, Hillel Yaffe, and stood for a long time, motionless, next to the counter, not taking part in the discussion, only his eyes darting here and there, checking out the corners of the store and the faces of the people coming in and going out. For some reason, Yehoshua liked the man even though he had never met him and even despite his almost vulgar curiosity. He did not understand how this man stood frozen, without changing his position, not joining in the debate, but also not becoming bored. As Yehoshua put on his brimmed hat and buttoned up his coat, looking for Olga to show her he was leaving, he decided, in any event, to stay a bit longer and move toward the stranger to get a good look at him. He stood on the opposite side of the counter and gazed at the stranger without catching his eye. He paid attention to the smoothly combed hair, the pure white collar, and the carefully folded coat hanging on his arm. Then, when he had finished examining him, he coughed, so as to draw the man's attention. The man turned slowly, and his face, adorned with a carefully trimmed goatee, was aimed directly at him, and small, brown eyes scanned him from top to bottom, with a friendly smile dancing in them, in complete contrast to his serious mien. The man held his hand out to him and gave his name; Yehoshua greeted him with a nod and left.

At night he asked about the man, and Olga, who knew all comers to Jaffa, told him about Haim Margaliot-Kalvarisky, "Brother-in-law to the doctor Hillel Yaffe. Margaliot is his family name, and he was dubbed Kalvarisky because the family came from Kalvarija."

"And what is a person from Kalvarija doing in Jaffa?" inquired Yehoshua.

"It's a long story," smiled his wife, but Yehoshua would not give up. This new character gave him no peace, and something told him that things were about to happen, and they were linked to the man with the goatee.

"They promised him to be the head of Bnei Moshe," Olga informed him, pleased to show her husband her knowledge. "But in the end, they preferred Hillel Yaffe, since he lives in Palestine, works in its colonies, and is well known by everyone, while the other fellow lives abroad and to bring him to Eretz Israel would cost a lot of money. But Kalvarisky did not wait for Yaffe's death so he could inherit from him but rather came to this land with a wife and her sister-in-law, and fortunately, the sister fell in love with just that doctor, Hillel Yaffe. Now, they are brothers-in-law, and there's no bitterness between them. They work together in the Association, and the secretary arranged a job for his brother-in-law as a teacher in

Mikveh Israel. He spent a year there and met David Haim and Joseph Niego, who were emissaries of the Baron, as well as of JCA, so it turned out that more than he taught, he would wander with David Haim in Galilee and Judea, where they would examine the colonies and then return to Jaffa—one reporting to the company about where to invest and to whom to lend money, while the other would ignite the imagination of the youth and cry out, "The time has come to become more advanced, to be more modern."

Now, Olga dragged a chair from the kitchen, stood up on it, and tried to imitate the movements of this activist, but Yehoshua wanted to hear more and took hold of her waist and took her off the chair, sat her down, and said, "Nu? Go on."

She was surprised by his seriousness and continued speaking, "Hillel Yaffe has had enough of his brother-in-law's roaming about Jaffa, and from those gossipy people who called him "idler," so he wrote to Paris, to the directorate of the new company, asking that it hire him. Recently, a rumor has spread that they are about to send him to Izmir to open a school for the study of nature and agriculture. "An intellectual," she finished her statement, "Manual labor isn't for him. So, he'll walk about Izmir like he did in Jaffa."

Yehoshua didn't want to be influenced by Olga's mockery, since he still believed in his feelings and wanted to know more, but Olga had nothing else to add.

A month went by, and Yehoshua continued to work in the store, but one thing changed in his routine: Every Friday, he would remain with the group and stand in the entrance, waiting for the stranger. Maybe he would come. When he asked the doctor where his brother-in-law was, the man told him, "Busy," and explained no more. Then, one Friday evening, Olga and Yehoshua were invited to Barzilai's home to celebrate his success in opening a new school in Jaffa in the new Jewish neighborhood of Neve Tzedek, a school in which a few subjects were taught in Hebrew. Israel Belkind was also invited. The founders remembered him from the time of the Kiryat Sefer School and now offered him to take the young children under his wing, but he refused. Olga wanted to meet with her brother and wear her best clothes, walking arm in arm with her husband, so she dragged Yehoshua along with her.

Yehoshua sat in the corner and listened to the conversations, smiling to himself at seeing people arguing about the status of Ahad Ha'am and insisting on calling him Asher Ginsberg to demonstrate their knowledge and their closeness to the man. Of course, Yehoshua tried to make conversation with Israel Belkind, but the latter was too busy with the Jaffa intelligentsia, who overflowed the room. In the wee hours of the night, Yehoshua decided to stand up and go home. When Olga asked to remain, Barzilai promised to accompany her back home. Yehoshua called to mind the gossip about Olga of long ago, in the days of Vladimir Tyomkin of long ago, so he winked to his wife, but it seemed she did not understand. He said his goodbyes and went out into the narrow streets of Neve Tzedek and Neve Shalom, whose houses, standing one opposite the other, formed a wall, and on Chelouche Bridge, linking the new Jewish neighborhood with long-standing Jaffa, he stopped. Located at the end of the bridge was the home of Aharon Chelouche, the buyer of the lands of the new neighborhood, and an oil lamp, which someone made sure to light before the beginning of the Sabbath, was burning at the entrance to the synagogue to light the lane on the Sabbath.

The circle of light cast by the oil lamp extended to the threshold of the home of Chaim Amzaleg, another dignitary who lived in the neighborhood. The many carriages standing near the entryway to his home attest that many people were guests of the man, who was British vice-consul in Jaffa. Yehoshua took a look at the ends of the street and sent a glance toward the railway track that passed under the bridge.

Someone greeted him. Yehoshua turned toward him and saw the stranger with the brimmed hat and goatee. The man was on his way to Barzlai's house and had lost his way. Now, he was happy to encounter Yehoshua, so he stopped for a while and leaned on the bridge railing together with Yehoshua. Yehoshua had not expected to meet him just there, even though, on second thought, it was reasonable, but he did not find the words to start a conversation. On the tip of his tongue were questions and notions that had amassed for quite a while. Finally, he cleared his throat, concluded forming a sentence, and said, "I've heard people say you were a teacher at Mikveh Israel, and maybe they will send you to a JCA school in Izmir?

Kalvarisky winked at him mischievously, saying, "You know better than me. I didn't know that I had been sent to Izmir!"

Confused, Yehoshua lowered his head to study the tips of his boots, "I only heard this," he stuttered.

The stranger drew a bit closer to Yehoshua. "They certainly said to you, an idler, going between Jaffa and Mikveh. I have heard all of this behind my back." He smiled and immediately continued, "They thought about opening a school in Izmir to teach agriculture to Jews from Eastern Europe and prepare them for settlement in JCA colonies. But in the meantime, the plans changed."

Yehoshua wanted to go on and ask, but he was embarrassed and afraid of making another mistake, so he waited for the man to make his own statement. Yet, the man kept quiet, staring at him, his thoughts carrying him far away. Then, suddenly, he blurted, "Tell me about Musa Sursuq and the Galilee land. Share with me everything you know.!"

At first, Yehoshua did not understand the connection between the stranger and Musa Sursuq and those Galilee lands. Had he asked about the land of the Jezreel Valley or that of the Zevulun Valley, he would have given him a clear answer, but Galilee? Moreover, he had only met this fellow twice, and the man was already asking and expecting a reply. What should he say to him?

But Kalvarisky would not let up. "You know Musa Sursuq. You can't deny that. So, you turned to him to buy the Jezreel Valley lands, and when the negotiations between you two did not go well, he offered you land in Galilee, and you refused, insisting on *the Valley* land."

A few years had passed since someone had mentioned to him the lands of *the Valley* and the negotiations, and the memories that now rushed him made his blood boil and opened a wound that had never properly healed. What should he say? He did not know where to begin. But the man guided him with his questions, and Yehoshua answered them until he needed no further ones and his speech flowed like a mighty river flowing strongly and taking with it the anguish of years.

Yehoshua depicted the strips of *the Valley* in green and brown colors and brought the lions at the gates of the Sursuq family home in Beirut to life. He spoke about long rides in *the Valley* and galloping on the hills of Shefaram, and as he went on speaking, Kalvarisky's eyes burned brighter from one minute to the next.

Yehoshua spoke for a long time, until the clanking of the shafts of a wagon passing over the bridge, one taking oranges to the Jaffa port, returned him to reality. Yehoshua halted his speech and was frightened by the ill manners he had shown while talking on and on, not letting the other man get a word in edgewise. He apologized and then continued, "It's late, and my wife will no doubt worry." So, he buttoned the last button on his coat and straightened his collar, getting ready to go, but the man stopped him and said, "A month from today, I am going up to Galilee. JCA has chosen me to be the administrator and director of the Mishmar Hayarden colony." He paused for a moment to allow his listener to absorb his words and then went on, "They all got together to send me away from Jaffa. My brother-in-law claims I should remove myself from here. Barzilai says that it's better to use my expertise in lands and crops. But they don't realize how limited my knowledge is of land in Palestine and its crops. I already heard about you a few years ago. You were unique, a speculator in land. Come with me to Galilee, be a clerk for JCA, and teach me about the rules and regulations for land rules, as well as the ins and outs of buying and selling."

Yehoshua paled, and his legs trembled and had it not been for the support of the bridge, he would have fallen. He took a deep breath to calm down, and then stammered in a whisper, "Agent for land matters, you said? Am I an agent?"

"I said it. I indeed said it," laughed the man.

"I'll speak with Olga," he said, giving himself a way out, to not answer immediately. Kalvarisky nodded in agreement, and the two of them turned around and walked together a ways, and then they each went in his own direction.

For four days, Yehoshua did not mention the name of the JCA nor that of Kalvarisky, and he did not tell her about the man's offer. Every day he waited for the next; maybe something would happen, and he would find out that Kalvarisky had only been joking. And Olga, who was used to his silences, did not sense his hesitations.

On Thursday afternoon, he went to Dr. Masie's office to walk Olga home and talk to her in the lanes, rather than in the confines of their room. Since she was busy, he sat down to wait impatiently for her, while planning what he would say to her. He laughed at himself a bit for needing foreign walls and unfamiliar corners to speak with his wife and ask for her support, and perhaps she would decide for him and save him the hesitation and unrest. When she finally came out of the room of the expectant mother and took off her apron, she saw him and was pleased. It was so very infrequent that he came to take her from the office. She passed by him and purposely rubbed against his clothes, leaving her scent behind. A few minutes later, they left together and walked in the street. From time to time they stopped, and Olga felt some fabric in one of the stores. She held it up to her face and asked him, "Is it all right?" adding, "I'll buy a few meters and sew new sheets. Winter will come all at once, and until one sheet is dry, it has to be replaced by another. Perhaps I will make a dress or a curtain." But when she saw that Yehoshua was not listening, she became quiet and walked alongside him, not stopping again on her way.

Yehoshua searched for the right word to start the conversation, and while he was still thinking, they reached Ajami. He noticed that the lanes in the new neighborhood were wider than those in Old Jaffa and that the walls of the houses were still free of dust and signs of aging, and they were set apart from each other. Nevertheless, he had not as yet opened the wellsprings of his heart; they ascended the steps to their room, and he as yet had not uttered a word. Olga hurried to the kitchen to prepare a meal, and Yehoshua followed her. He spoke to her back as she stood cutting pieces of potatoes, "I want to go to Galilee and be the person mediating between the owners of Galilee land and the new company, "JC."

Olga stopped what she was doing and turned to him, forcefully shaking her head and stamping her feet on the floor like a little girl. "No!" she cried.

"Why," he wondered.

"It's exile, exile from Jaffa and from me," she responded in a trembling voice. "You'll be a small functionary, not a land agent shaking hands and signing contracts. Other bureaucrats, higher up than you, will tell you what to do every day, hour by hour. You'll be involved in petty things and be dependent on orders from others. The officials of the new company are worse than those of the Baron. I heard they pressure, threaten, and track each person to check if he is operating according to the regulations. That's how they treat a farmer they support and the laborers working for them, as well as the clerk and the director. On top of all that, Baron Rothschild's bureaucrats are dealing with Palestine, while the new ones are busy with Argentina. And if JCA finds out that supporting farmers in Palestine is more expensive than the farmers in Argentina, in that case, they'll toss away the farmers in the Palestine colonies, hold them in contempt, and look for others who are more advanced and modern."

"I'll go with Kalvarisky," he said, trying to stop her eruption of words. "They have asked me to manage a colony in Galilee."

"Who will you go with?" she burst out. "With the man from Kalvarija? Such an intellectual. And what does he understand about Palestine matters?"

"Maybe he's not such an expert, but they did ask him to improve the colony of Mishmar Hayarden. A colony that is far away from the Yishuv (the Jewish community in Palestine) and cut off from the petty Jewish issues. There, they do not remember who Yehoshua was or who Tyomkin was, and they have never read about Pines and his machinations. So, come with me," he pleaded, "we'll start all over again."

"I will not go with you," she declared firmly. "Work by yourself, and I will wait in Jaffa. As usual, I will wait for your fall," her voice petered out, and tears filled her eyes.

"I will not fail," he shouted, his voice growing stronger. "Why do you see calamities? Didn't we promise each other to act together?"

She knew that this time she had overdone it when she had let loose with her bitterness, and she tried to control her flaring temper, so she said to him, "There are many births in Judea, more than in Galilee. So, you still have a large debt that has to be covered."

"The work in Galilee will pay for my debt," he tried to convince her, well aware that she did not believe what he said. Even though he was not certain about this, and he really wanted her support, but he realized he would have to decide by himself.

He sat on a low stool and looked at her hands cutting the onion and potato, her sadness reflected in her so very forceful, precise chopping. I won't go, he thought; he would stay in Jaffa and help in the store. And the land? Will he stay away from it? Will he leave it for others who don't understand a thing?

"They need my knowledge," he emphasized to her.

She laughed bitterly. "For sure, they need your expertise in all the land laws, but they will throw you out when they don't need you anymore."

He and she kept quiet. Then, when she served soup and cheese and put a cruet of oil and some fresh bread on the table, he broke off a piece of bread and dipped it in the oil. The bread stuck in his throat, choking him, and Yehoshua muttered in a strangled voice, "I will go. I will be a minor land agent, but I will be close to the land."

She did not respond, for what should she say—that his weakness was good for her, that she enjoyed his dependence on her? Was she pleased with his spending time with her every evening in the small room in Ajami? She thought he had gotten used to his work in the store and did not want to go back to being a big land agent known throughout Eretz Israel. When he sipped his cup of hot water and sucked on a slice of lemon, she broke her silence and told him, "Go, and may it be good without me, while I wait for you as usual. Go, go without me."

Yehoshua rose and stood behind her, stroking her hair, but he could not find the right words to tell her what he was feeling, so he bent down and kissed her neck. She lifted up her arms and embraced his neck as if trying to say to him, "See, I understand." But she said nothing, knowing that she really did love him and that he was her entire world, and it didn't matter how many years they had been together, how more years there would be, or how many crises they would weather. She was repeatedly excited and surprised to have to struggle, but always forgiving in the end.

❧

The days grew longer, and at the end of May, Kalvarisky moved with his family to Galilee to manage and improve the colony of Mishmar Hayarden. About a week later, the JCA took in Yehoshua Hankin, and he became a land agent for it, one of many.

Yehoshua met with Arab land traders, measured plots, negotiated and discussed purchase contracts with them. He galloped between arrays of basalt and on chalky rocks and started everything over from the beginning.

Merchants who returned from Galilee to Jaffa and frequented the store brought regards from Yehoshua and told Olga about the eccentric who walked among the hills, dragging his horse behind him, measuring with his feet, and staying with him the Arab *fellahin* and looking just like them. If it were not for his long hair, they would say, they would not make the connection between the tanned face plus the worn-out clothes and Mr. Hankin of Jaffa. Some brought a letter with them, and Olga would wait impatiently for people to leave her alone so that she could remain with the written words suffused with the scent of Galilee, and for just a moment, she would be able to be in the company of her beloved.

In the letters, he told her about the sun-washed black rocks that he used to stretch out on to absorb their warmth and about galloping in wadis that cut through pieces of land planted with sorghum and lupines, and about the protected olive trees whose withered fruit scattered on cracked land. Often, she read between the lines, discerning the feeling of a small agent and clerk was going through disappointment from insignificant acts and tasks he fulfilled for others, but he did not write this openly, only occasionally signing his letters, "Galilee exile," or citing over and over what Kalvarisky had once said to him, "Your actions are patchwork, piece by piece, and they will lead to great things," desiring to console himself with them.

The issues occupying Yehoshua were not major, but the time he spent in Galilee was lengthy. At the end of two years, Kalvarisky was transferred to act as administrator and director of the "Khan" in Sejera and live in Nazareth; in addition to managing the small colony of Mishmar Hayarden, he was given a new task to set up on the Sejera land a farm for training laborers. Yehoshua continued to wander about in Galilee and follow the instructions of the clerks over him. So it was that he roamed between the "Khan" in Sejera and Constantinople, between the lands of Deleika on the shore of the Kinneret and Beirut. So it happened that he came once to the gates of the Sursuq family home to sign a contract with them for transferring a bloc of Sejera land to the name of the new association, JCA, but he was only the messenger doing the work of others, and his name was forgotten.

Standing at the shaded entryway, he looked at the pair of lions, which for some reason, he saw as small and swallowed up among the bushes of Syrian myrtle that grew and closed in on all sides. The lad who opened the door did not recognize him. When he was led into the courtyard, he did not hear the splashing of the water in the channel, nor did he sense eyes peeping through the slits in the wood; he didn't even hear the drumming of his boot soles.

The door was opened by an unfamiliar stranger, the "secretary for the family's property and land matters," as he presented himself. When Yehoshua told him his name, he became excited, and his face muscles twitched, and he scanned the secretary's face and prayed that his name would make ripples in the frozen visage, but nothing happened. Finally, the secretary signed, and Yehoshua left there, embarrassed to show his face in the streets of Beirut. He wanted to flee to the remote hills in Galilee and be anonymous; he mocked himself that he was collecting pruta (coin) after pruta to pay his debt to the landowner, whose land he had wanted to buy ten years earlier in the huge valley and had failed, and now he was acting as the agent between those same owners and the purchaser, but the buyer was different. He hated what he was doing, but he persisted in carrying out his tasks, and the land continued to trap him and didn't leave him alone, and he did not try to break free.

Constantinople Prison, 1915

Near the market in the city's center stood the prison, which had previously been the residence of one of the dignitaries who belonged to the Seljuk Empire. Its walls were now mired in filth, so high that people said it would reach the turrets and make it easier for those seeking to escape—if they were not put off by the stink.

Owing to its being near the market, the prison held thieves waiting for amputation of their hand; alongside traitors accused of slandering the government and whose verdict has been removal of their tongue, as well as diplomats from the countries of the Ottoman Empire who now, owing to the war, were labeled "dangerous" and were on their way to Sivas, which was in the grip of the plague.

Among those "dangerous" ones were some more dangerous and some less. Ascribed to the "less dangerous" were wealthy individuals who filled the policemen's pockets, thereby gaining their favors and making it possible for them to be sent to Constantinople rather than get on the train heading northward toward Sivas. It was the latter that Yehoshua wanted to join. So, when they took them by wagon from the train station to the local jail, he tried to calculate whether he had enough money hidden in the lining of his coat to have them sent to Constantinople, or at least to bribe a guard to take a letter to the American ambassador Morgenthau, the son of a Jewish family. The latter was ready to listen to the pleadings of the exiles from Palestine.

In the Adana jail, the men were separated from the women. Yehoshua and Israel sat in a large hall with thieves, traitors, and various types of dangerous individuals. Understanding Arabic and Turkish, Yehoshua gathered news about the war, as well as about Palestine, from them. However, he never took his eyes off Israel, lest he falter and fear engulf him. While looking at him in that way, he thought to himself, "Now I am guarding the 'Shomer,' the guard. If the jail guards knew how strong Israel was and his great expertise in weapons and the wrestling moves he had introduced to the Galilee group, they would keep an especially sharp eye on him." But Israel's appearance did not raise suspicion but rather pity: he sat in the corner and kept his bent legs close to his body, hugging them and trembling.

Mania and Olga were put in the women's wing. Mania was used to jail, and when she was separated from Israel and Yehoshua, she promised to watch over Olga, and in exchange, she asked Yehoshua to look after Israel. "He's hallucinating," she said, "but when he comes to and doesn't find me next to him, he will go into a panic."

Their stay in the jail was longer than anticipated. Aside from the meals and the daily round in the closed courtyard, they did nothing. Israel took a long time eating and put dry bread in his pocket, and chewed its crumbs between meals. Yehoshua ate little and pushed some of his food to Israel's plate; he spent most of his time musing. He thought about his wife and Mania, as well as about ways to exchange the Sivas exile for a different one. At one of the meals, when it was Yehoshua's turn to receive his portion, he held out his plate, and when the cook was about to pour the food into it, he pulled his plate toward him, and the liquid spilled on his clothes and on the long wooden board separating the prisoners from the cook. The guard, who stood at the end of the line, was angered by the disturbance and sent Yehoshua to bring a bucket and a rag. This was the chance he had been waiting for. He began to clean up around the big pots, holding a heavy coin wrapped in a note in his hand, he moved close to one of the lads in charge of the pots.

The young man stood close to the pot, with eyes wide open to see if any prisoner was trying to cheat and stand in the line twice. Everyone knew that in exchange for guarding, the fellow received a plate of food, and if he caught a prisoner, he would be given extra. Yehoshua moved close to the iron pot and felt the warmth escaping from the metal, and when the lad bent down, Yehoshua hurriedly stuck the coin and the letter into his hand, praying that the fellow would not shout and call for help. The young man stood up in panic, his eyes darting in their sockets, looking at Yehoshua and the soldiers guarding the prisoners. On the one hand, he wanted the solid coin, while on the other, he was scared out of his wits. Finally, he went away from there, and Yehoshua left the kitchen and returned to the line of prisoners.

On the fifth morning of their jail stay, Yehoshua still did not know anything about the fate of Olga and Mania. No answer had come from the American ambassador, and from the ridicule of the guards, he was aware that they intended to send them to Sivas. During that morning's breakfast, Yehoshua took his bowl and sat on the filthy floor, waiting for Israel. When he approached, Yehoshua pulled him toward him and sat him down next to him. Israel also had the tasteless porridge in his bowl, and Yehoshua, who could not look at this food and most certainly not taste it, pushed his bowl toward him. Until Israel finished swallowing his portion, Yehoshua curled up in his coat and, as usual, concentrated on his thoughts.

The thunderous voice of the jailer made him tremble. The man stood next to a row of prisoners sitting on the floor. He examined each bowl and noticed that Yehoshua's tin vessel was near Israel's knees. He came near them and stood over them, standing upright with his pot belly sticking out, and kicked Yehoshua's bowl to return it to its owner. The porridge spilled out of the vessel as it slid toward Yehoshua and scattered on the floor. The other sitters moved so as not to get dirty, as if they were not sitting on layers of dirt that had accumulated on the floor. Yehoshua waited for the kick that would come and the thwack of the cudgel on his fingers; he lifted his eyes slowly and saw the jailer playing with the ends of the cudgel and motioning him with his little finger to stand up. Yehoshua did so with his knees knocking in fear of the punishment awaiting him, and the jailor looked him up and down without letting him lower his eyes, and if Yehoshua turned his head, the man would move it back with a light tap of the cudgel.

Yehoshua thought his letter had been discovered, or perhaps the time had come to transfer them to Sivas, and if neither this nor that, probably isolation awaited him for his bowl having been found near Israel. He remembered the swollen soles of Mania's feet and heard Israel's teeth chattering. After the passing of many nerve-racking minutes of quiet in the prisoner's hall, during which he felts how ants were walking the lengths of his legs and climbing up his spine, the warder broke the silence, "Yehoshua Hankin?"

Yehoshua nodded his head, and the guard added, with an insidious smile, "Traitor, danger to the government."

Yehoshua did not move his head, and the man repeated what he had said and his cudgel out, tapping it sometimes on Yehoshua's head and then on his chin, until Yehoshua was forced to move his head up and down. The warder laughed, and then all the prisoners chuckled—they had to laugh, for if not, he would repeat his actions over and over. Finally, when he had had enough of the game, he ordered Yehoshua to sit and handed him a letter bearing the seal of the American consul.

Only when the guard went away from them and after he had calmed Israel down did Yehoshua open the letter and read it aloud to his friend, without explaining his words, since the man did not understand what he was saying. "I received your message. The four of you are being transferred to the political prisoners' jail in Bursa. It is not possible to free you. You are considered agitators. But your knowledge and expertise in land matters worked in your favor. From now on, you will be considered only exiles, and the Turkish Sublime Porte has the right to use your knowledge. I will try to help in other ways. Sincerely, Henry Morgenthau, American Consul."

Yehoshua could scarcely believe it. Fear of a beating from the guard was now replaced by excitement and hope. The letter stated, "the four of you," which meant he would soon meet Olga. He sat down next to Israel, putting the letter in his hand and encouraging him, "We've been saved. We won't be threatened by death from the plague at Sivas." Israel did not say a word, but his trembling hands holding the letters revealed his joy.

Many hours later, the two were called and escorted to the courtyard. They set them down on earth moist from the morning rain and left them to wait. They grew chilled as they waited for the women, who had not yet appeared. Israel trembled again and took hold of Yehoshua's shoulder, painfully digging his nails in. Yehoshua tried to restrain himself, understanding Israel's great fear about Mania. But finally, he could not take the pain and stood up to call to the warder in Turkish, asking him for an explanation of their long stay outside. "Shut up!" the guard yelled to him. "Sit and wait. If not, they will put you back in your cell."

The afternoon hours crept by. In the courtyard, striking in its cleanliness in total contrast to the dining hall floor, the prisoners ran and stretched their backs before returning to their cells. The next to come were the cadets, whose faces displayed innocence and who had not yet managed to acquire the look of a threatening prison guard. After they finished exercising came the turn of the "dangerous ones," who were taken out at a light trot and then pushed back into the cells. For a moment, the yard was empty, with only a few birds looking for food. Then, a while later, it was time for further exercise, this time of the warders themselves. And so it went, until sunset, when it became cool, and the shadow of the walls surrounding the yard grew longer.

Close to nightfall, Olga was pushed into the courtyard. Yehoshua got up to meet her, but a blow from the guard sat him back down. "At least she's all right," he thought, and hastened to obey the order of the cudgel. Olga refused to be pushed and let out a string of Russian curses toward the pusher and, while doing so, sent a few words to Israel and Yehoshua, with her furious eyes aimed at the jailer. "They are interrogating Mania. They saw Hasan Bek's signature on the prisoner document accompanying her and read the reports of the trial conducted against her in Damascus."

Israel's shaking grew more violent, and his hand again took hold of Yehoshua's shoulder. Olga, who saw the effect of her words on Mania's husband out of the corner of her eye, went on with the intention of calming him down. "When they separated us, she was about to be interrogated for the last time. They won't keep her too long, and she will certainly join us in a few minutes. And Sivas?" she continued speaking in one breath, directing her question to Yehoshua.

Yehoshua nudged his head a bit to the right and the left, so as not to draw attention, and when Olga saw his head movements, she stopped her curses.

Olga was placed a great distance away from them, and now the three were waiting for Mania.

A single lantern hanging over a narrow opening in the prison wall illuminated the courtyard. Its light was augmented at regular times by a spotlight that passed over the faces of those sitting there. The darkness was heavy, and the guard came close to Israel and Yehoshua, trying to pierce the gloom with his eyes and discern every suspicious move. Yehoshua thought him contemptible for his fears. Didn't he see the high walls surrounding them? Another hour went by until the creaking of a door was heard, followed by the sound of heavy shoes and of weak legs. They could not see Mania but knew she was joining them.

Israel's trembling came again, and Yehoshua could hear his teeth chattering. He did not know what to say since he could not see Mania's face nor hear her voice. He certainly hoped that they had not beaten her again nor left scars on her body. The night was burdensome, and the cold seeped into their bones. He brought his knees up close, trying to shrink himself and cover up with the light coat that was not enough to warm him. He was waiting for morning and tried to imagine the thoughts of Olga, who was sitting opposite, but not close to, them; her glance was surely trying to reach them. But, unfortunately, the beam of light probing the courtyard did not illuminate faces, only the tips of limbs; a stretched-out foot, the hem of a skirt, no more. He thought about Mania again, not knowing how many times he had done so that night. Even though they had long been acquainted, he could not fathom her thoughts. She was like a closed book.

When Yehoshua had met Mania, she had been ill and frightened, in need of consolation, and now, a few years later, she was well known throughout Palestine and no longer needed anyone, while others needed her and depended on her. When he had first known her, she was still Mania Wilbuschewitz, but then she met Israel and had become Mania Shochat, but she had never lived happily with her husband in the bonds of matrimony foisted on her. Like a free gazelle, Yehoshua imagined her, who is striving for open space and rooted in the earth and hills, breaking through any barrier. "Mania in her desire for freedom resembled me," he thought, "and neither Olga nor Israel could understand her aspirations."

Jaffa, 1904

Israel Belkind settled down. First, he took a wife, then a permanent place was found for him, and he grabbed it. To his credit were the Jaffa school, his roaming, and his broad knowledge, and he was chosen to establish a school for orphans at Shefeya, a colony between the Carmel and the Zichron Yaakov. Initially, he ran the place by himself, but when many more orphans came, he was given help when they added a young man to the administration—Israel Shochat. Now, gathering together on Fridays in Sarah Hankin's store were three Israelis. All of Jaffa was chuckling and telling each other that they were dreamers and visionaries, and they mixed up the three of them, and no one cared. Finally, one day, Sarah resolved this by announcing to all of them that from now on, Israel Feinberg would be called Lolik, Israel Shochat would be known by his full name, and Israel Belkind would simply be Israel.

Israel Shochat was not alone. He had come to Palestine with his brother Eliezer, and both of them were considered instigators. Lolik used to say that in Rishon Lezion 20 years ago, no one knew what "rebel" meant, but were familiar with the concept "revolutionary." Now they were careful not to use any word that was not Hebrew, since a rebel was rebelling against anyone who did not speak Hebrew. Indeed, anywhere the brothers reached, a rebellion did break out: a mutiny against the JCA officials in the Galilee colonies, a rebellion against the farmers in Petach Tikva who refused to give work to a Jewish laborer, a revolt against a Jaffa school that refused to teach in Hebrew, preferring the German language or French manners.

The character of Palestine had changed, and now there was room for new rebels. No one remembered the land rush of some 15 years ago nor the names of the men who had been the center of the world of the farmers, the laborers, and regular Jaffa people. Life went on as usual. New colonies were founded, lands were acquired, support associations were established, Russians came and were given a new nickname, "Muscovites," to differentiate between them and Russians of the years of the Tyomkin rush. They differed not only in nickname but also in attire, status, and high rhetoric, which was not understood by all. They wore caps on their heads and red boots on their feet and could be seen from afar owing to the two stripes of embroidery on their shirts. They did not need Soup Kitchens or pots of food from righteous women. They organized themselves into communes and took care of themselves by dealing with food, finding work, or helping in times of sickness. They would rent one room and stuff it with ten laborers; some would go out to work, but most just laid down ill since they were not used to living in the new country. At night, they would read poetry and run high fevers and hallucinate and debate about the nation's path and about a just, egalitarian regime among people, while work scarcely existed for them.

The settlements' farmers did not want to employ the Muscovites who insisted on calling themselves "laborers" but dubbed them instead "students," "hooligans," "daydreamers." They preferred to take the Arab *harath*, sharecropping laborer, who would live in their yard and work on their farm for a few girsh, while his wife would be the washerwoman and cleaner, and their children follow the donkeys and act as shepherds. No one wanted the pale-faced Jewish worker with red hands laced with blisters between the fingers after the first time they used a hoe.

In Jaffa, they too did not like these new Russians—perhaps they reminded the long-term resident Jews of themselves and their weakness twenty years earlier, or maybe they were afraid of their calls for change and new values. The old-timers were satisfied with their status and achievements, and the two groups did not merge but rather stayed far apart from each other. In Neve Zedek, the newcomers opened a "Workers' House," where they conducted conversations in Hebrew and published a newspaper, further reinforcing their separatism.

Once, a group of newcomers went to Rishon Lezion and to Gedera to look for Biluim, since they saw themselves as continuing the path of these originators and wanted to find spiritual fathers. But the Gedera pioneers closed their doors in their faces and turned a deaf ear to them, not wanting to listen to remembrances from the distant past. Only with Fanny and Lolik did they find people willing to listen. These two had remained the same; their spirit had not flagged, and they were still looking for controversy and challenges, so they were enthusiastic about meeting new "revolutionaries." But, since their house was too small to host the group, they all returned to Jaffa, with Fanny and Lolik among them, too, ready to change their path and go back to wandering.

Avshalom, the son of Fanny and Lolik, had already reached 13, and the lad, who knew what he wanted, came to live with his grandmother Shifra in Jaffa. After Meir had died and Sonya had gone away to study medicine, Shifra was left by herself, and she refused to live with her sons or daughters. At that time, Fanny was still in Rishon Lezion, and when her neighbors asked her why she didn't go to spend time with her, Shifra would answer, "I'm used to Jaffa." But when they kept on inquiring, "And what about your other daughter, Olga?" She would respond that she had not been given her grandchildren to raise and was busy with her husband, who was still searching the whole time to find his way, and her attending to births, so if she went to stay with her, she would be in the way and just interfere.

Shifra was happy with Avshalom. The young man made a change in her dreary life, not only with the caprices of his adolescence. There was someone to cook for and to listen to and someone to talk about when her neighbors gathered. She had a lot to relate, since Avshalom was drawn to the Muscovites and often went to the Workers' House and then stayed up late with his grandmother, excitedly telling her about what he had heard and seen. He thought all of them were special intellectuals, visionaries.

That year Yehoshua Hankin turned 40 and Olga passed the age of 50, and Shifra was right; no one could have guessed her age. Olga was busy, yet found time for the new Russians, even though she did not become too involved with them. When she saw their rebellion against the conventions of the Palestine Jews, she wondered if their approach would be successful. Yehoshua was far away among the Galilee hills, and the nights were long, so Olga occasionally joined Avshalom when he went to the Workers' House in Neve Zedek, where she would listen with him to the readings of Pushkin's poems and feel homesick for Petersburg and a different type of life, and she took notice of the change that had begun in her sister's son. The boy loved to go with his aunt and be involved with the Muscovite group. He learned their language and quoted verses from the Bible, stressing the words in Ashkenazic pronunciation. He looked deeply into the meaning of the word "commune," became a supporter of socialist theories, and called for a revolution and change in people's way of life in society and in the country. On the one hand, he still spoke with the earnestness of youth and did not know what compromise meant, while on the other, he matured quickly. All the while, Olga watched him, yearning to be like him and to go back and start all over again. She pined for Yehoshua and the time of the intensity of first love, but he stayed in Galilee, and Galilee was far from Judea.

Yehoshua continued to measure the Galilee lands with his feet, ride among the hills, meet with bureaucrats, and suffer insults on the right and left. The daily battles wore him down, and his doubts about what he was doing kept growing, and he could not subdue them. He met with the JCA official in Beirut more than once, and enumerated places in Palestine for him, adding with somewhat of a stutter, that perhaps it might be worthwhile for the JCA to consider the possibility of acquiring the land. Once, he was even so brave as to utter to that man the names "Jezreel Valley, Wadi Hawarith, and Jidru Valley." But the official had no idea what he was talking about and sent him to get a haircut, trim his beard, and then come back to him "looking properly, like a land agent of a famous company."

Only rarely did Yehoshua discover a ray of light and feel himself rise above the triviality of his actions. One occasion was when he was sent to solve the matter of complex Ottoman law involved in acquiring the land of Atlit, so he went to the sea and the watermelon port of Abu Zabura. He stood there on the shore, watching the ships sailing to Egypt. Once again, he dreamed of a city at the mouth of the stream to the ocean, with a port and house high above the kurkar cliff—Olga's house. Another time was when an American Jew who called himself a Zionist came to him in Galilee and wanted to redeem land in Palestine for purposes of investment and profit. Yehoshua told that American about the large tract of Wadi Hawarith, and the man showed interest in it and returned with him to Jaffa; both of them met with the heirs of Antoine Bishara Tayyan. But nothing came from that meeting, since the father had died and only the sons remained, and they were highly irresponsible with their inheritance. They owed money to others and mortgaged the land to pay their gambling debts. The American went home, leaving Yehoshua a business card in case other land became available. But this did not happen, so Yehoshua returned to Galilee to examine the sources of the Litani waters and to ride the entire length of the banks of the Jordan. He no longer tortured himself over his failures; he became accustomed to them, which were just part of his routine life. In any event, he knew he might succeed and return to being the Second Joshua.

In the brunt of winter 1904/5, Yehoshua returned to Jaffa. The rains brought him back. By January, the amount of rain that had fallen equaled that of the entire usual winter, and the roads of Palestine were full of mud and puddles. It was impossible to ride a horse, since the bridges had been destroyed, and the water flow ran swiftly, finding new pathways for itself and sweeping away clay houses on their march. Yehoshua's stay in Jaffa grew longer owing to an ongoing, increasingly bitter dispute between the official Kalvarisky and his JCA superiors: the Galilee farmers had raised a hue and cry, demanding stone houses that could withstand floods, so he tried to intercede on their behalf, but his efforts did not satisfy them, and they said that he was a submissive slave to the company and not taking care of his nation and that he was only trying to maintain his status among the high officials. At the same time, the company was angered by his asking for additional funds and by his attempts to buy land without consulting it and without making it party to his decisions regarding acquisitions. Especially vociferous was the official Pariente, who was situated in Beirut, and he ranked second among the senior staff whose center was in Paris—a merchant who had been very successful but understood nothing about land or procedures of acquisition from the *fellahin* or from the effendis who owned large tracts of land. In one of the arguments, the official in Beirut forbid Kalvarisky from making new land purchases for JCA. So, once again, there was no work for Yehoshua, and he remained in Jaffa until early summer.

Mania came to their home for the first time during that rainy winter.

ᡧ

On the second night of Hanukkah, Doctor Masie told Olga about a girl who had moved into the coal hut standing in the house's yard opposite the office and was deeply depressed. A day earlier, she had come to the office to ask for medicine to control the trembling attacking her due to malaria. The doctor was frightened by her gaunt, fragile appearance and her parchment skin, and it seemed like she might fall at any minute to the floor and not be able to get up. He fed her soup, and when she recovered a bit, she told him about herself. Her story was very strange, and the doctor did not know whether or not to believe her. Maybe she was hallucinating. She had come by herself to join her brother, but he could not support her since he, too, was barely subsisting. After the Russian Revolution, the doctor said, Mania was accused of murder, and in the train wagon in which she was riding, she was carrying a crate with her which contained the victim's body. They tried her in absentia in Petersburg and returned a verdict of execution, so she was forced to disguise herself as a boy to escape her persecutors. She managed to reach Jaffa by circuitous means and was still talking about the Russian Revolution, not differentiating between Jaffa and Petersburg.

22. From right to left: Olga Hankin, Mania Vilboshevitz-Shochat, Sonia Belkind, Dobah Belkind, Shoshana Vilboshevitz, Jaffa 1913 • Source: Tanchum Hankin Private Archive.

When he finished the story, the doctor asked Olga to visit the girl and take care of her, so Olga went. She did not know what drew her to the tin hut—was it the strange tale or pity or perhaps the young age of the girl or accusation against her? She knocked on the coal hut door and did not wait for a reply. She entered and was shocked to see the girl's drawn face and large eyes who preferred to sleep and did not want to get up from her bed but only waited for her vitality to give way.

A look was sufficient to keep Olga in the cabin, but strong bonds, the meaning of which she herself did not understand, linked her to the young woman. She didn't even feel like herself, but every morning, before going to the clinic, she stopped in to visit the girl. She gave her something to drink as she had done for her husband at the time when he had been depressed, and she washed and combed her but did not show her any feelings of pity; she just waited for the girl to begin to recover so that she would open up by herself. In the evenings, too, she checked on her and chattered with her about the news of Jaffa and Palestine, depicting for her images of laborers, and she told her about Avshalom. She did not mention Yehoshua. For some reason, she did not wish to share the girl with him and wanted to keep her for herself for now.

But in January, Yehoshua returned, and she was no longer a master unto herself and had to find explanations. Suddenly, Olga felt the rain, the wind, the cold mornings, and the nights that fell early, which until now, she hadn't noticed. For two days, she restrained herself and did not go to visit Mania but stayed only with her husband to accustom herself again to a different way of life. After two days passed, her confidence in Yehoshua returned, and she had already learned the events of his long stay in Galilee and felt the quiet engulfing him, for failure could no longer touch him, and he accepted his fate in silence. On the third morning, while she was still in bed and refusing to take herself out of the warm quilt, she told him about Mania and asked him to collect her at the office in the evening so they could go together to visit the girl.

Yehoshua promised to come, but Olga felt he had not taken her very seriously. She spoke no more about the girl, and when they finished eating, she put on her coat and visited her patients. Before going to the office, she wanted to see the girl, so she knocked on the tin door of the coal hut. She heard no response from inside; she became frightened and pushed the door open. She found the girl sitting on the bed wrapped in a warm blanket, looking at the raindrops traveling down the windowpane; she scarcely noticed someone had entered.

The woman dragged a chair and sat down opposite her; she raised her voice to draw the young woman's attention. She still refused to look at her, and Olga understood that she was insulted that Olga had not come by for two days. Olga changed her tone of voice and continued to speak, this time about her husband. She talked about him as she had seen him before his collapse, and he was still a big land agent buying broad swaths of land and galloping among the hills of Shefar'am and examining the clods of earth in the huge Jezreel valley. She also told her of her horseback rides along the sea and among the dunes and swamps and about his promise to build a house in the dunes. The more she spoke, the more she understood how great her love was for her husband, and she realized Mania's thirst to hear more and more.

A strong cough from Mania brought Olga out of her memories. When she saw the sun shining outside the window, she was alarmed at her lengthy stay and hurried to make the bed and plump up the pillow. Then she left, promising to return in the evening.

Yehoshua came to take Olga from the office, as he had pledged. The doctor and the Arab midwife had already left, so Olga made tea from them before they continued on. Yehoshua wondered a bit about this delay but didn't say anything, and when they sat down to drink, Olga again described the girl to him, and Yehoshua sensed the excitement in her voice. He became fearful that she might be disappointed, since the minute the young woman would become stronger, she might toss away the friendship that had been offered to her and leave. In his mind's eye, he saw the girl differently from the way Olga conceived her. The story of the murder and the journey on the train, as well as the talk about a revolution, depicted a very strong figure for him. If her vitality had been sapped, it would only be for a short time, and she would recover and leave Olga behind.

"She's a young woman," he hinted to her. "Don't forget that."

Olga looked at him, trying to fathom his meaning, but when he didn't go into more detail, she replied, "If I could, I would want a daughter like her."

"You won't have a daughter," Yehoshua nodded and took her hand, "you will have a friend. And when she regains her strength, she will leave, and who knows if she will come back and remember your friendship with her."

"No," she burst out. "Mania won't leave Jaffa. She needs me and won't forget my friendship for her in the time of her suffering."

He let go of her hands and caressed her face. "I did not forget, and that's enough."

"You'll never understand," she replied and dropped her shoulders.

But Yehoshua understood her yearning and was angry at himself and his distance away from her for so long. So, he lowered his eyes and asked himself why didn't he just give in and stay with her, since anyway his life was full of ups and downs, becoming distant and returning, but she was always there, waiting.

"This is not the time to think about the two of us and our closeness," she read his thoughts. "We'll go see her. She's waiting, and I promised to hurry to her at nightfall."

When they came in, the girl was sitting with hair combed and rosy cheeks. The instant Yehoshua saw her, he immediately understood why Olga wanted to adopt her as a daughter. Mania interested him, and he could not take his eyes off her. They sat with her until the wee hours of the night. Then, for the first time in several days, Mania got out of bed and served the others. She did, of course, have to hold on to the back of the chair and walk slowly, but she managed to pour tea for them. When it was time to leave, she asked them to come again together and help her restore her strength and take her with them to meet Fanny and Lolik and visit the school at Shefeya and meet Israel Belkind. "Do they look like you?" she asked.

"Different, very different," both of them laughed', with Yehoshua adding, "It's better that way. If not so, things would be boring."

The winter was almost over. Mania grew stronger and often met with Yehoshua. Olga was busy at the clinic. As for him, his time was his own until the squabbles in Galilee between the bureaucrats there, and the higher-ranking officials in Beirut ended, and he would have to return to working as an agent, buying pieces of land a bit here, a bit there. He taught Mania to ride bareback, and the two of them rode a lot. Sometimes the three of them would ride; sometimes, only two of them. Mania quickly adjusted to the habits of the riders; she became familiar with the Arab *fellahin's* way of life, and she memorized the names of the lands. Yehoshua loved to spend time with her, and Olga encouraged him to do so, considering it something to do and especially the development of an ever-stronger connection, as well as instilling the hope that the day would come when they would be three and not only two. Yehoshua was afraid that the dream would come to nothing, but even though he knew how hard the break would be, he kept on reinforcing the connection.

On the Sabbaths, when Olga had time off from her work, she would take them to visit the Bedouin tribes scattered south of the Jaffa orchards and introduce them to the most recent infants she had delivered. First, she would lift the dark-skinned infants for them to see and show them sheikhs wrapped in jalabiyas. Then, when she would examine the women in the tent encampment, Mania and Yehoshua would sit with the men. Mania would ignore their looks of astonishment and take part in the discussion, spicing her statements with legends common among the tribes. Quite quickly, everyone would feel comfortable and forget they were sitting together with a woman.

Mania was different from any other woman Yehoshua had met; she had short hair and always wore riding breeches, with her shirt tucked in so tightly that her breasts did not show. She wore a brimmed hat if she wanted, making it impossible to tell if she was a woman or a man. The link between her and Yehoshua became stronger. But not in the way Olga had hoped for; he never saw Mania as a daughter but as an equal—a free spirit seeking wide open spaces and finding walls and narrow lanes insufferable. He made her party to his dreams. After a long while, he once again rode to the entrance to *the Valley* without fearing his dream and spread his hands wide to embrace the spaces; Mania's eyes grew wide in wonderment at every vista and each word he spoke. She believed in his faith and rode with him on the dunes and hills of Tul Karm and went up with him to the top of the Carmel, and glided down toward the Mediterranean Sea bay. They even reached the desert, stayed with the Turkish soldiers in Beersheba, and rode to El Arish from there, going so far as Jericho. Their trips came to an end one day when he took her to Nes Ziona to show her the remains of Reuven Lerer's farm and to introduce her to the workers who had united and built a colony there.

Yehoshua stood next to the brick house, drew water from the well, and breathed in the air of the orchards; he told Mania Mr. Lerer's story. At first, he did not realize Mania was no longer next to him; only when he turned to see if she had understood his story, did he find himself alone. He was embarrassed by the silence and from talking to himself, so he searched for her. When he didn't see her, he left the well and went to the colony, up the ascent of Tel Aviv Street; as he went down from the hill, he saw the Worker's House. He entered it and understood the meaning of her disappearance.

She was sitting with a group of young men in worn-out clothes but eyes ablaze, and she already belonged to them, and neither to him nor to Olga. He waited a bit, and when darkness crept into the room, he rose and left. Mania did not get up but told him she was staying with the laborers and would return alone in a few days, but he knew those days would turn into months.

Yehoshua returned to Jaffa by himself, saddened by the dream of friendship with Mania that had begun evaporating and afraid of Olga's reaction. Olga was angry and accused him of leaving her with the workers' group, but a few days later, she realized the young woman's needs differed from hers and that she did not want a mother's love or any kind of dependence but was looking for friendship. For a long time, the loss of the daughter she had never hurt her, though finally, she made peace with reality and tried to get used to it.

When Mania did come back to Jaffa, she had already changed. During the summer, she rode by herself, with a pistol carried in her boot and an ammunition belt around her chest. She did not limit herself to the Nes Ziona workers but also came to know the laborers of Petach Tikva. One day she left Jaffa and didn't even say goodbye to Olga and Yehoshua.

They did not hear from her for a long time, though once they did get some sort of regards incidentally through Israel Belkind, who was living in Shefeya and had seen her there with Israel Shochat. But, then, other rumors were rife linking her name with that of Shochat; people whispered that the two of them had founded a new association called "Bar Giora" and that the name had been written in blood on its flag. Also heard was that they were planning to settle the Jericho plains and to set up colonies of Jewish guards. Olga smiled and dismissed the gossip with one word, "Nonsense," but Yehoshua believed it. For a moment, he was sorry that he was not involved in the plan and not getting a taste of the empty plains. Still, when he saw Olga's calm, he reconciled himself to his situation. He enjoyed sitting together in the late-night hours in the kitchen adjacent to their rented room in Ajami. He spent this time with her, the two of them alone.

Change, 1905

At the end of the summer, Yehoshua was called to return to Galilee and to solve the problems of the quarrel between the Arab *fellahin* and the Jews over the lands of Mesha, Milhamia, and Yemma, some of which were purchased for the three colonies: Yavneel, Menahemia, and Kfar Tavor and were under the management of Kalvarisky. Work was not plentiful, and unwillingly Yehoshua became enmeshed in the farmers' spats in the matter of the director. The farmers were divided between those who loved Kalvarisky and those who hated him. In Yavneel, there were more haters than in the other colonies. Yavneel was already the center for all colonies in the Tiberias district. People often gathered there in its streets, sought medical services, visited the tool and implement storage area, or simply listened to gossip. The workers in the colony consisted mainly of Muscovites from among those new Russians whom Yehoshua had met in the winter when he was staying at his place in Jaffa. Yehoshua was, of course, invited to the Kalvarisky family house in Nazareth, but he preferred the laborers who dwelled in the yards overstaying in an orderly home.

At first, he would come at nightfall and sit with them, not getting involved with their group, while the Muscovites, who respected him, did not ask difficult questions and did not even wonder about his age or his long hair, deep-set eyes, and lengthy silence; they left him alone. A few of the farmers' families were not reconciled to his joining the workers and tried to discourage him from doing so. Still, Yehoshua did not want to take a stance regarding the Kalvarisky issue and realized that if he went to the home of one farmer, his name would immediately be linked to the lovers or haters camp—according to which group the farmer belonged. Later on, Yehoshua began to stay longer among the laborers, hum their tunes, and share their vision.

In September, many workers left the farmers' yards. They went to spread gravel on the road being paved from the train station at Samakh in the direction of the new colonies and toward Dalhamiya Bridge over the Jordan and turning from there to Daraa and Damascus. In Galilee, all that was left for Yehoshua was to deal with land measurements and marking borders and be subordinate to the whims of the official in Beirut who obliged him to present himself to him every month and to report what he had done. To pass the time, he joined the laborers and spread gravel with them, covering his face with dust and hearing again about Mania and Israel Shochat.

Right before the holiday season, Kalvarisky told him to come to him in Nazareth. There, he asked him to polish his boots, brush his coat, and go to

Beirut, and, if necessary, to Constantinople to obtain for the company sending him kushans for the Deleika land that stretched between the outlet of the Kinneret and the Jordan estuary. Yehoshua was happy about the change, being called Hawaja Hankin by the wagon driver, getting away from the dreaming youth, and slowly sobering up.

In Beirut, he did not approach the Sursuq family home, but he did spend a few days roaming between the lower and upper city and learned their lanes and people at his leisure. Then, after he had obtained the required agreement, he rode a train to Constantinople, made his way among high officials, and met the cronies who sat at the Ottoman Sublime Porte until he obtained the needed kushans and all the signatures.

The trip to Jaffa took a week, and until he reached Nazareth, two weeks had passed. But when he reached Kalvarisky's house, with the contract for the lands of Deleika in his pocket and the kushans registered in the name of the JCA, he was frightened by the downcast look on Kalvarisky's face. The letter put in Yehoshua's hand that bore the address of Pariente in Beirut, along with Kalvarisky's stormy face and his silence, explained everything clearly. Kalvarisky had fallen out of favor, and with his failure, he intended to drag Yehoshua down after him. JCA had refused to acquire all the lands of Deleika and demanded that he find buyers for half of it and informed him that he was leaving his job and moving to Rosh Pina to manage the established colonies there. "They kicked me upstairs," he told Yehoshua. "The fledglings I nurtured they have taken away from me. First, it was Sejera and now the new colonies." Yehoshua could not find words to console him. His own situation was far worse: what was his future? He placed the land documents on the table, and without asking for anything in exchange and without taking part in the official's pain, he fled from there. From the stable owner in Nazareth, he rented a horse and galloped to the entrance to the Jezreel Valley that opened wide toward the slopes of the Carmel to encounter his dream and grab on to making it real.

In the summer, *the Valley* lands, covered with straw and trampled thorns, were more exposed and broader, so riding on them was easy. He walked the length of al-Moqatta River, examining its springs and the disappearance of its water into the thirsty soil, and he skipped over the gray limestone rocks, forgetting his fears in doing so. When he reached the Bedouins, he stayed with them and roamed with their flocks. He discovered the secrets of a spring in the river whose length he had just covered. From there, he went to the *fellahin* living on the hills surrounding *the Valley* and slept in the huts. Then, he descended toward the watermelon patches. At night, they sat in a booth in a patch and guarded against Bedouins who invaded with their goats. The *fellahin* taught Yehoshua the secrets of the land and the ways to improve it and increase its yields. He worked ceaselessly and did not allow thoughts to engulf him again.

The fall festival of Sukkot passed, and the last watermelons were sent on the sailboats that were kept in the bays of the Mediterranean, at the west entrance of Jezreel Valley, to be loaded onto ships sailing for Egypt. All that time, Yehoshua did not think even once about his wife and refused to link the past with the present. One evening, Yehoshua sat with the *fellahin* who tilled the soil of Shunem in the Jezreel Valley and, while drinking the sweet coffee, listened to the stories about the ups and downs of the Turkish regime and the attempts of revolt by the Young Turk movement. He mused that they're young, and youth always rebel, remembering the revolt in Rishon Lezion, the laborers, and Mania, wondering to himself where she was now. Suddenly, he heard one of the *fallah* mention the name of Michel Sursuq, and his tale sounded like an old legend, so Yehoshua listened carefully, so as not to miss a word from the storyteller.

When the speaker saw the look on the face of the long-haired fellow, he began to speak slowly and draw out his words, "He was once a large landowner with his wealth, who negotiated with the elite among the people. He lived in Beirut, and dignitaries, merchants, and straightforward advice-seekers thronged to him. He had two sons, so when he saw he was getting old and could no longer watch over all his businesses, he decided to put his sons to the test. He sent each son to all the European countries with an escort loyal to his master, who would examine whether the son was worthy of being his heir and report back to him. Each son was given a pouch of money to pay for his activities with the instruction to return it full. One son arrived in Alexandria, Egypt, and did very well there. He bought a ship and sailed merchandise between ports and, about a year later, returned to Beirut with a great deal of money in his satchel. The other son made his way to Constantinople, stayed there, gambling over cards, shooting dice, racing pigeons, and becoming involved in cock fights. Close to a year later, he presented himself to his father with a large amount of money in his pocket. The father had no choice but to divide his property between his sons. But the brothers could not dwell together in peace. The one brother returned to Alexandria to expand his businesses, while the gambler stayed in his father's house and took control of the belongings and the real estate, the crops, and the money. Only one thing would the father, Musa Sursuq, not give him—the land of the big valley and his plot of the Jidru land that bordered the large sea.

"No one liked the gambling son, who was called by Beirut people, 'the little Sursuq.' He was double-chinned, much shorter than his elderly father, his body wrapped in the most precious materials, his eyes darting here and there, never looking straight ahead. His actions were few, but he took care to leave his name signed everywhere: in plaster carvings that decorated the wall of the courtyard in which his name was woven with verses from the Qoran and in old documents of his father's that he tore, replacing his father's signature with his name, 'Michel Sursuq,' in large letters. The young man continued to gamble, bringing competitors to his home, bragging about his talent and wealth, not caring about his reputation. His father, who could no longer see and now needed to use a cane, was silent and his statements were no longer heard in the courtyard of his home. He would just sit withdrawn in his corner."

The *fallah* halted his storytelling, but his eyes never left Yehoshua's face. Yehoshua was tense and knew that the words were aimed at him and attempting to reveal something, but he did not know what. The storyteller took a swallow from his glass and hummed under his mustache, his eyes still glued on the face of the bearded man sitting opposite him as if waiting for his pleas, but Yehoshua hesitated whether to respond to the speaker and go back to dealing with such faraway matters. Finally, he cast his eyes down and bent his head toward his knees with sudden fatigue that had engulfed him, and he only wanted to sleep and forget. When the narrator saw his motions, he put down his cup and continued telling in a whispery voice, "One day, the old father took ill and was on his deathbed. The son stood near the head of the bed every night and put a feather near his nose to check his breathing, waiting for a moment of clarity so he could have him sign for *the Valley* land and pass it on to him. But one night, with a full moon, the old mand suddenly sat up in bed, leaned on his pillows, and yelled at the son standing close by, 'The Valley land will never be yours! Before I die, I will do everything to sell it to others, better than you. No one will gamble over *the Valley* or dare to mortgage parts of it in exchange for a debt of cards and dice.' As soon as he had mentioned the word 'Valley,' color had returned to his cheeks, and he got up from the bed and no longer needed a cane."

The *fallah* finished speaking, and the others sitting in the circle stretched themselves and prepared to leave to go to bed, but Yehoshua realized that the man had hidden the end of the story from his listeners, so he got up and moved next to the *fallah*, sitting silently together with him. The others left, with just the two of them remaining, and only then did the peasant continue his story.

"Michel Sursuq got into money troubles, and his father could not withstand his crocodile tears, so he scoured all *the Valley* lands for a piece of it that he would not mind too much if he sold it, and the choice came to the Shunem land. Why Shunem precisely?" He pretended to be ignorant though he knew the answer, and like him, Yehoshua also knew.

"It is land destined for calamity: in the winter, the rains stand there; in spring, the mosquitos hover over it; in summer, the land is cracked; and in fall, the Bedouins swarm all over it. If the land were to be sold, the tenant farmers living on it would forgo it in exchange for money and land someplace else, without making any problems," he concluded and explained no more.

Yehoshua continued to sit motionlessly but still did not understand why the *fellah* had told him his story. He did not want to ask and seem eager, yet within himself, he prayed to find a smidgen of truth in the legend, perhaps even the whole truth. The *fellah* read his thoughts and suddenly broke out in thunderous laughter, "Hawadja Hankin, buyer of the Duran lands, strive for the tracts of the Jezreel Valley!"

Yehoshua wondered at what he was saying, for he did not know him, but the man looked at him and said, "The day will yet come when you will buy the land of *the Valley*, not piecemeal but a large, continuous tract, and you will be the great Yehoshua. It is Allah's will. The coffee grinds tell us …" At that point, the peasant had already gotten up and gathered the folds of his jalabiya, leaving while still chuckling.

Yehoshua returned to Jaffa and to Olga and their home in Ajami; he seldom traveled to Galilee. The *fallah's* story continued to fire his imagination, but for now, at least, it remained just a story. Yehoshua did not go to Beirut to meet with Michel Sursuq and ask about the Shunem land; he didn't have the nerve to deal with *the Valley* a second time and start everything all over again.

As usual, Jaffa again changed that winter; it changed colors and people and suffered the whims of the Turkish rulers who feared for their future. Certainly, new winds were blowing throughout the empire and penetrated Palestine, as well. They created a feeling among the local residents that they were the center of the world. Herzl had died a few years earlier, but he left behind the Zionist Congress, along with debates on the way to be followed and the Jewish National Fund that sought to buy land and preserve it for the Jewish people. Then, in 1908 the Young Turk Revolution broke out, and in Palestine, everybody said that it was clear now that a change was coming, and it would be possible to implement the decisions of the Zionist Congress and demand a charter and try to obtain Jewish autonomy.

One of the issues in the new place and time that they dealt with was a new office, the "Palestine Office," or in short, "the office." And as had happened in the days of Vladimir Tyomkin, now too, the wives of the colonies' farmers and the urban women discovered an issue in which they wanted to be involved. They would praise and glorify the officials of that new office and their wives. They spoke about the fashions in Berlin and Hague, the two cities where the offices were located, that the group of new officials and clerks had brought with them and about the recipes for baked goods, the wine tasting, and the new houses built for these officials in Jerusalem and Jaffa. Whoever was not well-versed in all of this had no reason to go to dine at others' homes or with others, because there was nothing to talk about. In time, the office was not sufficient, so they established a company—the Palestine Land Development Company. This time as well, the name was shortened, and people simply called it "the Company," and everyone knew who and what was meant.

Yehoshua and Olga could not help but hear about the office and the new company. The words were like a wake-up pill for Olga, but for Yehoshua—a passing fancy that did not concern him. Olga, unlike her husband, was able to specify the matters of the office and the company, and she spoke about capital stock, a plan for a cooperative, as well as a training farm. She distinguished between officials directing the Office and those managing the Company, and she repeatedly said, "These manage those, and they have but one goal—the settlement of Palestine."

One day, Sarah called Yehoshua and whispered to him, "The times of Tyomkin are returning for your wife, and she is looking for officials' parties she can attend, and she wants to be among those who go to the new directors' home."

But Yehoshua ignored what she said, so Sarah sighed and did not talk about this anymore, though others did speak. But Olga did not want to hear it and did not react. She became close with the wives of the new officials and began to prefer their company over that of the family and the frequenters of the store. Her chattering about all the matters of the Office and the Company increased and became the only topic of conversation that she now had with Yehoshua.

At first, he considered her speaking as a way to fill long evenings in which there was nothing much to say. But something happened to Olga—the closer she became to the new officials, the more her speech began to be infused with a new mocking tone against anyone who did not act with the same energy, maintain the same direction, speak in agreement with the line of thought that the Company and Office represented. At that time, she blossomed, and even though she was no longer so young, her age did not show. Yehoshua, in contrast, had everyone thinking he was old, a spineless idler to whom everyone said, "You have a fine wife," while raising their eyebrows. However, these utterances did not keep them apart, and Yehoshua accepted his fate and considered it a fair punishment for the years of suffering he had thrust upon her.

They spent less and less time together, even though Yehoshua was careful to return to Jaffa for Sabbaths and holidays and take a break from the land matters he was involved in, so as not to fortify the gossipy whispering. Olga, it seemed, enjoyed hearing how people praised her beauty and intelligence, and her close connection to the Jaffa elite; while simultaneously shaking their heads in pity toward her husband, saying, "Once he was great, a man with a lot of property, but who still remembers…"

And when she remembered her husband and came home late on the Sabbath nights to serve him hot water several times, she forgot her original intention and would share her experiences with him. Even when she lay next to him, she would continue talking about those same matters and not respond to his hesitant caressing or the warmth of his close body.

The time came when Yehoshua could no longer stand her estrangement and tried to bring her back to him. He responded to her words and mocked the Company that had come to development ground when it still did not have land. Olga, in response, would provoke him, "Why do you demand that others should buy land while you don't?" Then, she would protect the Company and declare that it did intend to be the middleman between the sellers and those interested in acquiring land. It was also going to find credit for whoever was striving to buy a plot for himself in Palestine but could not afford it.

"How will they obtain credit?" he would be asked bitterly. "Doesn't the Company need investors to raise capital, assemble an inventory of land, as well as look for buyers? And I, who was a big land agent, did not succeed in interesting others to buy land."

"You're jealous," Olga would make fun of him, "seeing the achievements of others and not accepting them."

The nighttime conversations became ever more vocal, and in her voice, Yehoshua heard the mockery, while in his—the insult. One evening, Olga returned from a meeting with the German-speaking director of the Office, under the influence of wine and with an unsteady gait. When she saw him, she giggled and said, "You're not like Dr. Ruppin. If you could only see his white shirt and his tailor-made coat. All of them are so respectable and important and so good-looking," she added as she went to wash her face.

"They all speak German," he rebutted. "Loafers from The Hague and Berlin," adding, "Perhaps ze effendi vud tell me how much dis land is vurth, pliz," trying to imitate a German accent.

"And what good did it do you to know Arabic or Turkish?" she ridiculed him, and the scent of her hair dripping water drove him crazy. "You remained a small clerk, a land agent nobody recognizes." She stood opposite him, with a penetrating stare, her words so staid and painful.

"For many years, you remained great, in my opinion, the Second Joshua. I shut my ears to the slanderous voices, and I waited for your return, always forgiving and understanding. Now, instead of freeing yourself from petty actions and doing great things and joining the new Office, the company that acquires land, you are jealous and insulted."

Yehoshua did not know what to answer and refused to admit she was right, even though he agreed with everything she said. Later, when the two were lying in bed, with their backs to each other and not uttering a word, Olga regretted her harsh words but refused to take them back. She so wanted his caresses and the feel of the stubble of his beard on her body. But she was still searching for words to rouse him and bring him out of the continuous helplessness that had taken hold of him.

In the morning, Yehoshua left the room in Ajami without saying goodbye and meandered through the lanes. Then, he sat at a street corner sipping coffee, with the discussions about the Company and about the Office slicing through his heart as if a sword was stabbing him. Quite a while went by, but finally, he got up and went on the path leading to Sharona, the German colony where one could rent a wagon. That very day he rode to Rosh Pina to plead with Kalvarisky to ask him to intercede on his behalf with his superiors in Paris. But Kalvarisky could not help. He, too, had been ripped away from the land he loved and banished from the settlements he had nurtured, and because of that, Kalvarisky answered him with a very bitter voice, "A curse lies on anyone who tries to be an important land speculator. The times of Tyomkin are over, an era when there was room for only one agent. Today, the only possibility is to operate within the framework of a company and to be a small, disciplined clerk. If JCA doesn't need you, find another company. Look for work with the Palestine Land Development Company."

Yehoshua left the Administration House broken-hearted and headed to ride in the mountains. For a month, he stayed by himself in far-flung places and slept in caves and niches the Bedouin and *fellahin* avoided and ate wild dates and chewed oat seeds, and in September, ultimately returned to Jaffa.

Yehoshua and Olga did not mention that difficult evening, and Olga, who saw the change in Yehoshua, wished to try to help him adjust and to support him. He actually had become someone else. He had made a decision to try to obtain a job as a land agent in the Palestine Land Development Company. During Hanukkah, he got up and went to the home of Dr. Arthur Ruppin, the director of the new Office, who determined and decided everything related to the PLDC.

The nature of Jaffa had changed, and the city had grown and become crowded together at the same time. As Yehoshua walked to Dr. Ruppin's house, he slowed his pace, looked around him, and remembered his going to meet the owners of the Hawarith land. He was astonished by how little he had accomplished in the past two decades—dubbed "patchwork deeds" by Olga—and he had not fought back or revolted against his situation.

Rolling in the drainage canal bisecting the street was a page from the newspaper *Hamelitz*, and Yehoshua bent down and picked it up. He straightened it out with his hand and wiped it on the edge of his coat to dry it off and read, "Ahuzat Bayit News."

"Another association seeking to improve and reform the residents of Palestine," he thought but went on reading anyway. "The association is seeking land on which to build a Hebrew neighborhood."

This interaction left a bitter taste in his mouth. These issues continued to move along, and he was already not a part of them. He went around the Jaffa port and climbed the hill that overlooked Andromeda's Rock, scanning the dunes, the orchards and the open sea at the same time. It was getting late, so he returned to the narrow streets of the old city and made his way among its neglected houses. He was saddened by the ugliness of the buildings and the filth accumulating in the yards. Perhaps he should return to Ajami and ask Olga to join him. He mused and sat down on a large stone to gather his thoughts. Olga knew Ruppin and would understand how to make it easier for him to arrange the first meeting. He felt how he was shaking all over and how weakness was spreading through his very marrow. He was also aware that if he turned to her, people would say about him that he depended on women. No, he had to muster his strength and prove his greatness to her. He stood up, continued walking, and entered the Christian neighborhood whose houses were roomy and not heaped on one another. Olga had actually told him that every self-respecting person went to live on the Christians' street, and she certainly meant to hint to him that the time had come to build a house for themselves, but he, as usual, had not understood her allusions. His behavior embarrassed him. They had been married for 20 years, and he still had not found time to build a home for himself and his wife, 20 years … and he decided to change and go back to being great, in her opinion, and in the meantime, he had come close where he was headed.

He quickly located the house serving as the Palestine Office by the many well-dressed people who had collected at its entrance and spoke in a Babel of languages: Russian, German, French, Yiddish, and the Hebrew holy tongue. The men wore jackets and displayed European manners, while the women were elegantly dressed as well, and minced about in pointy shoes. The crowd frightened him, so he passed by the building and turned up the collar of his coat, lest someone recognize him or greet him, and the knowledge that he was a failure stung him. Again, he did not tarry and returned to the neighborhood bordering the port.

In response to Olga's astonishment at his swift reappearance at home, he said, "They spoke German there, and I don't know German."

The wonder in her expression was replaced by anger. "Go back to Galilee," she spat out to him. "Maybe there, the strength to conduct negotiations will come back to you."

"I'll go tomorrow," he responded weakly. "Today, there were many people there."

She shook her head as if refusing to believe his evasive statements. "Coward, you don't want to compete. Ride to *the Valley*, go embrace your dream. Anything can happen in a dream. Go to the dunes and Wadi Hawarith and go into the Kabara Swamps and scream, 'I am Yehoshua Hankin, the buyer of the Duran land.' Only they remember you."

He did not know what to say, so he approached her, wanting to take hold of her shoulder, hug her, and draw strength from her, but she turned away from him and sank into the easy chair and pretended she was looking into a new book she had received from one of the women clerks at the Palestine Office. Yehoshua took another step toward her, wanting so very much to talk to her and explain his fears, but her back didn't move, not even an inch. His sadness choked him, so he left the room.

He quietly closed the door, and, hunched over, went to the dock at the port. He halted close to the edge of the water, standing opposite the strongly streaming waves, waiting for the tears and wails that would burst out.

The boats in the port swayed and from time to time were hurtled against the stone wall, with the rope securing them becoming taut. Yehoshua took hold of the rope and pulled it toward him when it was stretched, feeling it wounding his skin and the pain piercing his hand. He loved her so much, and he was so embarrassed to face her. They had no children, so they did not have to share their love, yet he had failed in that, too. The only thing he knew how to do was to acquire land, and he had not succeeded in that either. People said to him, "You have a pretty wife, smart, too," but behind his back, they added—she doesn't even look her age. At the same time, he was old and tired and couldn't find his place; he would go far from Jaffa and run away from her and from the land. Yehoshua let go of the rope and bent down to pick up a stone he had found between the torn pieces of fishing nets and threw it into the foaming, stormy water like the tempest raging in his heart. "If he could only change their course and stop their crashing," he thought.

Now, he felt the cold wind and wanted to button his coat, only to realize that the top button was broken. He turned away from the water and began running toward the house, to Olga. He found her sitting on their bed, with her head in her hands, so he put his arm around her and pulled her close; the heat of her body slowly thawed him out. Then, fully dressed, they went under the quilt. She patted his arm and curled his beard, and Yehoshua passed his fingertips over her eyelids and the folds of her cheeks and undid her hair. She burrowed her head in his chest and buttoned his shirt, damp from the sea breeze.

"I'm afraid," he whispered to her, "afraid of the new company's officials, afraid to be small among them."

She hushed him, and her body trembled with desire, and her skin quivered from his touch. "You won't be small," she whispered to him. "You will be great."

He so wanted to believe her and hoped for a change that would come. But, when he held her close, the room revolved for a few minutes; everything was forgotten, with only them and their love being there.

⚜

December went by, and the winter continued non-stop. The old-timers were already saying they did not remember such a harsh winter. At the end of January, Yehoshua rode to *the Valley*, and—besides his wife—no one knew anything about his going there. Then, one night a messenger came to their house to tell them that the Sursuq family had finally fixed a date for selling some of its land and had put the land of Fuleh up for sale. Alternate land had been found for the *fellahin* living on the land, and the family had published announcements in Tiberias and Nazareth about the sale, and now it was waiting for buyers. Yehoshua knew who had sent the man to him—the storytelling Arab *fallah*. He hurried to saddle his horse and left Jaffa at sunrise. Olga rose early and packed sesame-studded bread for him, and her eyes blessed him without saying a word.

Yehoshua urged his horse on so as to ride as much as possible in the dim light of the short winter's day, thinking only about the land. Nine thousand dunams had been offered for sale in *the Valley*, and he considered them the beginning of a change; he already imagined himself traveling to Beirut to meet with the Sursuq family. For a moment, he was afraid that the old Sursuq might not recognize him, for he had been told that he was already using a cane, and he would have to carry on negotiations with the hedonist son. But he immediately took hold of himself and convinced himself that he could conduct business even with people younger than he. "I will bring witnesses and move heaven and earth until *the Valley* will be acquired," he whispered to himself and goaded the horse.

Yehoshua bypassed Sheikh Munis and stayed far away from the fields and orchards, so as not to see early-rising farmers, and he debated with himself whether to go to Hadera and from there turn toward the low hills surrounding *the Valley* or to continue toward the dunes and up to the foot of the Carmel. Yehoshua remembered his two brothers—Tanhum and Mendel. Tanhum was already married and had a son, but he had not congratulated him; Mendel was still a bachelor. He wondered what had happened to the plot of the Hadera land, and again reminded himself of his promise to Olga to build her a house in the dunes. She was close to her mid-fifties, and he had not yet fulfilled his promise. He turned off the road and headed down toward the coast; he felt the salt penetrating his lungs and stinging his face.

He smelled the stench of egg water and followed it, trying to discern through the darkness the path leading to the holy tomb of Sheikh Sidna Ali. A blinding rain was raging, and when the horse found it difficult to see his way, Yehoshua dismounted and tried to find the stones arranged on both sides of the way and the wall surrounding the tomb.

When he finally found the tomb, he rang the bell and, to his surprise, the gate was opened immediately, and the guard stood under the arch. Seeing the astonished face of his guest, the old man smiled and said, "I heard the horse's hoofs striking the stones of the path. Few come to the tomb, and those who do visit are *fellahin* living in the villages of Jalil and al-Haram, and they would not come in the thick of night for fear of Liliths and all kinds of demons." The elderly guard led the horse to the stable and gave Yehoshua a straw pallet and provided him with a cup of steaming coffee and a plate full of rice; he then disappeared into his own corner. Yehoshua began to get ready to sleep.

The fierce cold made it hard for him to fall asleep, and thoughts about the anticipated meeting with Musa Sursuq, the old man, or his son, Michel Sursuq, kept pestering him.

At dawn, Yehoshua jumped up from the mat and washed his face in cold well water. The Arab guard had already risen and had warmed water in a copper pitcher over glowing coals and rolled a warm pita. Yehoshua sat next to the coals and poured himself some coffee and ate some pita, while the Arab sat and looked at him as he ate, with his fingers agilely moving the beads of the *misbaha*. When Yehoshua finished eating and dried his hands on his pants, the old man asked, "Land? Are you going to buy land?"

Yehoshua smiled slowly, and then his grin grew broader until it became riotous laughter. "Land! Land!" he cried.

The old man became caught up in the laughter and roared with him for quite a while until they both calmed down; the guard went to fetch a pitcher of water, and both of them drank from the clay spout and let the water dribble down the sides of their mouths and along their necks. When they finished, Yehoshua told him the story of *the Valley* land, and the old man held out his string of beads to him, and absentmindedly Yehoshua began toying with the beads, moving them from side-to-side. Only when the sun had risen a quarter of the way in the sky, and the horse had begun stamping, anxious to gallop, did Yehoshua return the beads to the Arab guard, mount his horse, and ride swiftly away. From time to time, he would turn his head and see the Arab standing in the entrance, moving the beads and muttering a prayer, until he was finally just a small dot and then no longer visible. The sun reached noon and started to decline. At the same time,

Yehoshua traversed the land of Wadi Hawarith and went around the houses of the Hadera colony, crossed the raging river, and continued going up the hills of Zichron Yaakov and Shefeya. As evening neared, he stopped at the Arab village of Fuleh and hurried to go into the house of the *fallah*, the teller of legends.

He spent two days in *the Valley* to examine the land intended for sale and the crop of barley seed it produced and also studied the water sources. He looked as well into the brittleness of the rocks in the area and asked many questions about the malaria-carrying mosquitos and the days of rain and days of sunshine. Finally, on the morning of the third day, he returned to Jaffa with the first drawing of the borders of the land in his pocket.

Now he prepared to meet the Sursuq family in Beirut, and Olga, even more, impatient than he, urged him to go down to the port to ask about a ship.

"If you don't go and offer a price, someone else will come and buy the land," she said. "And once more, the opportunity will slip through your fingers."

He refused her suggestion to accompany him to the port and wanted to do everything alone and to again become great in her eyes, and in his imagination, he already saw himself standing on the deck and waving to his wife, while holding a signed agreement between him and Sursuq.

The sea was raging, and Yehoshua lay down on a pile of ropes and felt how the weakness of 20 years of petty activity and forgetfulness overtook him. He had never felt as bad as he felt on this voyage, and he was afraid that this was a sign of things to come. The ship was delayed at sea, owing to the storm, and reached Beirut only after five days. Nevertheless, Yehoshua was pleased to find a clean shirt in his satchel, and placed among its folds was a new razor, and a slight grin spread on his gray face—his wife wanted him to look his best. Even during times of anger and insult, she knew what he needed and waited for his recovery to come from him, without the help of others. He was always in her mind, but she was not always in his, he thought and took fright from his musings, and the smile was wiped off his face, and his legs gave out.

When he disembarked, it was already afternoon, and Yehoshua tried to decide whether to look for a hotel for one night's lodging and go to the meeting fresh tomorrow, or whether to hurry to inform the Sursuq house of his arrival. Weakness resolved the dilemma for him, so he headed for a local hotel and signed with his full name, "Yehoshua Hankin," and added with an underscore, "Land Agent." Then he ate a full meal and felt better. Toward evening, he walked the Beirut lanes, with which he was well acquainted, climbed up the mountain, and returned to the port, where he entered a small barbershop and prepared for tomorrow's meeting.

While waiting for the barber to be able to deal with him, Yehoshua called the lad standing next to the bowl of soap, laundering towels, washing razors, drying, and sharpening them. He put a coin and a note in his hand, asking him to hand this note over at the entrance to the Sursuq house.

To gain the agreement of the barber to borrow the boy for a while, Yehoshua put another coin down on the counter opposite him, and then the lad was permitted to go on his task. In the meantime, Yehoshua sat down on his chair and closed his eyes, letting the fatigue from the journey engulf him, and didn't realize when the barber was available to deal with him.

When he opened his eyes, evening had already arrived. When he touched his face, he felt its smoothness and the trimmed beard, and smelled the scent of the aftershave. When he asked why the lad was taking so long, the barber smiled and asked him to be patient. Then, he offered him a glass of hot water with rose leaves floating in it. A short while later, the young man burst into the store, breathing heavily and panting, and explained why his task had taken him so long: first, he had fulfilled the mission of the distinguished client and given the message to the guard of the Sursuq home, but the guard had given him another job to do, and since it was getting late, he had rushed to his mother's house to say he would be late, and she had also given him a task, but there had been a line in the fish store ...

The barber laughed, but Yehoshua, who was impatient and wanted to know the guard's reply, tried to halt the flow of words.

"Nu," he prodded him.

"Tomorrow, at eleven o'clock, the young gentleman will be waiting for you," the lad replied with a smile on his face, proud of succeeding in his mission.

Yehoshua heard and trembled for a moment when he precisely remembered the young man's name—Michel Sursuq. He wanted to ask the barber and the lad what had happened to the old man, but he was afraid to exhibit enthusiasm lest a rumor spread throughout Beirut that there were buyers for the Fuleh land in the Jezreel Valley.

The next morning, he rose early, looked in the mirror, and saw his gaunt face and graying hair. He sadly recalled the young man who had come years earlier to the family, when he was full of self-confidence, and now he was weak, and his fate lay in the hands of the irresponsible, gambling young man.

An hour before the time set for the appointment, Yehoshua went to the Sursuq family home and stood in the shade of the nearby houses so that the watchman would not notice him and looked at the open-jawed lions. Then, precisely at eleven, he rang the bell. The gate was opened by a young guard in full uniform, wearing new shoes, and topped by a tarboosh, who reminded him of the young men opening the doors to guests at the hotels he had stayed in Constantinople.

The fountain in the courtyard no longer sprayed water, and the hall they entered no longer looked so big to him, since it was all piled up with furniture, the magnificence of the Sursuq family trade around the world. The old man was sitting among the furniture, sucking the hookah's mouthpiece, and not paying attention to those entering the room. Not far from him, sat a young man whose face was as smooth and round as a child's, and his chin looked as if it were attached to his chest. Owing to his heaviness, he did not rise, but he hinted to Yehoshua to sit on a pillow set before him, and then he ordered the boy to go out to call the servant to offer refreshments. Yehoshua sat down, his eyes running back and forth between the young fellow and the old man in the hope of catching the glance of the older gentleman and of finding some sign of recognition from him, but to no avail. The old man was frozen in place, and only the sounds of sucking attesting to his existence. He returned his look to the young man, and until the refreshments were offered, the matter had been concluded. Michel Sursuq was willing to sell Yehoshua Hankin nine thousand dunams of Fuleh land in the Jezreel Valley without witnesses to the signing and without an advance. Yehoshua was astonished at how everything had gone so smoothly and was afraid that something was not right here, but finally stammered, "Why did I deserve this?"

The younger man laughed and pointed to the old man — The silent one. "He made me swear to sell to you. He said it was an old debt he owed you. I don't know what his debt is, but I will do what he asked. I will wait a year, and by the end of that period, the sale must be executed. At the end of that time, all the money must be in my possession." He concluded and rose from his spot, indicating that the meeting was over.

Yehoshua got up and tried to go close to the old man, but the young man stopped him, "He's too old, and he's deaf, and his eyes are weak. It's better for you to leave quickly."

But Yehoshua could not restrain himself, and when he passed by the elderly man, he stopped for a moment opposite him and saw his eyes wandering from one spot on the wall and focusing on his face. He nodded to him and left there, knowing that the old man's eyes were accompanying him as he walked.

Summer, 1910

"Yehoshua, Yehoshua, Yehoshua ..."

Yehoshua didn't hear. He was standing next to the pole and helping a young man tie the boat to it, feeling how the rope was scratching his palms as he tried to battle the waves pushing the boat toward the open sea. He had stood precisely there two years earlier, and it seemed that nothing had changed since them. He was no longer young, and seemingly his ambition to restore himself had also weakened. For five months, he had worked in the store among women prattling about what was going on in Jaffa, and he wholeheartedly wanted to escape from them.

Whenever he could, he would leave the store to go down through the lanes to the dunes, and as he returned, he would pass by the frames of the houses growing out of the yellow sand and arranged around a leveled path, and this new residential neighborhood was called "Ahuzat Bayit." For five months, he had been trodding the same way and greeting people he met along the way, and they would respond with a hello to "the son of Sarah Hankin" or "husband of the midwife Olga Hankin." He did not want these bynames. With all his being, he wanted to go back to being called "land agent" and to be Yehoshua Hankin once again, but five months had passed since his return from Beirut with a deed for the Fuleh land, but there were no buyers.

The morning after he came back from Beirut, he went to the ICA office in Jaffa and tried to sell it the land. What didn't he say to convince them the band of officials, dressed in well-tailored suits, of the quality of the land? He praised it highly and sketched and showed them the possibilities for expanding the purchase and creating a large block of properties settled by Jews, but they rebuffed him, claiming the land was a swamp, and the company did not deal with land that required such heavy investment. Yehoshua mustered his courage and went to the home of the director of the Palestine Office and was crushed among a crowd. When he finally did sit opposite him, he did not know if the man was listening to him or understood. At least, he did not summarily dismiss him. At the end of their discussion, he sent him to another clerk to fill out forms and told him, "Go home, and we will discuss this. When we decide, we will answer you with a letter that will be brought by a messenger."

The messenger never came, so Yehoshua went to Galilee, to Sejera, to that same farm that had drawn Kalvarisky from Jaffa to Galilee and then sent him away from it—and he did not forgive the company's officials. Now, they had appointed Mania to be the farm's accountant while Israel worked in the dry crops and drove mules, so Yehoshua went to seek peace.

He quickly learned that the profession they had chosen for themselves was camouflage for other activities. At first, he was excited by their courage and the long nights around the campfire. After about a week, he noticed the dulling of senses that had engulfed them. A whole group, including irresponsible, reckless fellows along with laborers searching for their way in Palestine, had gathered around them, and the two had not noticed this. They shrugged their shoulders when he sought to take them away from the farm for a single day and bring them to see the Fuleh land. The land wasn't important at that moment; significant to them were only the revolution and change. He stayed with them a bit longer, but he could not help laughing at the jalabiya wrapped around them and the fantasy that alienated them from life in a vital, problem-filled land that demanded a different form of coping. Before he left, he tried to shake them free from their dream, but they didn't listen to him. They were so steeped in their new theory calling for linking the plow to the rifle and to solving difficulties in unpleasant ways rather than through lengthy negotiations. They spoke about labor and Jewish guarding, and inwardly, he mocked them—what would they guard? Where would they work? They had no land.

Yehoshua returned to Jaffa, still wondering about the girl Olga wanted to adopt and thinking about her so very strange path, and he found no peace for himself. He was sure he wouldn't meet her again and mourned his letting go of memory and experiences. Only when he saw the houses of the city drawing near did he manage to pull himself out of his sorrow. He decided to cope and wait for future developments and not escape into his imagination like those youths.

Now, he had been waiting for five months, and in the meantime, he had become steeped in work in the store and tried not to think nor to count the passing days. And he no longer mentioned the Fuleh land. Olga helped him with that. She did not speak about the land and spent a lot of time with him, cooked his meals, and told him some of the stories about the Palestine Office and the Palestine Land Development Company. One time she mentioned, while pouring steaming soup, that she had spoken about the Fuleh land with Dr. Ruppin, and he had promised to look into the matter. But when she saw her husband's impassive face, she realized that he did not want to grasp false hopes. Another time, late at night, when they hadn't fallen asleep and lay in bed awake, staring at the ceiling, she related that the Office was looking for land, so as to realize through it an old settlement idea—to build a cooperative there—and she had again mentioned his name and that of the land up for sale in the Jezreel Valley to the wife of a high official. This time a grin spread on his face, "Women understand one another. That's what you said when you went to meet Adelheid, the wife of Baron Rothschild." She tickled him and was happy to see the slight smile, but she knew he didn't take her words to heart.

Yehoshua didn't know that Olga considered the matter seriously. At every opportunity, she presented herself as "Olga, wife of Yehoshua Hankin, land agent." She intentionally encountered the wives of the Office officials. She sat and spoke about her husband—not about his 20-year exile within Palestine — but about the years when he had bought the Duran land and the Hadera land and had frequently journeyed to Constantinople and Beirut to meet with the wealthy people who owned the land and its assets.

Yehoshua …

Now, he heard the call, straightened his back, and gripped the rope, holding it fast so it should not slip from his hand and again slide into the turbid water and the boat disappear together with the pile of fabric rolls. He slowly turned toward the direction of the call and saw Olga running toward him, waving something she had in her hand.

This time, he didn't take his eyes off her. He waved to her with his free hand and hurried to tie the end of the rope to a peg stuck between the paving stones of the dock. He rushed toward her, astonished by her panic. The view of his wife running in his direction, her apron tucked into her belt, and the hem of her dress twisting around her curves elated him. To be sure, she was not a young woman, but her breasts were firm and her stomach flat since she hadn't given birth. Her shape hadn't thickened, and her body, the body of a mature woman, belonged only to him, and he hadn't had to share it with nursing babies.

"They want you," she called out as she approached him running. "They want to buy the Fuleh land, and not only it. They propose you to be the land agent in their company. You will be the Second Joshua," she added proudly, "Hankin, redeemer of the land."

Then they bumped into each other as they ran, and when she stopped, Yehoshua grabbed her by the waist and lifted her up, paying no mind to her weight, and twirled her round and round until they couldn't distinguish between the sky and the earth, between dancing sunspots and their smiling faces. Then, finally, when Yehoshua felt he was about to collapse, he stopped and put Olga down, while the world rotated around him. But Olga did not stop murmuring, "Yehoshua, Yehoshua," enjoying the enunciation of each letter separately and taking care to stress every letter of his name.

"Why were they waiting?" Yehoshua asked though she didn't know the real answer.

"They waited because they hadn't completely made up their minds," she finally said. "They did not know how to define the function of the office or the role of the company."

"The land is toying with me," he uttered skeptically, "Sometimes lifting me up and sometimes lowering me to the deepest netherworld."

And Olga, who saw his fears, put her hand out to take hold of him and encourage him. "The land won't best you again. I won't allow it."

He smiled at her, and he went on walking with her until the port dock and sat down in the shade of a pole to which people tied up boats. Piles of ropes and nets hid them from the eyes of the merchants and laborers running about the wharf. Olga leaned her back against the pole, while Yehoshua put his head on her shoulder and blinked his eyes owing to the strong light, but his eyes filled with tears, and he could not hold them back, sobbing the cry of years of silence and long exile. "Maniac," they called after him; "little speculator," they dubbed him, and all those years, he had not given in to his fate, nor had he rebelled against it.

The two sat that way, totally wrapped up in themselves and belonging only to each other, no one capable of interfering or bothering them. The weeping subsided slowly into only a strangled wail, and when he calmed down, Olga took her hand off his shoulder and took an envelope out of her apron pocket and gave it to Yehoshua. He straightened the piece of paper and couldn't take his eyes off the header at the top of the page: "The Palestine Land Development Company."

Yehoshua read quietly, then he read it a second time, but aloud, and when he finished, he rose and pulled his wife behind him, so that both stood facing the sea. Suddenly, Yehoshua could restrain himself no longer and called out toward the water, in a trembling voice, "Yehoshua Hankin!" Then he yelled once again in a steady, firm voice, "Yehoshua Hankin, land agent in Palestine Land Development Company!" He turned to face his wife, smiled, and prodded her, "Nu, how does that sound?"

"Too long," she laughed at him and pressed his hand. "For me, Jashiya and the Second Joshua are enough." He hugged her and drew her to him, whispering in his ear, "Dyevka, my Dyevka." She felt that his voice carried a plea and a call for forgiveness. Olga only embraced him without uttering a word, hoping that better times were in store for them. However, she knew that he was starting out on a new, obstacle-laden path, and she was aware she would still experience loneliness in their room in Ajami while her husband was roving among the hills seeking land. She had already lived half her life, and she was no longer jealous of the land and did not consider it a competitor. The corners of her mouth turned up in a smile, and Yehoshua saw and was surprised, but she did not return his astonishment.

Bursa, 1915

Night fell. The four exiles were still sitting in the jail courtyard, waiting for policemen to come to take them to their new prison. Now, they added them to a group and no longer kept a close eye on them. Yehoshua differed from the other three in the small group. The Bursa exile did not frighten him, since he was used to exiles, and the Turkish exile did not seem so bad to him. But unlike him, the others feared the distance of the prison from Palestine and worried about the threat of war. Mania stayed close to Olga and tried to doze, with her head on her friend's shoulder—gray hair mingling with brown, a broad face touching sharp cheekbones. The length of the trip had brought the two closer and closed the ten-year gap, and it seemed as if the alienation that had engulfed Israel and Mania Shochat during their stay in Galilee had been effaced. On the entire journey, none of them mentioned Sejera or the idea of the *shomrim*, and whatever was not common to the four of them was not a topic for discussion.

The quartet had actually met from time to time before the war, but the connection between them had been merely coincidental. Yehoshua had been sent to Galilee on behalf of the Palestine Land Development Company to examine land in the region, but he did not go to meet the couple and sufficed with rumors telling of the organizing of *Hashomer*, and if he was asked in Jaffa about what was true and what was false in the stories, he would answer, "All of this is none of my business." But, on the other hand, if someone should happen to mention the closeness of Israel and Mania to Olga and Yehoshua many years ago, Yehoshua would nod and say, "That was a long time ago."

When Mania was about to give birth to her first child, her daughter, she called Olga to come to help her with the delivery. Olga did go but returned from there in shock—she gave birth like a Bedouin on a straw mat, and Olga wrapped the newborn in scraps of cloth, because that is what she found there. Mania's breasts were shrunken, and she refused to nurse the child, while Israel, who was staying somewhere among the hills, did not even know that his daughter had been born. For Olga, this was the only time she saw her until their joint arrest, but she did speak about her again when Lolik died.

Israel Feinberg died, and Olga spent time with her sister Fanny to console her. The sisters spoke about Avshalom, and Fanny complained that her son had been captivated by eccentrics and called for opposing the Turkish regime. She wondered if the arguments between her husband and her son had hastened Lolik's death.

Olga was angry with her sister and tried to change her mind, but Fanny stood her ground, linking Mania's influence on Avshalom with Lolik's passing.

She reinforced Mania's guilt when she mentioned the wedding of their daughter, Shoshana, to Mania's brother, Nahum Wilbushevich, five years before Lolik's death. The family ties between the Feinberg family, and the Wilbushevich and Shochat families further strengthened Fanny's concerns about the impact of Mania and Israel Shochat on their son. Olga insisted that the paths of Avshalom and Lolik were different, but they had a similar nature: quick to anger, a love of wandering, and swept away by new ideas. Avshalom was not a Shomer; he wanted to create a different revolution—to bring the British closer to Palestine and, with their help, to achieve redemption. But Fanny did not differentiate between the ideas and did not change her mind.

Yehoshua didn't feel his eyes closing but suddenly woke up to the sound of screams. The courtyard was filled with mules harnessed to wagons and the smell of animal droppings mixed with that of hay and chaff. He felt the dampness seep into his bones and saw the fear in Olga's eyes, along with the wrinkles forming at the corners of her mouth. The gendarme already stood over them, yelling, and he kicked Israel Shochat, who didn't understand what they wanted from him. It took a while until Yehoshua realized that now they had come to take them from Adana to Bursa, and they had to get up and climb onto the carts. He rose slowly, straightened his knees, and heard his bones popping; then, he approached the guard and tried to stop him from beating the detainees.

The gendarme was pleased to meet someone who understood his language and was willing to grace him with a dressing down, unloading all of his anger on his listener about the task he had been given to accompany the prisoners to Bursa.

The four got into the wagons, whose opening had been covered with thick material and fastened from outside, but through the slits that remained, it was possible to see the crowded streets of the bustling city. Olga clung to her husband; "A long exile," she said to him, "if only it would be shortened."

"Why should it be shortened? Our being together is good, "he smiled at her in jest.

She grinned and replied in the same tone, "We are old, and your shopping list is long."

He stroked her hair and hid a white strand among the dark ones. "Of course, we are old, but our love is young," he said, and what are my 50 years and your

63? They don't even come to 120." But she whispered to him sadly, "Old, and old love. It's with us 30 years and certainly is already tired of us."

"Perhaps, it has had enough of us, but we have not had enough of it," he said, knowing that his words offered no comfort, so he looked for a way to change the subject.

"Let the exile be shortened," he declared, with the noise of the wheels swallowing his words. He put his mouth near her ear and added, "I will buy a lot of land and build houses, and on one of them, I will hang a sign, 'Hankin House,' and on the other 'Olga's House,'" and it will be a summer home, standing on the dunes near the sea."

"Dreamer! You are just a vision, and the exile is long and Bursa far away," she finally gave into him and could not stop laughing.

Mania and Israel cast them wondering looks as if trying to be part of their joke, but Olga and Yehoshua paid no attention to them.

"I have changed," Yehoshua told his wife. "No one will dare to call me 'maniac.' The entire country recognizes my image and knows about the long-haired, bearded agent, and some young people want to look like me and grow their hair long like I do."

He was quiet for a moment, and scrunched up his forehead as if wishing to arrange his thoughts, so she finished his statement for him, "You were different after the letter. I know."

"Of course, Ruppin's letter changed the course of my life," he agreed with her. Then, he looked at her and noticed the smile hiding in her dancing eyes and added, "You are the one who spoke to Ruppin about the Fuleh land and reminded him about the delayed answer. You went and spoke about me at every meeting and talked about the wonderful deeds I performed in the past. Things changed because of you and not because of fate. Everything was the act of a woman."

She put her fingers on his mouth and refused to hear more.

Indeed, after the letter reached Yehoshua, the Palestine Land Development Company stood by its word and bought the Fuleh land from Michel Sursuq with Yehoshua Hankin as the intermediary and established on it an experimental cooperative. The entire Yishuv was watching to see the result of the experiment. "If it succeeds," the hacks said, "We'll settle all the lands of Jews in Palestine with cooperatives." Since Yehoshua's name appeared on the list of dignitaries involved in the work of the cooperatives, it was again impossible to forget him. Above the door of the house in the Ajamai neighborhood, they hung a copper sign, similar to the sign that had been over Yehuda Leib's store but bigger. Alongside the words "Agent for Land Matters," they also wrote, "The Palestine Land Development Company."

Yehoshua became more moderate. Not once or twice, Olga told him, "You changed!"

Only family members noticed the change that had taken place in him. The others did not know a different Yehoshua. Twenty years had erased his past and sent memories of his previous deeds into oblivion.

"The time has come to toe the line," he would whisper to Olga, "to be like average Joe."

"It is high time," she agreed with him. "You're close to 50, and the end is not so far off."

"I won't have enough time," he voiced his fear.

She would repeat, "You most certainly will. You are unique, the Second Joshua."

🙣

The wagon left the city and turned northward. Sitting hunched over in the wagon had cramped muscles, and drowsiness attacked the riders. Fears of exile in Sivas were replaced by lack of knowledge about the nature of exile in Bursa, but the four understood how much better lack of knowledge was than certain death in a plague, yet it still made the long trip difficult, like a war whose end is not in sight.

At the end of another week, the four were taken down from the carts and housed in a stable together with the mules, breathing in the sour smell of the animal residue and sneezing from contact with straw. Olga played with the idea of lying down on the hay, and if it were not for the guard stationed at the entrance to keep an eye on them, her happiness would have been complete. But, instead, Olga pushed her body toward Yehoshua, and he caressed her face and removed stalks of straw from her hair. In those moments, she seemed like a young girl to him, forgetting the weightiness of age and mounding a sheaf for the two of them to put their heads down on.

"Woman-child," he said to her, "and once I promised you that I would be a son to you, the son you did not give birth to."

"You weren't a son," she laughed, "but a husband who alternately pulled far away and came ner." Then, she rushed to continue trying to soften what she had just said, "The Fuleh land was the start of success, presenting an opportunity to you and to me as well. It did not come easily, nor did it smoothly do away with the pain of years."

And she was right. For a long time, she found it difficult to believe in success, and the 20 years rested on her like a heavy yoke.

Olga was already asleep, but he stayed awake, remembering in his mind's eye his trip to Beirut with Ruppin; he enjoyed the memory and let it banish the troubles of the jail and the terror of the unknown.

Speculator and Redeemer

Yehoshua and Dr. Ruppin were quite different from each other — One always went about dressed in a pressed suit, tie, and hat; while the other's beard was wild, his coat old, and his hat tattered at the edges. But actions brought them together. On many an occasion, Yehoshua laughed when talking about his first venture to Ruppin's office and how he circumvented the building and did not dare to enter. The story of their joint journey was a humorous one that underwent many changes as people told one another; the two heard what others were saying but just smiled, saving the truth for themselves, since the story of the trip was the first event that brought them close to one another and turned them into friends.

The kaymakam, the head of Turkish rule in Nazareth, refused to authorize the transfer of the Fuleh land to the name of the representatives of the Palestine Land Development Company. Yehoshua spent a long time sitting with him, trying to convince him with sweet talk and gold coins that he gave him under the table. Nothing helped. The governor showed letters and telegrams between him and the government in Beirut and Constantinople forbidding the transfer of the land because of its proximity to the Heijaz railway.

"It is intended neither for *fellahin* nor for Jews," argued the governor. "Only Turks will settle on it." Yehoshua showed the authorized kushan he had and the signed agreement between him and the Sursuq family, but the man was not convinced. For some reason, he harassed Yehoshua and tried to create difficulties and cause him to fail. Maybe because he was not respectfully presentable, thought Yehoshua, and he went to the Palestine Office to meet Ruppin. For Yehoshua, this was the first time since the day he had been hired by the Company that he went to meet the director. He had no choice, since he had to find people more impressive than he in their appearance and in the way they spoke, who would go instead of him to conduct negotiations. At the entrance to the office, he stood and saw the back of the official wearing a well-tailored suit and was embarrassed by his own look. Finally, he cleared his throat, and the man turned to face him, his eyes greeting Yehoshua's eyes. The look in the man's eyes did not match Yehoshua's impression of him. These were portals expressing understanding and consideration, as well as encouraging his interlocutor to express what he felt. Ruppin invited his guest to sit, and from that minute, a friendship developed between the two.

As had been the case with Tyomkin, this time too, the connection had been made through Olga, but from the moment it formed, Olga was no longer part of it, only an observer on the side blessing their closeness. Yehoshua thought about this many times and wondered about his weakness in not daring to be the first to forge a link with others, while she, the woman, made up for his shortcomings, one by one.

Ruppin agreed to travel with Yehoshua to Sidon to convince the governor living there that the Turks would suffer no security damage if Jews would settle the Fuleh land.

"I will come with my mats," laughed Ruppin, "and you will bring your knowledge of Ottoman law. I will ride with you, and you will show me the beauty of the Hermon area and release me for a short while from my office tasks and dealing with paperwork and dry decisions."

The other officials in the office were not enthusiastic about the idea of Dr. Ruppin's trip, and they were particularly not avid about the idea of his riding along with the new land agent.

"You're too dignified to ride with him," they told him. "Stories abound from the distant past about your escort, and they are not nice to hear. Besides, the office can afford to let itself rent a carriage and car."

Ruppin laughed at their fears and did not believe any bad word said about Yehoshua. He was so eager to ride that he almost forgot about the purpose of the journey.

The two set out one wintry morning. Strong winds blew, and heavy rain beat at their faces. The doctor wasn't used to long rides. At first, he did not complain and rode alongside Yehoshua, hiding his face in a white scarf so that his companion would not hear his serious breathing difficulties. But after three days, next to the bridge spanning the thrashing waters of the Jordan and leading to the huge swamp in the Huleh Valley, he could not continue riding. His body was racked by chills and the reins kept falling out of his hands until Yehoshua had to tie his horse to Ruppin's and bind Ruppin to the saddle so he would not fall. The agent did not let the man fall asleep lest he faint, and he heard him hallucinating in German. He replied to him, even though he did not understand a word, so the man would hear his voice and go on talking. Finally, the two could make out the houses of the tiny colony of Yesud ha-Ma'alah. This was a colony with only a few houses and two dirt roads crossing it, but at that point, the settlement looked to Yehoshua like a luxurious royal courtyard.

They put Ruppin to bed in the house of one of the farmers, and Yehoshua went out to look for a local doctor. He did not find a Jewish physician, but he did bring an old sheikh, who lived in the tents of the swamp and understood winter fever. The man gave Ruppin a tonic made of plants and sat, praying in his language; he put a mouse's tail under the pillow. At midnight on the second day, Ruppin opened his eyes and smiled. The two remained in the settlement a few more days, until Ruppin gathered strength and was ready to continue riding. Before they were ready to get underway, Ruppin put the mouse tail in his pocket against the Evil Eye and tried to mount the horse, but he failed because his legs were weak and did not obey him. Yehoshua saw this and was sorry he had not taken the advice of the clerks to rent a carriage and car, but the colony had neither a wagon nor a wagon driver to take them. Yehoshua decided to abandon the whole idea and to leave Ruppin behind so he could go on alone, but the director would not let him do that.

"Without you, I will not stay," he croaked. "I am not willing to forgo seeing you conduct negotiations in Arabic." Then he asked for Yehoshua's help and mounted his horse. The two rode slowly and frequently stopped at water stations along the Jordan River to dip their faces in the cold waters that froze their fingertips but cooled their bodies from the sweat that had accumulated. At Tibnin, they bought a wagon and for a few girsh hired a lad to accompany them and keep watch over the doctor as their craft swayed on the journey while Yehoshua served as the driver. They traveled a long way, and the wagon sank in the mud since the narrow paths intended for a single horse were not fit for it. To make Ruppin forget the travails of the journey, the young man began to teach him Arabic and Turkish. First, he showed him the surrounding landscape and then taught him the names of the various object they saw. Next, he strung the words into sentences, and Ruppin repeated them after him. His heavy German accent amused Yehoshua, but he was happy with the lad's company, and the way was covered easily.

In Sidon, they did not find the governor, who had gone to Beirut two days earlier, and they, after all, had been delayed on the way. The money in Yehoshua's pocket dwindled, but he did not want to appear helpless to Ruppin. He left Ruppin with the young fellow and went to a moneylender who knew him from his first attempts to buy *the Valley* land. The businessman recognized him and gave him a few coins that would be enough to hire fresh mules for the wagon. The lad agreed to accompany them to Beirut—by now, he already called Ruppin Arthur, without adding *hawaja*.

Ruppin's knowledge of Arabic improved a bit, and the more he advanced, so did his mood. But the more they traveled northward, the winds grew stronger, and the temperatures dropped; once again, Yehoshua was worried about the director's health.

After a journey of four days, the group reached Beirut. Even though the mules moved slowly, Ruppin became very weak, and Yehoshua hurried to find a hotel where he could stay until he recuperated. All of his plans to meet with the governor together with the distinguished doctor—the one impressive in appearance and eloquence, the other well-versed in land issues and all facets of the law and registration—evaporated. Now, he needed other ways to convince the Turkish governor of the validity of the transfer of the land from the ownership of the Sursuq family to that of the representatives of the Jewish company. When standing at the gate to the governor's house in Beirut, Yehoshua planned what he would say and hoped the governor would understand that the Jews were capable of making the land of the Empire blossom and that traitors were not among them. Just then, while waiting for someone to open the gate, for some reason he remembered Avshalom, who was roaming among the capital cities of Europe, gaining expertise in foreign languages but finding no serenity. On a few occasions, he had heard him call to exploit the times of unrest throughout the Ottoman Empire and to rebel against the Turks. Yehoshua still considered him a child who needed guidance and wondered to himself what Avshalom would say if he could see him standing at the entrance to the governor's house to conduct negotiations with him about Palestine land.

When the gate was finally opened, he let his fleeting thoughts go and followed the guard, who put him in the foyer and did not allow him to enter until the governor would agree to see him. Like a beggar asking for a handout, he waited there for a long time, but the governor refused, and neither his name nor that of Ruppin nor the titles of each helped him. And again, Avshalom came to mind—but maybe the young man was on the right path? He tried to banish these difficult thoughts and returned humiliated to the hotel. Ruppin tried to take the blame: had he himself gone, maybe …; They discussed what to do and decided to write a letter. The letter was sent, and a few days later, they received a reply, which was replete with polite phrases and greetings along with praise for the builders of the Turkish Empire and for the workers within its bounds, improving its land, while in the margins of the page one line had been added: "Jews living in proximity to the railway present a security danger to the peace of the Empire, and for that reason, no negotiations can be conducted about land near the railway crossing in the Jezreel Valley."

Ruppin read the response and became depressed; he lost all interest in going on, and he had already announced that he would forget the matter of the Fuleh land and was ready to send Yehoshua to look for other property. But Yehoshua was not willing to give up—not now when he was on the brink of great success. So, he decided to write a letter on his own and provide details, not all of which he knew to be correct. Still, since he was familiar with the Turkish officials' way of thinking, he wrote them down. He hoped for the best, "The land next to the railway is intended solely for settlement by Jews who are Ottoman citizens faithful to the rulers in Constantinople. The form of settlement is still being tested, but if this trial should succeed, it will be possible to apply it to many settlements, and the Ottoman Empire will be strengthened and also flourish and gain from this."

A day later, he received a reply; this time, it was short and to the point: "The *fellahin* in *the Valley* say that the Jews intend to build on the site a fortress that will control the road and the railway, and the authorities believe what they are saying. They have lived in *the Valley* for decades, working the land of the Sursuq family and being loyal to the Turkish regime, while the Jews have as yet to step in its mud, not even a footprint, so that the land will remain in Ottoman possession."

Now, Yehoshua didn't know what else he could do and was even afraid to show the reply to Ruppin, but Ruppin could tell from the expression on his face that their mission had failed. His illness grew more intense; the ague struck him again. Palestine was far away, and Yehoshua was helpless. When, after two days, the fever had declined, Yehoshua went and knocked on the door of the Sursuq family. The young man opening the door was a new one, but his uniform was exactly like the one worn by the previous lad. Yehoshua nudged him a bit to pass by and not tarry at the gateway, but the fellow held his hands up. Yehoshua was sorry for his rashness and apologized. Then, he went out to the entrance to stand next to the two mute stone lions. Only after a long while, when the sun was about to set, was Yehoshua called to come in.

He did not see the elderly father, but was received by Michel Sursuq, who was sitting in the room crowded with furniture, waiting for his entrance. Yehoshua was sure he would wave the sales agreement and remind him that the period of a year that he had been allotted was about to end. But the man did not budge from his pillow nor bat an eyelash; he did not even motion to Yehoshua to sit beside him. He realized that the ceremonial precepts were of no interest to the younger son of the Sursuq line, so he immediately opened his mouth and told him about the obstacles being mounted against him and about the Palestine Land Development Company. "Please," he asked, "write to the governor. He will certainly listen to you more than to me."

"I will write," replied his host, "more than I need the governor, he needs me. But, in the meantime, bring the ill doctor accompanying you to my house, and he will be cared for properly, and his recovery will be seen to."

Yehoshua did not understand the reason for this about-face in Michel Sursuq's attitude toward him, and only later on did he find out just how much the man needed money to pay his gambling debts.

For seventeen days, Ruppin and Yehoshua waited for an invitation to the governor's house. Meanwhile, Ruppin gained strength, and the two of them began going out to walk among the crowded streets of the Old City and riding in a carriage to the suburbs spreading on the hills; they spent quite a time on the narrow seashore and asked the fisherman about their trade. They could have continued like this for much longer, but on the seventeenth day, the young Sursuq came into their room holding the authorization of the transfer of the land to the Jews, the representatives of the Palestine Land Development Company.

They both bombarded him with questions and forgot all the niceties of good manners, and the owner of the land became self-important and put his hands on his waist and leisurely told them how he had managed to get the document from the governor. He threatened that he would gather all the sharecroppers working the Fuleh land and the other family properties: in the large valley and the Jidru land and in Galilee, and forbid them to pay the Turkish government, as customary, one-fifth of their crop. The governor was actually frightened a bit because he needed the sharecropper's money, but on second thought, he replied to Sursuq that if the peasants would not pay the tax of the one-fifth, he would take double from the other landowners, and they would be sure to come and yell and bang on the doors of the Sursuq family. The landowner realized that the threat was not severe enough. So a day later, he returned to the governor and waved a pouch full of coins before him until the governor's eyes were whirling in their sockets, and he authorized the transfer of the land with no argument.

Yehoshua and Ruppin stayed two days longer and then returned from there in the Sursuq family wagon. Their entrance into Jaffa about 10 days later, in the light of day and in a luxurious carriage pulled by two mighty horses, stirred the interest of everyone in the city. The story of the Fuleh land sale made the round in the city among the officials, clerks, and simple folk for many days, and enhanced the connection between Yehoshua and Ruppin.

Second Exile

Yehoshua felt tired and wanted to fall asleep, but lying among the piles of straw was uncomfortable, and his arm, the one Olga was leaning on, had fallen asleep. He moved his hand, and Olga woke up.

"What are you thinking about?" she asked as she opened her eyes.

"I was steeped in memories," he replied.

She laughed, still half-dozing, and said, "Let me guess. You reminded yourself about the Fuleh land, and you going with Ruppin to Beirut."

"You read my thoughts, too," he noted, surprised at the precise guess. But Olga simply said, "After so many years, you can't be unreadable to me. Your luck is that you only think only of the ten thousand dunam that belong to the Fuleh land," she added, "and you are not thinking now of the other twenty thousand that abut it, or about the Shunem land that also belongs to the big valley, or about the tract of the Nuris lands that touches upon the Bet Shean Valley. For if that were not so, I would never finish thinking. My luck is that you are preoccupied with me and that I am no longer frightened by thousands of dunam of land." She completed her statement, turned on her side, and closed her eyes.

Yehoshua was still awake and still wondering about the numerous land acquisitions that he had begun before the war—until it had come and cut off negotiations. He thought about the change in his status since the purchase of the Fuleh land and the establishment of the cooperative at Merhavya. The rich Jews of the world turned to him; even the Rothschild family needed him and had forgiven him for the rebellion in Rishon Lezion and forgotten the nickname "Revolutionary" that had been added to his name. For a moment, Yehoshua was sad about the war that had prevented him from making the large deal in the Jezreel Valley so that he could not put into action the plan to plant thousands of dunam of sugar cane, but then he consoled himself — War by its nature comes to an end, he thought, but the quality of the land remains.

The exile grew longer. The four prisoners were placed together in an exiles' camp in Bursa with others banished from Palestine; some were acquaintances, others not. During the first year, little was found to occupy them in whiling away their imprisonment. They divided the small amount of money they had brought with them into three: one part for basic necessities; another part to use as bribes; a third for buying extras. The extras were thread and material and paper and ink. Using the thread, Olga tried to teach Mania tatting, but she soon realized that Mania's hands were not meant for any kind of embroidery and that it was better for her to join Yehoshua and spend her money on sheets of paper. Both of them had musings and plans, and they quickly filled the pages that soon became a large pile. Of the four of them, only Israel could not find a niche for himself. He did not touch his money and preferred to sit in the corner of the room and mumble, to the point that everyone thought he was going crazy.

A few months later, the money had run out, and in the small room, complaints began to be heard about hunger and cold. But just then, to their good fortune, the Turkish authorities needed to survey the lands in Palestine to map the area of the dunes and to examine possibilities for economic development, and Yehoshua came to mind.

At an early morning hour, knocking was heard at the door, and Mania, who woke up first, opened it. A policeman stood at the entrance holding a form, and two soldiers accompanied him. Initially, Mania was taken aback in horror, since she was sure they had come to take her. But the gendarme hurried to explain that he had come to take Hawaja Hankin to Talaat Pasha, the Turkish minister of the interior.

Neither Yehoshua nor the other three knew why he was being called to the minister. Olga was sure they would separate them now, and she would not see her husband for a long time. So, she rushed to hug him and did not notice the grin spreading on the policeman's face. Yehoshua did notice it but did not understand it. He tried to get him to talk, but the man did not answer, only urging the prisoner to hurry and not to take unnecessary items. Yehoshua put on his tattered coat, took of few of his papers, and said goodbye to the room's residents.

"Don't worry," he tossed out in Russian. "If they don't want me to take all my things, they intend to bring me back safe and sound after a short time."

Yehoshua returned in the evening to the surprise of the room's occupants. Olga burrowed into his neck and kissed every inch of available skin, wetting him with her tears until he was embarrassed in front of Mania and Israel. He took her hands off him, reproaching her, saying, "It is not proper to act that way at our age."

But Olga paid no attention to him. "It is oh so proper," she replied and embraced him again for a minute.

Half the night, Yehoshua told the story of his visit to the minister, and even Israel broke his silence and sat near Yehoshua, swallowing every word he heard.

They had taken him in an open carriage and sat him next to guards, a policemen on each side of him; that was how they traveled on the outskirts of

Bursa. From time to time, the wagon halted, and the driver would get off and buy everything he needed; he shared a bit with the guards and hid the rest under the prisoner's seat. After a long ride, they stopped at the Turkish administration center, and with dignity and splendor, they had led Yehoshua to the reception office.

"I felt like a condemned man being led to the gallows for whom they were fulfilling his final wish," he related. "In my rosiest dreams, I had never imagined seeing such wealth in the administration center of a provincial town."

A high-ranking official received Yehoshua, or so it seemed, because as soon as he came in, the guards stayed behind, and Yehoshua remained alone in the room. A royal feast was offered to the guest, and between sipping wine and puffing on the nargila, the minister entered, too, and told him of the Turkish plans to settle the breadth and width of the Empire, letting Yehoshua feel like the war was very far from there. The discussion was friendly and very polite, and they both spoke in a roundabout way, as customary among Oriental nations. Only a few moments before Yehoshua left, the demands of the high official became clear to him—to advise the clerks in his office on how to write plans and which calculations were necessary. Likewise, he had learned that he would have to travel to Constantinople to meet the Turkish minister and his advisors once a month. When Yehoshua climbed into the railway car, soldiers no longer sat on each side of him, but behind him. Out of respect, they were careful not to insult him and not to say an impertinent word, lest this should be reported to the high official.

From that day on, the lives of the captives changed. Once a month, a wagon halted next to the house and took Yehoshua to the train station, and from there, he would proceed to the capital, Constantinople. Very soon, he was no longer accompanied by the policeman, and it was enough to have a low-level clerk who went and returned with him three days later. All the other days of the month, the four of them dealt with the trip, the scenes along the way, and the stories Yehoshua brought about the war and its development. In Bursa, they did not feel the vicissitudes of the war, and life went on as usual. Except for the decline in the number of men in the streets and the rationing of a few basic items, the events of the war were simply rumors. In Constantinople, however, the war was more palpable, and Yehoshua's stories were not at all happy ones.

Yet, Yehoshua's standing hadn't changed at all. The minister became closer to him. He considered him an expert on settlement matters and sought ways to make his few days outside of Bursa as pleasant as possible. Once, Yehoshua dared to bring up a proposal to him to give the Jews a district so that they could settle it and create Jewish autonomy, and the minister didn't even get angry but only excused himself from giving a clear answer, "It's too early to talk about that. We'll meet after the war."

Yehoshua did not raise the plan again, but did put it on paper— that one, and many other programs— and added them to the pile on the table, until it was overflowing with them. Olga decided to buy a used crate and fill it with the pages of Yehoshua's plans. In those years, Olga enjoyed his being close to her and his staying with her. As she saw it, the jail in Bursa was not a period after a fall but rather a long rest for a great man on whom others were dependent, listening to him and accepting of his advice.

The second year passed, and Mania, more than the others, was disgusted with their captivity and began talking about escape. First, she told them about her flight from Petersburg and compared it to possibilities for fleeing by herself, and then more boldly, she began to talk about a joint escape. This talk had a good influence on Israel. His mumbling ceased, and he began taking part in the discussions, since he knew best of all of them how to hide and how to steal across a border.

Yehoshua and Olga tried to prevent Mania from taking any hasty step, but she only laughed at their fears and gave a terse reply, "I have done this more than once, and I always succeeded." Then, when she saw that the two were not cooperating with her, Mania became closer to her husband and whispered secrets to him, the young couple drawing away from the older one full of hesitation.

At the time of the lighting of the last Hanukkah candle in December 1916, Mania and Israel reached a decision and turned to Yehoshua to influence him to participate in their venture. However, they only asked him to help them pass a letter to Avshalom Feinberg during one of his trips to Constantinople. To the surprised Olga, they explained that the boy was helping the agronomist Aharon Aaronsohn in his battle against the locusts. When Olga asked what the connection was between the boy working with the agronomist and the escape, Mania laughed at the woman's lack of practical awareness, whose entire world consisted of her husband and who did not see what was going on around her. Olga was hurt by her unfounded comment and turned her back on her. Mania realized she had gone too far, so she approached her and tapped her on the shoulder in remorse.

"Jamal Pasha has appointed Aaron Aaronsohn as chief supervisor of the locust survey," she explained, "and because of that important job, he and Avshalom can ride between Constantinople and Damascus and between Cairo and Haifa. This is excellent camouflage for attempts to study where the concentrations of the Turkish army are located and how much weaponry there is as well as the number of vehicles and soldiers," she said, delicately adding, so as to not hurt her, "This is not new. You've certainly heard about the closeness between Avshalom and Aaron and his many trips to Egypt."

Olga, of course, did know about Avshalom's actions and his relationship with Aaron, but she had not expected to hear Mania speak with such defiance to justify his act, mainly not to speak openly about the spying by the two of them.

"And Fanny?" she asked. "Has anyone thought about what's going on with Fanny?"

"Fanny has no say in this," Yehoshua rubbed his wife's back, "Avshalom is no longer a child, and he does what he wants in line with what he thinks."

"He can be deterred," she spouted angrily. "His father is gone. His sister Tzila is an adolescent and cannot be relied on for support yet."

Israel, who, to this point, had not been involved, thundered, "No one was talking about Fanny. The letter does not concern her, but only Avshalom. Why mention unnecessary emotionality?"

His voice brought Olga back to their captivity. She missed Fanny so much and the little Avshalom and the other times when all of them would gather in the room above the store in Jaffa. She stayed out of the discussion, while Yehoshua wrote the letter and readied a coin to bribe the guard. On his next trip to Constantinople, the letter was sent.

A month went by, and behind Yehoshua's desk, work began on opening a breach. The four scraped the wall and collected the pieces of stone and dust, hiding them in their pockets. Whenever anyone went out to the lavatory, they would use the opportunity to empty their pockets.

The four usually dug when the guards were dozing, so their activities did not garner attention. They would divide into groups late at night: one would dig, another collected the dust, and two stood near the door and the window to watch for anyone outsider coming close to the building. Israel preferred to dig, and the others were happy to let him do it. The ineptness he had shown during the long days of imprisonment disappeared, and he returned to himself. Now, he spoke with Mania as if two others were not sharing the room with them.

Yehoshua and Olga did help, but they were not partners in the escape plan. They sincerely believed that the war would end, and they would be released and returned to the places from which they had come. At night, Olga would whisper to Yehoshua about how far the other two had distanced themselves from her, while he would murmur into her ears words of consolation, as he attributed the situation to their youthfulness. He did not believe the escape plan would succeed, but he was unable to stop them from what they were doing.

The week before Passover, the digging was finished, and the escape scheme was almost complete. Now, Israel turned silent and spent most of the daytime sitting near the desk, listening to what was going on outside the walls. Late one day, gentle knocking was heard on the wall. Yehoshua jumped up from his mat and wanted to light the oil lamp, but he saw Israel's silhouette leaning over him and signaling him not to move a muscle. The rapping continued, and Israel put his ear to the wall. Then silence reigned, and Yehoshua saw Israel drawing himself straight, standing up, and going back to bed without saying a word.

The next morning, Israel addressed Mania during breakfast. "We'll set a time," he told her. "The day after the seder." Mania sat in her place, keeping still, and the hand holding the spoon trembled. Israel saw her excitement and tried to calm her. "Yehoshua's visit to Constantinople will be moved up, and he won't travel in two weeks but immediately after the seder instead. A new wagon driver will come to take him from the room, and he will even choose a different route for driving to the station. Two guards, also new ones, will accompany the driver."

There were many details, and Israel drilled them into them so they would be etched in their memories. Yehoshua could not understand when this campaign was hatched, how the connections were made, or if all this was done because of the letter sent to Avshalom. He did not ask Israel anything, nor did Olga utter a word about this, but her eyes revealed her fears, when she understood that the escape of Mania and Israel was going to take place and that she and Yehoshua were part of the plan.

"The wagon will go toward the Bursa meat market," he said again. "Between the lanes, the driver will stop, because of overcrowding, as it were, and Yehoshua will ask to get off, so as to loosen his muscles that had cramped because of the ride. He will hurry to go behind one of the meat stores with the sign hanging, 'Fuad's Lamb.' He will stay there only a few minutes, and then they will come to take him. Someone will provide a keffiyeh and long jalibiyeh to cover his student's jacket and his long hair that stands out at a distance."

Yehoshua burst out laughing, and for a bit, the tension in the room melted. "Bursa is full of eccentrics, and no one tells them apart. A person could die on the street, and no one would approach him. A fight could break out between two people, and nobody would get involved, and you're asking me to hide my hair in a kefiyyeh and cover my tattered coat with a jalibiyeh!"

But Israel ignored what he was saying and went on with his idea. "At the same time, the two women and I will break out through the excavated space. Outside, our own Turkish guard will be waiting and take care of Turkish women's clothing and load us onto a covered wagon. The wagon will leave the city going west to the Aegean Sea, where a boat, in which Yehoshua will already be sitting, will be waiting for us."

That night the four of them did not sleep. Instead, Olga and Mania sat in one corner and talked, so as to repel their anxiety, and in another corner sat Israel and Yehoshua, trying to complete unfinished details and speaking anxiously about the uncertain plan.

"Avshalom will be waiting for us next to the boat with a letter from Morgenthau in his pocket authorizing our right to unimpeded movement throughout the empire," Israel explained. "The English are planning to reach Beersheba, and in Egypt, they are preparing camel and mule battalions. We will reach the Egyptian coast in the boat, and from there, we will find a way to enter Palestine without the Turkish soldiers noticing us."

"And under what guise is Avshalom entering Turkey?" Yehoshua remembered to ask.

"He is, of course, an informant in the British army, but the Turks do not know that, and he goes about freely all over the desert and among the offices of the high Turkish administration and reports about the distribution of the locust." Israel spoke in jest, but Yehoshua did not hear the mockery. He was too worried about Avshalom. To be sure, he did not like the Turkish rule, but he also did not trust the new governing of Palestine by a distant country.

The Passover Seder they held was rushed. The guards had provided matzot and wine in exchange for a few coins; they improvised all the rest, even though they left most of the meal for the guards.

They did not sleep a wink that night. In the morning, Yehoshua put on two pairs of pants in whose pockets he hid plans and pages, not to leave them behind. Over his student's coat, he wore a wide coat whose lining Olga had unraveled and then placed a few coins in the space; Yehoshua stuffed more pages in there, too.

Before he left the hut, the place of their imprisonment, Yehoshua kissed Olga, feeling sorry that she was not going with him. "If I could, I would show you the streets of Constantinople and tell you the history of each and every building in the city," he mumbled, holding her face in his hands.

It was a sunny day in early spring. The guards joked with Yehoshua and let him taste some of the dried fruit filling their bags. The lanes of Bursa were humming with people: villagers selling products; city folk wandering about while carrying baskets and looking for merchandise at bargain prices; formally dressed clerks; beggars looking for handouts; soldiers speaking a mixture of languages from the lands of the Empire—a combination of colors and voices. The heat began to overpower Yehoshua, and sweat poured down his body, wet his armpits, and made his hair stick to his face. For a moment, he wanted to remove one of his coats but then remembered his bulging pockets. The guards jested and shared their stories with Yehoshua between chewing dried figs and cracking almond shells. He laughed at their tales even though he did not hear a word. He was preoccupied—mainly busy with the wagon driver sitting in front of him. The wagoner, whose back was turned to him, looked different from the back of his usual driver, but he wasn't sure of that and attributed his thoughts to the heat and humidity. The oppressive heat bore down on Yehoshua so much that he felt weak. But before he thought about sitting straighter to make it easier to breathe, the wagon stopped, and Yehoshua slid in his seat.

The wagon halted in the center of the meat market. Stalls were scattered all around. Hanging on wooden hooks in the doorways were legs of meat and skinned lambs, and set out on the wide tables were ribs dripping blood, with clouds of flies flitting around them. The minutes seemed endless to him. Finally, he leaned over the wagoner and asked to alight to empty his bladder. The driver did not react but turned to the guards, and they hesitated, whispering among themselves, but finally, they agreed, and one of them escorted him.

Yehoshua looked for the meat store "Fuad's Lamb." To his surprise, it was right in front of his eyes. Yehoshua came close to it and saw pieces of skin and tendons on a wooden shelf dripping blood; he felt bad and nauseated. When the guard saw his green face, he took hold of his hips and broke out in laughter, grasping intestines and waving them in Yehoshua's face. Yehoshua turned his face away and hurried to the backyard, opened his belt, and unbuttoned his fly, taking, on purpose, a long time, and then he waited for the Turks who had to come to take him.

Yehoshua urinated, and when he finished, he rebuttoned his fly and tightened his belt—and no one came near him. Yehoshua reopened his buttons, and still nobody arrived. The guard came out of the store holding an oily paper bag and yelled to Yehoshua to hurry up. "Just a minute," Yehoshua said, looking for excuses to lengthen his delay. "My stomach aches."

The guard laughed and re-entered the store, and after some time, came out impatiently and took Yehoshua with him. When he climbed into the wagon, he again looked at the wagon driver's back that was turned to him, and he was certain this was a different person. When he sat down, he felt he had sat on a small object pricking him, but he acted as if comfortable in his seat, so as not to draw special attention to himself and carefully picked up the item on the bench. He found himself holding a small, paper-wrapped stone. Soon the wagon left the bustling market and set off on the main road, and from there to the train station. At the depot, people were surprised by their arrival and claimed that only military trains were leaving that day for Constantinople. The guards looked at each other in astonishment—such as thing had never happened to them before—and they returned the way they had come.

Since they now had a great deal of time and were not rushed to get on the road, the guards decided to go about the city and make use of this trip for various matters and tasks. They did not ask Yehoshua for his opinion—he was a prisoner, and they could do whatever they wanted to him. The more time passed, the more Yehoshua worried, and he began trembling. In the meantime, the wagon became loaded with vegetables, pitas, rolls of fabric, and bricks for building a room in the house of one of the guards. Yehoshua sat anxiously among the piling objects, and terrible thoughts overwhelmed him.

As evening darkness settled around them, the wagon returned to the fenced group of houses, the quarters of the exiles. Yehoshua rushed to climb down and march off toward his place of imprisonment. He was not surprised to see two new guards at the second camp gate. One demanded to search him and asked him to remove his coat, but the wagon driver whispered something to him. Yehoshua saw him push a banknote into his pocket. When he entered the room, he saw Olga sitting on the bed in the dark in deep mourning, with Mania and Israel sitting silently.

Mania was the first to speak. A short time after he left, she told him, another two guards had come and stood behind the house—no one could come in or go out. They knew something had gone wrong but not exactly what.

Now, Yehoshua remembered the paper-wrapped stone in his pocket, and he took it out and gave it to Mania. "Avshalom has disappeared in the desert. Maybe he has been hurt. Perhaps he was kidnapped, and no one knows where he is," Mania read in tears, while Olga, who had not digested the meaning, looked at her husband as if asking for denial, but he could find no words of consolation. Olga left the group and sat hunched over and then made a slit in the collar of her dress, and her body rocked forward and back as she sobbed, "Avshalom, Avshalom."

⁖

The failure of the escape attempt changed the way of life in the small room. Israel again lost his self-confidence and went back to endless mutterings, while Mania sank into melancholy and lost vitality. Yehoshua's trips to Constantinople stopped, but he continued to write plans, fearing that perhaps he would not have enough time to write it all down. Of the four, it was only Olga who retained complete sanity. From time to time, however, she would say, "I should have been next to Fanny," but then she would again strive to relieve the three others, for a short time, from their sense of utter ruin. The guards began to bandy about stories, and every one of them made the four of them even more miserable: Palestine was full of spies, they said. The Turks searched for them everywhere, and whoever was suspected of belonging to the Hashomer organization was arrested, beaten, and exiled. The prison in Damascus grew full of Jewish exiles. A group of spies who called themselves "Nili" was caught because of a homing pigeon whose leg bearing a message had become enmeshed in a net while flying from Athlit to Egypt.

The third year of their captivity began. The tales of the victories of the Ottoman Empire were now replaced by stories of defeat. Then the four were separated from each other. Mania and Israel were taken elsewhere. Mania's links with Hashomer and the accusation against Israel for instigation led to a renewal of the trial against them. They brought Mania's young child from Palestine so she could take care of him, but she was not happy to have him. She did not want him at her side at this time of her weakness. Olga could not help in any way. She and Yehoshua remained in Bursa and fervently hoped that Israel would abandon his apathy and support his wife and child. In those months, the guards began to take their job less seriously, and there was a feeling that they wanted to protect their own hides more than they feared prisoners' escapes. Now, they wanted to make a good impression on the captives, in case there would be a change in the ruling powers, and they would become prisoners of war and need advocates. At first, Olga liked the idea of their weakness, and she began to ridicule the guards. She wanted a basket of dates, she would tell them, and they made sure to fulfill her request. She made clear she was asking for a Turkish sweet, and they brought her a bulging bag of them.

Yehoshua asked her to stop. "Any minute things can go topsy-turvy," he argued. "The war will end, and it will turn out that the Turks won."

But Olga did not agree with her husband's thinking. "You don't hear or you don't want change," she told him. "You're used to the Turks and the way they think." And Yehoshua was angered by what she said even though he knew it was the truth.

At the end of that year, a messenger came from Constantinople to the captives' camp in Bursa and informed Yehoshua that he was released and could return to Palestine. They did not understand what had prompted the change in the Turks' attitude, but they didn't spend much time worrying about it. They packed their bags and tried to get away from the place and its memories as fast as possible.

They left the city in a conveyance similar to the one that had brought them to Bursa, but now it was not covered but open. Then they got on a train heading for Constantinople, where they embarked on a rickety ship that sailed to Beirut and from there to Haifa. Their trip was very long, and they were already impatient. Besides them, there were no other exiles on the ship but rather Turkish and Lebanese merchants whose anxiousness about their livelihood was greater than their fear of the war. Sailing on the sea were ships from different countries, and the captain would remove the ship's flag time and again and replace it with the flag of the ship it was nearing. From time to time, a warship would stop next to them, and soldiers came onto the deck to check names and documents. On occasion, they took someone off with them who was apparently wanted by them, or whom they only suspected was wanted. For Olga, this sail was one long nightmare, and she repeatedly told her husband that she was sure that near the end of the journey, they would still arrest them and return them to exile. But her fears were unfounded, and after three weeks, the ship reached Haifa.

When they came down the ramp from the ship, Olga breathed a sigh of relief. Yehoshua looked at her; the trip had worn her out; her wrinkles were prominent, her hair uncombed, her clothing unkempt, and Yehoshua was sorry to see her looking like that.

In Haifa, too, they were forced to wait, since no wagon would take them to Jaffa. A few days later, they did find a wagon driver who was going to Hadera, so they decided to travel with him and visit Mendel and Tanhum and the young family. Yehoshua was surprised by the forcefulness of his feelings when he thought he was about to see Hadera, though he did not know if the war had lessened the farmers' anger at him.

The wagon followed a difficult, unconventional route, and more than they rode, the passengers were forced to push it to move it out of the dips and holes it had sunk into. By evening, they had arrived in Hadera, and they stayed over in the house of the effendi similar to a khan that was used as storage areas and for rooms for the colonies' workers.

Olga stayed in their room to refresh herself and stretch out after the exhausting trip, but Yehoshua was impatient to meet Fanny, who had returned to her home in Hadera after Lolik's death, and to visit his two brothers, but especially to see what had happened to the plot that had been the source of the controversy between him and the Hadera people.

Yehoshua began to climb the sandy hill toward the houses sprouting at its top. Even though dark had already settled, he managed to discern the changes that had taken place on this site. The trees had grown taller, and he could no longer recognize the paths he had trod. From afar, he heard the reverberations of unidentified cannons. The front was near, and he was strolling along wrapped in darkness to look for a plot and to feel the clods of earth that belonged to him.

First, Yehoshua saw a row of farm structures in the center of the farmyard, and citrus, almond, and olive trees planted along the walkways linking the buildings. He recalled Aharon Eisenberg and the Duran land, his face expressing a smile. The years of exile had made him forget friends and big plans. While walking in the sands, he remembered how much Aharon had not been satisfied with the flourishing of one colony, and since he had succeeded in Rehovot, he had established one more company called "Agudat Neta'im," and asked Yehoshua to sell him parts of his land in the Hadera dunes. He wanted to plant in the land and then sell it, and for whoever would find it hard to immigrate to Palestine, the Aguda would work the land for him until the trees produced fruit. Then, the owner would aspire to immigrate and settle on the land he had bought and take charge of working it. Yehoshua was enthusiastic about the plan. He sold Aharon some of his land, held fast to his dream, and went on to say, "First, the citrus groves and almonds will be planted. Then, they will pave the roads, and colonies will be established, and in the end, a city will be built—Hephtzibah—and it is located along the coast." He remembered the name and smiled to himself. Olga had given the name to the plot on one of their visits there, and she added, "I wanted a house but didn't get one, but an estate I do have."

All this occurred before the exile and the long stay in the captives' camp in Bursa. Now, Yehoshua trod between the houses of the farm and was saddened by the neglect; he wondered where the workers and manager were. The farm had been a magnet for everyone who had a fiery love for Eretz Israel. Laborers and visionaries had spent time there; even Israel Belkind had lived there and brought the orphans of the Kishinev pogroms to it and sought to found for them his "Kiryat Sefer." But the experiment had failed, and Israel and the orphans were moved to Shefeya.

Yehoshua continued walking and crossed the rows of almonds and olives. He was deeply pained to see uprooted trees with their roots upended, and in the dark, they looked to him like accusing fingers. He left the plantations and climbed a kurkar cliff that rose above the manager's house and the workers' structures and tried to look out from there to the vista of the dunes with the waves licking their edges. However, the lack of light allowed him only to see the foam of the waves and the ruins of the watermelon harbor, Minat Abu Zabura. Yehoshua sat down on a rock and listened to the sounds of the night, reminding himself that Avshalom had wanted to build a fortress among the ruins of the harbor. But Avshalom was no more. The war had paralyzed the harbor, leaving only two sailboats stuck in the sand, serving as testimony to the many boats loaded with watermelons that used to sail on the river to the estuary; where many stevedores who waited for them would load the fruit on their shoulders and then walk into the water, roll the fruit and build up many piles of it on the decks of the ships setting sail for Egypt.

In the meantime, it had turned cool, and the trembling from the cold and his fatigue bested him, so he descended from the cliff and returned to Olga. He found her bundled up like an infant in the bed, sleeping the sleep of the just as if she had never had a troubled day in her life. Yehoshua sat at the end of the bed and caressed her face, wondering what he would have done without her. Finally, he lay down next to her in his traveling clothes and fell into a deep sleep.

Olga rose early. The noise made by the soldiers and the dust scattered by the mules that made their way into the room drew Olga out of her sound sleep. She turned over and saw Yehoshua lying at her side in his coat and worn-out pants and lightly tickled him, to examine every single move he made. Yehoshua tried to prevent her from waking him, took hold of her, and pulled her to him, and Olga covered him with her body and felt how new, fresh desire was awakening in her. He was still dozing, and his movements were clumsy, but she enjoyed each caress of his and every kiss very much.

When they calmed down and the day's heat burst into the room, she told him she would be happy to stay just like this at his side for many days. He pushed her off him gently and reminded her where they were coming from. She smiled and tried to forget the lengthy exile. It seemed to her that during all the time they had spent in Bursa, she had not savored the flavor of love as she was enjoying it now. The great discomfort, the fears, Israel's mumblings, and Mania's presence had taken Yehoshua away from her. Now, when only a few weeks had passed since the day they had left Bursa, she already felt the taste of a new life and of awakening love.

They washed their faces and put on clean clothes; Yehoshua never took his eyes off his wife when she combed her hair and wound it into a mound around her head. He no longer saw the wrinkles on her face nor the signs of aging but was only filled with love for her.

Late that same day, Yehoshua went to look for a wagon driver who would take them to Jaffa, but all the horses and mules had been taken for the army. He checked in the huts of the nearby Arab village, and among the clay houses, he met one peasant who had a herd of donkeys, someone he had known even in the days of Fuleh in the Jezreel Valley who rented out his donkeys to transport merchandise from the train station to the houses of the cooperative. When Yehoshua asked about his donkeys, the Arab told him that at the start of the war, he had fled with his flock of donkeys and hidden in the wadis on the slopes of the Carmel. When the front came close, the Arab had moved with his animals to the British side; now, they served as pack animals in the camps being set up all along the coast. With the profit from his donkeys, so he said, he had bought a new mule to plow his field. When the *fellah* heard about Yehoshua's predicament, he was happy to release the mule he had bought from the plow for a few days and put it at Yehoshua's disposal. Now, there was, to be sure, a mule, but there was no wagon. For two days, he searched for a wagon among the houses of the colony, but wagons had also been taken to be used by the army.

In the end, a wagon was located, one whose wheel axis was broken. Yehoshua, who had never repaired the shaft of a wagon nor hammered a nail, had no choice but to follow the Arab's instruction.

While they were still fixing the wagon, the front moved closer, and the English entered Hadera. In the midst of this tumult of soldiers fleeing and soldiers coming in along with farmers sequestering themselves in their houses, Yehoshua loaded his bundles on the wagon, and he and Olga left Hadera in the dark of night. Again, the way was long. The Arab who walked with them along the track said that this was the only safe way to Jaffa – there were no trains, the roads were ruined, and robbers roamed among the ways. The entire journey, Olga napped and did not see the landscape that had changed nor the diggings of the war, while Yehoshua never ceased looking at the scenery and being amazed by the changes that had taken place during the years of his absence.

They stopped in Kfar Saba. The colony was in ruins following the war, but work had already begun to reestablish it. At night, they slept in the yard of Schlusser, who was one of the first to have rebuilt his home. The man had decided to make a profit from the war and allotted rooms to the British soldiers. He had built a brewery in his yard, and the heady smells filled the tattered streets, inviting the British soldiers to his house. Unexpectedly, it was in Kfar Saba that Yehoshua felt his idleness. Until now, he had been occupied with the great wandering from Bursa to Palestine, but in Kfar Saba, he began to sense his closeness to Jaffa. He did not know what awaited him in the city, which officials were still there, who had been exiled, or who had come back. The years had distanced him from Ruppin, Thon, who was now the director of the Palestine Land Development Company, and the other officials, and Yehoshua was anxious about his becoming reacquainted with them.

When Yehoshua woke up, a new morning had started, and Olga came out from the shower room, wearing a clean outfit, and her smell intoxicated him.

"I dressed up in honor of Jaffa," she told him. "By tonight, we will be on the outskirts of the town."

Outside, Yehoshua searched for the Arab and the mules, and Schlusser told him that the man had left at dawn and hadn't waited for payment but only asked that Yehoshua try to intercede on his behalf with the clerks to give him work after the war.

"He followed the front," mocked Schlusser. "He'll find plenty of work for the mules and the wagon that came into his possession without paying."

The diligence they rode to Jaffa in was full of bundles and another eight passengers. They all sat crowded together, holding baskets, and between their legs were bundles smelling of onions and anise and boiled eggs. For Olga, this reminded her of another journey, the Purim trip to Duran. Yehoshua giggled and gently elbowed his wife, whispering to her, "The whole life of the Kfar Saba farmers revolves around feeding the residents of Jaffa." Olga pushed him back to hush him and noticed the way people were looking at them. She wondered if they identified her husband or were only astonished by their sitting close to each other. The closer they came to Jaffa, the more excited Yehoshua became. He had not thought that he would be so moved by the houses of the port city as he approached his house. At noon, the first houses of the city appeared—first the homes of the new neighborhoods, scattered among the dunes, the houses of Tel Aviv, and then those of Jaffa, blackened with age and blanketing the hill facing the port and the new neighborhoods. The diligence bounced on a path of pebbles and gravel next to the train track and entered the wadi crossing the borders between Neve Tzedek and the old city, and there, next to Chelouche's house, it halted.

Yehoshua and Olga were the last to alight. They were excited and afraid of making any unnecessary move lest the moment be cut short and lose its glory. But while they were still standing near the track, with their packets around them, reality confronted them. Suddenly, Jaffa looked so very small, crowded, and ugly. Sewage was puddled in its streets, and its channels were full of excrement and peels, leaves, and papers. And at the heart of this filth, the two stood, not knowing if the three years in Bursa had made them forget these city scenes or whether, perhaps, it was the war that had made Jaffa so unbearably ugly. Yehoshua saw his wife's sorrow and could not find the words to console her.

A porter looking for work approached them and offered to carry their belongings for them, but when they told him their address, his face fell. Apparently, the man had seen their many items and thought he had come upon wealthy people who would leave him a nice tip for his service. When Olga registered his disappointment, she was even sorrier.

"We will build a house in Tel Aviv," Yehoshua said, trying to encourage her. "A new, roomy house with a tap spouting flowing water and our water bowl will serve us as a fruit basket."

She smiled at him, and they both felt a bit relieved. They hurried to walk behind the porter, no longer looking around them.

❧

Slowly, Yehoshua and Olga came back to themselves and became used to the ways of Jaffa. But the city had changed and was no longer as it had been in the past. The room in Ajami was small, and they barely found space in it for the box overflowing with pages and plans that Yehoshua had brought from Bursa. They moved it every day, and wherever they put it, it looked clunky and out of place. Finally, they took out two chairs and made room for it. They didn't need the chairs, since they seldom had visitors. The family had become small—some had died, others had gotten old and could not abide the hardships of the way to the small room in Jaffa. Sarah had died while they were in exile, with only Mendel and Haya at her side when she closed her eyes.

She asked to be buried next to Yehuda Leib, and she ordered the store to be sold and to divide the property among the children. The fabric store became a fish store, and the sign it bore that said "Yehuda Leib Hankin" was removed. Soon no one remembered those Friday mornings when crowds thronged near the entranceway and argued about the place of the Palestine Land Development Company and the role of the Palestine Office, or whether the JNF had to provide credit for the settlers in Ahuzat Bayit or to deal strictly with land acquisition for the Jewish people. Fanny was now far away in the Hadera colony; she and her only daughter, without a son and without a husband, depressed and waiting for the day she would die. Olga wanted to bring her to Jaffa. But Fanny refused and asked to live with her memories and with the spirit of Lolik and Avshalom. Haya left Galilee, and she and her husband Eliyahu Krauze were housed at the agricultural school Mikveh Israel. Actually, they were the only ones who came every Friday evening for a joint Sabbath meal with Yehoshua and Olga.

Above all, Olga missed Sonia, but she was still in Paris. Now, she was a certified physician engaged in research. She was by herself, unmarried, and didn't have to answer to anyone about what she was doing.

When they first arrived, Olga tried to renew her connections, visit the wives of the officials, and return to the clinic to see if they still needed her. But there were new midwives and new methods, so the doctor politely refused her help, "Take it easy for a bit. We'll recuperate from the war, and the exiles will come back to Jaffa, and you will find a lot of work."

She was not sorry, for her hands had become clumsy, and she was no longer enthusiastic about working as a midwife but preferred to sit at Yehoshua's side and busy herself with small matters.

A few months after they had returned to Jaffa, Olga began to look for a new house in the new neighborhoods north of the Old City. She wandered for hours among the whitewashed houses and the gardens around them, seeing in her mind's eye the new house belonging to her and Yehoshua with a fence around it, and she imagined fruit trees standing in front of the house. But, while Olga had plenty of free time and her life progressed smoothly, Yehoshua's life changed drastically.

Immediately upon his return to Jaffa, success came back, too, knocking on his door. The land registry offices had not yet opened, and new directors for the Palestine Land Development Company had not yet been appointed. The rules and procedures for buying and selling land had also not yet been determined under the new government. Nevertheless, Yehoshua was already swamped with work. He became an expert and leader in Palestine on all matters related to real estate and land. He turned into a sought-after land agent, whether because of the scarcity of agents in the period right after the war or by virtue of the plans and experience he had brought with him from Turkey, or owing to his appearance, which convinced whoever saw him, or to his fluent Arabic—everyone offered him a job, in the Palestine Land Development Company and outside of it, and again there were none who did not recognize Yehoshua Hankin.

Yehoshua's lists and plans earned a good reputation in Palestine. A few people remarked, "These are only castles in the air," while most of the others said, "Big dreams, but they can be realized." His lists were printed and passed from one person to another. There were already those who read them at important assemblies and quoted them later on, and the words of Yehoshua turned into a vision. Letters were piled on the table in his home. Many framed certificates of appreciation hung on its walls, and the box they had brought from Bursa was filled to bursting and had no room for more pages. Yehoshua was invited to events, and everyone addressed him as "Sir," and with "Would Mr. Hankin be so kind as to deliver his speech?"

After so many years, he considered the honor showered on him as his due and did not reject it. He believed everything he said and was happy to share his plans with others. In his vision, he saw two hundred Jewish colonies and battalions of workers engaged in public works, and ten new cities and factories and chains of banks. And when asked why the Arab effendis were willing to sell him land, he enjoyed sharing his views with the inquirers—that every sale of land to Jews would enhance the villagers' standard of living. With the help of the payment for the land, they would improve the plots remaining in their hand and their methods of cultivation, thereby increasing their yields. "The effendis believe in me. They always did, and the *fellahin* rely on my opinion." While he spoke, his eyes were fiery as were the eyes of others, and Yehoshua, who was aware of this, learned in time to add hand motions and wave at the right time, as well as to sometimes whisper and at other times to raise his voice. Indeed, he was great, and he did not scorn the greatness that encompassed him.

Now, he no longer worked by himself; he was accompanied by clerks and specialists, and a wagon drove this large group everywhere. Wherever this noisy band arrived, they were received with drinks and sweets. They did not forget to invite the photographer to immortalize Yehoshua Hankin, sitting with the officials and experts at his side, along with whoever happened to be there. Yehoshua loved the tumult around him and enjoyed seeing how the experts heeded his advice and agreed with every word. He had already instituted a notebook for each specialist in which he would write down various details. But Yehoshua's notebook was supreme above all of them. The clerks would copy his style of notation: columns running the entire length, terms for types of lands in a slew of languages—kurkar rock, sand, or red soil; land good for irrigated crops, for dry crops, for orchards, and for vegetables. Wilkanski was experimenting with crops on his farm at Ben Shemen. The notebooks were an identifying mark for Yehoshua's escorts, to the point that the experts would walk about the city, on the paths of the colonies, their hands tucked in their armpits, with a notebook peeking out from their coat pockets, and everyone would say, "These fellows are working with Yehoshua Hankin."

Now, Yehoshua was the biggest land agent in Palestine, with no competitors. If Olga mentioned Pines's name or that of Broide, her husband would laugh and not believe that he had ever been fearful of them and their reactions. He was no longer afraid of anyone or of the gossip bandied about behind his back, and even not of other agents. There was only one "Yehoshua Hankin," with no need to add to his name any detailed description. It was enough to say "Yehoshua," and everyone knew who was being referred to.

The Palestine Land Development Company placated him, agreed to all his whims, and honored all his requests; it did not take a step or come to a decision without first consulting him. When the heads of the JNF once complained that Yehoshua was not meeting his obligations and was turning over land he had acquired to private individuals before asking their opinion and inquiring whether the JNF wanted the land, the Palestine Land Development Company directors responded—we considered his proposal and agreed with his choice, but they did not tell them that Yehoshua had acted solely on his own initiative and had not made the directors party to his decision.

To be sure, he was "unique." Everyone knew about his journeys, since he did not travel alone, but with the clerks and the other experts of the Palestine Land Development Company, but about his riding, only Olga knew. He was 60 and would still set out before dawn, return at dark, and ride over his lands, to those that were not yet acquired and to lands not yet for sale. Only there, among the dunes in the desert and atop the kurkar cliffs at the seashore, would he forget the greatness attributed to him and return to himself and his old love for a short time. He would dismount and bend over toward the clods of earth and crumble them in his hands and let the wind carry the dust, and then he sit himself in the furrow with his ear attuned to the sounds of the earth.

Olga sensed the change in her husband. In the first years after the war, she explained this as the sharp shift from long exile and idleness to excess activity and fear of encroaching age that would not allow him to manage to achieve his vision, fearing the lands would remain in the possession of foreigners, and not in Jewish hands, so he would not be able to see it covered with colonies and cities. After a number of years had passed, when a new regime had settled in Palestine, and the system for land acquisition and establishment of new settlements had been instituted, she did not understand why her husband was pulling so many strings in buying land and making plans as well as establishing companies and founding settlements instead of sharing all this with others. Of course, she loved the nickname that had been given to him, "redeemer of the land," but she rejected the addition appended to the nickname, "the deed of a single man," and was afraid of failure. Olga knew that one failure was all that was needed to wreak destruction on his name and all his acquisitions. But she kept her thoughts to herself and did not share them with Yehoshua.

In time, Olga began to become accustomed to the greatness surrounding Yehoshua and to adjust to being Mrs. Hankin, for whom doors were opened everywhere she turned and for whom a chair was offered, while inquiring about her welfare and her husband's deeds. Age had left its mark on her appearance and in the manner of her walking; the clumsiness of her movements made it easier for her to decide to make her peace with all of her husband's actions and to enjoy the honor she received thanks to him.

❧

One winter, Yehoshua returned after a lengthy ride, trembling from the cold and wet to the bone. As he sat in the small kitchen, sipping his glass of hot water, he told Olga of his decision, "I want to find land to build a gravesite," he declared.

This statement frightened Olga, and for a moment, she thought that he wanted to put up a monument so that everyone could point to it and say, "This is the grave of Yehoshua Hankin, redeemer of the land."

"What's wrong with the Jaffa cemetery," she protested. "We don't have children, and there is nobody who will come to say kaddish for you. It is better to be interred among Jews, so that we will benefit from a bit of kaddish recited over other graves." As soon as she had said this, Olga was sorry about it, especially when she saw the look on his face and his agitation. Hadn't he only asked to make sure she would be buried next to him in land belonging only to them, to which no one else would have access. He sought to keep her with him even after death, and she was rejecting the gift he had offered her. Olga got up, moving slowly, and came up behind him, embracing him with loving hands and turning his body toward her; she caressed his face and kissed his hairy cheeks.

"What would I do if you shaved your beard?" she asked him, trying to get him to smile.

"You aren't used to smooth cheeks," he replied. "I would be someone else, not the Second Joshua, and no one would remember my identity."

They both sat on the bed, sagging from their weight, and Yehoshua smiled at her. "We have gotten old, and desire has dulled," he told her.

"I have aged, but you are still virile," she replied in a quiet voice. "Now that you have spoken about a gravesite, I have realized something. Look, see the wrinkles gathered at the edges of my mouth, the age spots on my hands, and my white hair."

Yehoshua shook his head like a child refusing to hear unpleasant things and said, "I will be buried first, and you will still visit my grave and put a bouquet of flowers on it."

But Olga knew he was only trying to console her and to banish what he had remarked to her.

But the thought about the gravesite would not let go of Yehoshua, and he began to devote all of his trips and rides to looking for a fitting plot of land. He wanted a piece of land far off the beaten path, not exposed to the view of passersby. He did not want to be buried anywhere where people would wander by next to the tombstone and read the name etched in it, raising an eyebrow and wondering who was buried under the heavy stone. He was sure that after his death, no one would remember neither him nor Olga. He already had experience with that; for some 20 years, he had been considered dead, and nobody remembered his accomplishments. After a lengthy search, Yehoshua found the proper spot. This happened when he rode by himself to examine the Nuris land in the Jezreel Valley and measure its borders prior to entering negotiations for the purchase of the entire bloc of land. Yehoshua rode leisurely, breathed in the smell of the blooming spring, and closed the upper button of his old coat while letting the light wind caress his wrinkled neck and disturb his beard. *The Valley* was beautiful. The blue of its swamps was swallowed up by the green growth and intermingled with the brown blotches of mud; the horse trod slowly, churning up moist lumps of soil, for neither the horse nor the rider was in a hurry.

For a second, he was astonished by his status and his strength, but when he looked around and saw the expanses of land and the slopes of the hills that looked toward *the Valley*, he no longer wondered. The might of the land had been absorbed in it, and it was what directed his deeds and what brought him his greatness.

No Bedouin tents or houses of Jewish settlement could be seen in the surroundings, no booth abandoned in a field, and no herd of goats attesting to human settlers. But now, *the Valley* was being acquired piece by piece, and slowly the dream was coming to fruition. Yehoshua, deeply involved with his passing thoughts, did not realize the horse had stopped near a small pond; only when the horse bent its head down to the water did Yehoshua notice.

The pool had been formed by the outpouring of the flow of a spring, and the sun's rays that danced on the water's surface drew Yehoshua's attention. He decided to look for the source of the spring, left his horse grazing weeds next to the pool, and began climbing the hillside on a trodden path created by animals or *fellahin* who, like him, were searching for the place where the clear water gushed out. He climbed high and did not feel the sweat dripping from his forehead and running into his beard, ignored his heavy breathing, and halted only when he came to the mouth of a cave at which the path ended. He leaned toward it and heard the trickle of the water rising from under the large rocks that blocked the exits of the gushing.

For a brief time, he stood absolutely still and held his breath, so as not to interfere with the enchanted quiet, and then, he bent down and began moving the large rocks to free the spring's source and let the water flow ragingly. He went on digging until he felt his backache and a pain that spread from his fingertips to his arms and the sides of his body. As he slowly stood up, holding on to his waist with both hands, he saw before him the entire Valley, from the foot of the hills onward, and its end could not be seen. Yehoshua spread his two hands as if wishing to embrace wide-open spaces and to yell, "It's mine! It's mine!" but he did not want to break the total silence, so instead, he only whispered the words. Then he sat on one of the rocks, staying there until evening. When he heard the horse's neighing rising from the foot of the hill, he realized how late it was and remembered the distant settlement he had been supposed to reach before sunset. When he stood on the cave's dome, he knew that he had found a gravesite for him and for Olga.

After Yehoshua had finished the negotiations over the Shunem land, as well as that of Nuris and Ma'lul, and transferred the kushans to the name of the Palestine Land Development Company, he left one piece of land in his name and signed a separate contract with the owners. No one looked into this nor asked; he did not take Olga to show her the land intended for their gravesite for fear he would sadden her again. Only two years after he had bought it, when he had begun carving their grave in Mt. Gilboa, a mountain overlooking *the Valley*, near the Harod Spring and staying there longer – without returning home for quite a while – did he tell her about his parcel.

"I will build it like they built the tombs of the sages in the Jerusalem Mountains," he told her gently, so as to not depress her. "I will dig into the mountain and set up pillars of marble."

Olga was not frightened this time. "You are hastening my death," she laughed. But from then on they did not talk about the grave. Other events pushed this matter aside: building a new home and Sonia's return to Palestine, after graduation and the title of Doctor of Medicine was added to her name, and her marriage to Mendel, Yehoshua's brother.

When Sonia had come home, Olga said that from now on, she was the wife of an important man and a sister of a well-known doctor. Truly, only a few people remembered her private name or her family name before her marriage—Olga Belkind. Everyone called her Mrs. Hankin, and that was enough for her. Rolls of fat had thickened her body, and her walking became increasingly unwieldy. She usually walked on the streets of the new neighborhoods that sprouted from the dunes and became a new city. Palestine was not the same, and Olga was well past the age of 70. Jaffa was no longer the main artery of Jewish life. *Halutzim* had come as had "the barefoot ones," who wandered between the colonies and the cities. Merchants came, political parties and labor battalions were founded, and workers' cooperative settlements and kibbutzim settled her husband's lands. However, she saw this from afar but did not become involved, as she was already summing up the chapters of a long life.

1920s
Big Plans and Big land acquisitions:

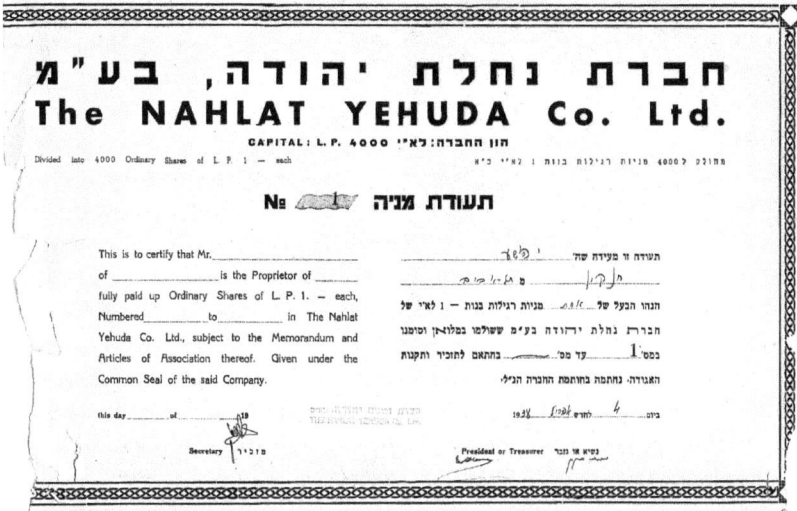

חברת נחלת יהודה, בע"מ
The NAHLAT YEHUDA Co. Ltd.
CAPITAL: L.P. 4000 :הון החברה: לא"י

תעודת מניה №

This is to certify that Mr._____
of _____ is the Proprietor of _____
fully paid up Ordinary Shares of L. P. 1. — each,
Numbered _____ to _____ in The Nahlat
Yehuda Co. Ltd., subject to the Memorandum and
Articles of Association thereof. Given under the
Common Seal of the said Company.

this day_____ of_____19___

Secretary   מזכיר

President or Treasurer   נשיא או גזבר

23. The Nahlat Yehuda Co LTD share certificate, 1938 • Source: Central Zionist Archives.

24. Yehoshua Hankin plan for purching lands for next 20 years, 1926 • Source: The National Library of Israel 34V4107.

Translation 14.5.?

L18/1169

40/5

AGREEMENT

Between Mr.Joshua Hankin of Tel-Aviv, hereinafter called the 1st party, and Mr.Asher Pierce and Mr.Yehiel Weizman as attorney for Sir Alfred Mond, hereinafter called the 2nd party.

1. The 2nd party orders from the 1st party and hereby empowers him to purchase in his name and on his account:-

    a. Part of the land comprising an area of about 3000(three thousand)dunams of the part indicated by N°.20 on the plan attached, signed by the two parties.

    b. Part of the land comprising an area of about 2500(two thousand)dunams of the part indicated by N°.7 on the plan attached.

    c. Part of the land comprising an area of about 7500(seven thousand)dunams,which is the part indicated by N°.8 on the plan attached.

NOTE: A Dunam is 919 sq.metres.

2. The 2nd party undertakes to pay as the purchase price of the a/m land:-

    a. Price per dunam of the part N°.20 = £P.3.500(Three Palestine Pounds & 500 mils),

    b. Price per dunam of the part N°.7 = £P.4.-(Four Palestine Pounds

    c.   "   "   "   "   "   "   8 = "3.-(Three   "   ").

NOTE: The a/m price includes the price of the land and all expenses together with the fees for registration of the transfer of the land at the Land Registry Office of the Palestine Government to the name of the 2nd party, the price being for every dunam of 919 sq.metres that will be legally transferred to the name of the 2nd party and handed over to him for use.

3. The 2nd party undertakes to pay to the Palestine Land Development Co.Ltd.6% of the price of the land that will be transferred to his name at the Land Registry Office of the Palestine Government as detailed.above.

4. The two parties agree to fix a time of from 1 - 2 years from the time of the signing of this agreement for the effectuation of the official transfer of the a/m parts in the Government Land Registry Office; but should the first party arrange the transfer of one of the complete parts as detailed in para.1 before the time determined upon as above, the 2nd party is obliged to accept the transfer not later than one month after receipt of a registered written notification of same.

And if after two years have elapsed from the time of the signing of this agreement,without the above mentioned parts-having-been-transferred lands have not been transferred to the name of the 2nd party or to any one nominated by him, the 2nd party has the right to refuse to accept the transfer after the two years, and the 1st Party will then be obliged to return to the 2nd party the sum received on account of the part, the transfer of which was delayed, within the period of one month together with 6% interest per annum from the time of the receipt of the money, and this must be done on receipt of written notification by ordinary letter from the 2nd party.

5. The 2nd party undertakes to pay the price of the lands in the following manner:-

    a. The sum of £P.800(Eight Hundred Palestine Pounds) on account of the part N°.20 at the time of the signing of this agreement.

    b. The sum of £P.700(Seven Hundred Palestine Pounds) on account of the part N°.7 at the time of the signing of this agreement.

    c. The sum of £P.2500(Two thousand five hundred Palestine pounds) on account of the part N°.8 at the time of the signing of this agreement.

25A. Land purchase agreement between Yehoshua Hankin, Lord Alfred Mond and Asher Pierce, 1926. • Source: Central Zionist Archives. L18/1169.

- 2 -

d. The balance remaining of the price of each part, to be paid at the time of the effectuation of the official transfer of that same part to the name of the 2nd party or to the name of any other person or persons as desired by the 2nd party.

NOTE: The first party cannot compel the 2nd party to accept the transfer of but a part of the area of each plot as determined above.

6. The 1st party undertakes to interest himself in the purchase and in the arrangement of the formalities in connection with the official transfer of the land in the books of the Government Land Registry Office to the name of the 2nd party or to that of any other person as desired by the 2nd party, and the 1st party also undertakes the responsibility for the title deeds that the 2nd party will receive on the a/m land, and to guarantee the 2nd party or his successors against any claim or mortgage, either existin-g or that may arise in the future on the a/m land, either whole or in part, and to hand over to the 2nd party the land that have been transferred to his name, in a legal manner, stating that they are free of incumbrance or dispute, and this not later than 15 days after the official transfer in the Land Registry Office.

7. The 2nd party appears as a single entity in mutual responsibility against the 1st party.

8. This agreement is made in triplicate to be as evidence in the hands of the two parties and is signed here at Tel-Aviv on Monday, the 14th of May , 1928.

Revenue Stamp.

Signed on behalf of Sir Alfred Mond by Yehiel Weizman,
  "   by Asher Pierce,
  "   " Joshua Hankin.

the terms of payment

(Conditions of payment depend on the reply of Sir Alfred Mond).

25B. Land purchase agreement between Yehoshua Hankin, Lord Alfred Mond and Asher Pierce, 1926. • Source: Central Zionist Archives. L18/1169.

26A. Planting the first citrus grove at Gan Haim, 1928 • Source: Pierce Family Private
Archive, Montreal, Canada.

26B. Planting the first citrus grove at Gan Haim, 1928
Source: Pierce Family Private Archive, Montreal, Canada.

26C. Gan Haim share certificate, 1929.
Source: Central Zionist Archives, A238/13.

27. Inauguration of Kalmania Farm, 1932.
Source: Gredinger Family Private Archive, London.

28A. Share Certificate of 'The Eretz-Israel Jewish Agricultural Trust Ltd.' 1942.
Source: Central Zionist Archives, A238-9.

28B. Meshek HaOtzar, 2020.
Source: Irit Amit Cohen Private Archive.

תזכיר ההתאגדות

של

«האוצר הארץ-ישראלי עברי לחקלאות בע"מ»

חברה מוגבלת במניות

1. שם החברה הוא: «האוצר הארץ-ישראלי-עברי לחקלאות» בע"מ.

2. המטרות שלשמן נוסדה החברה הן:

א) לאסוף הון אשר ישקע באפן שישמש מקור הכנסה קבועה לשם פעולות ההתישבות של יהודים בא"י.

ב) להשקיע את ההון ברכישת אדמת שלחין ולטעת אותה בעיקר תפוחי-זהב, גפנים ותאני חיה. אשר יהיו את הרכוש המיצע של החברה.

ג) לשלם לבעלי המניות דיבידנדה אשר לא תפלה על 6%, ובהדרגה לפרע לבעלי המניות על חשבון הערך הנומינלי של מניותיהם את אותם הסכומים שבעליהם יחליט החברה באספה כללית רגילה.

ד) לנהל בהכנסות ברכוש החברה את התישבית של משפחות אחרים, ולמשקיעים תהיה זכות קדימה הן בשביל עצמם והן בשביל קרוביהם. הן ביחס לקבלת עבודות בעבודות החברה והן ביחס להתישבות בהתאם לתקנות שתקבענה בנוגע לסדר בזכות הקדימה ובנוגע לבחינת בעלי הבקשות.

ה) לאחר שיסולקו שלשה רבעים מהערך הנומינלי של הון החברה, תחלק החברה את נכסיה בשלשה חלקים: שני שלישים מהרכוש ויקדשו לקרן-היסוד למטרת הקמת בנק להתישבות יהודים. ושליש אחד מהרכוש יוקדש לקרן הקים למטרת הקמת בנק יהודי לקרקעות. וכנגד זה תשלמנה קרן-היסוד וקרן-הקימת הנ"ל לחברה הראשונה הראשונה שני שלישים והשניה שליש אחד, כהחלק הרביעי הנותר והבלתי יפרע של הון בדרישת של החברה. אז תפרע חברה לבעלי מניותיה את החלק הרביעי מהערך הנומינלי של מניותיהם והחברה תפורק בהכרח.

ו) לנטע ולגדל תפוחי-זהב, לימונים, תאנים, ושאר פירות ולהמשיך ולנהל עסקים של מגדלי פירות מכל מין שהוא ותוצרות אחרות של וכו' להריא לשוק את התוצרת הזאת. ולמכור. להשתמש ולטפל בכל תוצרת כזו.

ז) לנהל עסקים של אכר, בעלי מרעה, משמרי פירות, נוטעים. בעלי מחצבות, בנאים, קבלנים לבנין בשביל עבודות צבוריות ופרטיות, סוחרים, אימפורטרים ואכספורטרים, בנקאים, בעלי אניות, סוכנים וכל עסקים אחרים שיראו כעלולים לפתח ישרות או בעקיפין את נכסי החברה.

ח) לקנות, לחכר או להחליף לשכר א ... כל נכסי-דלא-ניידי ודי-ניידי וכל זכויות או פריבילגיות שהחברה תמצא אותן לנחוצות או מועילות למטרות עסקיה וביחוד כל קרקע. שעבודים. חמרי מכונות. בניני אנונטר חי ומדמני סחורות.

ט) לפתח ולנצל את מקורות הקרקעות הבנינים והנכסיות שיהיו לחברה באפן שהחברה תמצא למתאים ובעיקר ע"י נקוי, יבוש. נטיעה בניה, השבחה, סדור משק הגברת העליה, יסוד ערים, כפרים ומושבים.

28D. Working in the packing house in 'Meshek HaOtzar', 1937.
Source: Irit Amit Cohen Private Archive.

1926

They bought the house on Allenby Street at a bargain price. Sonia and Olga found it and concluded the conditions of purchase with the owners. All Yehoshua and Mendel had to do was to come and sign the contract. On the day of the dedication of the house, they hung a copper tablet on the front of the building that faced the street. The letters sparkled in the stippled sunlight — "The Hankin House," with smaller letters underneath, "Office of the Land Agent Yehoshua Hankin and the Office of Dr. Sonia Belkind." Olga and Sonia stuck together. The house was large enough to allow for the arrangement of an office for Sonia to receive her patients, as well as an office for Yehoshua and to hang on its walls certificates of honor and receive dignitaries. Aside from the office and clinic, they divided the house into two separate units, one for each family. In the shared wall, they opened a window, so if Sonia or Olga needed each other, they turned the handle and called to one another.

Right after the clinic opened on Allenby Street, the name of the physician belonging to the Belkind family became well known, and there was a great deal of work. Olga, who besides seeing to the care and cleaning of the house, did not have much to do. She helped her sister with the kinds of tasks she had been used to before the war. But she quickly realized that the work methods had changed; modern equipment that Sonia had brought with her from Switzerland and Paris was put to use, but her own movements were too slow to allow her to become well integrated into the hectic pace of the clinic. When a young, experienced nurse joined the clinic, Olga quietly gave up her position, and from then on, sufficed with small jobs that did not require great expertise. She served tea to the patients, saw to the disinfecting of needles, and marked articles in medical journals that she felt deserved to be read, even though she never did so, and they were placed on the counter so Sonia could read them when she had the time. She spoke with the patients about what she had done in the past and about Yehoshua. Occasionally, the times were mixed up in her memory—a meeting with Mania at the start of the century seemed like it happened only yesterday, and the courting by the architect Papiermeister seemed to her like something everyone knew and talked about. None of the patients were familiar with the architect, nor did they know who Lolik and Adelaide were, but they loved to listen to her stories that made them forget their aching bodies. When she spoke about her husband, her whole body would relax and fill the entire chair; her face would glow with pleasure, her eyes sparkle, her voice trembled with excitement, and the listeners knew she was talking about the one and only, her Yehoshua. Everyone knew of Yehoshua Hankin, that he was an important director and land buyer and far away from the pettiness of Tel Aviv; Olga's stories brought him closer to the simple people, and they enjoyed penetrating his world and getting to know his other facets.

On occasion, it happened that Sonia stopped her work and joined the patients in listening to her sister's stories. She saw how old age was overcoming her and how her memory was failing, but she did not give it much thought. She was happy to spend time with her older sister and see the love prevailing between her and her husband. Her relations with Mendel were different. They both had married late, and each one had built a world of their own; the marriage was only intended to assuage the long hours of loneliness. She and Mendel had no children, but her barrenness did not trouble her too much. "I'm old," she repeatedly told herself, "too old to be dealing with toddlers."

434 IRIT AMIT COHEN & RUTH KARK

Of course, the busybodies whispered that there was a curse on the house of Hankin and that Mendel and Sonia should not have lived under the same roof with Yehoshua and Olga. Still, those gossiping took no note of the advanced age of those living in the house and did not understand how comfortable it was for the four of them in this situation. They became used to living without children. On the Sabbaths, when the children of Tanhum from Hadera or those of Haya from Mikveh Israel visited, the four of them waited for the minute they would leave, and quiet would be restored to their house. Here there was no need for children. Here they dreamed about large plantation estates conquering the red-sanded dunes and of boundless fields of wheat turning golden, as well as of a house facing the sea atop a kurkar cliff.

They had purchased the house on Allenby Street along with its furniture, and when they whitewashed the house, they put the furniture outside the door so people could walk off with it. Within two hours, the sidewalk was cleared. Sonia and Olga peeked from behind the shutter slats, so as to not embarrass the takers. They giggled at the sight of passers-by hesitating time after time, pretending just to happen to be walking by on the pavement, while in the meantime checking out of the corner of their eye to see that no one was watching them, so they could put out a hand to examine the quality of the furniture. Then, when they finally dared to take an object, they would hurry to run away from there without anyone seeing them.

Now that they had gotten rid of the old, they could run from store to store to buy new furnishings. As small girls, the two had done things together. Now, they wandered the familiar lanes of Jaffa for hours on end, stopped in at specialty stores, and stood under the tops of the market stalls, but they did not go to look at what had happened to the store that had once been Yehuda Leib's shop. They bargained with vendors in Polish, Russian, Romanian, and Yiddish—a veritable babel of languages, a mixture of faces, and all of them Jews dealing in trade. Olga would sigh, saying, "Once upon a time, everyone wanted to be a farmer," while Sonia would smile, "Times have changed."

They did not stuff the house with objects but only with what was necessary. Both loved the shine of the floor tiles and were satisfied with the small rugs that they spread near the chairs to warm their feet. Each hung pictures that matched their individual taste. Olga chose many photos that told the story of Yehoshua's life, while Sonia went to Jerusalem and brought pack drawings from the new school for the arts, Bezalel: a picture of a grove of olive trees, a picture of a shepherd piping, and a landscape of furrows opening toward a farmer sowing. When Olga would sit in her sister's unit and look at the pictures, she would repeatedly tell her, "You're constantly doing something new, while as for me—all my life is memories."

In the yard, Mendel planted saplings, one of an orange tree, the other lemon. He had taken them from seedlings in his Hadera orchard that had been planted in the early years of the colony, and the war had not uprooted. The trees grew and shaded the small yard and served as testimony to Sonia's agreement to marry Mendel.

Mendel was an expert citrus grower, and every seedling his hands touched developed leaves and flowered. Some people laughed at him, and about Yehoshua, they said that the land was his daughter and the orchard Mendel's son, and in the same way the two sisters were so close, the same was true of the brothers. Mendel would smile and immediately say modestly, "Right from the beginning, the orchard took hold in the ground." And when they didn't understand, he would hurry to tell that Yehoshua acquired the land near the Hadera colony because others didn't want it, and he gave plots to his two brothers to work. So together, Mendel and Tanhum planted a large, technologically advanced orchard that all Palestine talked about, but not because of the oranges as large as coconuts or because of the full harvest bushels, but because the plantation was the source of a dispute between the brothers and the farmers of Hadera. For many years, no decision was reached over ownership of the land or the orchard, not in the courts, not by mediators, not in the rabbinic courts, and not by an agreement among the farmers. For a bit, the war caused the quarrel to be forgotten, the orchard produced fruit, the water ran aplenty from the wells, and the success of Mendel and Tanhum became well known to all.

At that time, Tanhum married and had children, but Mendel remained a bachelor. The plethora of seedlings filled his world. In Mendel's way of life, there was no room for a wife, a well-kept home, or order and regimen. The soles of his shoes were always covered with mud; on the shelves and floor stood piles of scientific journals and cuttings from articles, and at night he would spend time among the trees, with a torch in hand, to catch a moth attacking the leaves or a worm gnawing at the tree trunk.

In those days, Mendel was considered quite a catch in the colonies. His sister Haya, who lived in Galilee for a long time—on the Sejera farm—tried to match him up with women. Rosa, who lived in Gedera, invited him to come to her house to meet the educated, French-speaking daughters of the farmers—but he rejected all of them. In time, when Aharon Eisenberg came and bought parts of Yehoshua's tract in Heftziba and invited the brothers to work on his plantation, he no longer responded to family invitations and kept his distance from all of them, staying close to his plantations. Tanhum became Yehoshua's manager at Heftziba, while Mendel became the agricultural instructor and organizer of tasks. He invested heart and soul in the farm and went to live in its huts, dreaming of seeing many orchards of olives and almonds, of lemons and citrons, stretching out in the dunes.

Until the war came and put an end to his dream. In the first years, the farm managed to survive, and Mendel and Tanhum did everything they could to manage it and increase their profits, but the debts ballooned, and the society that held the plantations ran into difficulties. The workers abandoned the plantations, and buyers were sought for Eisenberg's lands. Of course, Yehoshua now talked about fresh plans to establish a new city on this land and to pave access up to the beginning of the stream and to develop a port there, but Mendel loved the orchard and the plantation, and roads and trains and crowded neighborhoods were of no interest to him. Since it was not possible to dig trenches around the trees or prune the blossoms to increase the output of the tree, he left the Heftziba farm and gave in to Olga's insistent pleading to come and meet Sonia. When she ventured away to study medicine in Switzerland, she was still a young woman, and he did not remember her face.

One day, he accepted the invitation and appeared at his brother's house in Jaffa for a Sabbath meal. He came with two grafted seedlings that he wanted to plant in the yard, but Olga said, "It's a pity. I have already begun to look for a house in the new Jewish neighborhood Tel Aviv, north of the Old City." Mendel was sorry and did not know what to do with the seedlings, but just then, he heard a voice behind him, "You can put them in a vase and water them, and when a house is bought, we will call Mendel to plant the seedlings."

That's how Mendel's reacquaintance with Sonia began. Their decision to marry came quickly; "It's so logical," Sonia used to say, and the seedlings were actually planted by Mendel in the yard of the home on Allenby Street. Even though he changed his way of life, Mendel continued to dream about plantation estates, and now another sympathetic ear had been added to listen to his dream.

Mendel's orchard, his wide-ranging knowledge, and the plantations in Heftziba left Yehoshua no peace. "If I only had a large tract stretching from the Yarkon to the foot of the Carmel," he would share his thoughts with Mendel, "I would plant orchards on it and sell part of it to the world's wealthy who want to come to Palestine and rejuvenate it. But, of course, they aren't interested in settling on it but rather desire to increase its wealth. Those millionaires would set up on the red soil plantations tracts and turn them over to Jewish laborers, and the large swamps would disappear, and the wasteland would bloom."

In Palestine, in the meantime, the Third Aliyah had finished, and the Fourth was beginning. The scars of the war faded, plantations were restored, and "the barefoot" were replaced by the bourgeoisie, but wandering in the city streets were many unemployed laborers, while contrasting with them were capitalists who sought investment opportunities for their money and a way to gain a tidy profit. At the same time, they discovered the nature of the red sand and the levels of the groundwater. The region between Nahal Alexander and Nahal Auja and that from the Falik swamp to the foot of the Carmel became the focus of interest of moneyed people, as well as for laborers seeking work. These were the days Yehoshua and Mendel had been waiting for, and at the Sabbath evening dinner table, the idea of the large tract was discussed in detail. Olga was barely involved but only listened with shining eyes. Sonia, applying her common sense, calculated the costs and tried to dampen the rampant enthusiasm that had taken hold of the two brothers. She recalled the youth who had danced in Rishon Lezion a long time ago on a loaded wagon that went down to the vineyard to harvest the grapes without permission, and she smiled to herself. Since then, many years had gone by, and their lives had changed drastically. Now, no one dared give a peep against the Hankin family, and everyone recognized they were great experts on land matters, and there was also no one among the land agents who could compete with them. Yet, she wondered to herself whether they would succeed in realizing their dream in time.

Her thoughts took her aback. When she finally dared to let Mendel and Yehoshua in on her worries, both dismissed them, continuing to weave their dream, looking for an area of land they could sell in lots and plant orchards on it and establish estates between the dunes and the kurkar cliffs—a large plain covered with plantations as far as the eye can see. When she told them again that they had to consider the issue seriously, Yehoshua invited the Danin brothers to their house—the older one, Ezra, who was an expert on orchards, and the younger one, Hiram, who had just turned 20. The expert told them about the red, sandy land and about the level of groundwater in the Sharon and stressed that there was no better land than these two for growing citrus fruits. Sonia heard and did not interfere again with her husband's and her brother-in-law's actions.

The idea of large estates in the coastal plain began to take shape when Yehoshua Hankin entered negotiations for land north of the small colony of Kfar Saba and when it became clear that the JNF did not care about it. "It's expensive and split," its directors told him when he came to them to try to interest them in the land, "and many months, or even years, will go by, and there will be long trials and large expenses until the Fund will manage to acquire the land. You first have to complete buying the land of the Jezreel Valley and Zevulun Valley. The land of the plain can still wait."

But Yehoshua did not wait. When he told his family about the answer from the JNF directors and Olga posed the question of where the money would come from. He dismissed her doubts and refrained from looking directly at Sonia, and told them that, at that time, Jews had already bought lands and divided them into areas for plantations and sold them to people living abroad. So why shouldn't the Hankin family members realize their similar dream? Mendel had served as an adviser to others about orchards and yearned for one of his own, a large orchard that would take days to cross, and many workers' colonies would be established in it so they could work on it. And since fitting land had been found and the Palestine Land Development Company had not rejected his plan, the only thing left to do was to look for buyers for the land among those wealthy people, so as to bring his dream to fruition.

The first extended property of plantations did come into being, and Mendel was rejuvenated and went back to working in one. Stories about the new orchard filled many evenings in the Hankin home; Olga wanted to go to it to see its splendor. Yehoshua encouraged his brother and made sure to spread the word about the new lands and the plan to create large estates and increase the number of buyers for the new tract. Only Sonia still had doubts and continued to look at her brother-in-law, now over 65, and her sister, who was 78, and she prayed that her fears were baseless.

On the first anniversary of the founding of the initial plantations, a large celebration was organized. Many came to look at the young seedlings and saplings: local dignitaries, rich Jews, whoever considered himself a Zionist but didn't want to immigrate to the country and settle in a land that destroyed its inhabitants and sought ways to invest in it and silence his conscience. On that occasion, the president of the Zionist Organization was asked to give his name to the orchard. After he agreed and even bought shares, making him a partner, they called it "Gan Hayyim." It was a great honor to be counted among the buyers of a share in the new orchard, to be photographed alongside Yehoshua Hankin and Dr. Chaim Weizmann, give a speech, shake hands, and praise the redeemer of the land. The president's speech appeared in the press, and the descriptor "redeemer" was attached to Yehoshua.

When the four returned home, Yehoshua said, "I didn't have children, so streets and villages will bear my name." Tears welled in Olga's eyes, so Yehoshua went to her and took hold of her hands, "If it were not for you, even roads wouldn't be named for me," he added tenderly, yet Olga did not reply but sobbed even more. Suddenly, she patted her head and muttered to herself, "Avshalom, take it easy, Avshalom," and hummed a lullaby. The others were sure she had been overwhelmed by excitement and that momentarily had been overcome by memories. Sonia wiped away a tear, though she did not realize that her sister's sanity was perilously declining.

Yehoshua enjoyed being "the redeemer," new greatness adhered to him. Olga could no longer warn him or take him down from the big tree he had climbed up. Yehoshua noticed how old age had overtaken her and how she had become shorter, but he paid no attention to her forgetfulness, to her mixing up names, or to silences that went on too long. She still waited for his return in the evenings and baked him the round cookies that he liked, and put them on the plate and sat opposite him to watch how he dipped them in the cup of boiling water in which lemon peel floated and then sank whenever a spoon was stirred in it. When he asked for another cup, she was happy to get up and lean on the back of the chair and stretch her hand to take hold of the marble counter, so as to take as few steps as possible and fill the plate with the sugar-topped cookies arranged in a tin.

Yehoshua was not aware of all this. He was occupied with stories about new acquisitions and his success. In those days, he went south to the Negev to examine the land near Beersheba, took the young Hiram Danin with him, and taught him the way to buy land. The fellow learned from him and also told him about his love for Sarah Kolodny, and Yehoshua heard and smiled, remembering the days of his youth when he went for the first time to Shimshon Belkind's home to ask for Olga's hand. When he finished examining the lands of the south, he headed north and inspected the Huleh land and looked into the possibility of acquiring the land of Ramot Menashe. He saw only successes and great honor and esteem, to the point that he would brag to his wife, "I am familiar with all the lands of Eretz Israel, and I can buy them and also find buyers for them, settle them, and see them flourishing."

His eminence pushed the officials of the Palestine Land Development Company away from him. At first, it distanced from him those who sought to gain a taste of acquiring land for the company, but they couldn't because Yehoshua was always there ahead of them. Then, he fended off the clerks who wrote letters and the lawyers and the surveyors. They would approach him in awe and reverence, while he would not even look at them but only order them loudly and confidently to do what he said without asking any unnecessary questions. Yehoshua worked by himself, and the others would curse him behind his back. A feeling of power suffused him, and he proudly bore the nickname "the redeemer" and was not willing to let it go in favor of an "agent for land matters" or "an official of the Palestine Land Development Company." Olga would hear the stories of his achievements, but just like her senses were declining in other ways, she did not even discern the change that had taken place in Yehoshua.

The hubbub of a new city, developing at a fast pace and trying to accomplish in ten years what other cities had done over centuries, did not cross the threshold of the Hankin house. Sonia was occupied with her patients; Mendel was improving the plantations of "Gan Chaim" and helping create a new plantation, "Mata'ei Eretz Israel," and Olga had lost all sense of time. Near the house on Allenby Street, a few of the smaller homes were demolished, and new, taller ones were built; the open areas between the houses became smaller, and construction covered every piece of available land. Everyone was sure that the city was undergoing a binge of development and building that could not be stopped. Only a few dared to warn about unplanned construction and investments whose source could dry up one day.

Cafes popped up everywhere in Tel Aviv, and any worker who found a permanent job could allow himself to sit at them and leisurely drink tea and listen to the pianist and violinist and then stand in line for a motion picture or the theater, and incidentally argue with a merchant buying land and reprove him for not having left all the land for the nation, and in the heat of the debate, the two could forget to go into the performance or movie.

Sonia claimed that the noise from the street did not allow her patients to get the rest they needed, so she replaced the wooden entrance door with an iron one. Neither Yehoshua nor Olga were party to that decision—one just shrugged, while the other simply sank deeper into old age. The family was sealed in, and the events in Tel Aviv barely penetrated the house, and as in his home, outside too, Yehoshua refused to hear the criticism voiced against him. In those days, he renewed his connections with the sons of Antoine Bishara Tayyan, the owners of the Wadi Hawarith land, and completed their acquisition; the land was no longer called Wadi Hawarith but rather Hefer Valley. Since there were many times when he did not need the descendants of Antoine Bishara Tayyan, but they needed him, when he would come to them and ring the bell, the lad would run with alacrity and announce out loud, "Hawaja Hankin," "Hawaja Hankin." Yehoshua would not wait to be invited to sit but rather sit himself down and sip from the coffee as an equal among equals. Stories were told, legends grew, and Yehoshua enjoyed the great honor and did not bother to correct any exaggerations; he took pleasure in the numerous pats on the back he received and considered himself a legendary hero. In the evenings, when he was at home and not staying with the clerks in Haifa or Jerusalem, he continued to set himself opposite his wife and detail his own praise to her. He did not notice how her eyelids drooped during the conversation. Since he was so full of himself, he paid no attention to when she suddenly awoke from her napping, blurting out, "The wagon is bouncing, and Mania is groaning with labor contractions. Tonight, I will travel to Galilee."

He first became aware of the change to his wife, when he told her about a meeting he had had with Jacob Thon, the Palestine Land Development Company director, about acquiring the Huleh land. Olga did not know who he was talking about and wondered what the connection was between Yehoshua and land in the north. He grimaced and became angry that she was not a party to his overall enthusiasm about his successes, but a moment later, he noticed her furrowed brow, her befogged eyes, and her attempts to remember.

"She's too tired," he told himself, and his anger subsided.

"I will take you to bed," he said aloud and led her like a small child; she put her in the bed and covered her with the patchwork quilt. Then he lay down next to her, almost not touching her. He put his hand on her stomach and, for some reason, she was very far from him. He turned his face toward her and saw the wrinkles etched in her face and thick neck, and the wild white hair. Then he touched her wrinkled skin again and realized it was still soft; his fingers walked along her hands, and he felt the prominent veins and wanted to wake her and to see her open eyes, watching what he was doing and a smile of enjoyment spreading on her face at his touch. But Olga didn't feel a thing, only slept deeply, snoring gently. Yehoshua closed his eyes and remembered the day awaiting him. The meetings with the landowners in Jalil, near the holy tomb of Sidna Ali, and the *fellahin* in Kefr al-Haram. He recalled an old picture of Olga riding alongside him many years ago in his mind's eye, and this picture banished the troubling thoughts niggling at him.

After that occasion, Yehoshua frequently found Olga napping on the kitchen chair with her mouth slack and gurgling sounds filling the small room, and a plate and cup on the table, a pot containing a cooked dish on the stovetop. She had waited for his return and fallen asleep, without feeling the passage of time or realizing the smell of the burnt food. Their sitting together became less frequent; the situation still did not trouble him greatly. His life was so full, and it was enough for him to know that she was waiting for him in their home on the corner of Allenby and Ahad Ha'am Streets.

Olga's name gradually became forgotten. She infrequently joined Yehoshua when he was invited to events connected to the Palestine Land Development Company or the JNF, and if she did go with, she remained leaning on her husband's arm for the entire evening, not seeking honor, and considering the memories and honor of her husband enough. A layer of heavy armor overlayed her husband's sensitivity to those swarming around him. She did not see, nor did she pay attention to the fear and rage reflected in the officials' eyes. Moreover, she did not notice their jealousy over his successes. She was far distant for all of that, an old woman. In the first years that they lived in the new house, rural effendis and Bedouin sheikhs still remembered the kindness in her treatment in the pre-war years, and they brought her sacks of olives that had to be cured, bottles of olive oil, and baskets of dates. Olga only used a small amount of the bounty, since only four of them lived in the house, and there were no children or grandchildren. She distributed the rest among Sonia's patients, who were pleased to receive the gift, and thanked the pleasant elderly woman who talked a bit too much. In time, few presents came to her as those who knew her grew old or passed away, and their sons did not continue the tradition of their fathers. Olga was not saddened by this, since she had become tired of dealing with dividing the olives into packages. She rarely stirred to life and took an interest in any new matter, but even then, in a short time, she would sink back into desolation and the loss of a sense of time.

One morning, Yehoshua was sitting with Olga and brought up the idea of building a summer home for themselves next to the burial plot above Nahal Harod. "We'll escape the heat of the city and the bone-penetrating humidity of the muggy summer days," he said, trying to convince her.

"You're hastening my end. Why are you talking about graves?" she said to him. "And besides, you already spoke about that a few years ago, and, as usual, you do what you want, without asking anyone."

Yehoshua smiled at her and came out of his shell. "You are stronger than me and know me better than others do," he replied. "Look at your straight back. Listen to the clarity of your opinion. I will be buried long before you, knowing you are sitting above me. And when I hear your feet stamping, and the hem of your skirt dragging, I won't feel alone."

"I'm older than you, and you are talking nonsense," she dismissed his statements. "You are not thinking of me but only of yourself, afraid I won't wait for you."

He remained silent and rued bringing up the subject. Olga saw his stormy expression and bitterly recalled his promise to build her a house on the Hadera dunes. "You haven't finished one house, and you're already building another? Even if I live to be a hundred, I would not manage to split my time with you among three houses ..."

In mid-sentence, she broke off what she was saying, and she quickly forgot her talk with him, sunk into her chair with a smile on her face, and mumbled meaningless sentences in Russian. He left her in her mutterings, facing the window and warming herself in the rays of the sun, and went back to his usual matters.

From Olga's perspective, time stood still; it had stopped at some point in the distant past, and whatever had happened after that was erased and forgotten. Life outside the house continued to move noisily along, and Yehoshua kept thinking about the idea of building their burial plot in Jezreel Valley near the Harod Spring. An invisible force prodded him, and he admitted to no one—neither to himself nor others—that he had begun to worry that he would not manage to finish preparing it in time. He found two laborers from among the builders of the new colonies in Emeq Harod who were debating with themselves whether to be part of the idea of the "the large communal settlement," and to turn Palestine into one large commune or to suffice with paving roads with "Gedud haAvodah." the labor battalion, and to continue wandering between the colonies and the cities. Until they could come to a decision, they were happy to accept the suggestion of the "redeemer of the land" to work at building his gravesite. They reminded him of the time of his stay in Galilee when he went along with groups of workers under the leadership of Mania and Israel Shochat, and because of that, he preferred to stay longer with them next to Nahal Harod. There he could return to being the other Yehoshua, the one searching for his way and full of fears lest Olga should precede him, and he would be left with his loneliness.

The laborers promised to keep secret about the burial plot—that was the only condition to their getting the job. The burial cave did not lie on the main road, and he took care of their every need so they wouldn't have to leave the site, except for Friday when they needed a *minyan*, a prayer quorum, and went back to their comrades in the labor battalion. He considered the building of the burial plot his deed alone, a holy endeavor, one in which no one else should be involved. He stayed with the laborers for quite a while and observed them as they worked; he dug out the steps in the mountain with them and laid a steel pipe near the source of the spring's gushing.

Despite his fears, Yehoshua did not prod the laborers to finish the work. He did not pressure them, but from time to time, he did ask them to make a change and add another layer, and perhaps also raise the ceiling. He extended his stay there and delayed, as much as possible, his return to the house in Tel Aviv. After several days of sitting over the spring and in the shadow of the cave, his feeling of importance disappeared. He yearned for the days of his youth and the maturity of the woman marching along with him on the pathways of life, and he felt the pain of the reality knocking on his door, and he knew he could not push it off any longer.

The reality, however, was stronger than any of Yehoshua's attempts to escape. The events of 1929 came like a bolt out of the blue and changed the way of life in Palestine. But they were only the beginning; after them came the 1936 Arab Revolt. From time to time, Yehoshua was forced to remain in Tel Aviv and take part in the Palestine Land Development Company discussions, as well as those of the Zionist Executive, the Jewish National Fund, and Keren haYesod, which went on into the night. In the morning, he would hurry to complete negotiations over land before the Arab seller would change his mind over threats by the Palestine Arab Congress of Muslim-Christian Losses that tried to prevent the transfer of land into Jewish hands. At first, he did not adapt to the influence of the events on his work and still considered himself an important director whose approval was needed for every land purchase, but in the end, reality had to be reckoned with.

Not only did the events harm Yehoshua's dream: economic crises were added to them. First came the crisis of the bourgeoisie and then the Great Depression; all those investors who had wanted to build factories in Palestine to see profits from their efforts began to leave. The Stock Market crashed in New York. The capitalists went bankrupt and closed their businesses. Immediately after that, the orchard tracts, too, ran into difficulties. Yehoshua's hands were tied, and he was not given free rein to complete the acquisition of land and transfer it to the buyers, as well as to find new ways to deal with the crisis. New officials began shooting off their mouths and speaking pompously about a new settlement policy, the White Paper, and the need for organization of the Yishuv. However, Yehoshua was far away from all that and only knew the direct route to purchasing land—without institutions and by shaking hands and drinking coffee after the contract had been signed with a fingerprint.

In the winter after the 1936 revolts, Olga's situation deteriorated, and it was no longer possible to ignore it.

One night, after two weeks full of scurrying around the land of Qiri Qamun and Harithiya, to the east of the Carmel Mountains and on the border of Ramot Menashe, Yehoshua intended to go home and find Olga waiting for him in the kitchen, the soup bubbling in the pot and its aroma filling the rooms. Yehoshua climbed into a wagon, but the pouring rain forced him to stop in Hadera. The wagon could no longer make its way through the mud, and the horses stumbled. People suggested he stay over and continue in the morning by train. He had a premonition of something bad. Suddenly, he was afraid to cause Olga to worry. He had promised to return in the evening; maybe, she would be waiting for him impatiently in the kitchen. And if he would not arrive? She would go into a panic and not know what to do with herself on a stormy winter's night. Yehoshua did not understand what was happening to him nor where his fears were coming from. Neither of them had been in distress for a long time now, so why should he suddenly be so afraid of her responses? These thoughts pursued him, leaving him no peace. He walked among the houses like a crazy man looking for transportation that would take him to Tel Aviv, to the house on Allenby Street. Finally, close to midnight, thoroughly drenched, he found the owner of a vehicle who was willing to take him for a large sum of money. Yehoshua sat squeezing himself into one corner of the closed car, wrapped in his coat and trembling from cold and fear. Thoughts of old age perturbed him, and when he realized that he was now 70, he was frightened.

Fatigue overtook him, and he dozed lightly, not even feeling that they had reached the outskirts of the city. Only when the vehicle screeched to a stop at the entrance to the house did Yehoshua wake up and look at his watch. The hour of daybreak had arrived, but the thick cloud cover and the rain did not let the sun's rays breakthrough. Yehoshua hastened to pay the driver; he opened the door to the house whose frigid air froze him. Yehoshua wondered what this meant, since usually he was greeted with warm air blowing when he opened the entranceway. Both Sonia and Olga took care to maintain the heat in the room and lit the iron stove, and let it burn all night. He used to take off his boots as he came into the house and leave them there, walking to the kitchen wearing only his socks and putting on the woolen slippers that Olga had made sure to leave next to the stove. Olga had tried to convince him to leave his slippers near the entrance a few times, but he refused because he did not want to bring his mud-laden boots from outside near them. Even when she was generally forgetful, Olga did not forgo the heat of the stove, the same way she was particular to satisfy her husband's small wishes.

Now, he stood in the entranceway and called out her name over and over, but she did not reply. Maybe she had become deaf, he thought, for every day her responses changed. The silence was too thunderous. Yehoshua rushed up the stairs in his boots and damp coat and saw a strip of light under the door to their room. He took a deep breath and opened the door wide, but Olga was not in the neatly made bed. His heart began to beat wildly, and he let out a scream. He wanted to open the window in the joint wall and call Sonia and Mendel for help, but he held back; perhaps Olga was sitting in the kitchen, and he would find out that his foolishness and worry were unnecessary. The kitchen door was wide open, and Olga was actually sitting next to a cup of cold tea, staring at one spot on the ceiling. She did not notice him coming in and did not feel it when he embraced her shoulders and drew her to him.

Yehoshua looked at her and saw a smile frozen on her face; he waved his hand in front of her eyes, but she did not blink, only continuing to stare at the same place on the ceiling. Yehoshua looked for ways to bring her out of her numbness; he dragged a chair over and sat down next to her, whispering "Dyevka," "Dyevka," then he took her hands in his and pulled them toward him, but Olga still did not react.

"I will tell you about my activities during my last roamings," he muttered in a strangled voice. "I will tell you about my plans to establish a colony on the land of Qiri Qamun. I will find buyers for the land and not have to rely on the Palestine Land Development Company or the Jewish National Fund. I will do it by myself; I will pave roads, dig wells, divide the land among the farmers, and give them equally both mountain land and land on the plain. I will act as I did with Duran and Khudeira, alone, without the help of others, and you will be proud of me. Do you hear? Again I'll be the Second Joshua, only yours."

He spoke quickly, afraid to lose time, but Olga continued to sit in the same pose without reacting; only her eyes were closed now, and she was breathing heavily.

After that wintery night, Olga did not return to herself. She needed constant supervision; a nurse who worked in the office stayed with her during the long evenings until Yehoshua's return. Yehoshua did not have the time to sit for long next to Olga's bed, since he was at the beginning of new ventures and completing older ones. So, he was torn between his wife's bed and the lands located throughout Palestine. Each day the path between the house on Allenby Street and the lands grew longer, or so it seemed to Yehoshua, and he often traveled on it day and night, without feeling exhausted, without yet giving up, neither his wife nor the land.

After Passover 1938, Olga needed her sister more than she needed her husband. At first, Yehoshua refused to admit that and believed that if he would steadfastly hold her hand and share his body warmth with her, he would succeed in weaning her away from the pills piled on the small table next to the bed. He would sit at her side during long nights and not let his body droop or his eyes close, only hoping that she would respond and press his hand. He told her dozens of times about his attempt to obtain a concession to drain the swamps in the Huleh Valley and about his new acquisition near the lands of the Hefer Valley, so as to increase the land held by Jews there. He described to her the 50-year cycle of being together with her, with her always at his side in both success and failure. There were only two topics he never touched upon: he did not tell her about the new dispute and the conflicts over the land of Qiri Qamun abutting Wadi Ara nor about the gravesite nearing completion. To the land stretching over Ramot Menashe, he attributed the guilt for his wife's illness and the manor house—his great blindness and his dealing solely with himself.

29A. Plan for the Heftziba Suburb near the Hadera Colony, 1936, front cover page.
Source: Central Zionist Archives, A238/9.

29B. Plan for the Heftziba Suburb near the Hadera Colony, 1936.
Source: Central Zionist Archives, A238/9.

29C. Heftziba Farm near Hadera Colony, 1909.
Source: Irit Amit Cohen Private Archive.

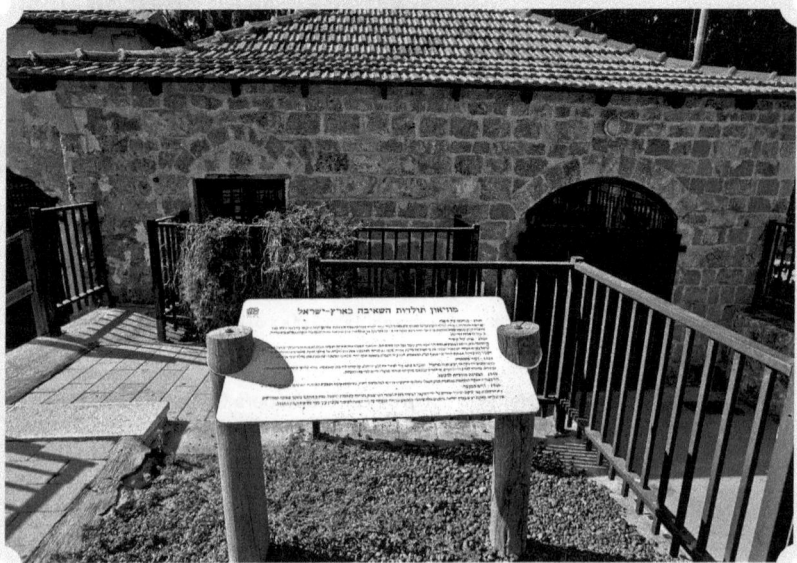

29D. Heftziba Farm Heftziba near Hadera, 2020.
Source: Irit Amit Cohen Private Archive.

‘6ॐ

Olga's condition worsened, as did the situation regarding acquiring land. Yehoshua had to stay in Beirut, Damascus, Haifa, and Tiberias, and every day he spent away from his wife, it seemed to him that she was calling him and needed him. He drove like a maniac. His face grew gaunt; his hair grew wild; his eyes sunk, and madness was reflected in them. He would reply angrily if he was asked how his wife was doing, interpreting the questions as gloating at her downfall. Now, he was seized by great fear that she would leave him without saying goodbye and leave him alone with the patchwork blanket Sarah had given them for their wedding day.

Sonia tried a number of times to restore him to sanity. "How can you help?" she would repeatedly ask. "She's an old woman, and old age has befogged her brain." But he refused to accept any logical explanation and refrained from meeting with Mendel or Tanhum; he did not want to see the faces of Haya or Rosa, who would come to visit them and ask to help—but their assistance was rebuffed.

"You want to see her death and my fall," he used to say to them, but they ignored his scathing remarks. Haya brought a card from "Ezra House" for uncurable patients and left it secretly on the table in his study. Yehoshua found it at the beginning of the week when he lifted his briefcase with the documents for the Harithiyeh and Qiri Qamun up from the table. The furor that engaged him was horrific to the point that he put it in an envelope and sent it to her addressed to Mikveh Israel and asked her to cease visiting them. Obviously, Haya did not listen to him and went on visiting Olga, but she didn't speak with Yehoshua. When she would come to call with her husband Eliyahu Krauze, Yehoshua would leave the house and wander the city streets or go back to his office in the Palestine Land Development Company building and sketch a plan of the future house to be built on the kurkar cliff on the Hadera dunes.

"I will build a house for Olga," he thought out loud, "and she will sit like the lady of the house on the veranda and look out at the waves touching the sand." But since he did not like the draft, he would crumple the paper, and start a new one with trembling hands.

No one understood him. Neither Sonia nor Haya realized that he was not asking for much but just to be near Olga, in their common bed and under the checkered blanket they had received for their wedding day, with it covering both of them. Only when he was alone on the Harithiya and Qiri Qamun plots did he dare scream out his pain. She was his entire world, and he did not believe he would be able to go on without her or bear the loneliness.

Only three years after Olga's illness had set in did Sonia's words begin to influence him. Once he understood how little he could be helpful, he began to stay away from the house more and more. He took a wagon and journeyed to visit his lands and kept away from the company of people, turning inward, closing himself up. He also hurried to conclude his land deals. He stopped reporting about his deeds to the officials and board of the Palestine Land Development Company. He acted on his own and did not ask for the help of his colleagues among the land agents and did not call for the surveyors to mark the borders, and did not attend meetings of the directorate. When he had some free time, he went to the Heftziba land and started to build the house he had promised to Olga.

"A hard man," people dubbed him, but secretly they added, "crazy coot," and grumbled to the directors, "The time has come to teach him that not all the land of Palestine is his."

But Yehoshua did not take part in those meetings, and when he later read the contemptuous, angry comments about his work method, he mocked the scoffers to himself. "The land of Eretz Israel is not redeemed by talking but by doing," and he went back to his travels, examining the price of the Galilee land and whether the foundations of his house in the dunes had been properly set. In the meantime, the officials who had accompanied him for years were replaced, and new ones took over, one who had not known Yehoshua in other times and did not know how to forgive. His insulting them and his working without partners began to stir reactions.

Dealing with the soil and constructing the house on the seashore did not make him forget the burial plot. He erected the house because he had promised her, but he built the gravesite because he now understood there was no longer any reason to try to repel death. Despite everything, he still hoped that Olga would be able to live in the house over the kurkar cliff and that the building of the burial plot would take a long time. He continued to sleep between the walls whose construction was not yet complete, and his body shook from the cold. When he returned home, he would stand for a long time in front of the doorway, afraid to open it and go up the stairs to their room. Then, finally, he would gather the courage, make the trek up, and look at his wife, seeing the shapeless body and the chin that had dropped to her neck and the neck joining her chest—all running together.

1938

Times changed. Seeing the wealthy German Jews, members of the Fifth Aliyah, willing to raise chickens in a white coat and arrange a concert at nighttime but in the daytime to wallow in cow manure, was no longer an amazing occurrence. Italy had fought Ethiopia; in Palestine, riots broke out again. The Arabs founded committees and forbade the sale of land to the Jews, threatening anyone they heard was conducting negotiations with them. Debts went unpaid; houses whose construction had begun remained skeletal, and there was no one to finish building them. The Depression was terrible. Just two years earlier, money had still been passed a hand over fist, and people had stood in line at the entrances to the banks and spoken about investment and profit. They offered land for sale, and it was immediately snapped up; they proposed an apartment house, and it was bought on the spot; they suggested a plantation and a strip of rocky ground—everything was taken. Like mushrooms after rain, agents popped up all over and pounced on the moneyed German Jews and on the American investors, and they promised a good, profit-returning investment.

Many of these agents sought to dupe the innocents, and they would sell the same lot to two wealthy people, and when the buyers ran into trouble, these agents would come and buy the lot from them and then sell it to a third person at an exaggerated price, and start the cycle again. But despite these frauds and the war, nobody pulled back, since the fear of losing out on profit was greater than their anxiety over the anticipated future.

But the Depression did arrive, ushering in the panic. The city streets were full of bankrupt merchants and homeowners with no one to buy their apartments, and German, Polish, and Romanian-speaking laborers. The "New," as well as the "veteran," were out of work and down and out. But this was only the beginning.

The riots that broke out in 1936 shunted aside involvement with the economic depression for a time. The entire Yishuv was occupied with committees of inquiry and the drawing of conclusions, White Papers, and the drafting of maps. There were many arguments over whether to hurry up the construction of the Tel Aviv port and no longer have recourse to the Jaffa port, or whether to pave a new road to Haifa that would cross the Jewish colonies and not pass through Arab villages. They spoke about "two-state partition" and discussed the "Arab revolt," and clandestinely, they told about the Beth Shean Valley and kibbutz Tel-Amal, as well as a new form of settlement—wall and stockade. But Yehoshua Hankin continued to maintain his distance from all of these. His isolationism only increased the hatred of the corporation's clerks against him, since they considered his habit as misplaced pride, as if he were defying them, saying, I am greater than all the current events.

Olga's situation deteriorated. He knew only this, and he perceived all the rest as incidental. From this point on, his land acquisitions were carried out only in her honor, and he strove to achieve as much as possible before she passed away. His land deals paralleled Olga's condition. Every success symbolized her cure, while each failure attested to her further decline. The debates about his actions were of no interest to him. As long as she continued to breathe in their shared room, Yehoshua went on to acquire land and bring to the Palestine Land Development Company contracts properly signed.

In those hard times, the Palestine Land Development Company often discussed the events of the moment and the new approaches that had to be implemented concerning land acquisition and selling property to buyers. Opinions were especially divided over the areas that should receive preferential treatment. The officials were split into those who supported buying land in the mountains that were not settled by Jews and those who favored reinforcing the settled regions on the plains and in the valleys; there were also some who said both to expand and bolster as well as to buy land in the mountains and make our mark, so that the Jews will have a foothold when the time comes for dividing Palestine between the two peoples. As time passed, they made it clear that Jewish settlement would expand in the mountains and not be concentrated solely on the plains.

Yehoshua avoided these discussions that never ended in explicit conclusions, and he held steadfast to his decisions and his method, which were always clear to him. He took little interest in the mountain land, since he still felt the bitter taste of his attempts to buy Galilee land with Kalvarisky 30 years earlier. He was well aware of the ownership situation there, the nature of the rocky soil, and the difficulty finding freely running water. So, he agreed to act as an agent for these lands only if there was a determined buyer who insisted on buying only mountain land, promising to settle it as well. Few such people could be found, since most of the buyers of Land of Israel property did not know precisely what they wanted and gave the agent a free hand to decide for them. They would come and say to him, "Buy us a plot in the area of Tel Aviv for us," and he would look for land for them there. But things had changed, and the wealthy had disappeared, leaving only the JNF that knew well what it wanted, and it did not always like Yehoshua's land acquisition method.

The public company made its attitude toward the method of land acquisition clear to the heads of the PLDC, and stormy reactions from the corporation. Yet, Yehoshua still kept himself away from all that while fighting against the tendrils of Olga's illness that were wrapped around him and drew him toward her; he held fast to his old system and was still not ready to accept the end. While Palestine was roiling the land trembling and people hesitating about whether to continue operating as usual, Yehoshua kept on dealing with the land of Qiri wa Qamun and the lands of the huge swamp in the Huleh Valley—and with his dream of establishing a city in the dunes of Hadera.

The gravesite next to the bubbling spring on the slopes of Mt. Gilboa was almost finished, and Yehoshua was taken aback by a sense of the end drawing near. Now, his opinion changed: he urged the laborers working on Mt. Gilboa to finish the construction and even promised to add to their payment if they would complete it ahead of schedule. However, he had them sign a new contract to carry out the building of the house in the sandy tracts and to finish it before the arrival of summer, and then to pave a road on the Heftziba land and lay the foundation for the construction of a new city in the dunes. The laborers held him in contempt and considered him a childless old man who was afraid of the summer, but they craved his money and rushed their work even though they did not know how serious he was about his plans.

Not only Yehoshua stayed far away from the tempests raging in Palestine, but the other members of the household on Allenby Street corner of Ahad Ha'am also ignored them. They dealt with the incurable ailing person, trying in vain to make her lengthy stay in bed pleasant, cooking delicacies for her to brighten her mood.

In the meantime, the turmoil in the PLDC kept growing. Buyers weren't found for the old land; new deals were not signed; the deadline for payment of debts had passed, and the treasury was empty. Official letters began to arrive at the Hankin house, and when they weren't answered, messengers came, but since they too were of no avail, the directors of the corporation knocked on the door and called for Yehoshua to consult with them. Yehoshua, however, did not stay home during the day, and at night, when the nurse taking care of Olga gave him his messages, he would laugh and reply, "I am not strong at discussion and debate. They want to decide, then let them decide. I will do my part—the land is bought through action and not with debates and reservations."

That's how it happened that Yehoshua did not take part in the PLDC meeting when they replaced the directors, set up new institutions, and assigned new functions within it. From the laborers working on the gravesite, he heard about the establishment of the new "Land Department" in the JNF institutions, which was increasingly taking over the roles of the PLDC and declaring that Palestine no longer needed a company to mediate the acquisition of land for private individuals as well as for the Jewish people. "Times have changed," the laborers said as they quoted the words of the new directors, "and a wealthy person avoids Palestine, leaving only the JNF to carry out buying of land and to look out for the Jewish people. As they spoke, they watched the face of Yehoshua Hankin, the great land agent, and expected a reaction. But Yehoshua did not listen and had no faith in changes, and since he was aware of the limitations of the JNF, the differences of opinion within it, and the struggles over the budgets for acquiring land, he belittled their stories and told them, "The land of Eretz Israel is not redeemed with an order from above, but through hard work and money."

One day, they told him, as if inadvertently, that a new director had been appointed as head of the JNF Land Department, and he represented a group of officials who called for giving priority to and hastening the acquisition of mountain lands — and if necessary, to give preference to the mountain over plains and valleys. Yehoshua knew the new director by name, but he preferred to call him "the Mountain Man" to himself. He did not believe in altering the age-old ways of doing things and establishing new rules for the negotiation process and the buying of land in Eretz Israel. When the workers were pouring the roof of the house in the dunes, he told them, "He only wants to demonstrate his power to others and to innovate, but he does not understand that it is forbidden to institute new things in Eretz Israel. Only an experienced agent, who has worked for decades in land acquisition and knows the follies of the land and the oddities of its owners will succeed."

Yehoshua now divided his time between the house being built on the dunes and the settlement that was to be established on the land of Qiri Qamun in Ramot Menashe that had even been given a name—Yoqneam—as well as between measuring the borders of the new lands in Western Galilee and Olga's sickbed. When he came to the festive laying of the cornerstone and naming of the new moshava on the land of Qiri Qamun (that is, Yoqneam), he met the "Mountain Man" in person.

Yosef Weitz was 30 years younger than Yehoshua, a man of about 40 with an upright bearing and penetrating eyes, a full head of hair, and a confident stride. Yehoshua could not stop looking at him, seeing his strength, and understanding his power. The new director offered him a hand and smiling, said, "You're the Second Joshua, they say?"

For a moment, Yehoshua did not understand how this man knew the nickname that was reserved for Olga. The man had hit his sore spot and didn't even know it. And Yosef saw the face of the man before him becoming clouded, and he did not know why, since he had meant to be respectful, not spiteful. So Yehoshua turned his back on him and left depressed, and his past was dragged along with him and made him trudge slowly.

About a month later, Yehoshua met him again. By that time, the JNF Land Department had become organized, and Yosef Weitz had divided Palestine into regions and appointed an agent for each one, so that he would become an expert on his own region and not have to move about and learn once again the names of places and the landowners nor the problems of the tenant farmers and of the wandering Bedouin tribes. The printed bulletin about the new decisions lay neglected for a full week on the table in the entrance to the Hankin home until Yehoshua came to his office at the PLDC and heard the vague sentences uttered behind his back. When he asked questions of the secretary, she looked surprised and inquired whether the minutes of the meetings of the JNF directorate had arrived at his home. Yehoshua recalled the envelope lying on his table and rushed home to open it; his anger knew no bounds. He hurried to the bed he shared with Olga and cried out, "He doesn't only stick his nose in my private affairs—he hinders all my actions. He works against me and makes decisions without considering me. He wishes to get rid of me so he will have no competitor, a person considered greater than he."

Sonia heard and took pity on him, and the woman lying like an edema-swollen, shapeless blob of flesh, stared at the ceiling, concentrating on one spot. And Yehoshua felt alone, so alone.

Sonia dragged over a chair and sat next to him, trying to comfort him. "Examine his intentions." she began, trying to ease his pain. "You yourself saw how the buyers are fleeing and refusing to invest in land. Look at the beggars, who just yesterday were 'laborers' and 'pioneers' and 'bourgeoisie.' The situation is tough, and actions are called for. He is trying to allot responsibilities and not concentrate on them, and you know well just how dependent the PLDC is on money from private individuals, and when they are not to be found—the company cannot exist. In troubled times, it is not the wealthy person who will buy land but the JNF that is afraid of partition of Palestine. If the Fund does not buy in Bet Shean Valley and Upper Galilee, there will be no Jewish foothold in these areas, and you know this better than me."

But Yehoshua did not want consolation or even to be a minor agent and take orders from a new, inexperienced director. To irritate that fellow, he fled to look after the pathway being paved in the Heftziba dunes. From there, he went far away to the raging Hermon streams that mingle into a strong stream and then drain into the great swamp. He did not see the desolation nor hear the wails of the coyotes, but in his mind's eye, he saw farming settlements and kibbutzim and patches of green and brown. When he left the swamp, he returned to the dunes and stayed there for a few days in the frame of the house being built on the kurkar cliff. He imagined Olga sitting there, supported by pillows, with the scent of the sea expanding her lungs, with him sitting next to her, holding her fragile hand in his and whispering his love to her. In the silence of the nights, his memory wiped away the picture of the ill woman, leaving only a proud woman walking on the moshava's paths in a roomy dress with puffed sleeves in European style.

Tanhum, who lived in the Hadera settlement and cultivated the family's land there and also saw to the sale of the land of the Heftziba farm, knew of Yehoshua's dream and of the paving of the roads in the dunes. And whenever Yehoshua came to visit him on his way to the house on the Kurkar hill, he became frightened anew. Yehoshua's appearance was like that of an unbalanced person: his hair was wild, his face gaunt; his coat had not been laundered for a long time; his eyes were burning and darting restlessly here and there; he jumped at every comment and worried that perhaps people were whispering about him. He would stay at Tanhum's for a short visit, tasting whatever his wife had cooked, and hurry to leave, so as not to waste time.

"We must finish building the city, deepening the port, and pouring the roof for the house on the cliff," he would explain when he took leave of them, with his eyes already looking outside, far above the roofs of the moshava. "Olga is waiting for me," he would add, "and I promised to return on time and take her with me and show her the house and the roads opening up in the dunes."

His enthusiasm was heartrending, and if it were not for his appearance, Tanhum would have become attached to him and followed him to the ends of the earth. But whenever Yehoshua returned to visit the settlement, the rumors were more rampant. "The man has gone crazy," the neighbors noted. "The old fellow is not ready to accept the authority of those younger than he," related a functionary close to the one of the JNF directors.

One time, Tanhum tried to hold Yehoshua back and read him parts of newspaper articles and talk about essential matters of import to the entire Yishuv, but Yehoshua was not willing to tarry. The dunes were stronger than Tanhum and attracted Yehoshua to them. Another time, Tanhum read about "The Eretz Israel-Hebrew Treasure for agriculture founded by Yehoshua Hankin" and about "Pardes Meretz," and he went especially to Tel Aviv to ask Sonia about these. The doctor shrugged her shoulders and refused to answer, sending him to her brother, "Ask Yehoshua. And if he refuses, ask Mendel." And this time, the youngest brother stayed and waited anxiously for his two older brothers.

From Mendel, Tanhum learned that for Yehoshua, the dunes of Heftziba had not been enough. "It's an old story," Mendel told him, "That started with the history of the plantation estates in the Sharon. At first, Yehoshua wanted to plant orchards with the money of the wealthy from all over, until the Great Depression hit, and the rich stayed away from Palestine. Yehoshua went and, with his own money, bought land north of Kfar Saba, created a farm there, and planted an orchard, calling his farm "HaOtzar haIvri" (The Hebrew Treasure). He liked this venture and bought another piece of land north of Emeq Hefer, where he also wanted to plant an orchard, enlarge it, and name it 'Pardes Meretz.' He asked Sonia and me to buy stock in both companies and to keep this a secret.

"'I am not buying the land for myself,' he explained to us. 'I do it to increase the areas of orchards on the coastal plain. And when the farm will grow and its capital increase, its money will be divided between Keren Hayesod (Palestine Foundation Fund) and the JNF, and each one will set up its own bank for financing settlement and land acquisition.'

"In order to not disappoint him, we bought a share in 'HaOtzar' company as well as in the "Meretz" company, and we were also witnesses when he registered the companies properly, but even so, we did not believe that the farm and orchard would last and show a profit. We didn't visit the 'HaOtzar haIvri' farm but only read the correspondence and the reports that came to the house from the court and attested to the legal problems Yehoshua was up against. He did not manage to transfer ownership of the land to his name, but he did find workers who were not afraid of the repeated harassment by the Arabs of Kalkiliya and from their attempts to drive them off the land."

"And what's going on with the orchards today?" wondered Tanhum.

"Pardes' Meretz' has become the colony Kadima, and we are all relieved of responsibility for it, while in the 'Otzar Eretz Israel' orchard workers are dying struggling to guard the land dividing between Kfar Saba and Kalkiliya," responded Mendel, with a look of bitterness in his eyes.

Tanhum heard and thought to himself that whoever was close to Yehoshua went crazy, and he left Mendel and Sonia, returning to Hadera with an aching heart.

Events concluded, including the Great Arab Revolt. The land regulations imposed by the British were severe. In response, settlements were established overnight, some on land bought by Yehoshua at the time he was considered unique, and a few on land acquired by the "new agents," as Yehoshua dubbed them, while others called them "the regional agents–employees of the JNF." War broke out in Europe, but in Palestine, little was known about it; the people became steeped more deeply in issues of land issues and settlements, attempting to study the decrees and find loopholes in them and, despite the rage and opposition of the British regime, to extend the Jewish foothold in Eretz Israel. And Yehoshua stayed even further away from the house on Allenby Street. This time he did so intentionally, so as to forget the image of the invalid and to engrave other faces in his imagination.

Sonia would report to Yehoshua about his wife's situation and also make sure to get letters to him through the company clerks who traveled to the north, passing through Hadera on their way. When those same fellows would return, and she would ask about his situation, they would tell her that not only was the man estranged from what was going on in Palestine. He was also stubborn, and whenever they would mention the name of Yosef Weitz, his obstinacy would grow stronger, and he would dismiss everything that the new director had planned and done.

Actually, Yehoshua rebuffed any attempt for a rapprochement between him and Yosef Weitz; instead, he kept himself fully occupied with work. As if driven by a demon, he had only one desire—to accomplish as much as possible before Olga would leave him.

But exhaustion was beginning to leave its marks. First, he lengthened his all-night stays next to the dung campfire, until he fell asleep. Then horseback riding became difficult for him, and he preferred to measure land on foot. He spoke at length with the fishermen and tried to convince them to deepen the port, and he spoke with the Bedouins who spread into the dunes of the planned city with their sheep and took over the paths, but they looked at him in astonishment and spurned him. Then he met with the *fellahin* who had invaded the land of Qiri Qamun and argued against him, "We are tenant farmers. Find a solution before our being removed from the land." The discussion soon became heated, and Yehoshua would get up and raise his voice and threaten with the cane he had received from the PLDC in honor of its jubilee celebrations. The Arabs would yell after him, "Majnun" [maniac], and he would hear this, take in the insult, and go off to investigate what was happening with the Huleh land. But when he could find no satisfaction even there, he would return to the coast.

One evening, he returned to the seashore and sat in a dip in the sand, moving close to the fire, but the dung fire did not manage to warm him. He muttered unclearly, and when the fisherman tried to ply him with an herbal drink, he spit it out and vomited. His forehead burned, and his body trembled. Those sitting around dug a wide niche in the sand with glowing dung at its edges and laid him in it to preserve his body warmth. In the early morning, they called the Bedouins living in Wadi Qabbani near Wadi Hawarith to take him to Tel Aviv.

This was at the end of the summer, and Yehoshua imagined that Tel Aviv was spreading a net to trap him within the walls of the house on Allenby Street and make every effort to prevent him from finishing the work he had begun. The city was overflowing with the homeless who wandered among unfinished houses and scrabbled through garbage cans to satisfy their hunger, and slept at night on benches on the boulevard. For Yehoshua, they were a new discovery, and he feared them more than he did the piles of minutes of the PLDC meetings and the new decisions that had accumulated on his table. When he recovered, he began to go out to tend to his dealings. He preferred not to stay long on the depressing streets but to call for a cab to take him where he wanted to go. In the house, he called for a carpenter to repair broken shutters and made sure to lock them during the daytime. He did not allow the noises from outside to penetrate into the house, and he often sat at Olga's bedside and listened to her labored breathing.

Olga had withdrawn deep into herself and did not allow the life going on around her to penetrate; Yehoshua envied the infinite calm engulfing her. By now, he had already taken note of her bloated body, but he continued to speak to her and share his sadness with her. Sonia took care to pile pillows under her sister's head and to direct her gaze to whoever was sitting next to the bed. When she did not close her eyes, her expression continued to be dull and fixed on one spot. The patchwork quilt spread over her was full of lively colors to the point of glaring. The man would sit by her side and put his hand under the blanket to feel for the shrunken, lifeless hand. Several times, he thought that she was seeking to punish him for not having fulfilled his promises on time and pushing them off, while preferring land to her and to the home in the dunes for just the two of them. In those moments, his talkativeness would overpower him, and he would enumerate for his the entire list of his acquisitions and all his most recent projects: paths paved in the Heftziba dunes; the casting of the roof of the house on the kurkar cliff; a moshava called Yoqneam founded on the lands of Qiri wa Qamun, a farm consisting of orchards north of Kfar Saba; negotiations for the permit to drain the swamps in the Huleh Valley, as well as the acquisition of the lands of Wadi Qabbani abutting the Hefer Valley.

"The curse levied on Feibush Dolnik came true," he brought his face close to her ear and whispered to her. "The land of Wadi Hawarith has been redeemed, and settlements have been established on it. A contract will be signed in a few months, and the land of the Hefer Valley and the lands of Wadi Qabbani will all be registered on Jewish names, and Feibush has no part of it."

Yehoshua did not tell her that he had heard the clerks saying, "This is Yehoshua Hankin's swan song." Also, he did not share with her his hatred for Yosef Weitz, and he did not tell her of his fear of crossing the street and encountering beggars nor even about the situation of the Palestine Land Development Company—all of these belonged to the present in which she had no part.

The collapse of the Palestine Land Development Company actually did occur at the same time as its officials ignored the actions of Yehoshua Hankin. First, they smeared his name over the failure to establish the moshava Yoqneam on the land of Qiri Qamun, and they said that since Yehoshua had failed to evacuate the tenant farmers and had exhibited shiftlessness during the negotiations, the PLDC had lost the possibility to continue acquisition of agricultural land for the JNF. Then, they said about it that he was old and no longer capable of carrying out a complex transaction, and it would be better if he would sit at home and write his memoirs. On several occasions, they hinted to him that the PLDC needed new blood and a fresh system and that the JNF's methods of using many agents was better than Yehoshua's system of doing everything by himself. Yehoshua heard the comments but did not accept them; he continued operating in his own way and inquiring about lands and possibilities for purchasing them as well as for lowering their price and solving the issue of land ownership and the matter of clearing the tenant farmers from the land—all by himself.

☙

In the PLDC, they said that Yosef Weitz did not want Yehoshua. He disturbed him with his work method: acting on his own accord, promoting or delaying everything as he sees fit, and not working together with anyone, as well as not reporting to the PLDC about his activities. In particular, Weitz refused to accept the common opinion that for years in Palestine, only one acquirer of land had been recognized; namely,

Yehoshua Hankin, and any other agent had no standing at all. He thought that rules and order should be instituted; each detail should be listed; things should be planned without deviating from the program one way or another. All land purchases had to be carried out according to rules predetermined by a number of officials, with each one of them having a function he had to carry out. And mainly—no land acquisition should be conducted by a single person, seeing that many people were good and had expertise in the Palestine land laws, in carrying out negotiations over property, and in methods for preparing, cultivating, and settling it.

Yehoshua and Yosef differed from each other—in appearance, age, plans, and loves. Yosef Weitz loved the mountains and wanted to cover them with Jewish settlements and wrote plans on how to remove the rocks and till and plant on a mountain. Yehoshua loved the valleys and the large plains. He did not believe in the mountains. He aspired to space and infinite horizons. When Sonia once asked him why he preferred the plain and the valley, he explained, "Fellahin settled the mountainous regions, and there was no room in them for a new settlement, while the valleys were sparsely inhabited and not considered by the Arabs as good land for cultivation."

In reality, Yehoshua had pursued land in the valley and on the plains all his life. He traveled to the ends of the earth to convince the landowners to sell it to him. He mortgaged his soul to make sure that the land of the plains would not slip through his fingers. For 20 years, the landowners in Damascus and Beirut had laughed at him and considered him a small speculator, but he did not give up and tried again to acquire the land. And when the war broke out, it seemed that his plans had come to an end, but after it, Yehoshua hurried to return to the plains and the valleys and would not quit. He looked for wealthy buyers to realize his vision. He did not distinguish between the JNF and people with large private capital, as long as there were individuals like that who were also willing to redeem his lands, improve and settle them, and turn them into a blooming garden.

Yehoshua did not agree with Yosef Weitz's system of acting in accordance with a set plan, discussing and voting on each issue, along with conducting mounds of correspondence before buying any piece of land. But after a great deal of hesitation, he gave in to Sonia and Mendel and asked for a meeting with Yosef Weitz so that he could explain his system to him in detail. Thus, one day,

Yehoshua came to the long hallways in the JNF offices in Jerusalem and waited for Mr. Weitz to be so kind as to listen to him. When he finally went in, he said to Weitz, "Your system for land acquisition is not good. Eretz Israel's land is bought through direct negotiation, with a promise, and a word of honor. There are no arguments and stalking out, leaving the negotiations, and then coming back and leaving again. Rather, you finish it and sign. If you don't do it that way, the price of a dunam will go up, and the JNF will no longer be able to buy the land, nor will private buyers be found for it."

The new director, who was sitting on a comfortable chair behind a table covered with maps marked with straight, precise lines, looked at him, and tossed out a statement to him, "You are a man of *the Valley*," adding with a snide giggle, "and since the purchase of the valleys have been completed, your task is finished. It'd be better for you to go home and write your memoirs and leave land acquisition to people younger than you."

He said this without knowing that, at that time, Yehoshua had nothing to do at home. He left there and went to solve the problems of the tenant farmers, wanting to remain attached to the land of Qiri Qamun and to expand the acquisition. Despite the intense anger of the "Mountain Man," he continued to operate according to his system — to come to an agreement with the seller, to sign, and then send out letters to find buyers. When he did find private buyers for the land, he promised him, as he had done with the Duran and Khudeira lands some 25 years ago, to build a settlement and pave roads in it and dig wells and divide the land into plots and decide where the public buildings would stand and where the street and houses would be. He wished with all his might for the outburst that he knew would come. He wanted it to break the monotony of his life. And when the letters were distributed, one of them reached the hands of a clerk, who hurried to present it at the weekly meeting of the representatives of the JNF and the PLDC.

In time, they told him about the events at that meeting and described for him how the director stood and screamed, his face red with rage, "That won't happen!" and then repeated, "The mountain land is destined to be under the ownership of the Jewish nation, and there is no room there for private holdings, and in that case, Yehoshua Hankin will not decide its future. He's passé. He should go home. He should go, he should go! ..."

After that outburst came the obstacles. Someone made sure that the Arab sellers of the Qiri Qamun would change their minds about selling large swaths of the land over which Yehoshua had conducted a long negotiation, and the guarantees Yehoshua had signed were of no help. The tenant farmers raided the lands registered in his name and hit his horse's hindquarters when he was riding between the furrows and seedlings that had just sprouted. He tried to send them away, but they laughed and mocked him.

The Duran net had come back and was wound around him: Pines' face turned into Broide's face, and Broide's face—into the visage of the "Mountain Man." They both disappeared as if they had never been, with one difference—Olga was no longer at his side to support him, to unravel the entanglement and set him free.

For some time, he still tried to rise up on his own, disregard what was happening, hold firm to his method and renew negotiations for other land. He went to acquire the big swamp land, the Huleh valley, but his legs slipped and sank in the mud, and his body was pulled ever lower. The same as what the speculators had done to him over the land of the big valley, the Galilee properties, and the Hefer Valley at the time of the great panic, now was perpetrated by the "Mountain Man" and his coterie of clerks over the swamp land. Over 50 years had passed since the land rush had erupted, but the fire had consumed it all, leaving behind only desolation and silence. Yet now, it was boiling over again with the sparks and awakening anew. Only he felt the wall of fire nor knew that with its spreading, a period was coming to an end. They would no longer buy large swaths of land but deal only in trivial acquisitions, crumbs of earth. The effendis who owned stretches of land would not want to deal with agents and would hold in contempt the clerks who operated only according to the book, and they would look for excuses to avoid negotiations. He did not continue to protest. There was no reason to. In any event, they would not believe him. Crazy, they called him, a crazy old man.

1940

During the summer's end heatwave, the land regulations were published that forbid selling land to Jews in most of the regions of Palestine. The phones ceased to ring in the PLDC offices. Tables remained devoid of documents; rooms were locked, and clerk after clerk was fired. Some of those sacked joined the JNF Land Department clerks and land agents, while others were added to the list of the unemployed. And whoever remained sat in meetings and whined sorely and smeared many names, while looking for someone to blame for the corporation's losses and the failure of its acquisitions.

In the fall, the land of the Huleh swamp was dropped from the company's possession. Negotiations for it were transferred to Yosef Weitz's Land Department. One after the other, areas of land went over to the JNF, and the spokesmen for the corporation and its agents and managers again had nothing to say. Their authority was taken away from them, and they were left with mere crumbs—to deal with urban properties. Yehoshua began to hear voices saying, "The acquisition of Qiri Qamun ruined the PLDC, an expensive purchase. Yehoshua gave the company a bad name"; "The work of one man, who does and acts as he sees fit"; "He wanted to be great, a redeemer he called himself"; "a speculator who put the profits in his own pocket while throwing the other clerks leftovers from a harlot's fee."

One morning, a letter arrived detailing the status of Yosef Weitz and the procedures of the Land Department as well as officially Yehoshua informing that from now on, the PLDC would deal only with property in the cities. Enclosed with the letter was a golden certificate "In Honor and Appreciation for Lifetime Achievement." There was also a card saying, "Honorary Chairman," party to votes of no consequence, but a seat at the table in the large hall had been saved for him. He hid the letter, the certificate, and the card, hid on his table beneath a pile of files on which work had not been finished. He went up to the bedroom, lay down next to his wife, and pulled the patchwork quilt to him. Then, he brought himself close to her inert body, crying very softly, until he was empty of feeling and pain. He knew he was no longer capable of contending with reality.

On Friday, a few days after receiving the letter, while everyone was still in the synagogue and preparing for the Sabbath evening meal, Yehoshua went and opened the door to his office in the PLDC building. After not having visited it for quite a while, for a moment, he was intoxicated by the scents arising from the papers and ink; he began to feel dizzy and leaned on the table for support. Once he was stable, he saw signed letters that had been sent to him sitting in their envelopes. He put himself down in his desk chair and leaned back, with his hands stroking the cardboard files and touching the rolls of maps.

Yehoshua closed his eyes, seeking serenity far from the frenzy of the street and the room overflowing with the smell of medicines, from the new administration that had not accepted his method, and from the land that had pursued him all his life. He sat like that for many hours, and the people's images passed before his eyes and the times intermingled in his mind, and only with the arrival of morning did he come to his senses and straighten his back; he rose from his chair and made a pile of signed files and lists and letters and then called for a taxi to come to collect him.

When the drowsy driver came, Yehoshua asked him to help him bring the files down, while he remained in the office for his final moments of leave-taking until the impatient driver began to honk and make noise in the street. Finally, he saw the old man coming down the stairs and throwing a key into the channel in the street, so he called out to him, "The key fell!" but when the man did not respond to him, "Crazy old man," the driver murmured and hurried to speed away from there.

The address the driver had been given meant nothing to him. He stopped with a squeal of brakes and, with definite unwillingness, took a pile of files without paying attention that one of the pages had fallen into the filth of the street and, with a slam of the door, drove away. Yehoshua turned on the light in his study and closed the shutter so that no daylight would penetrate there. He dragged a chair, placed it in the middle of the files on the floor, and sat down to sink into the past and search for consolation in it.

☙

The house on Allenby Street corner of Ahad Ha'am was now turned into an office with lights burning in it day and night. Yehoshua spent more time there than he did at Olga's bedside. He let no one in to disturb him, except for Sonia, who occasionally knocked on the door to remind him that the meal was ready, and the clerk who had been fired from the PLDC came three days a week to write letters and send out bills. In the first months, there was still work for her, since

Jews who still remembered him favorably came and looked for him among the rooms in the PLDC building, and the guard at the gate sent them to the house on Allenby Street. Among them were land-owning Jews—small traders who a few years earlier had dealt with land and passed it on from hand to hand, raising its price, and now their land was still available, and there were no buyers. They asked for Yehoshua to report their difficult situation to the JNF Land Department so that it would add them to its list, and when Yosef Weitz would decide that this land, and only this property, was of strategic importance, he would redeem their land. There were Arab effendis who came late at night for fear of the members of the Arab Higher Committee and land speculators who sought loopholes in the new land laws and decrees so they could sell land to a Jew as well as lawyers seeking advice. The secretary would note their requests, and Yehoshua would sign and add an opinion, and once a week, a taxi would come and take a pile of letters to the PLDC headquarters and the JNF Land Department. A few days later—not too soon, so no one would think that Yosef Weitz was rushing to reply to Yehoshua Hankin, but not too late, so that he should not let the matter be forgotten—a messenger would come to the house with a letter of reply. The two never did meet face to face, but each one knew of the other's actions and heard from different people what each thought of the other, and they gnashed their teeth.

Then, the visits dwindled, and the honorary roles increased, "Requesting your distinguished presence at the ribbon-cutting ceremony for a street named after you"; "Inviting you to sign on a copper plaque in honor of a village bearing your good name," and the like. Yehoshua refused to go and instructed his secretary to thank them in his name. He saw all of these as a sign of the end, attempting to turn him into a mere memory.

During Passover 1943, Olga passed away, almost in silence. Other than a sigh and the release of air from the body, nothing changed. Her eyes were open, staring at a single spot on the ceiling; the hands clenched, close to her body; and the patchwork quilt was wrapped around her well. Staying next to her bed were Mendel, Sonia, and Yehoshua, and when the doctor and the nurse came to take her away from there, Yehoshua hastened to pull off the patchwork blanket and wrap himself in it, covering his head and his face, and leaning over the bed, he breathed in the intermingling smells of the body and the medications.

A few hours later, he slammed the door and left there; he got on a bus going to *the Valley*, with nothing in his pockets other than coins for the fare and the patchwork quilt. He was going to prepare the grave on the slopes of Mount Gilboa, near Nahal Harod.

He stayed at the gravesite for two days and swept away the dust. When he was tired, he spread out a blanket, stared at the star-studded skies, and embraced the expanses of *the Valley* full of his touch and his steps. In the Tel Aviv house, Mendel and Sonia took care of the consolers, and on the third day after her death, a long caravan wended its way to the cave on Mount Gilboa. Yehoshua stood on the dome of the grave and waited for the mourners. Dignitaries and officials came, though none of them knew that that was exactly how Yehoshua had waited when the people of Jaffa had come to examine the Duran land. After a long prayer and speeches by others, the white shroud-wrapped body was interred, and Yehoshua stood at the edge of the pit, wrapped in the quilt, and no one saw his face.

Even when the shiva week ended, Yehoshua continued to be withdrawn into himself, though once a week, he went out to take part in the meetings of the PLDC directorate in the large building on Ahad Ha'am Street. The first time, he went after, Sonia had threatened him that if he did not go out by himself to see people, she would drag him by his beard, until he would respond. But when he stood in the structure's entrance, and a number of clerks gathered around him to console him and nod their heads, he was sorry that he had given in to her. He did not react to their sorrow or their expressions of sympathy; he did to want pity. Not from them, nor from the group of clerks that had betrayed them and let the "Mountain Man" run things and forget his deeds. He sat in his usual place next to the directors' table and stayed silent most of the time, and only when a decision had to be made would he express his opinion by raising his hand.

Once again, the PLDC had no extensive spaces to deal with. Only hotels, commercial centers, and city lots, but he did not consider them seriously. These were not the wide-open, horizonless spaces nor the dunes and valleys where the wind blows strongly. The JNF dealt with the expanses, while it left crumbs to the Company. The PLDC officials wanted to show that they still had work, so that banged their fists a lot, raised their voices, and interrupted each other.

But Yehoshua did not belong to their group. Without wide-open spaces, he had nothing to do. He considered them a group of cackling crows around a sliver of cheese whose holes are more than the cheese itself.

Again, Yehoshua was not great, neither in his own eyes nor in those of others, and they had almost forgotten his sitting at the table. However, they did remember him on his birthday, and they bought him a new cane, engraved his name on it, and added the nickname, "Redeemer of the Land." And Yehoshua needed a cane, since his walking had become slow. His life flowed slowly. A month passed since Olga's death, ten months, a year … During the winter, his limbs were afflicted, and Sonia examined him and his bones and saw to a wheelchair that fit his needs. Yehoshua continued to go once a week to the Company's meetings, but since there was no room at the table to position a wheelchair, which took the space of two chairs, they made sure to arrange a room for him on the floor above and drilled a hole in the floor so he could peek and hear and be part of all the Company's decisions.

Yehoshua felt good in the room. He enjoyed sitting above the hall and beating the floor with the cane, in order to express his opinion. He intentionally delayed striking with his cane so they would wait. The walls defended him, and he could hold the directors and officials of the Company in contempt and become great once again. They did not see him in his weakness, but he saw them through the peephole: small ants, who would lift up their eyes and wait like birdwatchers to find out on whose side he stood and to which opinion he would add his voice to tip the scales.

Summer, 1943

Yehoshua put his eye near the peephole again. He could not get up by himself and had to wait for the guards to come take him out of the room above the meeting hall.

How much they hated him, he thought. The officials had been sitting for hours, raising and lowering their hands and talking loudly, but they never lifted their eyes to the ceiling and never tried to hear his pounding with the cane or his beating with his fists on the bare floor. They were behaving like this intentionally. They wanted to humiliate him. Had they been courageous people, he knew, they would point an accusing finger toward the hole and yell, "It's all because of you.

It's your fault that we are officials of a company that is not functioning!" But they preferred to keep quiet, and he could not respond and prove his innocence.

"Cowards," he dubbed them. He had waited for a letter informing him that they no longer needed him, For quite a while. But when the letter never arrived, he was certain that they would find a way to take the cane away from him and break it. They hated the cane the same way they were fed up with him. Since they did not send a letter and had not touched the cane, he began to scorn them and bang over their heads, whether necessary or not, to inform them of his existence and his attentive ear. They could not ignore his knowledge or his expertise; he had no competitors in Israel. The more the decrees increased, and the more obstacles to acquiring land from Arabs piled up, the more they needed his advice.

When he first began to require a wheelchair, he was sure they would exploit the situation and find an excuse to leave him at home; that they would intentionally not remember to send a cab for him. But events were stronger than they were, and no one except him knew how to win over the heads of the Bedouin tribes throughout the desert so that they would sell their lands to the Jews and ignore the riots as well as the land decrees prohibiting its transfer to Jewish hands.

Twice a week, the taxi would stop at the entrance to the house on Allenby Street, and two guards would take him and the wheelchair toward the Company building. He did not always understand why they did this. They didn't always need him, yet they preferred to transport him, bring him to the room, and wheel his chair up to the hole in the floor. Of late, the thought passed in his mind that perhaps it was not out of consideration for his condition, nor owing to his broad knowledge, nor being afraid that there was no substitute for him. Rather, they acted that way to use the opening in the floor to humiliate him. At first, he was angry with himself for these notions. "Since Olga passed away, I have become paranoid," he would tell himself. "Nonsense. Am I not still unique, and there are no competitors among the other land agents and buyers of land."

Completion of the acquisition of the land in Wadi Qabbani and the creation of a contiguous bloc of land in the Hefer Valley repressed these thoughts. Still, he did not manage to forget them, and whenever he had nothing to do, these ideas kept gnawing at his innards and never let go.

Now, as he was lying on the floor, dependent on the kindness of others who were not coming to lift him up, the musing became a hard fact. "They have succeeded in humiliating me, placing me next to a peephole in the floor," he slammed his fists, and his finger joints hurt. And, actually, any reasonable person who entered the room and saw him in his ridiculous situation would burst out laughing.

He had to fall, he thought bitterly, to hear the vote conducted by the man he abhorred; he had to wallow in the dust on the floor to finally understand their convoluted way of thinking. Self-pity flooded him—he was so alone. Leaden weariness spread through his limbs, and each cell in his body longed for Olga, for the scent of the heavy body and the fingers that made their way into his tangled hair.

He did not know what to do with his heavy body and his troublesome thoughts. An old man with no future. Until she died, Olga loved to flee to her memories, and they soothed her in times of distress. When he recalled his past, she was sitting beside him, caressing him with her hand. She never left him by himself and never let him fall. But just now, when he needed her more than ever, she was not with him to give him support. She had passed away two months ago and left behind her mounting bitterness, and his memories were of no consolation but rather a burden, a net closing around him and strangling him slowly. Pity turned into fury, anger, growing against Olga. She left at the moment of his weakness, without being aware of the great hatred of the clerks for him. She went and did not see his fall and did not stay with him to share his days and nights. He stretched out his finger and tried to lift himself, but he was powerless and rolled on his back, continuing to lie there, with his eyes seeing the wheelchair lying on the floor and the patchwork quilt caught between its wheels.

Lying on the floor was very difficult for him, and the tips of his fingers became numb. Yehoshua stretched his neck and raised his head. Where his head had lain was a moist blot. His mind was empty of all thoughts. He finished his roster of memories, and now only Olga remained, and every attempt he made to forget her failed, for the patchwork quilt was there to remind him of her.

The darkness spread in the room; the lines of the furniture became blurred; the voices rising from below became unclear, and sleep overtook him. He spread his arms; he was so tired …

❧

Fury woke him. Despite the cold that had made its way into the room, his body was covered with sweat. He dreamt a nightmare and could not escape its influence until he opened his eyes. For a moment, he did not know where he was and imagined hearing the wind banging on the tin sign held by a single, unreinforced screw in the wall of the house on Allenby Street, and he peered concentratedly to see the worn letters on it. Many years earlier, all the inhabitants of the city recognized the "Hankin House," and they had no need for a tin sign shining from afar. But the sign was hanging there proudly, and every week Olga would call to one of the lads who passed by and offer him a few girsh to climb the length of the eaves and polish the letters. She would stand on the sidewalk, on the other side of the street, looking toward the house, nodding her head, and directing the young man as to where he had to continue polishing.

After Olga's death, there was no one who would call to one of those youths in the street, and Yehoshua stopped looking at the sign and did not glance above the threshold. Now, he was sorry about this and tried to banish from his thoughts the image of the worn letters and promised himself to make sure the screw was tightened and to clean the sign as well. He again tried to get up. "I won't let the sign fall," he repeatedly told himself. "I will not let them forget that this is 'Hankin House' and the owners—both the dead and the living fill it."

Yehoshua lifted one shoulder above the floor and pushed and rolled slowly until he was again lying on his stomach. Now, he filled his lungs with air, leaned on his elbows, and managed to push himself and crawl towards the chair. Next, he pulled his body and rested and then dragged it again. His eyes noticed the cane thrown on the floor, and he put out his hand and stretched his fingers until he could touch it. He was relieved. His breathing was labored, and he was sure that those sitting below in the large hall heard his heartbeats. When he tried to calm his breathing, he almost choked, and the air ejected from his mouth came out as a whistle and raised dust motes, which irritated his throat and made him burst out coughing.

When his body finally settled down, Yehoshua pulled the cane toward him, grabbed its top with one hand, and with the other, leaned on the floor, beginning to lift himself up. He raised himself slowly, so as not to lose his balance and fall again. When he eventually stood on his unstable legs, he only had to raise his chair, and his work would be done.

Yehoshua plopped into the chair like a rock and threw away the cane, which he no longer needed. He tightened the blanket around his legs, and heat streamed into his body, bolstering his confidence. Unclear voices were heard through the hole, and he did not know if they had finished talking about the land of Wadi Qabbani, but he no longer cared about that. The shadows lengthened, and he enjoyed the dancing of the headlights' reflections on the walls of the room, the toots of the horns, and the voices of men and women waking up to nightlife.

Now he was certain that the thugs would come to take him and not close the gates of the building, leaving him in the room on the second floor. He waited in his chair and slowly calmed down. After quite a while, the door did open noisily, and the silhouette of a large, burly man filled the space between the lintel and the threshold.

"Nu, did you stomp?" asked the thug but did not wait for an answer and approached the wheelchair. "It's late," he murmured as he released the brake and pushed the chair toward the doorway. "They loaded me down with so many drives. They all see themselves as important directors and measure their success and status according to the driver who comes to take them and bring them back," he hurried to add, "but at the last minute, when I was about to end my shift, I remembered you. Nu, anyway, you're not in a hurry, right?"

The driver did not apologize, nor did he wait for an answer. He just bounced the chair down the steps, but he did not bother to ask the person sitting in it if he was comfortable or if it hurt him. At the end of the steps, both stopped. At that moment, the last bureaucrats straggled out of the large hall, and the thug straightened the chair and let the others pass by and leave the building before him. Some of those exiting turned toward the man sitting in the wheelchair, muttering something and holding back to let the hooligan go ahead and leave by the door. But the thug didn't move, whether out of respect for them or because he was used to receiving orders. Yehoshua did not hear what was murmured to him and looked away from them, ignoring their presence. Right then, he was well aware of what he wanted, fully aware. And when he saw they were taking their time and sending looks his way, and the thug was doing nothing, he lost his patience and pulled the fellow's sleeve pushing the chair and raised his voice, "Out!"

The officials were frightened, and the thug was taken aback, trying to understand the meaning of the scream, and hurried to push the chair into the group crowding the exit. The gathering divided into two, and people stood on either side of the wheelchair facing each other, with the chair creating a path through them. A smile of victory spread on Yehoshua's face. Those standing reminded him of soldiers preparing for roll call and shaking like a leaf for fear of the commander's wrath. The taxi was already waiting at the gate, and the other thug, seeing his comrade's panic, hastened to open the door and carry the old man into the car.

The door was slammed, and the driver turned on the motor, intending to take the usual route to the house on Allenby Street.

"Stop!" Yehoshua called out, "You're driving the wrong way."

The alarmed driver stopped, turned off the motor, and turned his head toward the passenger, and the two thugs leaned over him in fright. "You don't want to go home? To your house?" asked the man, stressing his words like speaking to an infant who doesn't understand.

Yehoshua knitted his eyebrows and made an angry face, with the thug's panic increasing even more. Now, a few of the officials gathered around the car, wondering about the delay. Yehoshua saw the tumult around him and enjoyed the extra attention. Then, turning the handle of the window, he lowered the pane and called to the driver, "Drive out of the city!" The driver still hesitated, but Yehoshua raised his voice to him and knew that his yell was heard outside the car and the whole group standing there heard what he said.

The driver looked questioningly at the thugs, but they shrugged their shoulders, and one of them twirled a finger toward his forehead. Yehoshua saw this move and burst out in roaring laughter.

They considered him a crazy man. They didn't know that he was finally relieved. He was free of them, free of the "Mountain Man," as well as from the room and the hole in the floor.

"Drive!" he blurted. "Drive to the Gilboa!"

The driver turned the car on and stuttered, "I don't know the way."

"Leave the city, and I will direct you," Yehoshua responded; his laughter burgeoned, and he could no longer control himself. "They do not know the lands of Palestine. They are all ignoramuses, living but not knowing where they live." And in his mind's eyes, he saw dancing before him the picture of Lolik holding the chair, and both of them falling, chortling boisterously, and his laughter grew stronger.

The driver turned the wheel, and Yehoshua threw his cane out the window. It rolled on the road and landed between the legs of the officials standing at the entrance to the building, with Yehoshua's last call echoing and astounding them, "Drive to the *Valley*! Drive!"

Appendix:

1. Purchases of land by Jews in Eretz Israel in the years 1890–1940 in which Yehoshua Hankin was involved

In 1948, at the end of the Mandate period, Jews owned about 1,800,000 dunams of the Land of Israel (Eretz Israel/Palestine). Of these, 420,000 dunams had been purchased in the Ottoman period up to the end of the First World War (1918).

For fifty years, 1890–1940, Yehoshua Hankin purchased close to 600,000 dunams of Eretz Israel and was involved in purchase of another 400,000 dunams, a total of one million dunams.

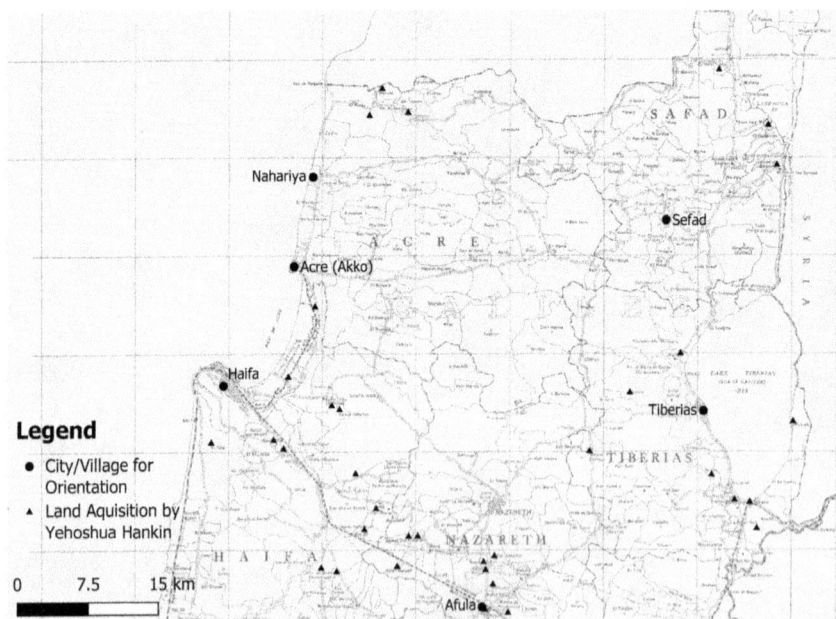

1.1 North

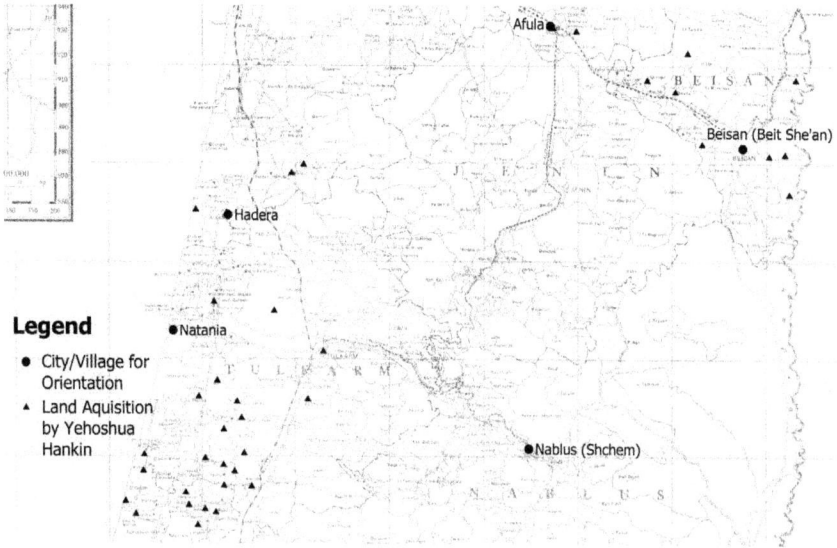

1.2a Center

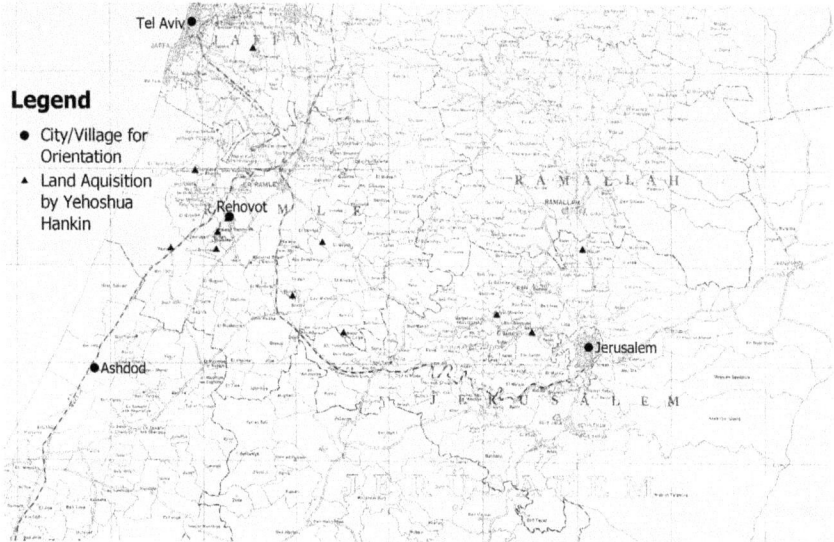

1.2b Center

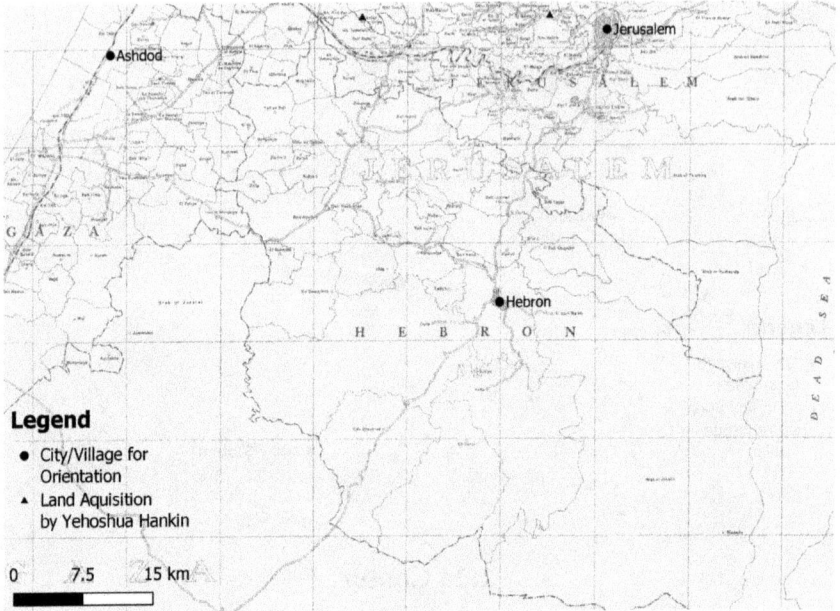

2.1a South

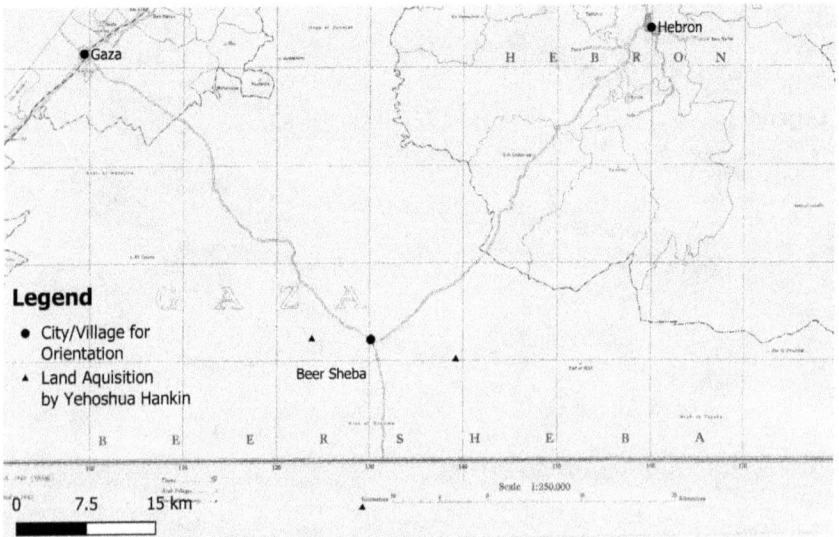

2.2b South

www.ingramcontent.com/pod-product-compliance
Lightning Source LLC
Chambersburg PA
CBHW071401090426
42737CB00011B/1307